---◇◇◇◇◇◇◇◇◇◇---

1905

---◇◇◇◇◇◇◇◇◇◇---

LEON TROTSKY

1905

Translated by Anya Bostock

RANDOM HOUSE

New York

ACKNOWLEDGMENTS

Studies in the Third World Books gratefully acknowledges
the care and diligence of Anya Bostock.
Without the selfless efforts of John Berger
this book could not have been published.
Editorial work of Professor Joan Mellen
and of Ralph Schoenman were indispensable.

ISBN: 0-394-47177-6
Library of Congress Catalog Card Number: 70-159382

Designed by Andrew Roberts

Manufactured in the United States of America
by The Colonial Press Inc., Clinton, Massachusetts

2 4 6 8 9 7 5 3

First Edition

Preface to the First Edition

The events of 1905 formed a majestic prologue to the revolutionary drama of 1917. For a number of years, when the reaction was triumphant, the year 1905 appeared to us as a completed whole, as *the Russian revolution*. Today it has lost that independent nature, without at the same time forfeiting any of its historical significance. The revolution of 1905 grew directly out of the Russo-Japanese war, just as the revolution of 1917 was the direct outcome of the great imperialist slaughter. In this way, both in its origins and in its development the prologue carried within it all the elements of the historical drama whose witnesses and participants we are today. But in the prologue these elements appeared in a compressed, not as yet fully developed form. All the forces engaged in the struggle of 1905 are today illuminated more clearly than before by the light cast back on them by the events of 1917. The Red October, as we used to call it even then, grew after twelve years into another, incomparably more powerful and truly victorious October.

Our great advantage in 1905 was the fact that even during this phase of revolutionary prologue, we Marxists were already armed with the scientific method of comprehending historical processes. This enabled us to understand those relations which the material process of history revealed only as a series of hints. The chaotic July strikes of 1903 in the south of Russia had supplied us with material for concluding that a general strike of the proletariat with its subsequent transformation into an armed rising would become the fundamental form of the Russian revolution. The events of January 9, a vivid confirmation of this prognosis, demanded that the question of revolutionary power be raised in concrete fashion. From that moment on, the question of the nature of the Russian revolution and its inner class dynamic became a burning issue among the Russian social democrats of that time.

It was precisely in the interval between January 9 and the October strike of 1905 that those views which came to be called the theory of "permanent revolution" were formed in the author's mind. This rather high-flown expression defines the thought that the Russian revolution, although directly concerned with bourgeois aims, could not stop short at those aims; the revolution could not solve its immediate, bourgeois tasks except by putting the proletariat into power. And the proletariat, once having power in its hands, would not be able to remain confined within the bourgeois framework of the revolution. On the contrary, precisely in order to guarantee its victory, the proletarian vanguard in the very earliest stages of its rule would have to make extremely deep inroads not only into feudal but also into bourgeois property relations. While doing so it would enter into hostile conflict, not only with all those bourgeois groups which had supported it during the first stages of its revolutionary struggle, but also with the broad masses of the peasantry, with whose collaboration it—the proletariat—had come into power.

The contradictions between a workers' government and an overwhelming majority of peasants in a backward country could be resolved only on an international scale, in the arena of a world proletarian revolution. Having, by virtue of historical necessity, burst the narrow bourgeois-democratic confines of the Russian revolution, the victorious proletariat would be compelled also to burst its national and state confines, that is to say, it would have to strive consciously for the Russian revolution to become the prologue to a world revolution.

Despite an interruption of twelve years, this analysis has been entirely confirmed. The Russian revolution could not culminate in a bourgeois-democratic regime. It had to hand power over to the working class. In 1905, the working class was still too weak to seize power; but subsequent events forced it to gain maturity and strength, not in the environment of a bourgeois-democratic republic, but in the underground of the Tsarism of June 3. The proletariat came to power in 1917 with the help of the experience acquired by its older generation in 1905. That is why young workers today must have complete access to that experience and must, therefore, study the history of 1905.

❖ ❖ ❖

As appendices to the first part of this book I have decided to print two articles, one of which (concerning Cherevanin's book) was published in Kautsky's journal *Neue Zeit* in 1908; while the other, devoted to expounding the theory of "permanent revolution" and a polemic against views on this subject which were dominant within Russian social democracy at the time, was published (I believe in 1909) in a Polish party journal whose guiding spirits were Rosa Luxemburg and Leo Jogiches. It seems to me that these articles will not only make it easier for readers to orient themselves in the debate among Russian social democrats during the period directly following the first revolution, but will also shed a reflected light on certain extremely important problems of the present day. The seizure of power in October 1917 was by no means an improvisation as the ordinary citizen was inclined to believe, and the nationalization of factories and plants by the victorious working class was by no means an "error" of the workers' government which, it is said, failed to give timely heed to the warning voice of the Mensheviks. These matters were discussed, and were solved in principle, over a period of a decade and a half.

The debate over the character of the Russian revolution had, even during that period, gone beyond the confines of Russian social democracy and had engaged the attention of the leading elements of world socialism. The Menshevik conception of bourgeois revolution was expounded most conscientiously, that is to say, most badly and candidly, in Cherevanin's book. As soon as it appeared, the German opportunists seized hold of it with glee. At Kautsky's suggestion I wrote an analytical review of Cherevanin's book in *Neue Zeit*. At the time, Kautsky himself fully identified himself with my views. Like Mehring (now deceased), he adopted the viewpoint of "permanent revolution." Today, Kautsky has retrospectively joined the ranks of the Mensheviks. He wants to reduce his past to the level of his present. But this falsification, which satisfies the claims of an unclear theoretical conscience, is encountering obstacles in the form of printed documents. What Kautsky wrote in the earlier—the better!—period of his scientific and literary activity (his reply to the Polish socialist Ljusnia, his studies on Russian and American workers, his reply to Plekhanov's questionnaire concerning the character of the Russian revolution, etc.) was and remains a merciless rejection of Menshevism and a complete theoretical vindication of the subsequent political tactics of the Bolsheviks, whom thickheads and renegades, with Kautsky today at their head, accuse of adventurism, demagogy, and Bakuninism.

As my third appendix I print the article *The Struggle for Power*, published in 1915 in the Paris newspaper *Nashe Slovo*, which is a presentation of the idea that those political relations which became clearly outlined in the first revolution must find their culmination and completion in the second.

◇ ◇ ◇

This book lacks clarity on the question of formal democracy, as did the whole movement it describes. And this is not surprising: even ten years later, in 1917, our party was not yet completely clear in its own mind on this question. But this ambiguity, or lack of complete agreement, has nothing to do with matters of principle. In 1917 we were infinitely far removed from the mystique of democracy; we envisaged the progress of revolution, not as the putting into operation of certain absolute democratic norms, but as a war between classes which, for their temporary needs, had to make use of the slogans and the institutions of democracy. At that time, we directly advanced the slogan of the seizure of power by the working class, and we deduced the inevitability of this seizure of power, not from the chances of "democratic" election statistics, but from the correlation of class forces.

Even in 1905 the workers of Petersburg called their Soviet a proletarian government. The name became current and was entirely consistent with the program of struggle for the seizure of power by the working class. At the same time we opposed to Tsarism a developed program of political democracy (universal suffrage, republic, militia, etc.). And indeed we could not have done otherwise. Political democracy is an essential phase in the development of the working masses—with the important proviso that in some cases the working masses may remain in this phase for several decades, whereas in another case the revolutionary situation may enable the masses to liberate themselves from the prejudices of political democracy even before its institutions have come into being.

The state regime of the socialist revolutionaries and Mensheviks (March–October 1917) completely and utterly compromised democracy, even before it had time to be cast in any firm bourgeois-republican mold. And during that time, although having inscribed on our banner: "All power to the Soviets," we were still formally supporting the slogans of democracy, unable as yet to give the masses (or even ourselves) a definite answer as to what would happen if the cogs of the wheels of formal democracy failed to mesh with the cogs of the Soviet system. During the time in which this book was written, and also much later, during the period of Kerensky's rule, the essence of the task for us consisted in the actual seizure of power by the working class.

The formal, legalistic aspect of this process took second or third place, and we simply did not take the trouble to disentangle the formal contradictions at a time when the physical onslaught on the material obstacles still lay ahead.

The dispersal of the Constituent Assembly was a crudely revolutionary fulfilment of an aim which might also have been reached by means of a postponement or by the preparation of elections. But it was precisely this peremptory attitude towards the legalistic aspect of the means of struggle that made the problem of revolutionary power inescapably acute; and, in its turn, the dispersal of the Constituent Assembly by the armed forces of the proletariat necessitated a complete reconsideration of the interrelationship between democracy and dictatorship. In the final analysis, this represented both a theoretical and a practical gain for the Workers' International.

◇　◇　◇

The history of this book, very briefly, is as follows. It was written in Vienna in 1908–1909 for a German edition which appeared in Dresden. The German edition included certain chapters of my Russian book *Our Revolution* (1907), considerably modified and adapted for the non-Russian reader. The major part of the book was specially written for the German edition. I have now been obliged to reconstruct the text, partly on the basis of sections of the Russian manuscript still in existence, and partly by means of re-translating from the German. In this latter task I have been greatly helped by Comrade Ruhmer, who has done his work with extreme conscientiousness and care. I have revised the whole text and I hope that the reader will not be plagued with those innumerable mistakes, slips, misprints, and errors of all kinds which today are a constant feature of our publications.

L. Trotsky

Moscow
12 January 1922

Preface
to the Second Edition

The present edition differs from the first Russian edition in two respects. 1) I have added the speech delivered by the author at the London party congress (1907) concerning the relationship of social democracy (as it then was) with the bourgeois parties involved in the revolution. 2) The volume now includes the author's reply to Comrade Pokrovsky on the subject of the special features of Russia's historical development.

10 July 1922

Preface
to the German Edition

The time has not yet come for an exhaustive historical appraisal of the Russian revolution; the relations are not yet sufficiently defined; the revolution continues, giving rise to new consequences all the time, and its full significance cannot be taken in at a glance. The book here presented to the reader does not claim to be a historical work; it represents the evidence of a witness and a participant, written while the traces of the events are still fresh in his mind, and illuminated from the author's party viewpoint— the author being a social democrat* in politics and a Marxist in science. Above all, the author has attempted to make clear to the reader the revolutionary struggle of the Russian proletariat which found its culmination—and, at the same time, its tragic conclusion—in the activities of the Petersburg Soviet of Workers' Dep-

* At the time this preface was written we still bore the name of social democrats.

uties. If he has succeeded in doing this, he will consider his main task to have been fulfilled.

◇ ◇ ◇

The introduction is an analysis of the economic basis of the Russian revolution. It covers Tsarism, Russian capitalism, agrarian structure, production forms and relations, and social classes: the landowning nobility, the peasantry, large capital, the petty bourgeoisie, the intelligentsia, the proletariat—in their relationships to one another and to the state. Such is the content of the "introduction," the purpose of which is to show to the reader in their static form those social forces which, subsequently, will appear before him in their revolutionary dynamic.

◇ ◇ ◇

The book makes no claim, either, to any completeness as to factual material. We have deliberately refrained from attempting to give a detailed description of the revolution in the country as a whole; within the limited framework of our work, we could, at best, have furnished a list of facts which might have been useful for reference purposes but would have told nothing of the inner logic of the events nor of the form they actually assumed in life. We chose a different method: having selected those events and institutions which, as it were, summed up the very meaning of the revolution, we have placed the center of the movement— Petersburg—at the center of our narrative. We leave the northern capital only to the extent that the revolution itself shifted its central arena to the shores of the Black Sea (*The Red Fleet*), to the villages (*The Peasant Riots*), and to Moscow (*December*).

◇ ◇ ◇

Having thus limited ourselves in space, we were compelled also to limit ourselves in time.

We have devoted most of the available space to the last three months of 1905—October, November, and December—the cul-

(xiv)

minating period of the revolution, which began with the great all-Russian strike and ended with the crushing of the December rising in Moscow.

As to the preceding preparatory period, we have extracted from it two moments which are essential for an understanding of the progress of events as a whole. In the first place, we have chosen to discuss the brief "era" of Prince Svyatopolk-Mirsky, that honeymoon of *rapprochement* between the government and "the public," when trust was the general watchword and when government announcements and liberal leading articles alike were written with pens dipped in a sickening mixture of aniline and treacle. Secondly, we discuss January 9, the Red Sunday unequalled in dramatic horror, when the atmosphere so saturated with mutual confidence was suddenly pierced by the scream of bullets fired from guardsmen's rifles and shattered forever by the curses of the proletarian masses. The comedy of the liberal spring had come to an end. The tragedy of revolution was beginning.

We pass over in almost complete silence the eight months between January and October. Interesting though that period was in itself, it does not add anything fundamentally new without which the history of the three decisive months of 1905 might not be understood. The October strike was almost as much a direct consequence of the January procession to the Winter Palace as the December rising was a consequence of the October strike.

The final chapter of the historical part sums up the events of the revolutionary year, analyzes the method of revolutionary struggle and gives a brief description of the political developments of the three years that followed. The essential conclusion of this chapter can be expressed thus: *La révolution est morte, vive la révolution!*

❖ ❖ ❖

The chapter devoted to the October strike is dated November 1905. It was written during the final hours of the great strike which drove the ruling clique into a blind alley and forced

Nicholas II to sign with trembling hand the manifesto of October 17. At the time, this chapter was published as an article in two issues of the Petersburg social-democratic paper *Nachalo*; it is reproduced here almost without change, not only because it draws the general picture of the strike with a degree of completeness sufficient for our present purpose, but also because by its very mood and tone it is, to some extent, characteristic of the political texts that were published in that period.

The second part of the book represents an independent whole. It is the history of the court trial of the Soviet of Workers' Deputies and, subsequently, of the author's exile to Siberia and his escape therefrom. However, there is an inner link between the two parts of the book; not only because at the end of 1905 the Petersburg Soviet of Workers' Deputies stood at the very center of revolutionary events, but also, and above all, because its collective arrest marked the opening of the era of counter-revolution. One after the other, all revolutionary organizations throughout the country fell victim to the counter-revolution. Systematically, step by step, with ferocious determination and bloodthirsty vengefulness, the victors eradicated every trace of the great movement. And the less they were aware of any immediate danger, the more bloodthirsty became their contemptible vindictiveness. The Petersburg Soviet of Workers' Deputies was brought before the court in 1906. The maximum sentence passed was privation of all civil rights and exile to Siberia for an unlimited period. The Yekaterinoslav Soviet of Workers' Deputies was not tried until 1909, but the results were very different: several dozen of the condemned were sentenced to forced labor and thirty-two death sentences were pronounced, of which eight were actually carried out.

After the titanic struggle and the temporary victory of the revolution came the epoch of liquidation: arrests, exiles, attempted escapes, dispersion over the entire world—and therein lies the connection between the two parts of my book.

We conclude this preface by expressing our warmest gratitude to Mrs. Zarudnaya-Kavos, the well-known Petersburg artist, who put at our disposal her pencil sketches and pen drawings made during the court trial of the Soviet of Workers' Deputies.

Vienna, October 1909

Contents

(xix)

Contents

PART TWO

Contents

(xxi)

PART ONE

CHAPTER 1

❖◇❖◇❖◇❖◇❖◇❖

Russia's Social Development and Tsarism

Our revolution* destroyed the myth of the "uniqueness" of Russia. It demonstrated that history does not have special laws for Russia. Yet at the same time the Russian revolution bore a character wholly peculiar to itself, a character which was the outcome of the special features of our entire social and historical development and which, in turn, opened entirely new historical perspectives before us.

There is no need to dwell on the metaphysical question of whether the difference between Russia and Western Europe is a "qualitative" or a "quantitative" one. But neither can there be any doubt that the principal distinguishing characteristics of Russia's historical development are its slowness and its primitive

---

* I am speaking of the revolution of 1905 and of the changes it introduced into Russia's social and political life: the forming of parties, representation in the Duma, open political struggle, etc.

nature. In point of fact, the Russian state is not all that much younger than the European states; the chronicle of Russia's life as a state begins in the year 862. Yet the extremely slow rate of our economic development, determined by unfavorable natural conditions and a sparse population, has delayed the process of social crystallization and has stamped the whole of our history with the features of extreme backwardness.

It is hard to tell how the life of the Russian state would have developed if it had taken place in isolation, influenced by internal tendencies alone. Suffice it to say that this was not the case. Russia's social existence was always under constant pressure from the more developed social and state relations of Western Europe, and as time went on this pressure became more and more powerful. Given the relatively weak development of international trade, a decisive role was played by military relations between states. First and foremost, the social influence of Europe found expression in the form of military technology.

The Russian state, having been formed on a primitive economic basis, was brought face to face with state organizations which had developed on a higher economic basis. Two possibilities presented themselves: the Russian state had either to fall in the struggle with those state organizations, as the Golden Horde had fallen in the struggle with Muscovite Tsardom, or it had to outpace the development of its own economic relations, swallowing up, under pressure from outside, a disproportionately large part of the nation's vital juices. The Russian national economy was no longer primitive enough to allow of the former solution. The state did not collapse; it began to grow, at the price of monstrous pressure upon the nation's economic forces.

Up to a certain point all the above also applies, of course, to any other European state. The difference is that in their mutual struggle for existence those states could draw on economic bases of an approximately equal kind, so that their development as states was not subject to such powerful and economically intolerable outside pressures.

The struggle against the Crimean and Nogayan Tartars involved immense effort; but that effort was, of course, no greater than that involved in the Hundred Years' War between France and England. It was not the Tartars who forced the Russians to introduce firearms and to form regular regiments of marksmen (*streltsy*); it was not the Tartars who, later, forced Russia to create a cavalry and an infantry. The pressure which brought this about came from Lithuania, Poland, and Sweden. In order to stand up to a better-armed enemy, the Russian state was compelled to create industry and technology at home; hire military specialists, official money-forgers, and gunpowder-makers; import textbooks on fortification techniques; set up naval schools; build factories; appoint "privy" and "active privy" councillors. And while it was possible to import military instructors and privy councillors from abroad, the material means had to be squeezed, at whatever cost, out of the country itself.

The history of Russia's state economy is an unbroken chain of efforts—heroic efforts, in a certain sense—aimed at providing the military organization with the means necessary for its continuing existence. The entire government apparatus was built, and constantly rebuilt, in the interests of the treasury. Its function consisted in snatching every particle of the accumulated labor of the people and utilizing it for its own ends.

In its search for material means, the government balked at nothing. It imposed arbitrary taxes on the peasants, taxes which at all times were intolerably heavy and to which the population was quite unable to adapt itself. It introduced the system of mutual guarantees in the villages. By pleas and threats, admonitions, and extortion it took money from the merchants and the monasteries. The peasants ran away from the land; the merchants emigrated. Seventeenth-century censuses show that the population was constantly decreasing. At that time, the total state budget amounted to 1.5 million roubles, of which 85 per cent was spent on the armies. At the beginning of the eighteenth century, Peter, owing to the cruel blows administered to him from abroad, was obliged to reorganize the infantry on a new pattern and to create a fleet. During the second half of the eighteenth century the budget already amounted to 16 to 20 million roubles, of which 60 to 70 per cent was spent on the army and navy. Nor did this figure fall below 50 per cent under Nicholas I. In the middle of the nineteenth century the Crimean War brought the Tsarist autocracy into armed conflict with the economically most powerful European states—England and France—as a result of which it became necessary to reorganize the army on the basis of universal conscription. Fiscal and military requirements played a decisive role in the semi-liberation of the peasants in 1861.

But the means available within the country were inadequate. As far back as under Catherine II the government was empowered to borrow money from abroad. Thenceforth the European stock exchange became increasingly the source from which Tsarism drew its finances. From that time on, the accumulation of vast amounts of capital on the West European money markets came to have a fatal effect on the progress of Russia's political development. The intensified growth of the state organization now found expression not only in an excessive increase in indirect taxation, but also in a feverish growth of the national debt. During the ten years between 1898 and 1908 this rose to 19 per cent and by the end of the period it had reached 9 billion roubles. The extent of the autocracy's dependence on the Rothschilds and the Mendelssohns is demonstrated by the fact that interest alone now absorbed approximately a third of the treasury's net revenue. In the preliminary budget for 1908, expenditure on the army and navy, together with the interest on repayment of the national debt, and costs connected with the ending of the (Russo-Japanese) war amounted to 1,018,000,000 roubles, that is, 40.5 per cent of the entire state budget.

As a result of this pressure from Western Europe, the autocratic state absorbed a disproportionately large share of the surplus product, which is to say that it lived at the expense of the privileged classes then being formed and thus restrained their development which, in any case, was a slow one. But that was not all. The state seized the essential product of the agricultural worker, snatched from him the very sources of his livelihood, and, by so doing, drove him from the soil on which he had hardly had time to become securely settled; this in turn inhibited population growth and restricted the development of productive forces. Therefore, as the state absorbed a disproportionately large part of the surplus product, so it inhibited the process—at any rate, a slow one—of class or estate differentiation; and, as it seized a significant part of the basic product, it destroyed even those primitive productive bases which were its only support.

But in order to exist and rule, the state itself had need of a hierarchical organization of estates. And that is why, while undermining the economic foundations of the growth of such organization, it strove at the same time to force its development by state-imposed measures—while endeavoring, like all other states, to turn this process to its own advantage.

In the play of social forces, the pendulum swung much further in the direction of state power than was the case in the history of Western Europe. That exchange of services—at the expense of the working people—between the state and the higher social groups, which is expressed in the distribution of rights and obligations, services and privileges, occurred less in favor of the nobility and the clergy in Russia than had been the case in the medieval estate organizations of Western Europe. Nevertheless it is a terrible exaggeration and a distortion of all perspective to say, as Milyukov says in his history of Russian culture, that while in the West the estates created the states, in Russia state power created the estates in its own interest.

Estates cannot be created by legislative or administrative means. Before a particular social group, assisted by state power, can become a fully-fledged privileged estate, it must form itself economically with all its social privileges. You cannot create estates in accordance with a previously devised "table of ranks" or with the charter of the *Légion d'honneur*.

One thing is certain: in its relationship to the Russian privileged estates, Tsarism enjoyed an incomparably greater degree of independence than European absolutism which had grown out of estate monarchy.

Absolutism reached the apex of its power when the bourgeoisie, having hoisted itself on the shoulders of the third estate, became sufficiently strong to serve as an adequate counterweight to the forces of feudal society. The situation in which the privileged and owning classes, by fighting one another, balanced one another, ensured maximum independence for the state organization. Louis XIV was able to say, *"L'état, c'est moi."* The absolute monarchy of Prussia appeared to Hegel as an end in itself, as the materialization of the idea of the state as such.

In its endeavor to create a centralized state apparatus, Tsarism was obliged not so much to oppose the claims of the privileged estates as to fight the barbarity, poverty, and general disjointedness of a country whose separate parts led wholly independent economic lives. It was not the equilibrium of the economically dominant classes, as in the West, but their weakness which made Russian bureaucratic autocracy a self-contained organization. In this respect Tsarism represents an intermediate form between European absolutism and Asian despotism, being, possibly, closer to the latter of these two.

But at a time when semi-Asiatic social conditions were transforming Tsarism into an autocratic organization, European technology and European capital were equipping that organization with all the means of a great European power. This enabled Tsarism to intervene in all the political relations of Europe, where its heavy fist came to play the role of a decisive factor. In 1815, Alexander I arrived in Paris, restored the Bourbons and himself became the incarnation of the idea of the Holy Alliance. In 1848, Nicholas I obtained an immense loan for the suppression of the European revolution and sent Russian soldiers against the rebellious Magyars. The European bourgeoisie hoped that the Tsar's troops would, on future occasions, again serve as a weapon against the socialist proletariat, as they had previously served European despotism against the bourgeoisie itself.

But historical development took a different course. Absolutism was smashed by capitalism, which it had itself so zealously nurtured.

During the pre-capitalist epoch, the influence of Europe on the Russian economy was, of necessity, limited. The natural— that is to say, the self-contained—character of the Russian national economy protected it from the influence of higher forms of production. As we have already said, the structure of our estates was not fully developed even at the final stage. But when capitalist relations finally became predominant in Europe, when finance capital became the incarnation of the new economy, when absolutism, fighting for its life, became the accomplice of European capitalism, then the situation changed utterly.

Those "critical" socialists who have ceased to understand the significance of state power for a socialist revolution should at least study the example of the unsystematic and barbaric activity of the Russian autocracy so as to realize the immensely important role which state power can play in the purely economic sphere when, generally speaking, it is working in the same direction as historical development.

By turning itself into a historical instrument in the capitalizing of Russia's economic relations, Tsarism was, first and foremost, shoring up its own position.

By the time that our developing bourgeois society began to feel a need for the political institutions of the West, the autocracy, aided by European technology and European capital, had already transformed itself into the largest capitalist entrepreneur, the largest banker, the monopoly owner of railways and of liquor retail shops. In this it was supported by the centralized bureaucratic apparatus, which was in no way suited for regulating the new relations, but was perfectly capable of applying systematic repression with considerable energy. The vast dimensions of the country were conquered by the telegraph, which gave the administration a sense of confidence, a certain homogeneity and great speed, while the railways enabled military forces to be transferred at short notice from one end of the country to another. The pre-revolutionary governments of Europe had practically no railways or telegraph at their disposal. The army at the disposal of absolutism is colossal, and although it proved inefficient in the serious trial of the Russo-Japanese war, it is still quite good enough for internal rule. Neither the government of France in the old days nor the European governments prior to 1848 had anything comparable to the Russian army of 1908–1909.

The financial and military power of absolutism oppressed and blinded not only the European bourgeoisie but also Russian liberalism, robbing it of any faith in the possibility of fighting absolutism by means of an open trial of force. It seemed as if the military and financial power of absolutism excluded every possibility of a revolution in Russia.

What actually took place was the exact opposite.

The more centralized a state is, and the more independent from the ruling classes, the more rapidly it is transformed into a self-contained organization placed above society. The greater the military and financial forces of such an organization, the more prolonged and more successful its struggle for existence. A centralized state with a budget of two billion roubles, a national debt of eight billion and with a million men under arms could have maintained itself for a long time after it had ceased to satisfy the most elementary needs of social development—including the need for military security, for the sake of which it had originally been formed.

Thus the administrative, military, and financial might of absolutism, which enabled it to continue existing despite and against social development, not only did not exclude the possibility of revolution—as the liberals thought—but, on the contrary, made revolution the only possible way of development; moreover, the fact that the growing power of absolutism was constantly widening the gulf between itself and the popular masses engaged in the new economic development guaranteed that the revolution would bear an extremely radical character.

Russian Marxism can be truly proud of the fact that it was alone in pointing out how things were likely to develop, and predicted the general forms of that development* at a time when Russian liberalism was living on a diet of the most utopian of "realisms" and Russia's revolutionary populists nourished themselves on fantasies and a belief in miracles.

* Even so reactionary a bureaucrat as Professor Mendeleyev is unable to deny this fact. Speaking of the development of industry, he remarks, "The socialists saw something in this, and even, up to a point, understood something of it, but they went astray because they clung too closely to their dogma, recommended violence, encouraged the animal instincts of the mob and strove for revolution and power."

CHAPTER 2

◇◆◇◆◇◆◇◆◇◆◇◆◇

Russian Capitalism

The low level of development of the productive forces, considering the predatory activities of the state, left no room for the accumulation of surpluses, for the widespread development of social division of labor, or for urban growth. The crafts were not separated from agriculture nor were they concentrated in towns; instead, they remained in the hands of the village population, in the form of home industries scattered over the entire countryside. It was precisely because of the dispersed nature of artisanal work that home craftsmen were obliged to work, not to order, like the craftsmen of European towns, but on the chance possibility of sale. The merchant or the traveler was the intermediary between the scattered producer and the scattered consumer. In this way the sparseness and poverty of the population and the resulting smallness of the towns determined the immense role of commercial capital in the organization of the national economy of old Muscovite Russia. But commercial capital, too, remained scattered and failed to create any major commercial centers.

It was not the village craftsman, nor even the rich merchant, but the state itself which finally came face to face with the necessity of creating a large-scale industry. The Swedes imposed on Peter the creation of a navy and a new type of army. But having made its military organization more complex, the Petrine state became directly dependent on the industries of the Hanseatic cities and Holland and England. Thus the creation of Russian manufactures to supply the army and the navy became an essential task of national defense. Before Peter, there was never a suggestion of factory production. At his death there already existed 233 large-scale state and private enterprises: mines, armaments factories, cloth, linen, and sailcloth factories, etc. The economic basis for these new industries was provided, on the one hand, by state funds and, on the other hand, by commercial capital. Furthermore, new branches of industry were frequently imported from abroad together with European capital which enjoyed corresponding privileges for a number of years.

Merchant capital played an important role in creating major industries in Western Europe. But there manufacture grew on the basis of collapsing artisanal trade, the previously independent craftsman being transformed into a hired industrial worker. In Muscovy the manufactures imported from the West found no free craftsmen on the spot and so were obliged to make use of the labor of peasant serfs.

That is why the Russian eighteenth-century workshop did not, from the very start, encounter any competition from urban artisanal trade. Neither was the cottage craftsman a rival to it: he was working for a popular consumer, while the manufacturing workshop, regimented from head to foot, worked primarily for the state and, to some extent, for the upper classes of society.

During the first half of the nineteenth century the textile industry broke the circle of serf labor and state regimentation. Factories based on freely hired labor were, of course, radically hostile to the social relations of the Russia of Nicholas I. For that reason, the serf-owning nobility's point of view was wholly that of the "free traders." As far as his sympathies were concerned, Nicholas himself entirely shared this viewpoint. Yet the needs of the state, including fiscal needs, forced him to adopt a policy of prohibitive taxes and financial subsidies to the factory owners. After the lifting of the embargo on the importation of machines from England, the Russian textile industry developed entirely on the basis of ready-made English models. During the 1840s and 1850s the German, Knopp, transferred 122 spinning factories, down to the last nail, from England to Russia. In the textile area there even used to be a proverb: "Where there's trouble, there's a cop, where there's a factory there's Knopp." Since the textile industry was working for a market, it put Russia in fifth place (on a world scale) as regards the number of spindles, despite the chronic shortage of skilled hands and even before the abolition of serfdom.

But the other branches of industry, especially ironmaking, developed hardly at all after the death of Peter. The main reason for this stagnation was slave labor, which rendered the application of new technology quite impossible. Cheap cotton is manufactured for the use of peasant serfs themselves; but iron presupposes a developed industry, towns, railways, railway engines. None of this was compatible with serfdom. At the same time serfdom was also holding back the development of agriculture, which, as time went on, was working more and more for the foreign market. Hence the abolition of serfdom became a pressing demand of economic development. But who could put it into effect? The nobility refused even to consider it. The capitalist class was as yet too negligible to achieve a reform of such vast scope by any pressure it could exert. The frequent peasant riots, which in any case bore no comparison with the peasant war in Germany or with the Jacquerie in France, remained mere scattered outbursts and, finding no leadership in the cities, were in themselves too weak to destroy the power of the landowners. The state had to pronounce the decisive word. Tsarism had to suffer a cruel military defeat in the Crimean campaign before it could, in its own interests, clear the way for capitalist development by means of the semi-liberation reform of 1861.

This point marked the beginning of a new period of economic development within the country, a period characterized by the rapid formation of a pool of "free" labor, a feverish development of the railway network, the creation of seaports, the incessant inflow of European capital, the Europeanization of industrial techniques, cheaper and more easily available credit, an increase in the number of limited stock companies, the introduction of gold currency, ferocious protectionism and an avalanche-like growth of the national debt. The reign of Alexander III (1881–1894), when the ideology of the "uniqueness" of Russia dominated the whole of public consciousness, starting in the revolutionary conspirator's hideout (the narodnik movement) and ending with the private chancellery of His Majesty himself (official "*narodnost*," or Russianness), was, at the same time, an era of ruthless revolution in production relations. By setting up major industries and by proletarianizing the muzhik, European capital was automatically undermining the deepest foundations of Asian-Muscovite "uniqueness."

The railways acted as a powerful lever for the country's industrialization. The initiative for building them was, of course, the state's. The first railway (between Moscow and Petersburg) was opened in 1851. After the Crimean catastrophe, the state yielded first place in railway construction to private entrepreneurs. Yet, like a tireless guardian angel, it always stood at the back of these entrepreneurs: it assisted the formation of stock and bond capital, it undertook to guarantee profits on capital, it showered the shareholders' path with all kinds of privileges and encouragements. During the first decade after the

peasant reform, 7 thousand *versts* of railways were built Russia, 12 thousand during the second decade, 6 thousand during
the third and, during the fourth, more than 20 thousand in European Russia alone and approximately 30 thousand in the empire
as a whole.

During the 1880s and especially the 1890s, when Witte appeared as the herald of the notion of autocratic police capitalism,
there was a renewed concentration of the railways in the hands
of the treasury. Just as, in the development of credit, Witte saw
a weapon in the hands of the finance minister to "guide the national industry in one direction or another," so state-controlled
railways were seen in his bureaucratic brain as a "powerful
means of controlling the country's economic development."
Stockbroker and political ignoramus that he was, he could not
understand that in fact he was gathering the forces and sharpen-
ing the weapons of revolution. By 1894 the total length of railway line amounted to 31,800 *versts*, including 17,000 *versts* of
state-owned line. In 1905, the year of the revolution, the railway
personnel who played such an immensely important political
role counted 667,000 men.

The customs policy of the Russian government, in which
fiscal greed was intimately bound up with blind protectionism,
almost completely barred the way to the ingress of European
goods. Deprived of the possibility of dumping its products on
Russia, European capital crossed the Eastern frontier in its most
invulnerable and attractive hypostasis: in the form of money.
Any animation on the Russian financial market was always determined by the contracting of new loans from abroad. Parallel
with this, the European entrepreneurs took direct possession of
the most important branches of Russian industry. Europe's finance capital, by assimilating the lion's share of the Russian state
budget, returned in part to Russian territory in the form of
industrial capital. This enabled it, through the intermediary of
the Tsarist fiscal system, not only to exhaust the productive
forces of the Russian muzhik, but also to exploit directly the

working energy of the Russian proletarian. During the final decade of the nineteenth century alone, and especially after the introduction of gold currency in 1897, not less than 1.5 billion roubles of foreign industrial capital flowed into Russia. Whereas during the forty years preceding 1892 the basic capital of limited stock companies increased by only 919 million roubles, during the succeeding decade alone it had increased by 2.1 billion roubles.

The importance of this golden flood from the West for Russian industry can be seen from the fact that whereas in 1890 the sum total of the production of all our factories and plants amounted to 1.5 billion roubles, by 1900 it had risen to between 2.5 and 3 billion. Parallel with this, the number of factory and plant workers increased during the same period from 1.4 million to 2.4 million.

While it is true that Russia's economy, as well as Russian politics, always developed under the direct influence—or rather, the pressure—of European politics and economy, the form and depth of this influence, as we have seen, changed constantly. During the period of artisanal and manufacturing production in the West, Russia borrowed Western technicians, architects, craftsmen, skilled workers of all kinds. When factory production displaced manufacture, machinery became the principal object of imitation and importation. And, finally, when serfdom had fallen under the direct pressure of state needs, giving place to so-called "free" labor, Russia opened herself to the direct influence of industrial capital, the path for which was cleared by foreign state loans.

The chroniclers tell us that in the ninth century we called upon the Varangians from across the sea to come and help us establish a state. Then came the Swedes to teach us European military skills. Thomas and Knopp taught us the textile trade. The Englishman, Hughes, implanted a metallurgical industry in the southern part of Russia, Nobel and Rothschild transformed Transcaucasia into a fountain of oil gushers. And at the same time the viking of all the vikings, the great, the international Mendelssohn brought Russia into the domain of the stock exchange.

While economic contacts with Europe were still limited to the importation of craftsmen and machines or even to loans borrowed for productive purposes, this was, in the last analysis, a question of making the Russian national economy assimilate certain elements of European production. But when free foreign capital, in its race for a high level of profits, flung itself upon Russia's territory, protected by customs duties which were like the Great Wall of China, it became a matter of making the capitalist industrial organism of Europe assimilate the national economy of Russia. That is the program which has filled the last decades of Russia's economic history.

Only 15 per cent of the total number of existing Russian industrial enterprises were created before 1861. Between 1861 and 1880, 23.5 per cent were created, and more than 61 per cent between 1881 and 1900, 40 per cent of all existing enterprises having been created during the last decade of the nineteenth century alone.

In 1767, 10 million *pouds* of pig iron were smelted in Russia. In 1866 (a hundred years later!) smelting still barely reached 19 million *pouds*. By 1896 it had already reached 98 million *pouds*, and in 1904, 180 million; moreover, while in 1890 the south accounted for only one-fifth of the total amount smelted, ten years later it accounted for one-half. The development of the oil industry in the Caucasus proceeded at a similar rate. In the 1860s, less than a million *pouds* of oil were produced; in 1870 the figure was 21.5 million *pouds*. Foreign capital entered upon the scene in the mid-eighties, taking possession of Transcaucasia from Baku to Batum and launching operations intended for the world market. By 1890 oil production had risen to 242.9 million *pouds*, and by 1896 to 429.9 million *pouds*.

Thus we see that the railway, coal-mining and oil industries of the southern part of the country, to which the economic center of gravity has been shifting with extreme rapidity, are only twenty or thirty years old. In this part of Russia, the development assumed from the very start a purely American character, and, within a very few years, Franco-Belgian capital has radically changed the appearance of the steppe provinces, covering them with giant enterprises of a size almost unknown in Western Europe.

Two conditions were necessary for this: European/American technology and the Russian state budget. All the metallurgical plants of the south—many of which were bought from America, down to the last bolt and screw, and transported across the ocean—had government orders guaranteed for several years ahead at the moment of going into operation. The Urals, with their patriarchal, semi-feudal traditions and "national" capitals, remained a long way behind and it is only recently that British capital has begun to eradicate barbaric "Russianness" in that part of the country as well.

The historical conditions of the development of Russian industry sufficiently explain the fact that, despite its relative youth, neither small-scale nor medium-scale production plays any significant role within it. Large-scale factory and plant production has not grown in Russia in any "natural" or organic manner. It did not grow gradually out of artisanal trade and manufacture, since artisanal trade itself had no time to grow out of the cottage industries and was doomed to economic death, even before its birth, by foreign capital and foreign technology. The cotton mill had no need to fight the craftsman weaver; on the contrary, it was the cotton mill that gave birth to cotton-producing cottage industries in the villages. Likewise, the ironmaking industry of the south and the oil industry of the Caucasus were not obliged to swallow up any small enterprises; on the contrary, such enterprises had to be brought into existence as a series of secondary and ancillary branches of the economy.

By reason of the pitiable state of our industrial statistics, it is quite impossible to express the correlation of minor and major production in Russia. The table reproduced below gives only an approximate picture of the real situation, since the information concerning the first two categories of enterprises, occupying up to 50 workmen, are based on materials which are extremely incomplete, or, to be more precise, accidental.

Mining and factory enterprises	Number of enterprises	Number of workers in 1,000 men & as a percentage	
Less than 10 workmen	17,436	65.0	2.5
Between 10 and 49 workmen	10,586	236.5	9.2
Between 50 and 99 workmen	2,551	175.2	6.8
Between 100 and 499 workmen	2,779	608.0	23.8
Between 500 and 999 workmen	556	381.1	14.9
1,000 workmen and above	453	1,097.0	42.8

The same question is vividly illuminated by a comparison of the profits obtained by different categories of commercial and industrial undertakings in Russia.

	No. of undertakings	Sum of profits in million roubles
Profits between 1,000 and 2,000 roubles	37,000 or 44.5%	56 or 8.6%
Profits over 50,000 roubles	1,400 or 1.7%	201 or 45.0%

In other words, about half of all undertakings (44.5 per cent) receive less than one-tenth of the entire profit, whereas one-sixtieth (1.7 per cent) of the enterprises received almost half of the whole surplus value (45 per cent). Moreover, there can be no doubt that the profits of the large enterprises as given in the table are considerably underestimated. To demonstrate the exceptional degree of concentration of Russian industry, we reproduce comparable data (excluding mining enterprises) for Germany and Belgium in the tables on the next page.

The first table, despite the incompleteness, already mentioned, of the data it contains, enables us to draw the following incontrovertible conclusions: (1) within homogeneous groups, the average Russian enterprise employs a considerably larger number of workers than a German one; (2) a considerably higher percentage of workers is concentrated in the large (51–1,000 workers) and very large (over 1,000 workers) enterprises in Russia than is the case in Germany. In the last group this difference is not merely relative but absolute. The second table shows that the same conclusions can be drawn in even more striking form from a comparison between Russia and Belgium.

We shall see further on the enormous influence this highly concentrated character of Russian industry had on the course of the Russian revolution, and indeed on Russia's whole political development.

At the same time we shall have to take into account another circumstance of a not less important nature: this highly modernized industry of a highly capitalistic type involves only a minority of the population, while the peasant majority continues to struggle under the net of class enslavement and pauperism. This fact, in turn, sets narrow limits on the development of capitalist industry in our country.

GROUPS OF FACTORIES AND PLANTS	GERMANY (CENSUS OF 1895)				RUSSIA (STATISTICS FOR 1902)			
	No. of enter-prises	*No. of workers*			*No. of enter-prises*	*No. of workers*		
		1,000	*%*	*average*		*1,000*	*%*	*average*
Between 6 & 50 workers	191,101	2,454.3	44	13	14,189	234.5	12.5	16.5
Between 51 & 1,000 workers	18,698	2,595.5	46	139	4,722	918.5	49.0	195.0
1,000 workers and above	296	562.6	10	1,900	302	710.2	38.5	2,351.0
	210,095	5,612.4	100.0	—	19,213	1,863.2	100.0	—

GROUPS OF ENTERPRISES	BELGIUM (CENSUS OF 1895)				RUSSIA (STATISTICS FOR 1902)			
	No. of enterprises	*No. of workers*			*No. of enterprises*	*No. of workers*		
		1,000	*%*	*average*		*1,000*	*%*	*average*
Between 5 & 49 workers	13,000	162	28.3	12.5	14,189	234.5	12.6	16.5
Between 50 & 499 workers	1,446	250	43.7	170.0	4,298	628.9	33.8	146.3
500 workers or more	184	160	28.0	869.0	726	999.8	53.6	1,377.0
	14,650	572	100.0	—	19,213	1,863.2	100.0	—

The breakdown of the industrially active population into agricultural and non-agricultural pursuits, for Russia and the United States of America, is given in the table below.

	RUSSIA (CENSUS OF 1897)		U.S.A. (CENSUS OF 1900)	
	1,000	*%*	*1,000*	*%*
Agriculture, forestry and similar	18,653	60.8	10,450	35.9
Mining and processing industries, commerce, transport, liberal professions, servants	12,040	39.2	18,623	64.1
Total	30,693	100.0	29,073	100.0

The number of people employed in industry in Russia, with its population of 128 million, is scarcely larger (30.6 million) than in the United States with a population of 76 million (29 million). This is a result of the country's general economic backwardness and the consequent tremendous preponderance of agricultural over non-agricultural population (60.8% as against 39.2%)—a circumstance which must inevitably mark all branches of the national economy.

In 1900 the factories, plants and large-scale manufacturing enterprises of the United States produced 25 billion roubles' worth of goods, whereas the corresponding figure in Russia was only 2.5 billion, that is, 10 per cent, which apart from anything else bears witness to extremely low productivity of labor. During the same year the following amounts of coal were extracted: 1 billion *pouds* in Russia, 1 billion *pouds* in France, 5 billion *pouds* in Germany and 13 billion *pouds* in England. The figures for iron production were: 1.4 *pouds* per worker in Russia, 4.3 *pouds* in France, 9 *pouds* in Germany and 13.5 *pouds* in England. "Yet," says Mendeleyev, "we could supply the entire world with our extremely cheap pig iron, iron, and steel. Our oil, coal, and other mineral reserves are virtually untapped."

But the development of industry corresponding to such wealth is unthinkable without an expansion of the domestic market and an increase in the purchasing power of the population: in other words, with an economic improvement in the life of the peasant masses.

Therein lies the decisive importance of the agrarian question for Russia's future as a capitalist country.

CHAPTER 3

✧✧✧✧✧✧✧✧✧

The Peasantry
and the Agrarian Question

According to calculations (which, by the way, are far from accurate), Russia's economic revenue from the extracting and processing industries amounts to between 6 and 7 billion roubles a year, of which some 1.5 billion, that is to say, more than a fifth, is absorbed by the state. This means that Russia is three to four times poorer than the European states. As we have seen, the number of economically active persons represents a very small percentage of the population as a whole, and, furthermore, the productive capacity of these economically active elements is very low. This is true of industry, whose annual product is far from proportional to the number of persons employed; but the productive capacity of agriculture, which absorbs approximately 61 per cent of the country's labor force and the revenue from which, despite this fact, amounts to only 2.8 billion roubles—that is, less than half the national product—is at an incomparably lower level still.

The conditions of Russia's agriculture (consisting over-whelmingly of peasant agriculture) were, in their essentials, predetermined by the nature of the so-called "liberation reform" of 1861. Carried out in the interests of the state, this reform was wholly adapted to the selfish interests of the nobility. The muzhik was not only cheated in the distribution of land but, also, was placed under the enslaving yoke of taxation.

The table reproduced below shows the land allotments turned over to the three main categories of the peasantry upon the liquidation of serfdom.

Categories of peasants	*No. of men in 1860*	*No. of dessyatins awarded*	*No. of dessyatins per man*
Landlord-owned	11,907,000	37,758,000	3.17
State-owned	10,347,000	69,712,000	6.74
Independent	870,000	4,260,000	4.90
Total	23,124,000	111,730,000	4.83 (average)

Assuming that the land allocation received by state-owned peasants (6.7 *dessyatins* per man) was, under the given economic conditions, sufficient to provide full occupation for the labor power of a peasant family—which roughly corresponds to fact —we are bound to conclude that landlord-owned and inde-pendent peasants received approximately 44 million *dessyatins* short of the required norm. Those areas of land which under serfdom were worked by the peasants for their own needs ab-sorbed only half of their labor power, since for three days of every week they were obliged to work for the landlord. Never-theless, some 2 per cent of the best land was cut off, in favor of the landlords, from these already inadequate land allocations (speaking very generally, with considerable variations between one part of the country and another). Thus agricultural over-population, which formed part of the fundamental condition of serfdom, was further aggravated by the nobility's appropria-tion of peasant land.

The half-century which has elapsed since the reform has brought about a considerable reshuffle in land ownership, land to the value of three-quarters of a billion roubles having passed from the hands of the nobility into those of the merchant and peasant bourgeoisie. But the mass of the peasantry has derived no benefit whatever from this fact.

In 1905, the distribution of the land area of the fifty provinces of European Russia was as follows:

1. Land allotments owned by:	*112 million dessyatins*
former state serfs	66.3
former landlord-owned serfs	38.4
2. Privately owned land owned by:	101.7
companies and associations (including 11.4 by peasant associations)	15.7
Private owners:	
up to 20 *dessyatins* (including 2.3 owned by peasant-owners)	3.2
Between 20 and 50 *dessyatins*	3.3
More than 50 *dessyatins*	79.4
3. Crown and independent lands	145.0
including non-forestry and arable land (approx.)	4.6
4. Lands belonging to the church, to monasteries, municipal institutions etc.	8.8

As we have already seen, the average allotment per male peasant after the land reform was 4.83 *dessyatins*. Forty-five years later, in 1905, the average area including any newly acquired pieces of land amounts to only 3.1 *dessyatins*. In other words, the total area of peasant-owned land has been reduced by 36 per cent.

The development of commercial and industrial activities, which absorbed not more than one-third of the annual growth

of the peasant population; the emigration movement to periph-
eral areas which, to some extent, reduced the peasant population in the center; and lastly, the activities of the Peasant
Bank, which enabled peasants of medium and higher levels of
prosperity to acquire 7.3 million *dessyatins* of land during the
period from 1882 to 1905—these factors proved incapable even
of counterbalancing the effect of the natural population growth
and preventing the exacerbation of land penury.

According to approximate calculations, some 5 million adult
men in Russia cannot find a proper outlet for their labor power.
Only a minority of this total consists of professional vagrants,
beggars, etc. The overwhelming majority of these 5 million
"superfluous men" belong to the black-earth peasantry. By applying their labor force to the land, which could be worked
just as well without them, they lower the productivity of peasant
labor by 30 per cent and, being absorbed in the mass of the
peasantry as a whole, avoid proletarianization by means of the
pauperization of still wider peasant masses.

Theoretically, a possible solution could consist in the intensification of agriculture. But for this the peasants need better education, greater powers of initiative, freedom from tutelage and
a stable legal order—conditions which did not and could not
exist in autocratic Russia. However, the principal obstacle to
the improvement of our agriculture has been, and still remains,
the lack of financial means. And this aspect of the crisis in the
peasant economy goes back, like landlessness, to the reform of
1861.

The peasants did not receive their inadequate land allocations free of cost. They were obliged to pay a redemption fee
to the landlords, with the state acting as intermediary, for the
pieces of land on which they had subsisted before, under serfdom, that is, their own pieces of land whose area, moreover,
had been further reduced by the reform. The fees were established by government agents working hand in glove with the
landowners—and, instead of 648 million roubles, a figure based

on the capitalized profitability of the land, they placed on the shoulders of the peasantry a debt of 867 million roubles. Thus in addition to paying for their own land, the peasants in fact had to pay the landlords an additional 219 million roubles as the price of their liberation from serfdom. To this, as a result of landlessness, were added extortionate land rents and the monstrous work of the Tsarist fiscal organization. For example, direct land tax per *dessyatin* of allotted land amounts to 1.56 roubles and for privately-owned land to 23 kopecks (0.23 roubles). Hence almost the entire weight of the state budget is borne by the peasantry. Devouring the lion's share of the peasants' profits from agriculture, the state gives to the villages virtually nothing in exchange by way of raising their cultural level and developing their productive capacities.

The local agricultural committees set up by the government in 1902 established that from 50 to 100 per cent, and sometimes more, of the net agricultural profit of peasant families is swallowed up by direct and indirect taxation. This leads, on the one hand, to an accumulation of hopeless arrears and, on the other hand, to stagnation and even deterioration of the level of agricultural activity. Both technology and crops over the vast expanse of central Russia today are the same as a thousand years ago. The average crop of wheat from a hectare of land amounts to 26.9 hectoliters in England, 17.0 hectoliters in Germany, and 6.7 hectoliters in Russia. To this should be added that crops on peasant lands are 46 per cent below those on landowners' lands, and that this difference is the greater, the worse the year's harvest. Our peasant has long ago forgotten even how to dream of saving a reserve of grain for a rainy day. The new commodity and financial relations on the one hand, and fiscal obligations on the other, compel him to transform all his natural reserves and economic surpluses into ready cash which is immediately swallowed up by the payment of rents and taxes. The feverish race for ready money forces the peasant to do constant violence to his land, depriving it of fertilization and rational husbandry.

Every bad harvest, which is the earth's vengeance for its own maltreatment, has the effect of an elemental, devastating disaster on the villages which, as we have seen, possess no stock of reserves whatsoever.

But even in so-called "normal" years, the peasant masses cannot emerge from a state of semi-starvation. Here is the peasant budget which ought to be engraved on the golden foreheads of the European bankers, the creditors of Tsarism: every member of a peasant family spends 19.5 roubles per annum on food, 3.8 roubles on lodging, 5.5 roubles on clothing, 1.4 roubles on other material needs and 2.5 roubles on spiritual and intellectual needs! A single skilled American worker spends, directly and indirectly, as much as two Russian families of six members each. Yet to cover this type of expenditure, which no state moralist could call excessive, the peasantry's income from agriculture is more than a billion roubles short each year. Cottage industries bring in about 200 million roubles' profit to the villages. If this sum is deducted, peasant agriculture shows an annual deficit of 850 million roubles, which is precisely the sum which the state fiscal organization snatches each year from the hands of the peasantry.

In our description of peasant agriculture we have until now ignored the economic differences between different regions, which, in actual fact, are of the greatest significance and have found powerful expression in the forms of the agrarian movement (see the chapter entitled *The Peasant Riots*). If we concentrate on the fifty provinces of European Russia, and set aside the northern forest strip, the remainder of the area can, from the viewpoint of peasant agriculture and of economic development in general, be divided into three large regions:

1. The industrial region, including Petersburg province in the north and Moscow province in the south. This northern capitalist area, dominated by Petersburg and Moscow, is characterized by factories (especially textiles), cottage industries, flax cultivation, and commercial agriculture—

in particular, market gardening. Like all other industrial regions, this area does not grow sufficient grain for its needs and is obliged to import it from the south.

2. The southeastern region adjoining the Black Sea and the lower reaches of the Volga: the Russian America. This area, in which serfdom was almost non-existent, played the role of a colony in relation to the central part of Russia. So-called "wheat factories," using modern agricultural machinery and exporting their grain to the industrial region in the north and to foreign countries in the west, sprang up rapidly in the free expanses of the steppe, attracting a large number of immigrants. Parallel with this there took place a transfer of labor power to the processing industries, the flourishing of heavy industry and feverish urban growth. In this area, the differentiation within the peasant community goes extremely deep, the peasant farmer standing at one end of the scale and the agricultural proletarian, in many cases an immigrant from the black-earth provinces, at the other.

3. Between the old industrial north and the new industrial south there lies the broad strip of black earth, the Russian India. Its population, which was relatively dense even under serfdom and was engaged in agriculture in its entirety, lost 24 per cent of its land area as a result of the reform of 1861, the best, essential parts of the peasants' allotments being turned over to the landowners. Land prices rose rapidly, the landlords engaged in a purely parasitic economy, partly cultivating their lands with the peasants' stock and partly leasing them to the peasants, who were thus bound inescapably to slavish rent conditions. Hundreds of thousands of peasants are leaving this region for the industrial area in the north and for the south, where they bring down the level of labor conditions. In the black-earth strip there is neither large-scale industry nor capitalist agriculture. Here, the capitalist farmer cannot

compete with the pauper tenant-farmer, and the steam plow is defeated in the struggle with the physiological resilience of the muzhik, who, having paid as rent not only the entire profit on his "capital" but also a large part of his wages, exists on a diet of flour mixed with wood shavings or ground tree-bark. In some places the poverty of the peasants is assuming such proportions that even the presence of bedbugs or cockroaches in an *izba* is regarded as an eloquent sign of relative wealth. It is an actual fact that the rural doctor Shingarev, today a liberal deputy to the Duma, has found that in the homes of landless peasants investigated by him in some areas of Voronezh province no bedbugs are encountered at all, whereas among other categories of the village population the number of bed-bugs encountered is largely proportional to the family's "wealth." The cockroach, it appears, is less of an aristo-crat, but it, too, requires a higher standard of comfort than the Voronezh pauper: in 9.3 per cent of peasant fam-ilies, cockroaches are not found on account of the pre-vailing starvation and cold.

Under such conditions it is futile to speak of any develop-ment of agricultural technology. The peasants' stock, including beasts of labor, is sold to pay the rents and taxes, or else is eaten. But where there is no development of the productive forces, there, too, no social differentiation can take place. Equality of pauperism reigns within the black-earth community. Compared with the north and south, the stratification of the peasantry is highly superficial. Above the embryonic class differences stands the acute estate antagonism between the pauperized peasantry and the parasitic nobility.

The three areas described do not, of course, correspond ex-actly to the geographical limits of the regions concerned. The unity of the state and the absence of internal customs barriers exclude any possibility of formation of separate economic or-ganisms. During the 1880s the semi-serfdom relations in agri-

culture which were dominant in the twelve provinces of the
central black-earth area prevailed, also, in five provinces outside
the black-earth strip. On the other hand, capitalist agricultural
relations predominated in nine black-earth provinces as well as
in ten non-black-earth provinces; and, lastly, in seven provinces
the two systems were roughly equivalent.

The struggle between tenant farming and capitalist agriculture—a struggle which, though it involves no shedding of
blood, claims countless victims—has been continuing, and still
continues without cease; capitalist agriculture is far from being
in a position to boast of victory. The peasant, caught in the
mousetrap of his land allotment and deprived of the means of
earning money on the side, is obliged, as we have seen, to rent
the landlord's land at any price. He not only relinquishes all
profit, not only cuts down his own consumption to the lowest
minimum, but also sells his own agricultural stock, thus lowering
still further the already very low technological level of the
economy. Large capital is powerless in the face of these fatal
"advantages" of small-scale farming: the landlord will have
nothing to do with rational methods of cultivation, and cuts his
land up into minute portions so as to let it out to peasants. By
raising land rents and prices, the surplus population of the central part of the country, at the same time, lowers wages throughout the country as a whole. In so doing it renders unprofitable
the introduction of machinery and modern techniques, not only
in agriculture but also in other branches of production. During
the last decade of the nineteenth century, profound economic
decay had already extended to a considerable part of the southern region, where, parallel with the growth of land rents, there
was a progressive reduction in the number of the peasants' beasts
of labor. The crisis in agriculture and the progressive pauperization of the peasantry is narrowing still further the basis of Russian industrial capitalism, which is obliged to work principally
for the domestic market. Inasmuch as heavy industry is fed by
state orders, the progressive impoverishment of the muzhik

has become a terrible menace to heavy industry because it under-
mines the very foundations of the state budget.

These conditions are sufficient in themselves to explain why
the agrarian question has become the axis of Russia's political
life. All the country's oppositional and revolutionary parties
have already received cruel wounds from the sharp edges of the
agrarian problem: this was true in December 1905, in the first
Duma, and the second Duma. Today the third Duma is scurry-
ing around the agrarian question like a squirrel in a wheel. Tsarism, too, runs the risk of smashing its criminal head against the
same problem.

The government of the nobility and the bureaucracy, even
with the best intentions, is powerless when it comes to carrying
out a reform in an area where palliatives have long since lost all
meaning. The 6 or 7 million *dessyatins* of good land which are
today at the government's disposal are utterly inadequate, given
the presence in the country of 5 million surplus male workers.
But even if the state were to sell this land to the peasants, it
would have to do so at prices which it would have to pay itself
to the landowners: which means that even if these millions of
dessyatins were to pass rapidly and entirely into peasant hands,
every muzhik rouble, instead of finding productive use in the
economy, would drop into the bottomless pocket of the nobility
and the government.

The peasantry cannot make the leap from poverty and hunger into the paradise of intensive and rational agriculture; to
make such a transition possible at all, the peasantry must immediately, under the existing conditions of its economy, receive adequate land to which to apply its labor power. The transfer of
all large and medium lands into the hands of the peasants is the
first and essential prerequisite of any profound agrarian reform.
Compared with the tens of millions of *dessyatins* which, in the
hands of the landowners, serve only as a means of extorting
usurers' rents from the peasants, the 1,840 pieces of land, extending over 7 million *dessyatins*, where relatively rational large-

scale agriculture is being conducted, are hardly significant. Yet the sale of this privately owned land to the muzhiks would change the situation only very little: what the muzhik now pays as rent, he would then have to pay in the form of purchase price. There remains confiscation.

But it is not difficult to show that even confiscation of large lands would not, by itself, save the peasantry. The overall profit from agriculture amounts to 2.8 billion roubles, of which 2.3 billion are derived from peasants and agricultural laborers and approximately 450 million from the landowners. We have already mentioned that the peasantry's annual deficit amounts to 850 million roubles. It follows that the income which would be derived from the confiscation of the landowners' lands would not even cover that deficit.

Those who oppose the expropriation of landowners' lands have often based their arguments on calculations of this kind. But they ignore the main aspect of the problem: the real significance of expropriation would be that a free farming economy at a high technological level, which would multiply the overall income from the land, could be developed on the estates torn from the idle hands which now possess them. But such American-type farming is only conceivable in Russia if Tsarist absolutism with its fiscal demands, its bureaucratic tutelage, its all-devouring militarism, its debts to the European stock exchanges, were totally liquidated. The complete formula for the agrarian problem is as follows: expropriation of the nobility, liquidation of Tsarism, democracy.

That is the only way in which our agriculture can be shifted from its present stagnation, increasing its productive forces and at the same time raising its demand for industrial products. Industry would receive a mighty impulse for further development and would absorb a considerable proportion of the surplus rural population.

None of this, of course, can provide a final solution to the agrarian problem: no solution can be found under capitalism.

But, in any case, the revolutionary liquidation of the autocracy and feudalism must precede the solution which is to come.

The agrarian problem in Russia is a heavy burden to capitalism: it is an aid to the revolutionary party and at the same time its greatest challenge: it is the stumbling block for liberalism, and a *memento mori* for counter-revolution.

CHAPTER 4

◇◇◇◇◇◇◇◇◇◇

The Driving Forces
of the Russian Revolution

A population of 150 million people, 5.4 million square kilometers of land in Europe, 17.5 million in Asia. Within this vast space every epoch of human culture is to be found: from the primeval barbarism of the northern forests, where people eat raw fish and worship blocks of wood, to the modern social relations of the capitalist city, where socialist workers consciously recognize themselves as participants in world politics and keep a watchful eye on events in the Balkans and on debates in the German Reichstag. The most concentrated industry in Europe based on the most backward agriculture in Europe. The most colossal state apparatus in the world making use of every achievement of modern technological progress in order to retard the historical progress of its own country.

In the preceding chapters we have tried, leaving aside all details, to give a general picture of Russia's economic relations and social contradictions. That is the soil on which our social classes grow, live and fight. The revolution will show us those classes at a period of the most intensive struggle. But there are consciously formed associations which intervene directly in a country's political life: parties, unions, the army, the bureaucracy, the press and, placed above these, the ministers of state, the political leaders, the demagogues and the hangmen. Classes cannot be seen at a glance—they usually remain behind the scenes. Yet this does not prevent political parties and their leaders, as well as ministers of state and their hangmen, from being mere organs of their respective classes. Whether these organs are good or bad is by no means irrelevant to progress and the final outcome of events. If ministers are merely the hired servants of the "objective intelligence of the state," this by no means relieves them of the necessity of having a modicum of brain inside their own skulls—a fact which they themselves are too often apt to overlook. On the other hand, the logic of the class struggle does not exempt us from the necessity of using our own logic. Whoever is unable to admit initiative, talent, energy, and heroism into the framework of historical necessity, has not grasped the philosophical secret of Marxism. But, conversely, if we want to grasp a political process—in this case, the revolution—as a whole, we must be capable of seeing, behind the motley of parties and programs, behind the perfidy and greed of some and the courage and idealism of others, the proper outlines of the social classes whose roots lie deep within the relations of production and whose flowers blossom in the highest spheres of ideology.

The Modern City

The nature of capitalist classes is closely bound up with the history of the development of industry and of the town. It is true that in Russia the industrial population coincides with the urban population to a lesser extent than anywhere else. Apart from the factory suburbs which, for purely formal reasons, are not included within the boundaries of towns, there exist several dozen important industrial centers in the countryside. Of the total number of existing enterprises, 57 per cent, employing 58 per cent of the total number of workers, are located outside the towns. Nevertheless the capitalist town remains the most complete expression of the new society.

The urban Russia of today is a product of the last few decades. During the first quarter of the eighteenth century Russia's urban population was 328,000, that is, approximately 3 per cent of the total population of the country. In 1812, 1.6 million people were living in towns, which still represented only 4.4 per cent of the total. In the middle of the nineteenth century the urban population amounted to 3.5 million people, or 7.8 per cent. Finally, according to the census of 1897, the urban population by then already amounted to 16.3 million or approximately 13 per cent of the total. Between 1885 and 1897 the urban population had grown by 33.8 per cent, whereas the rural population had increased by only 12.7 per cent. The growth of individual cities during this period was more dramatic still. The population of Moscow rose from 604,000 to 1,359,000, that is, by 123 per cent. The southern towns—Odessa, Rostov-on-Don, Yekaterinoslav, Baku—developed at an even faster rate.

Parallel with the increase in the number and size of towns, the second half of the nineteenth century saw a complete transformation of the economic role of the town within the country's internal class structure.

Unlike the artisanal and guild towns of Europe, which fought with energy and often with success for the concentration of all processing industries within their walls, but rather like the towns of the Asian despotic systems, the old Russian cities performed virtually no productive functions. They were military and administrative centers, field fortresses or, in some cases, commercial centers which, whatever their particular nature, drew their supplies entirely from outside. Their population consisted of officials maintained at the expense of the treasury, of merchants, and, lastly, of landowners looking for a safe harbor within the city walls. Even Moscow, the largest of the old Russian cities, was no more than a vast village dependent on the Tsar's private lands.

The crafts occupied a negligible position in the towns, since, as we already know, the processing industries of the time took the form of cottage industries and were scattered over the countryside. The ancestors of the four million cottage craftsmen listed in the census of 1897 performed the productive functions of the European town artisan but, unlike the latter, had no connection whatever with the creation of manufacturing workshops and factories. When such workshops and factories did make their appearance, they proletarianized the larger part of the cottage craftsmen and placed the rest, directly or indirectly, under their domination.

Just as Russian industry has never lived through the epoch of medieval craftsmanship, so the Russian towns have never known the gradual growth of the third estate in workshops, guilds, communes, and municipalities. European capital created Russian industry in a matter of a few decades, and Russian industry in its turn created the modern cities in which the principal productive functions are performed by the proletariat.

The Big Capitalist Bourgeoisie

Thus large-scale capital achieved economic domination without a struggle. But the tremendous part played in this process by foreign capital has had a fatal impact on the Russian bourgeoisie's power of political influence. As a result of state indebtedness, a considerable share of the national product went abroad year by year, enriching and strengthening the European bourgeoisie. But the aristocracy of the stock exchange, which holds the hegemony in European countries and which, without effort, turned the Tsarist government into its financial vassal, neither wished nor was able to become part of the bourgeois opposition within Russia, if only because no other form of national government would have guaranteed it the usurers' rates of interest it exacted under Tsarism. As well as financial capital, foreign industrial capital, while exploiting Russia's natural resources and labor power, had its political basis outside Russia's frontiers— namely, the French, English, and Belgian parliaments.

Neither could our indigenous capital take up a position at the head of the national struggle with Tsarism, since, from the first, it was antagonistic to the popular masses—the proletariat, which it exploits directly, and the peasantry, which it robs indirectly through the state. This is particularly true of heavy industry which, at the present time, is everywhere dependent on state activities and, principally, on militarism. True, it is interested in a "firm civil rule of law," but it has still greater need of concentrated state power, that great dispenser of bounties. The owners of metallurgical enterprises are confronted, in their own plants, with the most advanced and most active section of the working class for whom every sign that Tsarism is weakening is a signal for a further attack on capitalism.

The textile industry is less dependent on the state, and, furthermore, it is directly interested in raising the purchasing power of the masses, which cannot be done without far-reaching agrarian reform. That is why in 1905 Moscow, the textile city *par excellence,* showed a much fiercer, though not perhaps a more energetic, opposition to the autocratic bureaucracy than the Petersburg of the metalworkers. The Moscow municipal duma looked upon the rising tide with unquestionable goodwill. But when the revolution revealed the whole of its social content and, by so doing, impelled the textile workers to take the path that the metalworkers had taken before them, the Moscow duma shifted most resolutely, "as a matter of principle," in the direction of firm state power. Counter-revolutionary capital, having joined forces with the counter-revolutionary landowners, found its leader in the Moscow merchant Guchkov, the leader of the majority in the third Duma.

The Bourgeois Intelligentsia

European capital, in preventing the development of Russian artisanal trade, thereby snatched the ground from under the feet of Russia's bourgeois democracy. Can the Petersburg or Moscow of today be compared with the Berlin or Vienna of 1848, or with the Paris of 1789, which had not yet begun to dream of railways or the telegraph and regarded a workshop employing 300 men as the largest imaginable? We have never had even a trace of that sturdy middle class which first lived through centuries of schooling in self-government and political struggle and then, hand in hand with a young, as yet unformed proletariat, stormed the Bastilles of feudalism. What has Russia got in place of such a middle class? The "new middle class," the professional intelligentsia: lawyers, journalists, doctors, engineers, university professors, schoolteachers. Deprived of any independent significance in social production, small in numbers, economically dependent, this social stratum, rightly conscious of its own powerlessness, keeps looking for a massive social class upon which it can lean. The curious fact is that such support was offered, in the first instance, not by the capitalists but by the landowners.

The Constitutional-Democratic (Kadet) party, which dominated the first two Dumas, was formed in 1905 as a result of the League of Landed Constitutionalists joining the League of Liberation. The liberal *fronde* of the Landed Constitutionalists, or *zemtsy*, was the expression, on the one hand, of the landowners' envy and discontent with the monstrous industrial protectionism of the state, and, on the other hand, of the opposition of the more progressive landowners, who recognized the barbarism of Russia's agrarian relations as an obstacle to their putting their land economy on a capitalist footing. The League of Liberation united those elements of the intelligentsia which, by their "decent" social status and their resulting prosperity, were prevented from taking the revolutionary path. The landed opposition was always marked with pusillanimous impotence, and our Most August dimwit was merely stating a bitter truth when, in 1894, he described its political aspirations as "senseless dreams." Neither were the privileged members of the intelligentsia, those directly or indirectly dependent on the state, on state-protected large capital or on liberal landownership, capable of forming a political opposition that was even moderately impressive.

Consequently, the Kadet party was, by its very origins, a union of the oppositional impotence of the *zemtsy* with the all-around impotence of the diploma-carrying intelligentsia. The real face of the agrarians' liberalism was fully revealed by the end of 1905, when the landowners, startled by the rural disorders, swung sharply around to support the old regime. The liberal intelligentsia, with tears in its eyes, was obliged to forsake the country estate where, when all is said and done, it had been no more than a fosterchild, and to seek recognition in its historic home, the city. But what did it find in the city, other than its own self? It found the conservative capitalist bourgeoisie, the revolutionary proletariat, and the irreconcilable class antagonism between the two.

The same antagonism has split to their very foundations our smaller industries in all those branches where they still retain any importance. The craft proletariat is developing in a climate of large-scale industry and differs only little from the factory proletariat. Other Russian craftsmen, under pressure from large-scale industry and the working-class movement, represent an ignorant, hungry, embittered class which, together with the *lumpenproletariat*, provides the fighting legions for the Black Hundreds demonstrations and pogroms.

As a result we have a hopelessly retarded bourgeois intelligentsia born to the accompaniment of socialist imprecations, which today is suspended over an abyss of class contradictions, weighed down with feudal traditions and caught in a web of academic prejudices, lacking initiative, lacking all influence over the masses, and devoid of all confidence in the future.

The Proletariat

The same factors of a world-historical nature which had transformed Russia's bourgeois democracy into a head (and a pretty muddled head at that) without a body, also determined the outstanding role of Russia's young proletariat. But, before we inquire into anything else, how large is that proletariat?

The highly incomplete figures of 1897 supply the following answer:

NUMBER OF WORKERS:

A. Mining and processing industries, transport, building and commercial enterprises	3,322,000
B. Agriculture, forestry, fisheries and hunting	2,725,000
C. Day laborers and apprentices	1,195,000
D. Servants, porters, janitors etc.	2,132,000
Total (men and women)	9,272,000

In 1897, the proletariat, including dependent family members, comprised 27.6 per cent of the total population, that is, slightly over one-quarter. The degree of political activity of separate strata within this mass of workers varies considerably, the leading role in the revolution being held almost exclusively by workers in group A in the table above. It would, however, be a most flagrant error to measure the real and potential significance of the Russian proletariat by its relative proportion within the population as a whole. To do so would be to fail to see the social relations concealed behind the figures.

The influence of the proletariat is determined by its role in the modern economy. The nation's most powerful means of production depend directly on the workers. Not less than half the nation's annual income is produced by 3.3 million workers (group A). The railways, our most important means of transport, which alone are able to convert our vast country into an economic whole, represent—as events have shown—an economic and political factor of the utmost importance in the hands of the proletariat. To this we should add the postal services and the telegraph, whose dependence on the proletariat is less direct but nonetheless very real.

While the peasantry is scattered over the entire countryside, the proletariat is concentrated in large masses in the factories and industrial centers. It forms the nucleus of the population of every town of any economic or political importance, and all the advantages of the town in a capitalist country—concentration of the productive forces, the means of production, the most active elements of the population, and the greatest cultural benefits— are naturally transformed into class advantages for the proletariat. Its self-determination as a class has developed with a rapidity unequaled in previous history. Scarcely emerged from the cradle, the Russian proletariat found itself faced with the most concentrated state power and the equally concentrated power of capital. Craft prejudices and guild traditions had no power whatsoever over its consciousness. From its first steps it entered upon the path of irreconcilable class struggle.

In this way the negligible role of artisanal crafts in Russia and of minor industry in general, together with the exceptionally developed state of Russia's large-scale industry, have led in politics to the displacement of bourgeois democracy by proletarian democracy. Together with its productive functions, the proletariat has taken over the petty bourgeoisie's historical role as played in previous revolutions, and also its historical claims to leadership over the peasant masses during the epoch of their emancipation, as an estate, from the yoke of the nobility and the state fiscal organization.

The agrarian problem proved to be the political touchstone by which history put the urban political parties to the test.

The Nobility and Landowners

The Kadet (or, rather, former Kadet) program of enforced expropriation of large and medium landholdings on the basis of "just assessments" represents, in the Kadets' view, the maximum of what can be achieved by means of "creative legislative effort." But in reality the liberals' attempt to expropriate the large landed estates by legislative means led only to the government's denial of electoral rights and to the coup d'état of June 3, 1907. The Kadets viewed the liquidation of the landowning nobility as a purely financial operation, trying conscientiously to make their "just assessment" as acceptable as possible to the landowners. But the nobility took a very different view of the matter. With its infallible instinct it realized at once that what was at stake was not simply the sale of 50 million *dessyatins*, even at high prices, but the liquidation of its entire social role as a ruling estate; and, therefore, it refused point blank to allow itself to be thus auctioned off. Count Saltykov, addressing the landowners in the first Duma, cried: "Let your motto and your slogan be: not a square inch of our land, not a handful of earth from our fields, not a blade of grass from our meadows, not the smallest twig on a single tree from our forests!" And this was not a voice crying in the wilderness: the years of revolution were precisely the period of estate concentration and political consolidation for the Russian nobility.

During the time of darkest reaction, under Alexander III, the nobility was only one of our estates, even if the first among them. The autocracy, vigilantly protecting its own independence, never for a moment allowed the nobility to escape from the grip of police supervision, putting the muzzle of state control on the maw of its natural greed. Today, on the other hand, the nobility is the commanding estate in the fullest sense of the word: it makes the provincial governors dance to its tune, threatens the ministers and openly dismisses them, puts ultimata to the government and makes sure that these ultimata are observed. Its slogan is: not a square inch of our land, not a particle of our privileges!

Approximately 75 million *dessyatins* are concentrated in the hands of 60,000 private landowners with annual incomes of more than 1,000 roubles; at a market price of 56 billion roubles, this land produces more than 450 million roubles' net profit per annum for its owners. Not less than two-thirds of this sum is the nobility's share. The bureaucracy is closely linked with land ownership. Almost 200 million roubles are spent annually on maintaining 30,000 officials receiving salaries of more than 1,000 roubles. And it is precisely in these middle and higher ranges of officialdom that the nobility is noticeably preponderant. Lastly, it is once more the nobility which is in full control of the organs of rural local government and the incomes derived therefrom.

Whereas, before the revolution, a good half of the rural administrations were headed by "liberal" landowners who had come to the fore on the basis of their "progressive" activities in the rural sphere, the years of revolution have entirely reversed this situation, so that, as a result, the leading positions are now occupied by the most irreconcilable representatives of the landowners' reaction. The all-powerful Council of the United Nobility is nipping in the bud all attempts by the government, undertaken in the interests of capitalist industry, to "democratize" the rural administrations or to weaken the chains of estate slavery which bind our peasantry hand and foot.

In the face of these facts, the agrarian program of the Kadets as a basis for *legislative agreement* has proved hopelessly utopian, and it is hardly surprising that the Kadets themselves have tacitly abandoned it.

The social democrats criticized the Kadet program principally on the grounds of the "just assessment," and they were right to do so. From the financial viewpoint alone, the purchase of all landed estates bringing in a profit of over 1,000 roubles a year would have added a round sum of 5 to 6 billion roubles to our national debt, which already amounts to 9 billion roubles; which means that interest alone would have begun to swallow up three-quarters of a billion roubles a year. However, what matters is not the financial but the political aspect of the question.

The conditions of the so-called liberation reform of 1861, with the help of the excessive redemption fees paid for peasant lands, in fact compensated the landowners for the peasant "souls" lost (roughly to the extent of one-quarter of a billion roubles, that is, 25 per cent of the total redemption fees). On the basis of a "just assessment" the important historical rights and privileges of the nobility would really have been liquidated; the nobility therefore preferred to adapt itself to the semi-liberation reform, and was quickly reconciled to it. At that time, the nobility showed correct instinct, as it does today when it resolutely refuses to commit suicide as an estate, however "just" the "assessment." Not a square inch of our land, not a particle of our privileges! Under this banner the nobility has finally acquired dominance over the government apparatus so badly shaken by the revolution; and it has shown that it is determined to fight with all the ferocity of which a governing class is capable in a matter of life or death.

The agrarian problem cannot be solved by means of parliamentary agreement with the landed estate, but only by means of a revolutionary onslaught by the masses.

The Peasantry and the Towns

The knot of Russia's social and political barbarism was tied in the countryside; but this does not mean that the countryside has produced a class capable, by its own forces, of cutting through that knot. The peasantry, scattered in 500,000 villages and hamlets over the 5 million square versts of European Russia, has not inherited from its past any tradition or habit of concerted political struggle. During the agrarian riots of 1905 and 1906, the aim of the mutinous peasants was reduced to driving the landowners outside the boundaries of their village, their rural area and finally, their administrative area. Against the peasant revolution the landed nobility had in its hands the ready-made weapon of the centralized apparatus of the state. The peasantry could have overcome this obstacle only by means of a resolute uprising unified both in time and in effort. But, owing to all the conditions of their existence, the peasants proved quite incapable of such an uprising. Local cretinism is history's curse on all peasant riots. They liberate themselves from this curse only to the extent that they cease to be purely peasant movements and merge with the revolutionary movements of new social classes.

As far back as the revolution of the German peasantry during the first quarter of the sixteenth century, the peasantry placed itself quite naturally under the direct leadership of the urban parties, despite the economic weakness and political insignificance of German towns at that time. Socially revolutionary in its objective interests, yet politically fragmented and powerless, the peasantry was incapable of forming a party of its own, and so gave way—depending on local conditions—either to the oppositional-burgher or to the revolutionary-plebeian parties of the towns. These last, the only force which could have ensured the victory of the peasant revolution, were however (although based on the most radical class of the society of that time, the embryo of the modern proletariat) entirely without links with the rest of the nation or any clear consciousness of revolutionary aims. They were without them because of the country's lack of economic development, the primitive means of transport, and state particularism. Hence the problem of revolutionary cooperation between the mutinous countryside and the urban plebs was not solved at that time because it could not be solved; and the peasant movement was crushed.

More than three centuries later, correlations of a similar kind were seen again in the revolution of 1848. The liberal bourgeoisie not only did not want to arouse the peasantry and unite it around itself, it actually feared the growth of the peasant movement more than anything else, precisely because this growth would have the primary effect of intensifying and strengthening the position of the plebeian, radical urban elements against the liberal bourgeoisie itself. Yet these elements were still socially and politically amorphous and fragmented and consequently were unable to displace the liberal bourgeoisie and place themselves at the head of the peasant masses. The revolution of 1848 was defeated.

Yet, six decades previously, the problems of revolution were triumphantly resolved in France, precisely through the cooperation of the peasantry with the urban plebs, that is, the proletariat, semi-proletariat, and *lumpenproletariat* of the time. This "cooperation" took the form of the Convention, that is, of the dictatorship of the city over the countryside, of Paris over the provinces, and of the sans-culottes over Paris.

Under contemporary Russian conditions, the social preponderance of the industrial population over the rural population is incomparably greater than at the time of the old European revolutions, and further, a clearly defined industrial proletariat has replaced the chaotic plebs. One thing, however, has not changed: only a party which has the revolutionary urban masses behind it, and which is not afraid, out of pious respect for bourgeois private property, to revolutionize feudal ownership, can rely on the peasantry at a time of revolution. Today only the Social Democrats are such a party.

The Nature of the Russian Revolution

So far as its direct and indirect tasks are concerned, the Russian revolution is a "bourgeois" revolution because it sets out to liberate bourgeois society from the chains and fetters of absolutism and feudal ownership. But the principal driving force of the Russian revolution is the proletariat, and that is why, so far as its method is concerned, it is a proletarian revolution. Many pedants who insist on determining the historical role of the pro-

(49)

letariat by means of arithmetical or statistical calculations, or establishing it by means of formal historical analogies, have shown themselves incapable of digesting this contradiction. They see the bourgeoisie as the providence-sent leader of the Russian revolution. They try to wrap the proletariat—which, in fact, marched at the head of events at all stages of the revolutionary rising—in the swaddling-clothes of their own theoretical immaturity. For such pedants, the history of one capitalist nation repeats the history of another, with, of course, certain more or less important divergences. Today they fail to see the unified process of world capitalist development which swallows up all the countries that lie in its path and which creates, out of the national and general exigencies of capitalism, an amalgam whose nature cannot be understood by the application of historical clichés, but only by materialist analysis.

There can be no analogy of historical development between, on the one hand, England, the pioneer of capitalism, which has been creating new social forms for centuries and has also created a powerful bourgeoisie as the expression of these new forms and, on the other hand, the colonies of today, to which European capital delivers ready-made rails, sleepers, nuts and bolts in ready-made battleships for the use of the colonial administration, and then, with rifle and bayonet, drives the natives from their primitive environment straight into capitalist civilization: there can be no analogy of historical development, certainly, but there does exist a profound inner connection between the two.

The new Russia acquired its absolutely specific character because it received its capitalist baptism in the latter half of the nineteenth century from European capital which by then had reached its most concentrated and abstract form, that of finance capital. The previous history of European capital is in no way connected with the previous history of Russia. In order to attain, on its native ground, the heights of the modern stock exchange, European capital had first to escape from the narrow

streets and lanes of the artisanal town where it had learned to
crawl and walk; it was obliged, in ceaseless struggle with the
Church, to develop science and technology, to rally the entire
nation around itself, to gain power by means of uprisings against
feudal and dynastic privileges, to clear an open arena for itself,
to kill off the independent small industries from which it had itself emerged, having severed the national umbilical cord and
shaken the dust of its forefathers from its feet, having rid itself
of political prejudice, racial sympathies, geographical longitudes
and latitudes, in order, then, at last to soar high above the globe
in all its voracious glory, today poisoning with opium the Chinese craftsman whom it has ruined, tomorrow enriching the
Russian seas with new warships, the day after seizing diamond
deposits in South Africa.

But when English or French capital, the historical coagulate
of many centuries, appears in the steppes of the Donets basin, it
cannot release the same social forces, relations, and passions
which once went into its own formation. It does not repeat on
the new territory the development which it has already completed, but starts from the point at which it has arrived on its
own ground. Around the machines which it has transported
across the seas and the customs barriers, it immediately, without
any intermediate stages whatever, concentrates the masses of a
new proletariat, and into this class it instills the revolutionary energy of all the past generations of the bourgeoisie—an energy
which in Europe has by now become stagnant.

During the heroic period of French history we see a bourgeoisie which has not yet realized the contradictions of its own
position, a bourgeoisie upon which history has placed the leadership of a struggle for a new order, not only against the outdated
institutions of France, but also against reactionary forces in Europe as a whole. The bourgeoisie, personified by all its factions
in turn, gradually becomes conscious of itself and becomes the
leader of the nation; it draws the masses into the struggle, gives
them slogans to fight for, and dictates the tactics of their fight.

Democracy unifies the nation by giving it a political ideology. The people—the petty bourgeoisie, the peasants and the workers —appoint the bourgeoisie as their deputies, and the orders issued to these deputies by the communes are written in the language of a bourgeoisie becoming conscious of its Messianic role. During the revolution itself, although class antagonisms become apparent, the powerful momentum of revolutionary struggle nevertheless consistently removes the most static elements of the bourgeoisie from the political path. No layer is stripped off before it has handed its energy over to the succeeding layers. The nation as a whole continues during all this time to fight for its objectives, using increasingly more radical and decisive means. When the uppermost layers of the property-owning bourgeoisie cut themselves off from the national nucleus which had thus been set in motion, and when they entered into an alliance with Louis XVI, the democratic demands of the nation, now directed against the bourgeoisie as well, led to universal franchise and to the Republic as being the logically inevitable form of democracy.

The great French Revolution was truly a national revolution. But more than that: here, within a national framework, the world struggle of the bourgeois order for domination, for power, and for unimpaired triumph found its classic expression.

By 1848 the bourgeoisie was already unable to play a similar role. It did not want to, and could not, assume responsibility for a revolutionary liquidation of the social order which barred the way to its own dominance. Its task—and this it fully realized— consisted in introducing into the old order certain essential guarantees, not of its own political dominance, but only of co-dominance with the forces of the past. It not only failed to lead the masses in storming the old order; it used the old order as a defense against the masses who were trying to push it forward. Its consciousness rebelled against the objective conditions of its dominance. Democratic institutions were reflected in its mind, not as the aim and purpose of its struggle, but as a threat to its well-being. The revolution could not be made by the bourgeoisie, but only against the bourgeoisie. That is why a successful revolution in 1848 would have needed a class capable of marching at the head of events regardless of the bourgeoisie and despite it, a class prepared not only to push the bourgeoisie forward by the force of its pressure, but also, at the decisive moment, to kick the political corpse of the bourgeoisie out of its way.

Neither the petty bourgeoisie nor the peasantry were capable of this. The *petty bourgeoisie* was hostile not only to the immediate past, but also to the possible future—to the morrow. Still fettered by medieval relations, but already incapable of resisting "free" industry; still centering itself on the cities, but already yielding its influence to the middle and higher bourgeoisie; sunk in its prejudices, deafened by the roar of events, exploiting and exploited, greedy and impotent in its greed, the provincial petty bourgeoisie was incapable of directing world events.

The *peasantry* was deprived of independent initiative to a still greater extent. Dispersed, cut off from the cities which were the nerve centers of politics and culture, dull-minded, its intellectual horizons hedged in like its meadows and fields, indifferent towards everything that the cities had created by invention and thought, the peasantry could not assume any leading significance. Appeased as soon as the burden of feudal tithes was removed from its shoulders, it repaid the cities, which had fought for its rights, with black ingratitude: the liberated peasants became fanatics of "order."

The *democratic intellectual*, devoid of class force, trotted after the liberal bourgeoisie as after an older sister. It acted merely as its political tail. It abandoned it at moments of crisis. It revealed only its own impotence. It was confused by its contradictions—which had not yet fully ripened—and it carried this confusion with it wherever it went.

The *proletariat* was too weak and had too little organization, experience, and knowledge. Capitalist development had gone far enough to necessitate the destruction of the old feudal relations, but not far enough to advance the working class, the product of the new production relations, to the position of a decisive political force. The antagonism between the proletariat and the bourgeoisie had gone too far to enable the bourgeoisie to assume the role of national leadership without fear, but not far enough to enable the proletariat to grasp that role.

Austria provided a particularly acute and tragic example of this political unreadiness in the revolutionary period. The Vienna proletariat in 1848 gave evidence of selfless heroism and great revolutionary energy. Again and again it faced the fire of battle, driven solely by an obscure class instinct, having no general idea of the objective of the struggle, groping its way blindly from one slogan to the next. Surprisingly, the leadership of the proletariat passed into the hands of the students, the only democratic group which, because of its active nature, enjoyed considerable influence over the masses and, consequently, over the events.

But although the students could fight bravely on the barricades and fraternize sincerely with the workers, they were quite incapable of directing the general progress of the revolution which had handed over to them the "dictatorship" of the streets. When, on the twenty-sixth of May, the whole of working Vienna followed the students' call and rose to its feet to fight against the disarming of the "academic legion," when the population of Vienna took *de facto* possession of the city, when the monarchy, by this time on the run, had lost all meaning, when, under the people's pressure, the last troops were removed from the city, when it seemed that Austrian state power could be had for the asking, no political force was available to take over. The liberal bourgeoisie consciously did not wish to seize power in so cavalier a fashion. It could only dream of the return of the Emperor, who had betaken himself from orphaned Vienna to the Tyrol. The workers were courageous enough to smash the reaction, but not organized nor conscious enough to become its successors. The proletariat, unable to take over, was equally unable to impel the democratic bourgeoisie—which, as often happens, had made itself scarce at the most crucial moment—to take this historic and heroic action. The situation which resulted was quite correctly described by a contemporary writer in the following terms: "A de facto republic was established in Vienna, but unfortunately, no one saw this . . ." From the events of 1848–49, Lassalle drew the unshakable conviction that "no struggle in Europe can be successful unless, from the very start, it declares itself to be purely socialist; no struggle into which social questions enter merely as an obscure element, and where they are present only in the background; no struggle which outwardly is waged under the banner of national resurgence or bourgeois republicanism, can ever again be successful."

In the revolution whose beginning history will identify with the year 1905, the proletariat stepped forward for the first time under its own banner in the name of its own objectives. Yet at the same time there can be no doubt that no revolution in the past has absorbed such a mass of popular energy while yielding such minimal positive results as the Russian revolution has done up to the present. We are far from wanting to prophesy the events of the coming weeks or months. But one thing is clear to us: victory is possible only along the path mapped out by Lassalle in 1849. There can be no return from the class struggle to the unity of a bourgeois nation. The "lack of results" of the Russian revolution is only the temporary reflection of its profound social character. In this bourgeois revolution without a revolutionary bourgeoisie, the proletariat is driven, by the internal progress of events, towards hegemony over the peasantry and to the struggle for state power. The first wave of the Russian revolution was smashed by the dull-wittedness of the muzhik, who, at home in his village, hoping to seize a bit of land, fought the squire, but who, having donned a soldier's uniform, fired upon the worker. All the events of the revolution of 1905 can be viewed as a series of ruthless object lessons by means of which history drums into the peasant's skull a consciousness of his local land hunger and the central problem of state power. The preconditions for revolutionary victory are forged in the historic school of harsh conflicts and cruel defeats.

Marx wrote in 1852,

Bourgeois revolutions storm swiftly from success to success; their dramatic effects outdo each other; men and things seem set in sparkling brilliance; ecstasy is the everyday spirit; but they are short-lived; soon they have attained their zenith, and a long crapulent depression lays hold of society before it learns soberly to assimilate the results of its storm-and-stress period. On the other hand, proletarian revolutions . . . criticize themselves constantly, interrupt themselves continually in their own course, come back to the apparently accomplished in order to begin it afresh, deride with unmerciful thoroughness the inadequacies, weaknesses and paltrinesses of their first attempts, seem to throw down their adversary only in order that he may draw new strength from the earth and rise again, more gigantic, before them, recoil ever and anon from the indefinite prodigiousness of their own aims, until a situation has been created in which all turning back is impossible, and the conditions themselves cry out:

Hic Rhodus, his salta!
(*The Eighteenth Brumaire of Louis Bonaparte*)

CHAPTER 5

◇◇◇◇◇◇◇◇◇◇◇

The Spring

I

General Dragomirov, now deceased, once wrote in a private letter about Sipyagin, then Minister of Internal Affairs: "What sort of internal policies can he possibly have? He's only a cavalry n.c.o. and a blockhead at that." This description is so correct that we can overlook its rather mannered rough-and-ready soldier's tone. After Sipyagin we saw the same position occupied by Plehve, then by Prince Svyatopolk-Mirsky, then Bulygin, then Witte-Durnovo. Some of these differed from Sipyagin only by the fact that they were not cavalry n.c.o.'s, while others were intelligent men, in their way. But all of them, one after the other, abandoned the scene, leaving behind them alarm and bewilderment above and hatred and contempt below. The cavalry n.c.o. of little brain, the professional detective, the benevolent but dim-witted gentleman, the stockbroker devoid of conscience and honor, all of them, one after the other, arrived with the firm intention of putting an end to sedition, restoring the lost prestige of authority, maintaining the foundations of the state—and every one of them, each in his own way, opened the floodgates of revolution and was himself swept away by its current.

Sedition grew as though according to a majestic plan, constantly expanding its territory, reinforcing its positions and demolishing obstacle after obstacle; while against the backdrop of this tremendous effort, with its inner rhythm and its unconscious genius, appeared a series of little mannikins of state power, issuing new laws, contracting new debts, firing at workers, ruining peasants—and, as a result, sinking the governmental authority which they sought to protect more and more deeply into a bog of frantic impotence.

Reared in an atmosphere of office conspiracies and departmental intrigues, where insolent ignorance vies with bare-faced perfidy; having not the smallest notion of the course or meaning of contemporary history, the movement of masses, or the laws of revolution; armed with two or three pathetic programmatic ideas for the information of Paris stockbrokers, such men try—harder and harder as time goes on—to combine the methods of eighteenth-century mercenaries with the manners of the "statesmen" of the parliamentary West. Abjectly hoping to ingratiate themselves, they chat with newspaper correspondents from the Europe of the stock exchanges, expound to them their "plans," their "forecasts," their "programs," and each one expresses the hope that he, at last, will succeed in solving the problem against which his predecessors' efforts were in vain. If only, before anything else, they can stop the sedition! They all start differently, but they all end up by issuing the order to fire point-blank on sedition. But, to their horror, sedition remains unkillable. It is they who end in shameful collapse. If a terrorist's obliging bullet does not release them from their sorry existence, they survive to see sedition, with that elemental genius which is its own, turn everything they planned and forecast to its own triumphant advantage.

Sipyagin fell to a revolutionary's bullet. Plehve was torn to pieces by a bomb. Svyatopolk-Mirsky was transformed into a political corpse on January 9. Bulygin was thrown out, like an old boot, by the October strikes. Count Witte, utterly exhausted by workers' and soldiers' risings, fell without glory, having stumbled on the threshold of the State Duma which he himself had created.

In certain circles of the opposition, especially in the milieux of the liberal landlords and the democratic intelligentsia, vague hopes, expectations and plans were invariably associated with the succession of one minister by another. And indeed it was by no means irrelevant to the propaganda of the liberal newspapers or the policies of the constitutionalist landowners whether it was Plehve, the old police wolf, or Prince Svyatopolk-Mirsky, the "Minister of Confidence," who held the reins of power.

Of course Plehve was as powerless against sedition as his successor, but he was a terrible scourge against the kingdom of liberal newspapermen and rural conspirators. He loathed the revolution with the fierce loathing of a police detective grown old in his profession, threatened by a bomb from around every street corner; he pursued sedition with bloodshot eyes—but in vain. And so he found a substitute target for his rancor in professors, rural constitutionalists, journalists, in whom he pretended to see the legal "instigators" of the revolution. He drove the liberal press to the utmost limits of humiliation. He treated the journalists *en canaille**: not only exiling them and locking them up, but also wagging his finger at them as though they were schoolboys. He treated the moderate members of the agricultural committees organized on Witte's initiative as though they were mutinous students instead of "respectable" country gentlemen. And he got what he wanted: liberal society trembled before him and hated him with the inarticulate hatred of impotence. Many of the liberal pharisees who tirelessly condemn "violence from the left" as well as "violence from the right" welcomed

* In French in the original.

the bomb of July 15 as though it were a message from the Messiah.

Plehve was terrifying and loathsome as far as the liberals were concerned, but against sedition he was no better and no worse than any of the others. Of necessity, the movement of the masses ignored the limits of what was allowed and what was forbidden: that being so, what did it matter if those limits were a little narrower or a little wider?

II

The official writers of reactionary panegyrics tried hard to represent Plehve's regency, if not as a period of universal happiness, at least as one of universal calm. But in fact this favorite of the Tsar was unable to establish even a police-controlled calm. No sooner had he assumed power and had the idea—with all the Orthodox fervor of the double convert—of visiting the sacred relics of the Lavra Monastery, than he was compelled to rush southwards because a major agrarian movement had flared up in the Kharkov and Poltava provinces. Peasant disorders on a smaller scale never stopped occurring thereafter. The celebrated Rostov strike in November 1902 and the July days of 1903, which extended over the whole of the industrial south, prefigured all the future actions of the proletariat. Street demonstrations succeeded one another without cessation. The debates and decisions of committees concerned with the needs of agriculture served as a prologue to the agrarian campaign which was to follow. The universities, even before Plehve, had become centers of extreme political turbulence, and they continued to remain so under his rule. Two congresses held in Petersburg in January 1904—the technical and the Pirogov congresses—played the role of a vanguard strike for the democratic intelligentsia.

Thus the prologue to the social "spring" occurred during Plehve's rule. Fierce reprisals, imprisonments, interrogations, house searches, sentences of exile provoked terrorism but were unable to paralyze completely even the mobilization of liberal society.

The last six months of Plehve's rule coincided with the beginning of the Russo-Japanese war. Popular discontent quietened down, or rather entered a latent phase. A book called *Vor der Katastrophe* (Before the Catastrophe) by the Viennese journalist Hugo Ganz gives an idea of the mood which reigned in bureaucratic circles and in the upper reaches of Petersburg liberal society during the first months of the war. The predominant mood was one of bewilderment approaching despair. "Things cannot continue as they are!" But where was the way out? No one knew the answer: neither the high officials in retirement, nor the famous liberal lawyers, nor the famous liberal journalists. "Society is utterly powerless. A revolutionary movement of the people cannot even be thought of; and even if the people did move, they would not move against authority, but against the gentry as a whole." Where, then, lay hope of salvation? In financial bankruptcy and military defeat.

Hugo Ganz, who spent the first three months of the war in Petersburg, reports that the common prayer not only of the moderate liberals, but also of many conservatives was: *"Gott, hilf uns damit wir geschlagen werden"* (Please God, let us be beaten). This did not, of course, prevent liberal society from simulating a tone of official patriotism. In a whole series of addresses, the *zemstvos* and the dumas, one after the other, all without exception, swore their loyalty to the throne and undertook to lay down their lives and property—knowing well that they would not have to do it—for the honor and power of the Tsar and Russia.

The *zemstvos* and the dumas were followed by a shameful queue of professorial bodies. One after the other they responded to the declaration of war by addresses in which the floweriness of the style—a style acquired in priests' seminaries—harmonized with the Byzantine imbecility of the content. This was not an oversight or a misunderstanding. It was a tactic based on a single principle: rapprochement at any price! Hence the efforts to make the emotional drama of reconciliation a little easier for absolutism. To organize, not in the cause of fighting the autocracy, but in the cause of serving it. Not to defeat the government, but to seduce it. To deserve its gratitude and confidence. To become indispensable to it. A tactic which is as old as Russian liberalism and which has not grown wiser nor more dignified with the years. From the very start of the war the liberal opposition did everything to ruin the situation. But there was no stopping the revolutionary logic of events. The Port Arthur fleet was destroyed, Admiral Makarov was killed, the war shifted to the mainland; Yalu, Kin-Chzhou, Dashichao, Wafangou, Liaoyan, Shakhe—all these were different names for one thing only, the humiliating defeat of the autocracy. The government's position was becoming more difficult than ever before. Demoralization in the government ranks made consistency and firmness in domestic matters an impossibility. Hesitation, compromise, conciliation were becoming unavoidable. Plehve's death offered a favorable pretext for a change of policy.

III

Prince Svyatopolk-Mirsky, former chief of the gendarmerie corps, was called upon to establish the governmental "spring." * Why? He would have been the last to be able to explain his own appointment.

This statesman's political personality emerges most clearly from interviews he gave about his program to foreign newspaper correspondents.

"What is the opinion of the Prince," asks the correspondent of *Echo de Paris*, "concerning the opinion held by the public

* This name, which acquired great popularity, was given by Suvorin, the editor of *New Times* (*Novoye Vremya*), to the "epoch of rapprochement between the authorities and the people."

to the effect that Russia needs ministers responsible to the public?"

The Prince smiles.

"Any such responsibility would be artificial and nominal."

"What are your opinions, Prince, on questions of religious freedom?"

"I am an enemy of religious persecutions, but with certain reservations."

"Is it true that you would be inclined to give more freedom to the Jews?"

"Happy results can be achieved by kindness."

"Generally speaking, Mr. Minister, would you describe yourself as being on the side of progress?"

Answer: the Minister intends "to concert his actions with the spirit of true and broad progress, at least to the extent that this is not incompatible with the existing order." These are his exact words.

But even the Prince himself did not take his program seriously. It is true that the "most immediate" objective of the government was "the good of the population entrusted to our care," but he confessed to Mr. Thomson, an American correspondent, that, in substance, he did not yet know what use he would make of his powers.

"I would be wrong," said the Minister, "if I were to say that I already have a definite program. The agrarian question? Yes, yes, we have vast materials relating to this question, but so far, I am acquainted with it only through the newspapers."

The Prince cajoled the Tsar at Peterhof, comforted the liberals, and gave assurances to foreign correspondents which bore witness to the kindness of his heart but hopelessly exposed his lack of statesmanlike gifts.

And this helpless, gentlemanly figure wearing a gendarme's epaulettes was seen—not only in the eyes of Nicholas II, but also in the imagination of the liberals—as the man whose destiny was to remove the century-old bonds cutting into our great nation's flesh!

IV

Everyone, it seemed, received Svyatopolk-Mirsky with enthusiasm. Prince Meshchersky, editor of the reactionary *Grazhdanin* (Citizen), wrote that a day of rejoicing had come for the "vast family of decent people in Russia," because, at last, "an ideally decent man" had been appointed to the post of minister. "An independent man is a man of noble mind," wrote the aged Suvorin, "and we have great need of men of noble mind." Prince Ukhtomsky in the *Peterburgskie Vedomosti* (Petersburg Gazette) drew attention to the fact that the new minister was a descendant of "an ancient princely family going back to Ryurik through Monomakh." The Viennese *Neue Freie Presse* noted, with satisfaction, that the Prince's outstanding characteristics were the following: "humaneness, justice, objectivity, a sympathetic attitude towards enlightenment." The *Birzhevye Vedomosti* (Stock Exchange Gazette) pointed out that the Prince was only 47 years old and that, therefore, he had not yet had time to become steeped in bureaucratic routine.

Verse and prose offerings were published telling us how "we had been asleep" and how, by a liberal gesture, the former commandant of the special gendarmerie corps had awakened us from sleep and pointed the way for a "rapprochement between authority and the people." When you read these outpourings you have the impression of breathing the gas of stupidity at a pressure of 20 atmospheres.

Only the extreme right managed not to lose its head in this "bacchanalia of liberal delight." The *Moskovskie Vedomosti* (Moscow Gazette) ruthlessly reminded the Prince that, together with Plehve's portfolio, he was also taking over his problems. "If our internal enemies in the underground print shops, in various public organizations, in the schools, in the press, and in the streets with bombs in their hands, have raised their heads high to prepare for their assault of our internal Port Arthur, this is possible only because they are befuddling society, as well as certain ruling circles, with utterly false theories to the effect that it is necessary to remove the surest foundations of the Russian State—the autocracy of its Tsars, the Orthodoxy of its Church, and the national self-awareness of its people."

Prince Svyatopolk tried to steer a middle course: autocracy, but made a little less rigid by legality; bureaucracy, but with public support. *Novoye Vremya*, which supported the Prince because the Prince was in power, assumed the task of a semi-official political procuress. A favorable opportunity for this was evidently at hand.

The Minister, whose benevolence failed to meet with an appropriate response among the camarilla which ruled Tsar Nicholas, made a timid attempt to seek support among the *zemtsy:* this was the object of the proposed conference of representatives of rural councils. But the excitement rising within society and the heightened tone of the press made the outcome of the conference appear increasingly dangerous. By October 30 *Novoye Vremya* had definitely changed its tune. "However interesting and instructive the decisions reached by the members of the conference may be, it should not be forgotten that, by reason of its composition and the method of issuing invitations, it is quite rightly viewed in official circles as a private meeting, and its decisions have only academic significance and carry only moral obligations."

In the end the conference of the *zemtsy*, which was supposed to provide a basis of support for the "progressive" Minister, was forbidden by that self-same Minister and was held semi-legally in a private apartment.

V

On November 6–8, 1904, a hundred personalities prominent in the *zemstvos* formulated, by a majority of 70 to 30 votes, a demand for public freedom, personal immunity, and popular representation with participation in legislative power, without, however, pronouncing the sacramental word *constitution*.

The liberal European press noted this tactful omission with respect: the liberals had found a way of saying what they wanted while at the same time avoiding the word which might have rendered it impossible for Prince Svyatopolk to accept their declaration.

This is a perfectly correct explanation of the meaningful omission in the *zemstvo* declaration. In formulating their demands, the *zemtsy* had in mind only the government with which they had to seek agreement, but not the popular masses to whom they might have appealed.

They worked out various points for a political compromise bargain, but they had no slogans for political agitation. In this they did no more than remain faithful to themselves.

"The public has done its work, now it is the government's turn!" the press exclaimed in a tone of challenge mingled with subservience. Prince Svyatopolk-Mirsky's government took up the "challenge," and promptly issued a warning to the liberal journal *Pravo* (Right)—for making the subservient appeal quoted above. The newspapers were forbidden to print or discuss the resolutions of the *zemstvo* conference. A modest petition from the Chernigov *zemstvo* was declared "insolent and tactless." The governmental spring was nearing its end; the spring of liberalism was only just beginning.

The *zemstvo* conference was a safety valve for the oppositional mood of the "educated public." Admittedly the conference did not consist of official representatives of all the *zemstvos*, but it did include the chairmen of town councils and many "authoritative" personalities (whose crass ignorance alone gave weight and significance to their views). Admittedly, the conference was not legalized by the bureaucracy, but it did take place with the bureaucracy's knowledge, and therefore the intelligentsia, reduced to extreme timidity, now believed that its innermost constitutional desires, the secret dreams of its sleepless nights, had been granted semi-official approval. And nothing so encouraged liberal society as the sense—even if it was an illusory one—that its demands were rooted in legal soil.

A season of banquets, resolutions, declarations, protests, memoranda, and petitions began. Corporations and associations of all kinds started out with professional and local events and jubilee celebrations and ended up with the same formulation of constitutional demands as appeared in the henceforth celebrated "11 points" of the *zemstvo* conference's resolution. The democrats hastened to form a choir around the *zemstvo* choir leaders to emphasize the importance of the *zemstvo*'s decisions and increase their influence upon the bureaucracy. For liberal society, the entire political task of the moment was reduced to exerting pressure on the government from behind the *zemtsy's* backs. At first it looked as though the resolutions themselves might, like Whitehead's mine, blow up the bureaucracy. But this did not happen. The resolutions began to become overfamiliar to those who wrote them as well as to those against whom they were written. The press, whose throat was being gripped more and more tightly by the Ministry of Internal Confidence, gradually became irritable without any definite object for its irritation.

At the same time the opposition began to become fragmented. More and more frequently, impatient, ill-mannered, intolerant persons came forward to take the floor at the banquets —an intellectual one day, a worker another—and harshly attacked the *zemtsy* and demanded that the intelligentsia's slogans be more clearly worded and its tactics more definite. People tried to calm down these persons, to conciliate them, to flatter them, to scold them, to shut them up, to mollify them, to cajole them; finally, they threw them out; but the impatient persons continued to do their work, pushing the left-wing elements of the intelligentisia on to the path of revolution.

While the right wing of the public materially or ideologically connected with liberalism was trying to prove the moderation and loyalty of the *zemtsy's* conference and appealed to Prince Svyatopolk's statesmanlike reason, the radical intelligentsia, predominantly composed of young students, joined the November campaign with the purpose of steering it off its pitiful course, giving it a more militant character and linking it with the revolutionary movement of the urban workers. This gave rise to two street demonstrations: one in Petersburg on November 28 and one in Moscow on December 5 and 6. These demonstrations of the radical "sons" were a direct and inevitable consequence of the slogans advanced by the liberal "fathers": once the decision to demand a constitutional order had been taken, it was necessary to plunge into the struggle. But the "fathers" showed no inclination whatever to accept such consistent political thinking. On the contrary, they immediately took fright lest excessive haste and impulsiveness break the delicate cobweb of confidence. The "fathers" did not support the "sons"; they handed them over, hand and foot, to the liberal Prince's cossacks and mounted gendarmes.

Neither, however, did the students receive any support from the workers. This made it manifestly clear how limited, in reality, was the "banqueting campaign" of November and December 1904. Only the thinnest, uppermost layer of the proletariat's aristocracy joined it, and "real workers," whose appearance gave rise to mixed feelings of hostile fear and curiosity, could be counted at the banquets of this period in single or at most double figures. The deep inner process taking place in the consciousness of the actual masses was not, of course, in any way linked with the hastily conceived actions of the revolutionary students.

And so the students were, in the final analysis, left almost entirely to their own resources.

Nevertheless these demonstrations, after the long political truce caused by the war—demonstrations which, given the critical internal situation created by military defeat, bore a sharply political character and which the telegraph quickly reported to the world at large—made a much stronger impression on the government, purely as a symptom, than all the wise admonitions of the liberal press. The government pulled itself together and made haste to show its mettle.

VI

The constitutional campaign which began with a meeting of several dozen *zemtsy* in Korsakov's elegant apartment and ended with the incarceration of several dozen students in the police stations of Petersburg and Moscow met with a twofold response from the government: a reformist "ukase" and a police "announcement." The ukase of December 12, 1904, which remains the finest fruit of the "confidence policy" of the so-called "spring," made the safeguarding of the basic laws of the Empire an essential condition for any further reformist activity. Generally speaking, the ukase formulated what had already been contained in Prince Svyatopolk's newspaper interviews, which were so filled with good intentions and cautious reservations.

This gives a sufficiently clear idea of its value. The government announcement issued two days later possessed an incomparably higher degree of political clarity. It described the November conference of the *zemtsy* as the prime source of a subsequent movement "alien to the Russian people," and reminded the dumas and the *zemstvos* that in discussing the resolutions of the November conference they were acting against the law. The government pointed out further that its lawful duty consisted in defending state order and the public peace; for that reason, all gatherings of an anti-government character would be stopped by all legal means at the authorities' disposal. If the Prince enjoyed little success in his efforts directed towards the peaceful reconstruction of the country, he was quite strikingly successful in fulfilling the more general task which was, in fact, the reason why history had placed him for a time at the head of the government: the task of destroying the political illusions and prejudices of the average citizen.

The era of Svyatopolk-Mirsky, which opened to the fanfare of the trumpets of conciliation and ended with cossacks' whips whistling through the air, had the effect of raising to unparalleled heights the hatred of absolutism among all elements of the population possessing even a modicum of political consciousness. Political interests took a more sharply defined form; discontent became more profound and more a matter of principle. What had, only yesterday, been but primitive thought, today threw itself avidly into the work of political analysis. All manifestations of evil and arbitrary rule were rapidly reduced to their fundamentals. Revolutionary slogans now frightened no one: on the contrary, they found a thousandfold echo and were transformed into popular sayings. As a sponge absorbs moisture, so the consciousness of society absorbed every word which rejected or condemned absolutism.

Now absolutism could do nothing more with impunity. Every awkward step was counted against it. Its attempts to ingratiate itself met with scorn. Its threats provoked hatred. True, Prince Svyatopolk's ministry made considerable concessions to the press, but the range of interests of the press grew much more rapidly than the mild tolerance of the Central Directorate for Press Affairs. The same was true in all other domains: the half-freedom granted as a form of charity proved no less irritating than total enslavement. That is generally the fate of concessions in a revolutionary epoch: they fail to satisfy, but only give rise to more stringent demands. More insistent demands were made in the press, at meetings and congresses, and these in their turn irritated the authorities, who were rapidly losing their "confidence" and sought aid in repression. Meetings and congresses were closed down, a hail of blows rained down upon the press, demonstrations were dispersed with merciless brutality. Finally, as if to help the common citizen to appreciate the true meaning of the ukase of December 12, on December 31, Prince Svyatopolk issued a circular explaining that the examination of measures concerning the peasantry, which had been announced in the liberal ukase, would now be carried out on the basis of Plehve's plan. That was the government's last act in 1904. The year 1905 opened with events which drew a fatal boundary between the past and the present. With a line of blood they put an end to the "spring," to the childhood of Russia's political consciousness. Prince Svyatopolk, his kindness, his plans, his confidence, his circulars—all were rejected and forgotten.

CHAPTER 6

◇◇◇◇◇◇◇◇◇

January Ninth

Headman of the Streltsy

Great Sire,
We cannot hold the people back—
They burst in, crying:
"We want to bow to Tsar Boris,
We want to see the Tsar."

Boris

Fling wide the doors:
Between the Russian people and the Tsar
There is no barrier.

A. Tolstoy, Tsar Boris

I

Sire! We workers, our children and wives, the helpless old people who are our parents, we have come to you, Sire, to seek justice and protection. We are in great poverty, we are oppressed and weighed down with labors beyond our strength; we are insulted, we are not recognized as human beings, we are treated like slaves who must suffer their lot in silence. And we have suffered it, but we are being driven ever deeper into beggary, lawlessness, and ignorance. Despotism and arbitrary rule are strangling us, and we are suffocating. Sire, our strength is at an end! The limit of our patience has been reached; the terrible moment has come for us when it is better to die than to continue suffering intolerable torment.

Thus began the celebrated petition of the Petersburg workers. In these words the proletarian threat may ring more true than the pleading of loyal subjects. The petition went on to describe all the oppressions and insults which the people had to suffer. It listed everything, from unheated factories to political lawlessness in the land. It demanded amnesty, public freedoms, separation of church from state, the eight-hour working day, a fair wage, and the gradual transfer of land to the people. But at the head of everything it placed the convening of a Constituent Assembly by universal and equal suffrage.

The petition ended,

These, Sire, are our greatest needs which we bring before you. Command and swear that they will be satisfied, and you will make Russia great and glorious and imprint your name eternally upon our hearts and the hearts of our descendants. But if you do not grant them, if you fail to hear our plea, we shall die here, in this square in front of your palace. We have nowhere else to go and no other cause to serve. Before us lie only two paths: to freedom and happiness, or to the grave. Sire, point either of those paths to us and we shall follow, even if it is the path towards death. Let our lives be sacrificed for long-suffering Russia. We are not sorry to make this sacrifice; we shall make it willingly."

And they made the sacrifice.

The workers' petition not only replaced the hazy phraseology of liberal resolutions with the incisive slogans of political democracy, but also filled those slogans with class content by demanding the right to strike and the eight-hour day. Its historical significance lies, however, not in the text but in the fact. The petition was only a prologue to an action which united the working masses. They were united momentarily in their appeal to an idealized monarchy; then, in the recognition that the proletariat and the *real* monarchy were mortal enemies.

The course of events is still alive in the memories of all. It covered only a few days and it unfolded in a strange way, as though according to a plan. On January 3 a strike broke out at the Putilov works. By January 7 the number of strikers had reached 140,000. The culminating point of the strike was on January 10. By the thirteenth, work was already resuming. Thus, there was first an economic strike sparked off by incidental causes. It spread to tens of thousands of workers and so became transformed into a political event. The strike was organized by the "Association of Factory and Plant Workers," an organization which had its origins in the police. The radicals, whose banqueting policy had reached a dead end, were burning with impatience. Dissatisfied with the purely economic character of the strike, they pushed Gapon, its leader, forward to a more political position; but he found such discontent, anger, and revolutionary energy among the workers that the petty plans of his liberal backers were completely swamped. The social democrats moved to the fore. Met with hostility at first, they quickly adapted themselves to their audience and took control of it. Their slogans were taken up by the masses and incorporated in the petition.

The government withdrew into complete inactivity. For what reason? Cunning provocation? Pathetic confusion? Both. The bureaucrats of Prince Svyatopolk's type lost their heads stupidly. Trepov's gang, anxious to put an end to the "spring" and for that reason consciously hoping for a massacre, let events develop to their logical conclusion. The telegraph was allowed complete freedom to inform the entire world about every stage of the January strike. Every Paris concierge knew three days in advance that there was going to be a revolution in Petersburg on Sunday, January 9. And the Russian government did not move a finger to avoid the massacre.

Meetings went on incessantly in eleven sections of the workers' "Association." The petition was drafted and plans for the march to the palace were discussed. Gapon went from section to section; the social-democratic agitators grew hoarse and dropped to the floor with exhaustion. The police did nothing to intervene. The police did not exist.

As agreed, the march to the palace was a peaceful one, without songs, banners, or speeches. People wore their Sunday clothes. In some parts of the city they carried icons and church banners. Everywhere the petitioners encountered troops. They begged to be allowed to pass. They wept, they tried to go around the barrier, they tried to break through it. The soldiers fired all day long. The dead were counted in the hundreds, the wounded in the thousands. An exact count was impossible since the police carted away and secretly buried the bodies of the dead at night.

At midnight on January 9, Georgiy Gapon wrote:

"My pastor's curse upon the soldiers and officers who are killing their innocent brothers and their wives and children, upon the oppressors of the people. My blessing on those soldiers who help the people to strive for freedom. I absolve them from their military oath to the traitor Tsar who ordered the shedding of innocent blood."

History used Gapon's fantastic plan for its own ends—and all that was left for Gapon to do was to sanction its revolutionary conclusion with his authority as a priest.

At a meeting of the Committee of Ministers on January 11, Count Witte, not then in power, proposed that the events which had taken place on the ninth and the measures "for the future prevention of such regrettable events" be discussed. Witte's proposal was rejected as "not falling within the Committee's competence and not included in the agenda for the present meeting." The Committee of Ministers allowed the beginning of the Russian revolution to go unnoticed because the Russian revolution was not on its agenda.

II

The forms taken by the historic events of January 9 could not, of course, have been foreseen by anyone. The priest whom history had so unexpectedly placed for a few days at the head of the working masses imposed the imprint of his personality, his views and his priestly status on the events. The real content of these events was concealed from many eyes by their form. But the inner significance of January 9 goes far beyond the symbolism of the procession to the Winter Palace. Gapon's priestly robe was only a prop in that drama; the protagonist was the proletariat. The proletariat began with a strike, united itself, advanced political demands, came out into the streets, drew to itself the enthusiastic sympathy of the entire population, clashed with the troops and set off the Russian revolution. Gapon did not create the revolutionary energy of the workers of St. Petersburg; he merely released it, to his own surprise. The son of a priest, and then a seminarian and student at the Aeligious Academy, this agitator, so obviously encouraged by the police, suddenly found himself at the head of a crowd of a hundred thousand men and women. The political situation, his priestly robe, the elemental excitement of the masses which, as yet, had little political consciousness, and the fabulously rapid course of events turned Gapon into a "leader."

A spinner of fantasies on a psychological subsoil of adventurism, a southerner of sanguine temperament with a touch of the confidence man about him, a total ignoramus in social matters, Gapon was as little able to guide events as he was to foresee them. Events completely overtook him.

The liberals persisted for a long time in the belief that the entire secret of the events of January 9 lay in Gapon's personality. It contrasted him with the social democrats as though he were a political leader who knew the secret of controlling the masses and they a doctrinaire sect. In doing so they forgot that January 9 would not have taken place if Gapon had not encountered several thousand politically conscious workers who had been through the school of socialism. These men immediately formed an iron ring around him, a ring from which he could not have broken loose even if he had wanted to. But he made no attempt to break loose. Hypnotized by his own success, he let himself be carried by the waves.

But although, on the very next day after Bloody Sunday, we ascribed to Gapon a wholly subordinate political role, we all undoubtedly overestimated his personality. With his halo of holy anger, with a pastor's curses on his lips, he seemed from afar almost to be a Biblical figure. It seemed as though powerful revolutionary passions had been awakened in the breast of this young priest employed at a Petersburg transit prison. And what happened? When the lights burned low, Gapon was seen by everyone to be the utter political and moral nonentity he really was. His posturing before socialist Europe, his pathetic "revolutionary" writings from abroad, both crude and naïve, his return to Russia, his conspiratorial relations with the government, the pieces of silver dealt out by Count Witte, Gapon's pretentious and absurd interviews with representatives of the conservative press, and finally, the wretched betrayal which caused his end —all these finally destroyed any illusions concerning the Gapon of January 9.

We cannot help recalling the shrewd words of Viktor Adler, the leader of the Austrian social democrats, who, on reading the first telegram which announced Gapon's departure from Russia, said: "A pity. . . . It would have been better for his name in history if he had disappeared from the scene as mysteriously as he had come upon it. We would have been left with a beautiful romantic legend about the priest who opened the floodgates of the Russian revolution. There are men," Adler added with the subtle irony so characteristic of him, "whom the role of martyrs suits better than that of party comrades."

III

"There is not yet such a thing as a revolutionary people in Russia." Thus wrote Peter Struve in his paper *Osvobozhdenie* (Liberation), published abroad, on January 7, 1905—precisely two days before the guards regiments crushed the Petersburg workers' demonstration.

"There is no such thing as a revolutionary people in Russia," said Russian liberalism through the lips of a renegade socialist, having managed to persuade itself in the course of a three-months' banqueting jamboree that it was the principal actor on the political scene. The statement had not had time to reach Russia before the telegraph wires carried to all corners of the earth the great news of the beginning of the Russian revolution.

We had waited for it; we had never doubted it. For long years it had been for us the only logical conclusion of our "doctrine" which was mocked by nonentities of every political hue. They did not believe in the revolutionary role of the proletariat; instead, they believed in the force of the *zemtsy's* petitions, in Witte, in Svyatopolk-Mirsky, in jars of dynamite. There was no political prejudice in which they did not believe. Our belief in the proletariat was the only thing they regarded as prejudice.

Not only Struve, but also that "educated public" whose service he had lately joined were taken by surprise. With eyes gaping in terror and impotence they watched through their windows the unfolding of the historical drama. The intelligentsia's intervention in the events was truly pitiful and negligible. A deputation of several literary men and professors visited Prince Svyatopolk-Mirsky and Count Witte "in the hope," as the liberal press explained, "of illuminating the problem in such a way that the use of military force might be avoided." A mountain was moving against another mountain and meanwhile this democratic handful believed that a visit to a couple of ministerial ante-rooms would suffice to avoid the inevitable. Svyatopolk refused to receive the deputation. Witte only gestured hopelessly. And then, as though availing themselves of Shakespeare's license to introduce an element of farce into the greatest tragedy, the police declared the pathetic deputation to be the "provisional government" and dispatched it to the Fortress of Peter and Paul.

Yet the January days drew a sharp dividing line across the amorphous blurred field of the intelligentsia's political conscience. The intelligentsia temporarily relegated to the archives our traditional liberalism with its faith in the happy succession of governmental personalities. Svyatopolk-Mirksy's foolish reign

had been the era of such liberalism's finest flowering, the reformist ukase of December 12 its ripest fruit. But January 9
swept away the "spring," replacing it by a military dictatorship
and giving unlimited powers to Trepov, the unforgotten general,
whom the liberal opposition had only just removed from the
post of Moscow's police chief. At the same time the distinction
between democrats and the official opposition became increasingly clear in liberal society. The workers' action strengthened
the position of the radical elements within the intelligentsia, just
as the *zemtsy's* conference had earlier put a trump card in the
hands of the opportunist elements. The question of political
freedom took on concrete form for the first time in the consciousness of the left wing of the opposition. They saw it in
terms of struggle, the balance of forces, the onslaught of powerful popular masses. And now, the revolutionary proletariat—
yesterday's "political fiction of the Marxists"—was seen to be a
powerful reality.

"Is this the moment," wrote the influential liberal weekly
Pravo, "after the bloody January days, to cast doubt on the historic mission of the Russian urban proletariat? It is evident that
this question, for the present moment in history at least, has been
solved—not solved by us, but by those workers who, during the
memorable January days, by the force of the terrible and bloody
events, wrote their names in the sacred book of Russia's social
movement." Only a week had passed between the publication
of Struve's article and the writing of those lines; yet a whole historical epoch lies between them.

IV

January 9 was a turning point in the political consciousness of
the capitalist bourgeoisie.

During the years just preceding the revolution and to the
great dissatisfaction of capital, a whole school of government
demagogy (the so-called Zubatov school) had come into being.

Its aim was to provoke workers towards economic clashes with the manufacturers and thus divert them from a clash with the state. But now, after Bloody Sunday, the normal course of industrial life came to a complete standstill. Work was only done in snatches, in the intervals between moments of unrest. The enormous profits from deliveries to the armed forces did not go to industry, which was in a state of crisis, but to a small group of privileged and predatory monopolists. There was nothing to reconcile industry with the state of growing chaos. One branch of industry after another passed to the opposition. Stock-exchange associations, industrial congresses, so-called "consultative bureaus"—that is to say, camouflaged syndicates—and other organizations of capital, politically virginal only yesterday, now vented their distrust of the autocratic police-state system and began to speak the language of liberalism. The city merchant showed that in the cause of opposition he had nothing to yield to the "enlightened" landowner. The dumas not only joined the *zemstvos* but, in some cases, placed themselves at their head. And the Moscow duma, which was an organization of merchants, moved into the front rank.

The struggle of various branches of capital among themselves for the favors and bounties of the Ministry of Finance temporarily receded in face of the universal demand for the renewal of civil and state order. Instead of simple notions about concessions and subsidies, or side by side with these, more complex ideas about the development of productive forces and the expansion of the domestic market began to emerge. Side by side with these dominant ideas, a sharp interest in calming the worker and peasant masses made its appearance in all the petitions, memoranda and resolutions of the employers' organizations. Capital was disillusioned with the panacea of police repression, which is like a rope that lashes at the living bodies of the workers with one end and whacks the industrialists' pockets with the other; and so it arrived at the solemn conclusion that the peaceful course of capitalist exploitation needed a liberal regime. "Et tu, Brute!"

the reactionary press howled as it watched the Old Believer merchants of Moscow, pillars of ancient tradition, supporting the constitutional "platforms." But the howling did not bring the Brutus of the textile industry to a stop. He had to describe his political parabola, in order, at the end of the year, when the proletarian movement reached its apex, to claim once more the protection of the holy, the one and indivisible policeman's whip.

V

But the most profound and significant effect of the January massacre was upon the Russian proletariat. A tremendous wave of strikes swept the country from end to end, convulsing the entire body of the nation. According to approximate calculations, the strike spread to 122 towns and localities, several mines in the Donets basin and 10 railways. The proletarian masses were stirred to the very core of their being. The strike involved something like a million men and women. For almost two months, without any plan, in many cases without advancing any claims, stopping and starting, obedient only to the instinct of solidarity, the strike ruled the land.

At the height of the storm of strikes, in February 1905, we wrote:

After January 9 the revolution knows no stopping. It is no longer satisfied with the hidden underground work of continually arousing new strata of the population; it is now making an overt and urgent roll call of its fighting companies, its regiments, battalions and divisions. The proletariat is the main force of its army and that is why the revolution has made the strike its means of carrying out this roll call.

Trade after trade, factory after factory, town after town are stopping work. The railway personnel act as the detonators of the strike; the railway lines are the channels along which the strike epidemic spreads. Economic claims are advanced and are satisfied, wholly or in part, almost at once. But neither the beginning of the strike nor its end is fully determined by the nature of the claims made or by the form in which they are met. The strike does not occur because the economic struggle has found expression in certain well-defined demands; on the contrary, the demands are chosen and formulated because there has to be a strike. The workers have to reveal to themselves, to the proletariat in other parts of the country, finally to the nation at large, their accumulated strength, their class responsiveness, their fighting readiness. Everything has to be submitted to the universal revolutionary appraisal. The strikers themselves and those who support them, those who fear them and those who hate them, all realize or dimly sense that this furious strike which leaps from place to place, then takes off again and rushes forward like a whirlwind—that this strike is not merely itself, that it is obedient to the will of the revolution which has sent it down upon the land. Over the operational area of the strike—and that operational area is the country at large—there hangs something menacing, sinister and defiant.

After January 9 the revolution knows no stopping. Without a care for military secrecy, openly, noisily, mocking the routine of life, dispelling its drugged dullness, the revolution leads us to its own culminating point.

CHAPTER 7

~~~~~~~~~~~~~~~~~~~~~~~~

The Strike in October

So you think the revolution is coming?
It's coming!
            Novoye Vremya, 5 May 1905

Here it is!
            Novoye Vremya, 14 October 1905

I

The fact that perfectly free popular gatherings were taking place within the walls of universities while Trepov's unlimited terror reigned in the streets was one of the most astonishing political paradoxes of the autumn months of 1905. A certain General Glazov, old and ignorant, who for no known reason found himself holding the post of Minister of Education, created—much to his own surprise—these islands of freedom of speech. The liberal professors protested that the universities are for study and the street has no place in the academics. Prince Sergey Trubetskoy died with this truth upon his lips. But for several weeks the doors of the universities remained wide open. "The people" filled the corridors, lecture rooms and halls. Workers went directly from the factory to the university. The authorities were confounded. They could crush, arrest, trample and shoot workers while they remained in the streets or in their homes. But as soon as the worker crossed the threshold of the university he promptly became inviolable. The authorities were thus given an object lesson in the advantages of constitutional law over the law of autocracy.

The first free popular meetings took place on September 30 in the universities of Petersburg and Kiev. The official telegraph agency, horrified by the audience which gathered in the assembly hall of Vladimir University, reported that apart from students. the crowd consisted of "a multitude of extraneous persons of both sexes, secondary school pupils, adolescents from the town's private schools, workers and a miscellaneous rag, tag, and bobtail."

The revolutionary word had escaped from underground and was filling the university halls, lecture rooms, corridors and quadrangles. The masses were greedily taking in the slogans of revolution, so beautiful in their simplicity. The unorganized, accidental crowd which seemed like "a miscellaneous rag, tag, and bobtail" to the fools of the bureaucracy and the hacks of the reactionary press showed a moral discipline and a political sensibility which amazed even bourgeois journalists.

A columnist wrote in *Rus*:

Do you know what astonished me most of all at a university meeting? The extraordinary, exemplary order. Soon after I arrived, an interval was announced in the assembly hall, and I went for a stroll down the corridor. A university corridor is rather like a street. All the lecture rooms off the corridor were full of people, and independent sectional meetings were taking place inside them. The corridor itself was filled to overflowing; crowds were moving back and forth. Some people sat on the window sills, on benches, on top of cupboards. They smoked; they talked in low voices. One might have thought that one was attending a reception, only a rather more serious one than these affairs usually are. And yet this was the people—the real, genuine people, with hands coarsened by hard manual work, with that earth-colored complexion which people get from spending days in unhealthy, airless premises. And all of them had shining eyes set deeply in their orbits. . . . For these undersized, thin, badly nourished people who had come here from the factory or the plant, from the workshop where steel is smelted or iron is cast, where the heat and smoke are stifling, the university is like a temple, lofty, spacious, dazzlingly white. And every word spoken here has the ring of a prayer. . . . The freshly awakened desire for knowledge absorbs any and every theory like a sponge.

No, this inspired crowd did not absorb any and every theory. Had those reactionary windbags who claim that no solidarity exists between the extremist parties and the masses attempted to address this crowd—but no, they did not dare. They sat tight in their holes-in-the-ground and waited for a breathing space in which they might renew their slanderous attacks on the past. But not only they—even the politicians and spokesmen of liberalism failed to address this vast, forever changing audience. Here the spokesmen of revolution reigned supreme. Here the social democrats forged indissoluble, vital political bonds to unite innumerable people. Here they translated the great social passions of the masses into the language of formulated revolutionary slogans. The crowd which left the university was no longer the crowd that had entered it. . . . Meetings took place every day. The mood of the workers mounted higher and higher, but the party issued no appeal. A popular action was expected to take place considerably later—coinciding with the anniversary of January 9 and the convening of the State Duma, due on January 10. The railwaymen's union threatened to refuse to allow the deputies of Bulygin's duma to enter Petersburg. But events developed more rapidly than anyone had foreseen.

The typesetters at Sytin's print-works in Moscow struck on September 19. They demanded a shorter working day and a higher piecework rate per 1,000 letters set, not excluding punctuation marks. This small event set off nothing more nor less than the all-Russian political strike—the strike which started over punctuation marks and ended by felling absolutism.

The police department plaintively reported that an association called the Union of Moscow Typographers and Lithographers, banned by the government, had taken advantage of the strike at Sytin's. By the evening of September 24, fifty printing works were on strike. A program of claims was drawn up on the twenty-fifth at a meeting permitted by the city governor. This program was interpreted by the city governor as an "arbitrary action of the Soviet of print shop deputies," and in the name of the personal "independence" of workers menaced by such "arbitrary" proletarian action, this police satrap tried to put down the print-workers' strike with his clumsy fist.

But the strike which had arisen over punctuation marks had already had time to spread to other branches. The Moscow bakers struck, and struck so solidly that two companies of the First Don Cossack Regiment, with the heroic courage characteristic of that particular arm of the Tsar's forces, were obliged to take Filippov's bakery by storm. On October 1 telegraphic messages were received from Moscow stating that the strikes at factories and plants were beginning to die down. But they were only drawing breath.

I I

On October 2 the Petersburg typesetters decided to demonstrate their solidarity with their Moscow comrades by means of a three-day strike. Moscow telegraphed that industrial plants in the city were "continuing the strike." There were no street incidents; heavy rain acted as the surest ally of law and order.

The railways, which were to play such a tremendous part in the October struggle, issued a first warning. On September 30 ferment began in the workshops of the Moscow-Kursk and Moscow-Kazan railways. These two railways were prepared to open the campaign on October 1. They were held back by the railwaymen's union. Basing itself on the experience of the February, April, and July strikes of various individual lines, the union was preparing a general railway strike to coincide with the convening of the State Duma; for the present it was against partial action. But the ferment continued unabated. On September 20, an official conference of railwaymen's deputies had opened to discuss the question of pension funds. This conference spontaneously extended its terms of reference and, applauded by the railway world as a whole, transformed itself into an independent trade union and political congress. Greetings to the congress arrived from all sides. The ferment increased. The idea of an immediate general strike of the railways began to gain hold in the Moscow area.

On October 3 we received a telephone message from Moscow to the effect that the strikes in the factories and plants were gradually diminishing. On the Moscow-Brest Railway, where the workshops were on strike, there was a noticeable movement in favor of resumption of work.

The strike had not yet made up its mind. It was still pondering and hesitating.

A meeting of workers' deputies from the printing, engineering, cabinet-making, tobacco, and other trades adopted a decision to form a general council (Soviet) of all Moscow workers.

During the next few days everything seemed to point to conciliation. The strike in Riga came to an end. On October 4 and 5 work was resumed in many of the Moscow printing works. The newspapers appeared once more. A day later the Saratov editions appeared after a week's interruption; nothing seemed to indicate the events that were to come.

At a university meeting in Petersburg on the fifth a resolution was adopted calling for the termination of "sympathy" strikes by a given date. The Petersburg typesetters returned to work after their three-day solidarity strike. On the same day the city governor of Petersburg was already announcing complete order on the Schlisselburg highway and full resumption of work. On the seventh, half the workers of the Neva shipbuilding plant resumed work. All plants beyond the Nevsky gate were working, with the exception of the Obukhov plant which had proclaimed a political strike until October 10.

Everyday life seemed about to return—revolutionary everyday life, of course. It looked as if the strike had made a few disorganized attempts, had abandoned them, and had departed. But that was only how it looked.

III

In reality the strike was preparing to go into action at full tilt. It meant to do its work in the briefest possible time—and immediately tackled the railways.

Influenced by the tension prevailing on all lines, particularly those centered on Moscow, the central office of the railwaymen's union decided to declare a general strike. In so doing it had in mind only a trial mobilization of its fighting forces everywhere; the battle itself was still planned for January.

The decisive day was October 7. "The heart spasms have begun," wrote *Novoye Vremya*; the Moscow railways were dying, one after the other. Moscow was becoming isolated from the country. Anxious telegrams raced one another along the telegraph wires: Nizhny Novgorod, Arzamas, Kashira, Ryazan, Venev, all complained that the railways were failing.

On October 7 the Moscow-Kazan Railway entered the strike. The Romodanov branch struck at Nizhny. On the next day the strike spread to the Moscow-Yaroslav, Moscow-Nizhegorod and Moskow-Kursk lines. Other central points, however, did not respond at once.

On October 8, at a meeting of employees of the Petersburg Railway center, it was decided to proceed actively with the organization of an all-Russian railwaymen's union (which had first been proposed at the April congress in Moscow) in order subsequently to submit an ultimatum to the government and to support its claims by a strike of the entire railway network. Yet here too the strike was deferred to the indefinite future.

The Moscow-Kiev-Voronezh, Moscow-Brest, and other lines struck on October 9. The strike took control of the situation and, feeling the ground firm under its feet, overturned all moderate, procrastinating decisions which were hostile to it.

On October 9, at an extraordinary meeting of the Petersburg delegates' congress of railway personnel, the slogans of the railway strike were formulated and immediately disseminated by telegraph to all lines. They were the following: eight-hour day, civil liberties, amnesty, Constituent Assembly.

The strike began confidently to take over the country. It finally bade farewell to indecision. The self-confidence of its participants grew together with their number. Revolutionary class claims were advanced ahead of the economic claims of separate trades. Having broken out of its local and trade boundaries, the strike began to feel that it was a revolution—and so acquired unprecedented daring.

The strike rushed forward along the rails and stopped all movement in its wake. It announced its coming over the wires of the railway telegraph. "Strike!" was the order of the day in every corner of the land. On October 9 the newspapers informed all Russia that a certain electrician named Bednov had been arrested with proclamations on the Kazan Railway. They still hoped to stop the strike by confiscating a bundle of proclamations. Fools! The strike swept ahead.

It followed a grandiose plan—that of halting industrial and commercial life in the country at large—and in following this plan it did not overlook a single detail. Where the telegraph refused to serve it, it cut the wires or overturned the telegraph poles. It halted railway engines and let off their steam. It brought the electric power stations to a standstill, and where this was difficult it damaged electric cables and plunged railway stations into darkness. Where it met stubborn resistance, it did not hesitate to disrupt lines, break signals, overturn engines, put obstacles across lines or place railway carriages across bridges. It penetrated into lift systems and stopped the hoisting winches. It halted goods trains wherever it found them, while passenger trains were usually run to the nearest junction or to the place of destination.

Only for its own purposes did the strike allow itself to break the vow of immobility. When it needed news bulletins of the revolution it opened a printing works; it used the telegraph to send out strike instructions; it let trains carrying strikers' delegates pass.

Nothing else was exempt: the strike closed down industrial plants, chemists' and grocers' shops, courts of law, everything.

From time to time its attention wearied and its vigilance slackened, now here, now there. Sometimes a reckless train would break through the strike barrier: then the strike would set off in pursuit of it. The guilty train, like a criminal on the run, raced through dark and empty stations, unannounced by the telegraph, leaving a wake of fear and uncertainty behind it. But in the end the strike would catch up with the train, stop the engine, immobilize the driver, let off the steam.

It used every possible means. It appealed, convinced, implored; it begged on its knees—that is what a woman orator did at the Kursky Station in Moscow—it threatened, terrorized, threw stones, finally fired off its Brownings. It wanted to achieve its aim at whatever cost. It staked too much: the blood of fathers, the bread of children, the reputation of its own strength. An entire class obeyed it; and when a negligible fraction of that class, corrupted by the very forces it was fighting, stood in its path, it is scarcely surprising that the strike roughly kicked the obstacle aside.

IV

The country's motor nerves were dying. The economic body was growing numb. Smolensk, Kirsanov, Tula, Lukoyanov complained helplessly of complete immobility on the railways. On the tenth almost all lines centered on Moscow fell idle, including the Nikolayev Railway as far as Tver—and Moscow was utterly lost in the center of a boundless plain. The Savelovsk Railway, the last of those centered on Moscow, struck on the sixteenth.

On the evening of the tenth, striking railway employees met in the hall of Moscow University and resolved to continue the strike until all their claims were satisfied.

From the center, the railway strike spread to the periphery. The Ryazan-Ural line struck on the eighth, the Bryansk line of the Polessky Railway and the Smolensk-Dankov line on the ninth, the Kursk-Kharkov-Sevastopol and Yekaterininsk railways and all those centered on Kharkov on the tenth. Prices of foodstuffs began to rise rapidly everywhere. By the eleventh, Moscow was complaining of a milk shortage.

On that day the railway strike spread still further. Traffic on the Samara-Zlatoust Railway began to come to a halt. The Orel center was immobilized. The largest stations of the South-West railways—Kazatin, Birzula and Odessa—as well as Kremenchug on the Kharkov-Nikolayev Railway joined the strike. Only three trains reached Saratov throughout the day, and those trains carried no passengers other than the strikers' elected deputies. The telegraph reported that these delegates' trains were met with enthusiasm everywhere.

The railway strike spread inexorably, involving more and more lines, more and more trains. On October 11 the governor-general of Kurland issued an urgent decree making the cessation of work on the railway punishable by three months' imprisonment. The answer to the challenge came immediately. By the twelfth no trains were running between Moscow and Kreizburg; the line was on strike; the Vindava train did not arrive.

Traffic came to a halt on all branches of the Vistula region on the night of October 11–12. In the morning, trains for Petersburg failed to leave Warsaw. On the same day—the twelfth—the strike encircled Petersburg itself. Revolutionary instinct prompted it to adopt the correct tactics: first it aroused the workers in all the provinces; then it bombarded Petersburg with thousands of frightened telegrams, thereby creating the "psychological moment"; it terrorized the central authorities; and only then arrived personally on the scene to deliver the *coup de grace.* On the morning of the twelfth the cessation of work on all railways which centered on Petersburg was adopted with complete unanimity. Only the Finland line still operated, awaiting the revolutionary mobilization of the whole of Finland; this line did not stop until four days later, the sixteenth. On October 13 the strike reached Revel, Libava, Riga, and Brest. Work ceased at Perm station. Traffic was halted on a part of the Tashkent Railway. On the fourteenth, the Brest center, the Trans-Caucasian Railway and the Ashkhabad and Novaya Bukhara stations on the Central Asian Railway struck in their turn. On the same day the strike spread to the Siberian railways; starting at Chita and Irkutsk and moving from the east westwards, it reached Chelyabinsk and Kurgan by the seventeenth. Baku Station struck on the fifteenth and Odessa on the seventeenth.

For a time, this paralysis of the motor nerves was accompanied by a paralysis of the sensory nerves: on the eleventh telegraphic communications were interrupted in Kharkov, on the thirteenth in Chelyabinsk and Irkutsk, on the fourteenth in Moscow and on the fifteenth in Petersburg.

Because of the railway strike, the postal system was forced almost entirely to refuse inter-city correspondence.

A horse-drawn *troika* with an old-fashioned forged shaft-bow was seen on the old Moscow highway.

Not only all the Russian and Polish railways, but also the Vladikavkaz, Trans-Caucasian and Siberian railways were at a standstill. The entire army of the railways—three-quarters of a million men—was on strike.

V

The bread, commodities, meat, vegetables, fish and other markets began to issue worried communiqués. Prices of foodstuffs, especially meat, rose rapidly. The money exchange trembled. Revolution had always been its mortal enemy. Now that they were face to face with one another, the exchange began to behave like a thing possessed. It rushed to the telegraph, but the telegraph maintained a hostile silence. The post office, too, refused to serve. The exchange knocked on the door of the State Bank, but was told that the Bank could not guarantee transfers at a fixed date. Shares of railway and industrial enterprises left their perches like a flock of frightened birds, and flew off—only not upwards, but downwards. Panic, accompanied by the gnashing of teeth, reigned in the shadowy world of stock-exchange speculation. Money circulation was obstructed, payments from the provinces to the two capitals ceased to come in. Firms operating on a cash basis stopped their payments. The number of protested bills began to increase rapidly. All the issuers of checks and bills of exchange, all the guarantors, the payers and the payees began to fret and fuss and demand the changing of laws created for their use, because *it*—the strike, the revolution—had infringed upon all the laws of economic exchange.

But the strike was not content with the railways. It aimed at becoming universal.

Having let the steam out of the engines and put out the station lights, it joins the crowds of railway workers on their way to town. It halts trams, stops the horses of hackney carriages and obliges the passengers to dismount, closes down shops, restaurants, cafés and taverns, and confidently approaches the factory gates. Inside, they are already waiting. The alarm whistle starts, work stops, the crowd in the street swells. The strike marches forward, now carrying a red banner. The banner proclaims that it wants a Constituent Assembly and a republic, that it is fighting for socialism. It passes the editorial offices of a reactionary newspaper. It glances back with hatred at that infected ideological source and, if a stone happens to be handy, it hurls it at a window. The liberal press, which thinks that it is serving the people, sends a deputation to the strike, promising to work for "conciliation" and begging for mercy. Its pleas are left unheeded. The type cases are closed, the compositors come out into the street. Offices and banks are closed down. The strike rules over everything.

On the tenth of October a general political strike was proclaimed in Moscow, Kharkov and Revel; on the eleventh, in Smolensk, Kozlov, Yekaterinoslav and Lodz; on the twelfth, in Kursk, Byelgorod, Samara, Saratov and Poltava; on the thirteenth, in Petersburg, Orsha, Minsk, Kremenchug and Simferopol; on the fourteenth, in Gomel, Kalish, Rostov-on-Don, Tiflis and Irkutsk; on the fifteenth, in Vilna, Odessa and Batum; on the sixteenth in Orenburg; on the seventeenth in Yuriev, Vitebsk and Tomsk. Riga, Libava, Warsaw, Plotsk, Byelostock, Kovna, Dvinsk, Pskov, Poltava, Nikolayev, Mariupol, Kazan, Chenstokhovo, Zlatoust and others also struck. Industrial life, and in many places also commercial life, collapsed everywhere. Schools and universities closed down. "Unions" of the intelligentsia joined the strike of the proletariat. In many places juries refused to sit, lawyers to plead, doctors to attend patients. Justices of the peace closed down their courts.

VI

The strike organized colossal meetings. The tension of the masses and the dismay of the authorities grew simultaneously, each feeding the other. The streets and squares were filled with mounted and foot patrols. The cossacks provoked the strike to offer resistance; they charged crowds, slashing with whips, striking with sabers, shooting from behind corners without warning.

Then the strike showed, wherever it could, that it was not a merely temporary interruption of work, a passive protest made with folded arms. It defended itself and, in its defense, passed to the offensive.

In a number of towns in the south it erected barricades, seized gun shops, armed itself and offered a heroic if not victorious resistance.

In Kharkov on October 10, after a meeting, the crowd seized a gun shop. On the eleventh, barricades were erected by workers and students near the university. Telegraph poles were torn down and laid across the streets; iron gates, shutters, grilles, packing cases, planks, and logs were piled on top, and the lot was bound together with telegraph wire. Some barricades were built on stone foundations. Heavy slabs dug up from the pavements were piled on top of logs. By 1.00 P.M. ten barricades had been built according to this simple but noble architecture. Windows and passages in the university were also barricaded. The university area was declared to be in a state of siege, and command of the area was entrusted to a certain, no doubt valiant, Lieutenant-General Mau. However, the governor accepted a compromise solution and honorable conditions for surrender were worked out, the liberal bourgeoisie acting as mediator. A militia was organized and enthusiastically welcomed by the citizens. The militia restored order. Petersburg then demanded that this order be crushed by force. The militia was dispersed almost as soon as it had come into being, and the town was once more in the power of thugs on horseback and on foot.

In Yekaterinoslav on October 11, after cossacks had treacherously fired on a peaceful crowd, barricades first appeared in the streets. They were six in number. The largest stood on Bryansky Square. Carts, rails, poles, dozens of small objects—all the things which, as Victor Hugo put it, the revolution can find to hurl at the head of the old order—were used in building it. The skeleton of the barricade was covered with a thick layer of earth, ditches were dug on either side, and wire obstacles were erected in front of the ditches. From morning, several hundred people were present on each barricade. The first attack of the armed forces was unsuccessful; only at 3:30 P.M. did the soldiers seize the first barricade. During the attack, two bombs were thrown, one after the other, from the housetops; among the soldiers there were dead and wounded. By evening, the troops had taken all the barricades. On the twelfth, the peace of the graveyard reigned in the town. The army was cleaning its rifles while the revolution buried its dead.

October 16 was the day of the barricades in Odessa. From morning, tramway carriages were overturned on Preobrazhenskaya and Richelieu streets, shop signs were taken down, trees were felled and street benches were gathered into a pile. Four barricades surrounded by barbed-wire obstacles were set across the entire width of the streets. They were taken by the soldiers after a fight, and were pulled down with the help of janitors.

Street clashes between strikers and soldiers and attempts to erect barricades occurred in many other towns. But by and large the October days remained a political strike, a revolutionary exercise, a simultaneous review of all the revolution's fighting forces, but not an armed rising.

VII

And yet absolutism gave in. The tremendous tension gripping the entire country, the confused reports arriving in vast numbers from the provinces, the total uncertainty as to what the next day had in store—all created unbelievable panic in the government's ranks. There was no full and unconditional confidence in the army; soldiers were seen at meetings; officers who spoke at meetings claimed that a third of the army was "with the people." Furthermore, the railway strike created unsurmountable obstacles to military pacification measures. And, finally, there was the European stock exchange. It understood that it was dealing with revolution, and declared that it was not prepared to tolerate such a state of affairs any longer. It demanded order and constitutional guarantees.

Absolutism, in its utter confusion, began to make concessions. A manifesto was issued on October 17. Count Witte became Prime Minister—thanks (let him deny this if he can) to the victory of the revolutionary strike, or, more precisely, thanks to the *incompleteness* of that victory. During the night of October 17–18 people marched in the streets with red banners, called for an amnesty, sang "Eternal Memory" at the sites of the January massacres and shouted "Anathema!" outside Pobedonostsev's house and the offices of the *New Times*. On the morning of the eighteenth came the first killings that were to take place during the constitutional era.

The enemy had not been stifled. He retreated only temporarily before the unexpected onslaught. The October strike showed that the revolution was now capable of bringing the whole of urban Russia simultaneously to its feet. This was a tremendous step forward, and the reactionary ruling clique showed a proper appreciation of this fact when it responded to the October trial of strength by, on the one hand, issuing the manifesto of October 17 and, on the other hand, by mobilizing all its fighting cadres in the cause of the Black Terror.

VIII

Ten years ago* Plekhanov said at the London socialist congress that the Russian revolutionary movement would triumph as a workers' movement or not at all.

On January 7, 1905, Struve wrote: "There is no such thing as a revolutionary people in Russia."

On October 17 the autocratic government put its signature to the first serious victory of the revolution—and that victory was won by the proletariat. Plekhanov had been right: the revolutionary movement triumphed as a workers' movement.

True, the October strike took place not only with the material help of the bourgeoisie, but also with its direct support in the form of a strike by the liberal professions. But that does not alter the situation. A strike of engineers, lawyers, and doctors could not have any independent significance, and it increased the political significance of the workers' strike only to a very

* Written in 1905 (Author).

small extent. What it did do was to underline the unquestionable and unlimited hegemony of the proletariat in revolutionary struggle. The liberal professions, which after January 9 had adopted the principal democratic slogans of the Petersburg workers, in October adopted the actual method of struggle typical of the proletariat: the strike. The students, the most revolutionary wing of the intelligentsia, had long since begun to carry the strike from the factories to the universities—accompanied by solemn protests by the entire body of liberal university professors. The further growth of the revolutionary hegemony of the proletariat spread the strike to the law courts, the chemists' shops, the rural administration offices and the town dumas.

The October strike was a demonstration of the proletariat's hegemony in the bourgeois revolution and, at the same time, of the hegemony of the towns in an agricultural country.

The old power of the land, deified by the Narodnik movement, gave place to the *despotism of the capitalist town.*

The town became master of the situation. It concentrated colossal wealth within itself, it attached the villages to itself by the iron bond of rails; along these rails it gathered into its entrails the finest forces of initiative and creative power in all spheres of life; both materially and spiritually, it put the entire country in its thrall. In vain the reactionaries would calculate the small percentage of the urban population, comforting themselves with the thought that Russia was still an agricultural country. The *political* role of the modern town cannot be measured by the number of its inhabitants any more than its *economic* role can be. The retreat of reaction in the face of the towns on strike—the countryside remaining silent all the while—is the best proof of the dictatorship of the towns.

The October days showed that in revolution the hegemony belongs to the towns and, in the towns, to the proletariat. But at the same time they revealed that *the consciously revolutionary towns were cut off from the spontaneously aroused countryside.*

The October days posed, in practice and on a colossal scale, the question: On whose side is the army? They showed that the destiny of Russian freedom depended on the answer to that question.

The October days of revolution led to the October orgy of reaction. The black forces took advantage of a moment of revolutionary ebb for launching a bloody attack. This attack owed its success to the fact that the revolutionary strike, having laid down the hammer, had not yet taken up the sword. The October days showed the revolution with a terrible logic that it needed arms.

To organize the countryside and bind it to itself; to establish close links with the army; to arm itself: those were the great and simple conclusions which the October struggle and the October victory dictated to the proletariat.

It is on these conclusions that the revolution rests.

◇ ◇ ◇

In our essay *Before January 9,* written during the period of the liberal "spring," we attempted to map out the course of the future development of revolutionary relations. In doing this we put the greatest emphasis on the mass political strike as the inevitable method of the Russian revolution. Certain people—who, one should add, are estimable in every respect—accused us of trying to provide a recipe for revolution. These critics explained to us that the strike, being a specific method of *proletarian class struggle,* could not play the role we were "forcing upon it" under the conditions of a *national bourgeois revolution.* Events as they have turned out in defiance of many a profound thinker's clichés have long ago relieved me of the necessity of replying to these estimable critics.* The general strike in Petersburg, on the basis of which the drama of January 9 took place, occurred while the above-mentioned essay was not yet printed: evidently our "recipe" was a simple plagiarism from actual revolutionary development.

* The persons meant here are Menshevik writers such as Martov, Dan, *et al.*

In February 1905, at the time of the chaotic disconnected strikes provoked directly by Bloody Sunday in Petersburg, we wrote:

After January 9 the revolution knows no stopping. It is no longer satisfied with the hidden underground work of continually arousing new strata of the population; it is now making an overt and urgent roll call of its fighting companies, its regiments, battalions and divisions. The *proletariat* is the main force of its army; and that is why the revolution has made the *strike* its means of carrying out this roll call.

Trade after trade, factory after factory, town after town are stopping work. The railway personnel act as the detonators of the strike; the railway lines are the channels along which the strike epidemic spreads. Economic claims are advanced and are satisfied, wholly or in part, almost at once. But neither the beginning of the strike nor its end is fully determined by the nature of the claims made or by the form in which they are met. The strike does not occur because the economic struggle has found expression in certain well-defined demands; on the contrary, the demands are chosen and formulated because there has to be a strike. The workers have to reveal to themselves, to the proletariat in other parts of the country, finally to the nation at large, their accumulated strength, their class responsiveness, their fighting readiness. Everything has to be submitted to a universal revolutionary appraisal. The strikers themselves and those who support them, those who fear them and those who hate them, all realize or dimly sense that this furious strike which leaps from place to place, then takes off again and rushes forward like a whirlwind—that this strike is not merely itself, that it is obedient to the will of the revolution which has sent it down upon the land.

We were not mistaken. The great October strike grew on the soil prepared by the nine months' strike campaign.

For the liberals with their incurably superficial view, the October strike was as unexpected as the ninth of January had been. These events did not enter their preconceived schema of history; they cut into it like a wedge. But after-the-fact liberal thought accepted these events. More than that: before the October strike, liberalism placed its trust in *zemstvo* congresses and contemptuously ignored the idea of a general strike; after October 17 the same liberalism, as represented by its left wing, placed its entire trust in the victorious strike and rejected all other forms of revolutionary struggle.

"This peaceful strike," Mr. Prokopovich wrote in *Pravo*, "this strike which involved a far smaller number of victims than the January movement, and which culminated in profound governmental change, was a revolution that radically altered the state structure of Russia.

"History," he continues, "in depriving the proletariat of one of the means of struggle for people's rights—the street rising and the barricades—gave it a still more powerful means, the political general strike." *

The foregoing quotations show the great importance we attached to the mass political strike as an inevitable method of the Russian revolution, at a time when the radical Prokopoviches were still placing their trust in the *zemstvo* opposition. But we are quite unable to admit that the general strike canceled or replaced the earlier methods of revolution. It merely modified and supplemented them. And likewise, however highly we assess the significance of the October strike, we are quite unable to admit that it "radically altered the state structure of Russia." On the contrary: all subsequent political developments can only be explained by the fact that the October strike left the state structure unchanged. More than that, the strike could not have achieved profound governmental change. Qua political strike it completed its mission by putting the opponents face to face.

The railway and telegraph strike indisputably introduced extreme disorganization into the mechanism of government, and this disorganization became greater as the strike continued. But a prolonged strike causes disintegration of economic and social life as a whole and inevitably weakens the workers themselves. In the end the strike could not but come to an end. But as soon

* *Pravo*, 1905, No. 41.

as the first engine began to steam and the first Morse apparatus began to click again, the state power (which was still in being) was able to replace all the broken levers and, generally speaking, to renew the worn-out parts of the old state machinery.

In struggle it is extremely important to weaken the enemy. That is what a strike does. At the same time a strike brings the army of the revolution to its feet. But neither the one nor the other, in itself, creates a state revolution.

The power still has to be snatched from the hands of the old rulers and handed over to the revolution. That is the fundamental task. A general strike only creates the necessary preconditions; it is quite inadequate for achieving the task itself.

The old state power rests on its material forces and, above all, on the army. The army stands in the way of real, as opposed to paper, revolution. At a certain moment in revolution the crucial question becomes: on which side are the soldiers—their sympathies and their bayonets?

That is not a question you can answer with the help of a questionnaire. Many useful and appropriate comments can be made concerning the width and straightness of streets in modern towns, the characteristics of modern weapons, etc., etc., but none of these technical considerations can supersede the question of the revolutionary takeover of state power. The inertia of the army must be overcome. The revolution achieves this by pitting the army against the popular masses. A general strike creates favorable conditions for such conflict. It is a harsh method, but history offers no other.

CHAPTER 8

❖❖❖❖❖❖❖❖❖

The Creation of the Soviet of Workers' Deputies

October, November, and December 1905 was the period of revolutionary culmination. It began with a modest strike of Moscow's typesetters and ended with government troops crushing the ancient capital of the Russian Tsars. But with the exception of the final moment—the Moscow rising—Moscow did not occupy first place in the events of that period.

The role of Petersburg in the Russian revolution cannot be compared in any way with that of Paris in the French Revolution. The economically primitive nature of France (and, in particular, of the means of communication) on the one hand, and administrative centralization on the other, allowed the French Revolution to be localized—to all intents and purposes—within the walls of Paris. The situation in Russia was entirely different. Capitalist development in Russia had created as many independent centers of revolution as there were centers of major industry

(103)

—independent, that is, but also intimately linked with one another. The railways and the telegraph decentralized the revolution despite the centralized character of the state; but, at the same time, they brought unity to all its scattered manifestations. If, as the result of all this, we recognize that Petersburg had the leading voice in the revolution, it does not mean that the revolution was concentrated in Nevsky Prospect or outside the Winter Palace, but only that the slogans and fighting methods of Petersburg found a mighty revolutionary echo in the country as a whole. The type of organization adopted in Petersburg, the tone of the Petersburg press, immediately became models for the provinces. Local provincial events, with the exception of the risings in the navy and the fortresses, had no autonomous significance.

If, then, we are to recognize the capital on the Neva as the center of the events of the final months of 1905, in Petersburg itself we must recognize the Council (Soviet) of Workers' Deputies as the cornerstone of all these events. Not only because this was the greatest workers' organization to be seen in Russia up until that time. Not only because the Petersburg Soviet served as a model for Moscow, Odessa, and a number of other cities. But, above all, because this purely class-founded, proletarian organization was the organization of the revolution as such. The Soviet was the axis of all events, every thread ran towards it, every call to action emanated from it.

What was the Soviet of Workers' Deputies?

The Soviet came into being as a response to an objective need—a need born of the course of events. It was an organization which was authoritative and yet had no traditions; which could immediately involve a scattered mass of hundreds of thousands of people while having virtually no organizational machinery; which united the revolutionary currents within the proletariat; which was capable of initiative and spontaneous self-control—and most important of all, which could be brought out from underground within twenty-four hours. The social-democratic organization, which welded together a few hundred Petersburg workers, and to which several thousand more were ideologically attached, was able to speak for the masses by illuminating their immediate experience with the lightning of political thought; but it was not able to create a *living* organizational link with these masses, if only because it had always done the principal part of its work in clandestinity, concealed from the eyes of the masses. The organization of the socialist revolutionaries suffered from the same occupational disease of clandestinity, further aggravated by instability and impotence. Internal friction between two equally powerful factions of the social democrats on the one hand, and the struggle of both factions with the socialist revolutionaries on the other, rendered the creation of a *non-party* organization absolutely essential. In order to have authority in the eyes of the masses on the very day it came into being, such an organization had to be based on the broadest representation. How was this to be achieved? The answer came of its own accord. Since the production process was the sole link between the proletarian masses who, in the organizational sense, were still quite inexperienced, representation had to be adapted to the factories and plants. Senator Shidlovsky's commission served as the organizational precedent.*

On October 10, at the moment when the largest of the strikes was imminent, one of the two social-democratic organizations in Petersburg took upon itself the task of creating a revolutionary workers' council of self-management. The first meeting of what was to become the Soviet was held on the evening of the thirteenth, in the Technological Institute. Not more than thirty to forty delegates attended. It was decided immediately to call upon the proletariat of the capital to proclaim a political general strike and to elect delegates. The proclamation

* One delegate was elected for every 500 workers. Small industrial undertakings combined into groups for election purposes. The young trade unions also received representational rights. It must be said, however, that numerical norms were not observed too strictly; in some cases delegates represented only a hundred or two hundred workers, or even fewer.

drafted at the first meeting states: "The working class has re-
sorted to the final, powerful weapon of the world workers'
movement—the general strike.

". . . Decisive events are going to occur in Russia within
the next few days. They will determine the destiny of the working class for many years ahead; we must meet these events in
full readiness, united by our common Soviet . . ."

This immensely important decision was adopted unanimously—and, what is more, without any discussion of principle
concerning the general strike and its methods, aims, and possibilities, although precisely these questions shortly thereafter provoked a passionate ideological struggle in the ranks of our party
in Germany. There is no need to explain this fact by differences
of national psychology; on the contrary, we Russians are almost
pathologically prone to tactical sophistries and the most detailed anticipation of events. The reason lay in the revolutionary
nature of the moment. From the hour it came into being until
the hour it perished, the Soviet stood under the mighty, elemental pressure of the revolution, which most unceremoniously
forestalled the work of political consciousness.

Every step of the workers' representation was determined
in advance. Its "tactics" were obvious. The methods of struggle
did not have to be discussed; there was hardly time to formulate
them.

❖ ❖ ❖

The October strike was confidently nearing its climax. At its
head marched the metal workers and the print-workers. They
had been the first to enter the fight, and on October 13 they
clearly and unequivocally formulated their political slogans.

"We proclaim a political strike," stated the Obukhov plant,
a citadel of the revolution, "and will fight to the last for the
summoning of a Constituent Assembly on the basis of universal,
equal, direct, and secret suffrage to introduce a democratic republic in Russia."

The workers of electric power stations advanced the same slogans and declared: "Together with the social-democrats, we shall fight to the end for our demands, and we proclaim before the entire working class our readiness to fight, weapons in hand, for the people's complete liberation."

In sending their deputies to the Soviet, the print-workers formulated the tasks of the moment in even more resolute terms:

"Recognizing the inadequacy of passive struggle and of the mere cessation of work, we resolve: to transform the army of the striking working class into a revolutionary army, that is to say, to organize detachments of armed workers forthwith. Let these detachments take care of arming the rest of the working masses, if necessary by raiding gun shops and confiscating arms from the police and troops wherever possible." This resolution was not just empty words. Armed detachments of print-workers were extraordinarily successful in seizing the city's largest print shops for the printing of *Izvestia Sovieta Rabochikh Deputatov* (Tidings of the Council of Workers' Deputies) and performed invaluable services in organizing the postal and telegraph strike.

On October 15 the majority of the textile factories were still at work. The Soviet worked out a complete range of methods, from verbal appeals to forcible coercion, to involve non-strikers in the strike. But it turned out to be unnecessary to resort to extreme methods. Where a printed appeal had no effect, it was enough for a crowd of strikers to appear on the scene—sometimes only a few men—and work was immediately interrupted.

"I was walking past the Pecliet factory," one of the deputies reported to the Soviet. "I saw it was still working. I rang and asked to be announced as a deputy from the Workers' Soviet. 'What do you want?' the manager asks me. 'In the name of the Soviet I call for the immediate closing down of your factory.' 'Very well, we shall stop work at 3:00 P.M.'"

By October 16, all the textile factories were out. Trade still continued only in the center of the town; in the working-class areas all shops were closed. By spreading the strike, the Soviet expanded and consolidated itself. Every striking factory elected a representative and, having equipped him with the necessary credentials, sent him off to the Soviet. The second meeting was attended by delegates from 40 large plants, 2 factories and 3 trade unions—those of the print-workers, shop assistants and office clerks. At this meeting, which took place in the physics auditorium of the Technological Institute, the author of these lines was present for the first time.

This was on October 14, when the strike on the one hand and the split in the government on the other were inexorably approaching the moment of crisis. That was the day of Trepov's famous order: "No blank volleys, and spare no bullets." Yet on the next day, October 15, the same Trepov suddenly recognized that "a need for gatherings has ripened in the people," and, while forbidding meetings within the walls of higher educational establishments, promised to set aside three municipal buildings for the purpose of meetings. "What a change in 24 hours!" we wrote in *Izvestia*. "Yesterday we were ripe only for bullets, today we are ripe enough for popular meetings. The murderous villain is right, in these great days of struggle the people of Russia are maturing by the hour."

Despite the ban, on the evening of the fourteenth the higher educational establishments were overflowing with people. Meetings were held everywhere. "We, gathered here, declare"—such was our reply to the government—"that the mousetraps which General Trepov has set for us are not large enough to hold us. We declare that we shall continue to meet in the universities, in factories, in the streets and in all other places, wherever we may see fit." From the assembly hall of the Technological Institute, where the need for demanding that the city duma should arm a workers' militia was discussed, we moved into the physics auditorium.

Here we first saw the Soviet of Deputies, which had been formed the day before. About a hundred workers' representatives and members of revolutionary parties were seated on the amphitheater benches. The chairman and secretaries were installed at the demonstration table. The meeting resembled a council of war more than a parliament. There was no trace of magniloquence, that ulcer of representational institutions. The questions under discussion—the spreading of the strike and the demands to be addressed to the duma—were of a purely practical nature and were debated briefly, energetically and in a businesslike manner. One felt that every atom of time was accounted for. The slightest tendency towards rhetoric was firmly checked by the chairman with the stern approval of the entire meeting.

A special deputation was instructed to submit the following demands to the city duma: 1) that measures be taken immediately to regulate the flow of food supplies to the workers; 2) that premises be set aside for meetings; 3) that all food supplies, allocations of premises and funds to the police, the gendarmerie, etc., be discontinued forthwith; 4) that funds be issued for the arming of the Petersburg proletariat in its fight for freedom.

Given the fact that the duma was composed of state officials and householders, approaching it with radical demands of this kind was a purely agitational step. It goes without saying that the Soviet entertained no illusions on that score. It neither expected nor obtained any practical results.

On October 16, after a number of adventures, attempted arrests, and so forth—let me remind the reader that all this happened before the publication of the constitutional manifesto—the Soviet's deputation was received "in private conference" by the Petersburg city duma. Before anything else was done, the deputation, energetically supported by a group of the duma's own members, demanded that the duma should decide, in the event of the arrest of any workers' deputies, to send the mayor to the city governor with a declaration stating that the duma would consider such arrest as an insult to itself. Only then did the deputation present its demands.

This is how the deputation's speaker, Comrade Radin (Knuniants, now deceased), concluded his speech:

The revolution taking place in Russia is a bourgeois revolution; the property-owning classes, too, have an interest in it. It is in your own interest, gentlemen, that it should be completed as soon as possible. If you are capable of any degree of far-sightedness, if you have a broad understanding of what is of advantage to your own class, you must do everything in your power to help the people towards the most rapid victory possible over absolutism. We want neither resolutions of sympathy nor platonic support for our demands. We demand that you show your collaboration by a series of practical actions.

Because of our monstrous electoral system, the property of a city with a population of a million and a half is in the hands of the representatives of a few thousand property-owning persons. The Soviet of Workers' Deputies demands—and it has a right to demand, not to ask, since it represents several hundred thousand workers, inhabitants of this city, whereas you represent only a handful of electors—the Soviet of Workers' Deputies demands that the property of the city be placed at the disposal of all the city's inhabitants for the satisfaction of their needs. And since the most important public task today is the struggle against absolutism, and for that struggle we need places where we can meet, open to us our municipal buildings!

We need funds for continuing the strike: allocate municipal funds for this purpose, not for supporting the police and the gendarmerie!

We need arms to gain our freedom and preserve it. Allocate funds for the organization of a proletarian militia!

The deputation left the meeting under the protection of certain members of the duma. The duma rejected all the principal demands of the Soviet and expressed confidence in the police as the guardian of law and order.

❖ ❖ ❖

As the October strike developed, so the Soviet naturally came more and more to the political forefront. Its importance grew literally hour by hour. The industrial proletariat was the first to rally around it. The railwaymen's union established close relations with it. The Union of Unions, which joined the strike from October 14, was obliged to place itself under the Soviet's authority almost from the start. Numerous strike committees—those of the engineers, lawyers, government officials—adapted their actions to the Soviet's decisions. By placing many disconnected organizations under its control, the Soviet united the revolution around itself.

The split in the government ranks was growing at the same time.

Trepov was for stopping at nothing, his finger on the trigger. On October 12 he compelled Nicholas to place him at the head of all the troops of the Petersburg garrison. On the fourteenth he was already issuing the order to "spare no bullets." He divided the capital into four military areas with a general at the head of each. In his capacity as governor-general he threatened all foodstuff dealers with expulsion from the city within twenty-four hours in the event of closure of their shops. On the sixteenth he closed down all Petersburg's higher educational establishments and had them occupied by troops. Without any formal proclamation of martial law, he in fact imposed it. Mounted patrols terrorized the streets. Troops were everywhere —inside government establishments, public buildings, in the courtyards of private houses. At a time when even artists of the Imperial Ballet were joining the strike, Trepov persisted in filling the empty theaters with soldiers. He grinned and rubbed his hands in anticipation of a good fight.

But he was mistaken in his calculations. The victory was won by the bureaucratic faction which was opposed to him, and which hoped to make a cunning deal with history. It is for this purpose that Witte was called in.

On October 17 Trepov's henchmen dispersed the meeting of the Soviet of Workers' Deputies. But the Soviet found a way of meeting again, decided to continue the strike with redoubled energy, advised the workers to pay no rent nor to pay for goods received on credit until the resumption of work, and called upon landlords and shopkeepers not to claim rents or cash payments from workers. On that day, October 17, the first issue of *Izvestia Sovieta Rabochikh Deputatov* came out.

And on the same day the Tsar signed the constitutional manifesto.

CHAPTER 9

◇◇◇◇◇◇◇◇◇

October Eighteenth

October 18 was a day of great bewilderment. Vast crowds moved in disarray through the streets of Petersburg. A constitution had been proclaimed. What next? What was allowed and what was not?

During those troubled days I slept at the house of one of my friends, who was in government service.* On the morning of the eighteenth he greeted me with the *Pravitelstvenny Vestnik* (Government Herald) in his hand, a smile of happy excitement at odds with the customary skepticism on his intelligent face.

"They've issued a constitutional manifesto!"

"It isn't possible!"

"Read this."

We started reading aloud. First the paternal heart's sorrow

* A. A. Litkens, senior medical officer at the Konstantinovsk Artillery School.

in the face of the unrest, then an assurance that "the people's grief is our grief," finally the categorical promise of all liberties, of the legislative rights of the Duma and of a broadening of the electoral laws.

We exchanged a silent look. It was hard to express the contradictory thoughts and feelings evoked by the manifesto. Freedom of assembly, personal immunity, control over the administration. . . . These, of course, were only words. But they were not the words of a liberal resolution, they were the words in a Tsar's manifesto. Nicholas Romanov, Most August patron of the pogromists, Trepov's Telemachus, was the author of these words. And this miracle had been wrought by the general strike. When, eleven years earlier, the liberals had submitted a humble petition asking for closer bonds between the autocratic monarch and the people, the crowned Junker had tweaked their ears for such "senseless dreams." Those had been his very words! Now he was standing at attention before the striking proletariat.

"Well, what d'you make of that?" I asked my friend.

"They're scared, the fools!" was the reply.

That was a classic phrase of its kind. We went on to read Witte's Most Loyal Report bearing the Tsar's resolution: "adopted in principle."

"You're right," I said, "the fools are really scared."

Five minutes later I was in the street The first person I met was a student, out of breath and carrying his cap in his hand. He was a party comrade,[1] who recognized me.

"Last night the troops fired on the Technological Institute. People are saying a bomb was thrown at them from inside . . . obviously a provocation. . . . Just now a patrol dispersed a small meeting in Zabalkansky Prospect, using sabers. . . . Professor Tarle, who was the speaker, was badly wounded with a saber. They say he's dead. . . ."

"Well, well. Not bad for a start."

* A. A. Litkens, the Doctor's younger son, a young Bolshevik, who died shortly thereafter following severe shock.

"Crowds of people are wandering everywhere, waiting for speakers. I'm on my way to a meeting of party agitators. What do you think? What should we talk about? Is amnesty the most important subject?"

"Everybody will be talking about amnesty without us. Demand the removal of troops from Petersburg. Not a single soldier within a radius of 25 *versts*."

The student ran on, waving his cap in the air. A mounted patrol passed by in the street. Trepov was still in the saddle. The shooting at the Institute was his comment on the manifesto. The good fellow had wasted no time in destroying any constitutional illusions the people might have entertained.

I walked past the Technological Institute. It was still locked and guarded by soldiers. Trepov's old promise that no bullets would be spared hung on the wall. Someone had pasted the Tsar's manifesto next to it. Small groups of people huddled on the pavements.

"Let's go to the University," someone said, "there'll be speeches."

I went with them. We walked rapidly and in silence. The crowd grew every minute. There was no sense of joy, but rather of uncertainty and disquiet. No more patrols were to be seen. Isolated policemen kept timidly out of the way of the crowd. The streets were decorated with tricolor flags.

"Herod's got his tail between his legs," a worker in the crowd said loudly.

Sympathetic laughter greeted the remark. The mood was noticeably rising. A boy snatched a tricolor flag with its staff from above a house-gate, ripped off the blue and white strips, and raised the red remainder of the "national" flag high above the crowd. Dozens of people followed his example. A few minutes later a multitude of red flags were waving above the mass of people. White and blue scraps of material lay everywhere and the crowd trampled them with their feet. We crossed the bridge to Vasilyevsky Island. A huge bottleneck of people formed on the quay, through which a countless mass poured. Everyone was trying to push their way through to the balcony from which the orators were to speak. The balcony, windows, and spire of the University were decorated with red banners. I got inside with difficulty. My turn to speak came third or fourth. The picture which opened before my eyes from the balcony was extraordinary. The street was packed with people. The students' blue caps and the red banners were bright spots among the hundred-thousand-strong crowd. The silence was complete; everyone wanted to hear the speakers.

Citizens! Now that we have got the ruling clique with its back to the wall, they promise us freedom. They promise us electoral rights and legislative power. Who promises these things? Nicholas the Second. Does he promise them of his own good will? Or with a pure heart? Nobody could say that for him. He began his reign by congratulating his splendid Fanagoriytsy* on the murder of the workers of Yaroslav, and stepping over corpse after corpse, he arrived at Bloody Sunday, January 9. It is this tireless hangman on the throne whom we have forced to promise us freedom. What a great triumph! But do not be too quick to celebrate victory; victory is not yet complete. Is a promise of payment the same thing as real gold? Is the promise of liberty the same as liberty itself? If anyone among you believe in the Tsar's promises, let him say so aloud —we'd all be glad to meet such a rare bird. Look around, citizens; has anything changed since yesterday? Have the gates of our prisons been opened? The Peter and Paul Fortress still dominates the city, doesn't it? Don't you still hear groans and the gnashing of teeth from behind its accursed walls? Have our brothers returned to their homes from the Siberian deserts?

"Amnesty! Amnesty! Amnesty!" comes the shout from below.

If the government had sincerely decided to make up its quarrel with the people, the first thing it would do would be to proclaim an amnesty. But, citizens, is an amnesty all? Today they will let out hundreds of political fighters, tomorrow they will seize thou-

* A cossack regiment. (Author)

sands of others. Isn't the order to spare no bullets hanging by the side of the manifesto about our freedoms? Didn't they use their sabers this morning on people peacefully listening to a speaker? Isn't Trepov, the hangman, master of Petersburg?

"Down with Trepov!" came the answering shout.

Yes, down with Trepov! but is he the only one? Are there no villains in the bureaucracy's reserves to take his place? Trepov rules over us with the help of the army. The guardsmen covered in the blood of January 9 are his support and his strength. It is they whom he orders not to spare bullets against your breasts and heads. We cannot, we do not want to, we must not live at gunpoint. Citizens! Let our demand be the withdrawal of troops from Petersburg! Let not a single soldier remain within a radius of 25 *versts* from the capital! The free citizens themselves will maintain order. No one shall suffer from violence and arbitrary rule. The people will take everyone under their protection.

"Out with the troops! All troops to leave Petersburg!"

Citizens! Our strength is in ourselves. With sword in hand we must stand guard over our freedom. As for the Tsar's manifesto, look, it's only a scrap of paper. Here it is before you—here it is crumpled in my fist. Today they have issued it, tomorrow they will take it away and tear it into pieces, just as I am now tearing up this paper freedom before your eyes!

There were two or three more speakers, and all of them concluded with a call to assemble in the Nevsky at 4:00 P.M. and from there to march to the prisons with a demand for amnesty.

CHAPTER 10

Witte's Ministry

On October 17, the Tsarist government, covered in the blood and curses of centuries, capitulated before the revolutionary strike of the working masses. No efforts at restoration can rub out this fact from the history books. The sacred crown of the Tsar's absolutism bears forever the trace of the proletarian's boot.

Both in the internal and the external struggle, the herald of Tsarist capitulation was Count Witte. A plebeian *parvenu* among the noble ranks of the upper bureaucracy, closed, like all bureaucrats, to the influence of any general ideas or political and moral principles, Witte held an advantage over his rivals precisely because, as a *parvenu*, he was not bound by the traditions of the court, the nobility or the cavalry stables. This fact helped him to develop into the ideal bureaucrat, free not only from nationality, religion, conscience, and honor, but also from caste prejudice. The same fact made him more responsive to the elementary demands of capitalist development. Among the hereditary imbeciles of the calvalry regiments he appeared as a statesman of genius.

Count Witte's constitutional career was built wholly on revolution. For ten years the autocracy's uncontrolled bookkeeper and cashier, he was relegated in 1902 by his antagonist, Plehve, to the powerless post of chairman of the pre-revolutionary committee of ministers. When Plehve himself had been "retired" by a terrorist's bomb, Witte, with the help of obliging journalists, began to put himself forward, not without success, in the role of Russia's savior. It used to be said, with suitably grave mien, that he supported all Svyatopolk-Mirsky's liberal steps. Confronted with defeats in the East he perspicaciously shook his head. On the eve of January 9 he told the terrified liberals: "You know that power is not mine." In that way terrorist assaults, Japanese victories, and revolutionary events cleared the path before him. From Portsmouth, where he had signed a treaty dictated by the world stock exchange and its political agents, he returned in triumph. Anyone might have thought that not Marshal Oyama but he, Witte, had won all the victories in the Asian East. The attention of the entire bourgeois world was centered on this providential man. The Paris *Matin* exhibited in its window a piece of blotting paper which Witte had used to blot his signature at Portsmouth. Everything thenceforth attracted the interest of the rubbernecks of public opinion: his tremendous height, his shapeless trousers, even his half-sunken nose. His audience with the Emperor Wilhelm confirmed still further his aureole of a statesman of the highest rank.

On the other hand, his conspiratorial chat with the émigré Struve testified to his success in taming the seditious liberals. The bankers were thrilled: here was a man who would make sure that interest was punctually paid. On his return to Russia, Witte resumed his powerless post with apparent confidence, made liberal speeches in the committee and, obviously gambling on revolution, called a deputation of railwaymen on strike "the country's finest forces." He was not mistaken in his calculations: the October strike raised him to the post of autocratic minister of constitutional Russia.

In his programmatic "Most Loyal Report" Witte struck his highest liberal note. The report tries to rise above the court lackey's, the fiscal bureaucrat's point of view, and to achieve the heights of political generalization. It recognizes that the unrest which is gripping the country is not simply the result of incitement but is due to the disturbed balance between the ideological aspirations of Russia's "thinking public" and the outward forms of its life. But if one forgets for a moment the intellectual level of the milieu within which and for which the report was written, if one takes it as the program of a statesman, one cannot but be struck by the paltriness of its thought, the cowardly evasiveness of its form and the pathetic bureaucratic inadequacy of its language. The statements concerning public freedoms are made in a form whose vagueness is merely underlined by the energy of the limiting explanations.

Summoning up the courage to take the initiative of constitutional reform, Witte does not pronounce the word "constitution." He hopes to bring it about in practice without anybody noticing, because his power rests on the support of those who cannot bear to hear its name. But to do this he needs a period of calm. He declares that although arrests, confiscations, and shootings will still be carried out on the basis of the old laws, they will henceforth be carried out "in the spirit" of the manifesto of October 17. With his trickster's simplemindedness he hoped that the revolution would immediately capitulate before his liberalism, just as, the day before, the autocracy had capitulated before the revolution. In this he was severely mistaken.

Witte came to power as a result of the victory, or rather of the incomplete nature of the victory, of the October strike. But the same conditions put him into an absolutely hopeless position from the very start. The revolution proved insufficiently strong to destroy the old machinery of the state and construct a new one out of the elements of its own organization. The army continued to remain in the same hands. All the old administrators, from governor to village policeman, who had been originally selected to serve the needs of the autocracy, remained in their posts. Likewise, all the old laws remained inviolate pending the issuing of new ones. Thus absolutism as a material fact was preserved in its entirety. It was preserved even as a name, since the word *"samoderzhets"*—autocrat—was not removed from the Tsar's title. True, the authorities were ordered to apply the laws of absolutism "in the spirit" of October 17. But this was the same as telling Falstaff to lead his dissolute life "in the spirit" of chastity.

As a result, the local autocrats of Russia's sixty satrapies completely lost their heads. They trailed in the wake of revolutionary demonstrations and saluted the red flag, they parodied Gessler and insisted that the population should take off their hats before them because they represented His Majesty's sacred person, they allowed the social democrats to march at the head of troops going to take the oath, they openly organized counterrevolutionary beatings. Complete anarchy reigned. No legislative authority existed, and it was not even known when and how such an authority would be set up.

Doubt as to whether the Duma would ever be convened increased. And above all this chaos there hung Count Witte, trying to deceive both Peterhof and the revolution and succeeding most of all, perhaps, in deceiving himself. He received endless deputations, both radical and reactionary, was equally courteous with both, developed his plans incoherently in front of Western correspondents, wrote daily government communiqués tearfully admonishing high-school boys not to participate in anti-governmental demonstrations and recommending to all schoolboys and all classes of society that they pull themselves together and return to work. In short, he completely lost his head.

On the other hand, the counter-revolutionary elements of the bureaucracy were hard at work. They had learned to value the support of "public forces," were calling pogrom organizations into being everywhere and, ignoring the official bureaucratic hierarchy, were organizing themselves into a unified body, having their own man—Durnovo—inside the cabinet itself. This most foul specimen of the Russian bureaucracy's foul mores, this thievish official whom even the unforgettable Alexander III himself was obliged to throw out with the energetic words: "remove this swine," this Durnovo was now brought out of the rubbish bin to provide a counterweight to the "liberal" Prime Minister in the capacity of Minister of Home Affairs.

Witte accepted this collaboration—an indignity even to someone like himself—and, presently, it reduced his own role to the same fictitious level as the actual practice of the bureaucracy reduced the manifesto of October 17. Having published a wearisome series of liberal-bureaucratic commonplaces, Witte arrived at the conclusion that Russian society was bereft of elementary political sense, moral strength, and social instincts. He became convinced of his own bankruptcy and foresaw the inevitability of a bloody policy of reprisals as a "preparation" for the introduction of a new regime. But he did not consider himself destined to implement such a policy, lacking the "necessary capabilities," and promised to cede his place to another person. Here, too, he proved a liar. He was to retain his post of powerless premier, despised by all, throughout the period of December and January, while Durnovo, the master of the situation, rolled up his sleeves and got on with his bloody work as the counter-revolution's butcher.

CHAPTER 11

❖◇❖◇❖◇❖◇❖◇❖

The First Days
of the "Freedoms"

The Soviet's attitude toward the manifesto was expressed very bluntly and precisely on the day of its publication. The representatives of the proletariat demanded amnesty, dismissal of the police at all levels of rank, withdrawal of troops from the city and the creation of a people's militia. Commenting on this decision in a leading article in *Izvestia*, we wrote: "And so we have been given a constitution. We have been given freedom of assembly, but our assemblies are encircled by troops. We have been given freedom of speech, but censorship remains inviolate. We have been given freedom of study, but the universities are occupied by troops. We have been given personal immunity, but the prisons are filled to overflowing with prisoners. We have been given Witte, but we still have Trepov. We have been given a constitution, but the autocracy remains. Everything has been given, and nothing has been given." They wanted a period of

(123)

calm. They would not get it. "The proletariat knows what it wants and what it does not want. It wants neither the police hooligan Trepov nor the liberal stockbroker Witte, neither the wolf's jaws nor the fox's tail. It does not want a whip wrapped in the parchment of a constitution." The Soviet resolved: the general strike continues.

The working masses proceeded to carry out this resolution with extraordinary unanimity. Smokeless factory chimneys stood as silent witnesses to the fact that the constitutional illusion had failed to make any headway in the working-class areas. Yet, despite everything, after October 18 the strike lost its directly militant character. It was transformed into a colossal *demonstration of non-confidence*. But the provinces, which had come out before the capital, now started going back to work. The Moscow strike ended on the nineteenth. The Petersburg Soviet decided to end the strike on October 21 at noon. The last to leave the field, it organized an astonishing demonstration of proletarian discipline by calling hundreds of thousands of workers back to their lathes at the same hour.

Even before the ending of the October strike the Soviet was able to test the tremendous influence it had acquired within a single week. This was when, at the demand of countless masses, it placed itself at their head and marched with them through the streets of Petersburg.

At 4:00 P.M. on the eighteenth, hundreds of thousands of people gathered by the Kazan Cathedral. Their slogan was amnesty. They wanted to march to the prisons. They wanted leaders and started out to where the Soviet was sitting. At 6:00 P.M. the Soviet elected three representatives to lead the demonstration. They appeared at a second floor window wearing white bands around their heads and arms. Below, a human ocean was seething. Red banners waved upon it like sails of the revolution. Tremendous shouts welcomed the chosen three. The whole Soviet walks downstairs and enters the crowd. "Speaker!" Dozens of arms stretch out towards the speaker; an instant later his feet are resting on someone's shoulders. "Amnesty! To the prisons!" Revolutionary anthems, shouts . . . In Kazansky Square and by Alexandrovsky Square, they bare their heads; here the procession is joined by the ghosts of the victims of January 9. The crowd sings "Eternal Memory" and "You Have Fallen Victim." Red banners outside Pobedonostsev's house. Whistling, curses. Does the old vulture hear them? Let him look out of the window without fear; they will not touch him at this hour. Let him gaze with his old, guilty eyes at the revolutionary masses, masters of the streets of Petersburg. Forward!

Two or three more streets, and the crowd is outside the House of Preliminary Confinement. News is received that a strong army ambush is waiting there. The leaders of the demonstration decide to set out on a reconnaissance. At the same time a deputation—as it turned out later, largely self-appointed— arrives from the Union of Engineers and announces that the amnesty decree has already been signed. All places of imprisonment have been occupied by troops, and the Union has been reliably informed that in the event of the masses approaching the prisons, Trepov has been given a free hand; bloodshed is therefore inevitable. After brief consultation, the leaders disperse the crowd. The demonstrators undertake, should the decree not be published, to meet again at the Soviet's summons and march on the prisons.

The struggle for amnesty went on everywhere. In Moscow on October 18 a crowd many thousand strong compelled the governor-general to release all political prisoners immediately; a list of their names was handed to a deputation of the strike committee* which supervised their release from the prisons. On the same day a crowd in Simferopol smashed the gates of the prison and drove the political prisoners away in carriages. In Odessa and Revel prisoners were released at the insistence of demonstrators. In Baku, an attempt to achieve the release of

* The committee was soon to develop into the Moscow Soviet of Workers' Deputies. (Author)

prisoners led to a clash with the troops which resulted in three dead and eighteen wounded. In Saratov, Vindava, Tashkent, Poltava, Kovno—everywhere large demonstrations marched to the prisons. Amnesty! Not only the paving-stones, the Petersburg city duma itself echoed the cry.

"Well, God be praised! My congratulations, gentlemen!" said Witte as he left the telephone, addressing three workers, representatives of the Soviet. "The Tsar has signed the amnesty."

"Is the amnesty complete or partial, Count?"

"The amnesty has been granted with all due prudence, but nevertheless it is sufficiently broad."

On October 22 the government at last published the Tsar's decree concerning the "relief of the fate of persons who, prior to the issuing of the manifesto, had perpetrated criminal acts against the state"—a pathetic, niggardly, mercenary document with its careful grading of "mercy," a true product of a power in which Trepov represented state authority and Witte stood for liberalism.

But there was a category of "state criminals" whom this decree did not and could not affect. They were those who had lost their lives by being tortured, by being slashed with sabers, by being strangled, by being pierced with bayonets, by being shot with bullets, all those murdered in the people's cause. At the same moment during the October demonstration when the revolutionary masses in the blood-stained squares of Petersburg were reverently honoring the memory of those killed on January 9, the steaming cadavers of the first victims of the constitutional era already lay in the police mortuaries. The revolution could not give life back to its new martyrs; it decided to put on mourning and solemnly inter their bodies. The Soviet announces a universal funeral demonstration for October 23.

A proposal is made that the government should be notified in advance, and precedents are quoted: in one case, at the demand of a deputation from the Soviet, Count Witte had arranged the release of two arrested leaders of a street meeting, in another he had ordered the opening of the state-owned Baltiysky plant which had been closed down in reprisal for the October strike. Despite warnings from the official representatives of the Social Democrats, the Soviet decides to inform Count Witte through a special deputation that the Soviet will assume responsibility for order during the demonstration, and demands the withdrawal of the police and troops.

Count Witte is very busy, and has just refused to receive two generals, but he receives the Soviet's deputation without protest. A procession? He personally has nothing against it: "Such processions are permitted in the West." But the matter is not within his competence. The Soviet should apply to Mr. Trepov, since the city is under his protection.

"We cannot apply to Trepov, we have not been authorized to do so."

"A pity. You might have found out for yourselves that he is not at all the monster people say he is."

"What about the famous order to 'spare no bullets,' Count?"

"Oh, that just slipped out in the heat of the moment."

Witte rings up Trepov, respectfully conveys his wish that "there should be no bloodshed," and waits for a decision. Trepov arrogantly refers him to the city governor. The Count hastily writes a few words to the latter and hands the letter to the deputation.

"We will take your letter, Count, but we reserve our freedom of action. We are not sure that we shan't have to make use of it."

"Of course, of course. I have nothing against that." *

Here is a living example of life in October. Count Witte congratulates the revolutionary workers on the signing of the

* "At Count Witte's," a documentary essay by P. A. Zlydniev, a member of the deputation, in the collective work *History of the Soviet of Workers' Deputies of Petersburg,* 1906. The Executive Committee, having heard the report of the deputation, decided "to instruct the chairman of the Soviet of Workers' Deputies to return the letter to the chairman of the Council of Ministers."

amnesty. Count Witte wants things to go off without bloodshed, "just like in Europe." Uncertain whether he will succeed in pushing Trepov off his perch, he attempts, in passing, to reconcile the proletariat with Trepov. The highest representative of power asks a workers' deputation to act as his intermediary in begging the city governor to take the constitution under his protection! Cowardice, trickery and stupidity were the watchwords of the constitutional cabinet.

Trepov, on the other hand, did not shilly-shally. He announced that "at these troubled times, when one section of the population is prepared to rise up in arms against the actions of another section, no political demonstrations can be allowed in the interests of the demonstrators themselves," and invited the organizers of the demonstration "to abandon their project . . . in view of the possibly extremely grave consequences of the drastic measures to which the police authorities may be compelled to resort." This was as sharp and clear as a saber stroke or the report of a rifle. Arm the scum of the city in the police stations, let them loose against the demonstrators, create confusion, and then take advantage of the scuffle to order the police and troops to intervene; sweep through the city like a storm, leaving blood, fire, and devastation in your wake. Such was the invariable program of the police scoundrel to whom the crowned imbecile had entrusted his country's destiny. At that moment, the scales of power began to oscillate: Witte or Trepov? To expand the constitutional experiment, or to drown it in a pogrom? Dozens of cities, in those honeymoon days of the new policy, were to become the arena of blood-curdling events, and the threads of those events were held in Trepov's hand. But Mendelssohn and Rothschild were for the constitution; the laws of the stock exchange, like those of Moses, forbid the consumption of fresh blood. Therein lay Witte's strength. Trepov's official position began to totter; and Petersburg was his last throw of the die.

It was a moment of extreme responsibility and importance.

The Soviet of Deputies had no interest in supporting Witte, nor any desire to do so, as it was to show clearly a few days later. But it was still less inclined to support Trepov, and to come out into the streets was to fall in with his plans. The political situation was not, of course, merely a matter of a conflict between the stock exchange and the police bullies. It was possible to rise above the plans of both Witte and Trepov and consciously to invite a clash in order to get rid of them both. That was the general trend of the Soviet's policy; it went towards the inevitable conflict with its eyes open. But it did not feel itself called upon to accelerate the conflict. The later, the better. To make the decisive struggle coincide with a funeral demonstration at a moment when the titanic tension of the October strike was already beginning to slacken and yield to a temporary psychological reaction of satisfied fatigue would have been to commit a monstrous error.

The author of this book—he considers it necessary to mention this fact, since afterwards he was often severely rebuked on this score—introduced a proposal to cancel the funeral demonstration. At an emergency meeting of the Soviet, past 1:00 A.M. on the morning of October 22, after passionate debate, the resolution we had submitted was adopted by an overwhelming number of votes. Here is its text:

The Soviet of Workers' Deputies intended to hold a solemn funeral for the victims of the government's villainies on Sunday, October 23. But the peaceful intention of the workers of Petersburg brought all the murderous representatives of the dying system to their feet. General Trepov, who rose to power on the corpses of January 9 and who has nothing more to lose before the face of the revolution, today threw down the final challenge to the Petersburg proletariat. Trepov insolently implies in his declaration that he means to set gangs of the Black Hundreds, armed by the police, against the peaceful procession, and then, in the guise of pacification, once more to cover the streets of Petersburg in blood. In view of this diabolical plan, the Soviet of Deputies states: The Petersburg proletariat will give final battle to the Tsarist government not on the day of Trepov's choice, but when the proletariat itself, organized and armed, considers it appropriate. For that reason, the Soviet of Deputies resolves: to replace the mass funeral procession by large and widespread meetings in honor of the victims, remembering that our fallen brothers, by their very death, have imposed on us the solemn duty to increase our efforts tenfold to arm ourselves and to bring the day closer when Trepov, together with the entire police gang, will be dumped on the rubbish heap of the monarchy's remnants.

CHAPTER 12

◇◇◇◇◇◇◇◇◇◇

The Tsar's Men at Work

The Soviet brought the strike to an end during those terrible
black days when the cries of slaughtered infants, the frenzied
curses of mothers, the dying gasps of old people, and savage
howls of despair rose to the heavens from every corner of the
country. A hundred of Russia's towns and townlets were transformed into hells. A veil of smoke was drawn across the sun.
Fires devoured entire streets with their houses and inhabitants.
This was the old order's revenge for its humiliation.

It recruited its fighting battalions everywhere, from every
alley, every slum. Here was the petty shopkeeper and the beg-
gar, the publican and his perennial clients, the janitor and the
police spy, the professional thief and the amateur housebreaker,
the small artisan and the brothel doorkeeper, the hungry, dumb
muzhik and yesterday's villager deafened by the roar of the ma-

chine. Embittered poverty, hopeless ignorance, and debauched corruption placed themselves under the orders of privileged self-interest and ruling-class anarchy.

These people had acquired their first experience of mass street actions during the so-called "patriotic" demonstrations at the beginning of the Russo-Japanese war. It was then that their basic props came to be known: the Tsar's portrait, a bottle of vodka, a tricolor flag. Since that time, the planned organization of society's rejects had been developed on a colossal scale. Whereas the mass of the pogromists (if "mass" is the right word) remained more or less haphazard, the nucleus was always disciplined and organized in para-military style, receiving its slogans and its watchwords from above and deciding the time and scope of every murderous operation. Komissarov, an official of the police department, said: "It is possible to arrange any kind of pogrom, involving 10 people if you like, or 10,000 if you like." *

Everyone knows about a coming pogrom in advance. Pogrom proclamations are distributed, bloodthirsty articles come out in the official Provincial Gazettes, sometimes a special newspaper begins to appear. The town governor of Odessa issues a provocational proclamation in his own name. When the ground has been prepared, a visiting company of "specialists" appears. They spread sinister rumors among the ignorant masses: the Jews are planning an attack on the Russians, some socialists have defiled a holy icon, some students have torn up the Tsar's portrait. Where there is no university, the rumor is made to fit the liberal rural council or even the high school. The wildest news travels along the telegraph wires, sometimes bearing an official stamp. Meanwhile the preparatory technical work is accomplished: lists are drawn up of people, houses are singled out for special attention, a general strategic plan is drawn up, on an ap-

* This fact was reported in the first Duma by Prince Urusov, former Deputy Minister of Home Affairs. (Author)

pointed date the hungry mob is called from the suburbs. On that date a special service is held in the cathedral. The bishop makes a solemn oration.

A patriotic procession starts out, with the clergy in the front, with a portrait of the Tsar taken from police headquarters, with many national flags. A military band plays without cease. At the sides and at the rear of the procession march the police. The governor salutes, the police chief publicly embraces the leading members of the Black Hundreds. Churches along the way of the procession ring their bells. "Hats off!" Visiting "instructors" and local policemen in civilian clothes, though frequently still wearing their uniform trousers which they have not had time to change, are scattered among the crowd. They keep a watchful eye on the proceedings, excite the crowd and urge it on, giving the impression that everything is allowed, and all the time looking for a pretext for open action. To start with a few windows are smashed, a few passers-by beaten up; the wreckers enter every tavern on their way and drink, drink, drink. The band never stops playing "God Save the Tsar," that hymn of the pogroms.

If no pretext is at hand they create one: someone climbs into an attic and fires on the crowd, usually with blank cartridges. Patrols armed with police revolvers make sure that the anger of the crowd is not paralyzed by fear. They respond to the provocateur's shot with a volley at the windows of previously selected apartments. A few shops are raided and stolen cloth and silk is spread on the ground at the feet of the patriotic procession. If any resistance is offered, regular troops come to the rescue. With two or three volleys they shoot down the resisters or render them powerless by not allowing them within range. Protected in the front and rear by army patrols, with a cossack detachment for reconnaissance, with policemen and professional provocateurs as leaders, with mercenaries filling the secondary roles, with volunteers out for easy profit, the gang rushes through the town, drunk on vodka and the smell of blood.*

The doss-house tramp is king. A trembling slave an hour ago, hounded by police and starvation, he now feels himself an unlimited despot. Everything is allowed to him, he is capable of anything, he is the master of property and honor, of life and death. If he wants to, he can throw an old woman out of a third-floor window together with a grand piano, he can smash a chair against a baby's head, rape a little girl while the entire crowd looks on, hammer a nail into a living human body. . . . He exterminates whole families, he pours petrol over a house, transforms it into a mass of flames, and if anyone attempts to escape, he finishes him off with a cudgel. A savage horde comes tearing into an Armenian almshouse, knifing old people, sick people, women, children. . . . There exist no tortures, figments of a feverish brain maddened by alcohol and fury, at which he need ever stop. He is capable of anything, he dares everything. God save the Tsar!

Here is a young man who has seen the face of death: his hair has turned white within an instant. Here is a ten-year-old boy who has gone mad over the mutilated corpses of his parents. Here is an army doctor who went through all the horrors of the siege of Port Arthur, but who, unable to stand a few hours of pogrom in Odessa, has sunk into the eternal night of madness. God save the Tsar! The victims, bloodstained, charred, driven frantic, still search for salvation within the nightmare. Some put on the bloodstained clothes of people already dead, lie down in

* "In many cases policemen themselves directed the crowd of hooligans in their wrecking and robbing of Jewish houses, apartments and shops, equipped the hooligans with cudgels made from cut-down trees, participated in the destruction of property, robberies and killings, and themselves controlled the actions of the crowd." ("Most Loyal Report" by Senator Kuzminsky concerning the Odessa pogrom.) The town governor Neidgart admits that "crowds of hooligans engaged in wrecking and robbing" greeted him "enthusiastically, with cries of hurrah." Baron Kaulbars, commander of the local troops, addressed the police with a speech beginning with the following words: "Let's call a spade a spade. Let's admit that all of us, in our heart of hearts, sympathize with this pogrom!"

a pile of corpses and stay there for a whole day, for two or three days. . . . Others fall on their knees before the officers, the policemen, the raider, they stretch out their arms, crawl in the dust, kiss the soldiers' boots, beg for mercy. In reply they hear only drunken laughter. "You wanted freedom? Here, look, this is it."

In these words is contained the whole infernal morality of the pogrom policy. The doss-house tramp, gorged with blood, rushes further. He is capable of everything, he dares everything, he is king. The White Tsar has permitted him everything: long live the White Tsar! * And the tramp is not mistaken. None other than the autocrat of all the Russias is the supreme protector of this semi-official gang of pogromists and thieves which weaves in and out of the official bureaucracy, which can call more than a hundred major local administrators its own, and whose headquarters is among the court camarilla. Dull-witted and scared, an all-powerful nonentity, the prey of prejudices worthy of an Eskimo, the royal blood in his veins poisoned by all the vices of many generations, Nicholas Romanov, like many others of his profession, combines filthy sensuality with apathetic cruelty. By tearing every sacred veil from his person on January 9, the revolution finally corrupted him. The times when he was content to remain in the shadows, using Trepov as his secret service agent in pogrom affairs,** have gone.

Now he flaunts his connections with the savage scum of the taverns and convict labor gangs. Trampling underfoot the foolish fiction of the "monarch who stands above all parties," he exchanges friendly telegrams with well-known thugs, grants

* In one such procession the tricolor flag was carried in front, the Tsar's portrait immediately behind, and directly behind the portrait a silver dish and a sack containing stolen goods." (Report by Senator Turau.) (Author)
** According to widespread opinion, Trepov reports to His Majesty on the state of affairs . . . and influences the policy line. . . . On his appointment to the post of palace commandant, General Trepov demanded and received the allocation of special funds for secret service expenses." (Letter by Senator Lophukhin.)

audiences to "patriots" despised by everyone and, at the demand of the Union of the Russian People, pardons without exception all the killers and robbers condemned by his own courts of justice. It is hard to imagine a more bare-faced mockery of the solemn mystique of the monarchy than the behavior of this monarch whom any court in any country would be obliged to condemn to forced labor for life, always provided that it recognized him as being of sound mind.

During this black October bacchanalia, compared with which St. Bartholomew's night looks like the most innocent piece of theater, 3,500 to 4,000 people were killed and as many as 10,000 maimed in 100 towns. Material losses, amounting to tens if not hundreds of millions of roubles, were several times greater than those suffered by the landowners as a result of agrarian riots. Thus did the old order avenge its humiliation!

What was the workers' role in these devastating events?

At the end of October the president of the Federation of North American Trade Unions sent a telegram addressed to Count Witte in which he energetically called upon Russian workers to take a stand against the pogroms which represented a threat to their newly-won freedom. "On behalf not only of the three million organized workers," the telegram ended, "but also of all the workers of the United States, I beg you, Count, to transmit this dispatch to your fellow citizens, our brother-workers." But Count Witte, who had only recently posed as a true democrat in the United States, declaring that "the pen is mightier than the sword," now found a sufficient reserve of shamelessness within himself to let him put the dispatch quietly away in a secret drawer of his desk. Not until November did the Soviet, by devious ways, hear of its existence. However, it should be said to the honor of the Russian workers that they did not have to wait for the warning from their friends across the ocean to intervene actively in the bloody events. In a number of towns they organized armed detachments which offered active, and in some places heroic, resistance to the thugs; and wherever the troops behaved in a more or less neutral fashion, the workers' militia found no difficulty in putting an end to the hooligans' excesses.

Nemirovich-Danchenko, an old writer very far away from socialism or the proletariat, wrote during those days:

Side by side with this nightmare, this Walpurgis Night of a dying monster, see how majestically, with what astonishing fortitude, order and discipline, the workers' movement developed. They did not defile themselves with murders or robberies; on the contrary, they came to the aid of the public everywhere, and, needless to say, protected the public far better than the police, the cossacks, or the gendarmes from the destructive delirium of the blood-gorged Cains. The workers' armed detachments appeared wherever the hooligans began their foul work. This new force, entering the historical arena for the first time, showed itself calm in the consciousness of its right, moderate in the triumph of its ideals of liberty and goodness, organized and obedient like a real army that knows that its victory is the victory of everything for whose sake humanity lives, thinks, and rejoices, fights and suffers.

◇ ◇ ◇

No pogrom took place in Petersburg. But overt preparations for a pogrom went on at full strength. The Jewish population of the capital was in a state of constant dread. After the eighteenth, students, worker agitators, and Jews were beaten up daily in different parts of the city. Separate gangs, yelling and whistling, attacked not only in the suburbs but in the Nevsky itself, using knuckledusters, jackknives and whips. Several attempts were made on the lives of deputies to the Soviet, who lost no time in equipping themselves with revolvers. Police agents urged shopkeepers and shop assistants to attack the funeral procession planned for October 23. It was not the fault of the Black Hundreds that, nevertheless, they had to content themselves with guerrilla action.

The workers made active preparations to defend their city. In certain cases whole plants undertook to go out into the streets at any threat of danger. The gun shops, ignoring all police restrictions, carried on a feverish trade in Brownings. But revolvers cost a great deal and the broad masses cannot afford them; the revolutionary parties and the Soviet had difficulty in arming their fighting detachments. Meanwhile rumors of a pogrom were growing. All plants and workshops having any access to iron or steel began, on their own initiative, to manufacture side-arms. Several thousand hammers were forging daggers, pikes, wire whips and knuckledusters. In the evening, at a meeting of the Soviet, one deputy after another mounted the rostrum, raising their weapons high above their heads and transmitting their electors' solemn undertaking to suppress the pogrom as soon as it flared up. That demonstration alone was bound to paralyze all initiative among rank-and-file pogromists. But the workers did not stop there. In the factory areas, beyond the Nevsky Gate, they organized a real militia with regular night watches. In addition to this they ensured special protection of the buildings of the revolutionary press, a necessary step in those anxious days when the journalist wrote and the typesetter worked with a revolver in his pocket.

By arming itself against the Black Hundreds, the proletariat was automatically arming itself against Tsarist power. The government could not fail to understand this, and it raised the alarm. On November 8, the *Pravitelstvenny Vestnik* (Government Gazette) informed the public of facts which everyone knew anyway: namely, that the workers "have recently begun to arm themselves with revolvers, sporting guns, daggers, knives and pikes. Out of these armed workers," the government communiqué continued, "whose number, according to available information, reaches 6,000 men, there has been formed a so-called self-defense force or militia, numbering approximately 300 men, who walk the streets at night in groups of ten under the pretext of defense; their real aim, however, is to protect revolutionaries against arrest by the police or troops."

A regular armed campaign against the militiamen opened in

Petersburg. The workers' detachments were dispersed, their arms confiscated. But by that time the danger of a pogrom had already passed, to be replaced by another, far greater danger. The government was giving temporary leave to its irregular troops and putting into action its regulars—the cossack and guards regiments. It was preparing for war on a wide front.

CHAPTER 13

✦✧✦✧✦✧✦✧✦✧✦

Storming the Censorship Bastilles

The Petersburg Soviet wages a splendid campaign—well organized, politically perfect and victorious—in defense of the freedom of the press. Its faithful comrade in this struggle was a young but united political and trades organization, the Union of Print-Workers.

"Freedom of the press," said a working-class speaker at a large meeting of the Union preceding the October strike, "is necessary to us not only as a political right. It is an economic claim. Literature freed from the clamp of censorship will extend the printers' trade and other related branches of the industry." From that moment on, the print-workers opened a systematic campaign against censorship restrictions. Even earlier, throughout 1905, illegal literature had been printed in legal print shops; but this was done clandestinely, on a small scale and with the greatest caution. From October on, the mass of rank-and-file typesetters were drawn into the work of publishing illegal literature. Conspiratorial methods within the print shops disappeared almost entirely. The workers' pressure on the publishers increased at the same time. The typesetters insisted on newspapers being published in disregard of the conditions of censorship, threatening otherwise to withhold their services. A meeting of representatives of periodical publications took place on October 13. At this meeting, the reptiles from *Novoye Vremya* sat side by side with extreme radicals. And this Noah's Ark of the Petersburg press decided "not to address any claim for freedom of the press to the government, but to institute such freedom without preliminary permission." The resolution breathes civic courage! Luckily the general strike helped the publishers by making it unnecessary for their valor to be put to the test; and, afterwards, the "constitution" came to their aid. The Golgotha of political martyrdom happily receded before the more tempting prospect of agreement with the new ministry.

The manifesto of October 17 was silent on the freedom of the press. Count Witte explained to liberal deputations, however, that this silence was a sign of consent and that the proclaimed freedom of speech extended also to the press. But, the Premier added, censorship proved as impotent as he himself. Its fate was decided, not by the publishers, but by the workers.

The Soviet stated on October 19,

The Tsar's manifesto proclaims "freedom" of speech in Russia, yet the Central Directorate of Affairs of the Press still exists, the censor's blue pencil is still in force. . . . Freedom of the press still has to be won by the workers. The Soviet of Deputies resolves that only those newspapers may be published whose editors ignore the censorship committee, refuse to submit their issues for censorship, and generally act in the same way as the Soviet in publishing its own newspaper. For this reason typesetters and other workers of the press will work only after editors have declared their readiness to put the freedom of the press into practice. Until that time newspaper workers will remain on strike, and the Soviet of Deputies will take all necessary measures to pay the comrades on strike all wages due to them. Newspapers which fail to accept the present resolution will be confiscated from their sellers, and any workers who do not accept the decision of the Soviet of Deputies will be boycotted.

This resolution, extended a few days later to all journals, brochures, and books, became the new press law. The type-setters' strike, together with the general strike, continued until October 21. The Union of Print-Workers resolved not to inter-rupt the strike even in order to print the constitutional manifesto, and this decision was strictly observed. The manifesto appeared only in the Government Gazette, which was printed by soldiers; apart from that, only the reactionary *Svet* (Light) issued the Tsar's underground proclamation of October 17 without the knowledge of its own typesetters. *Svet* was to pay a heavy price for this action: its print shop was wrecked by factory workers.

Is it possible that only nine months had passed since the January pilgrimage to the Winter Palace? Was it only the previ-ous winter that these same people had entreated the Tsar to grant them freedom of the press? No, our old calendar lies! The revolution has its own system of chronology, where months are decades and years are whole centuries.

Among twenty thousand workers, the Tsar's manifesto could not find a single loyal printer to print it. But social-democratic proclamations containing reports of the manifesto and com-menting upon it were disseminated in enormous numbers as early as October 18; and the second issue of the Soviet's own *Izvestia*, published on the same day, was distributed at every street corner.

After the strike, all the newspapers announced that hence-forth they would be published without censorship. Most of them, however, failed to breathe a single word about the real initiator of their decision. Only *Novoye Vremya*, through the pen of its Stolypin—brother of the future Premier—timidly expressed its indignation: we were quite prepared to make this sacrifice on the altar of a free press, but they came to us, they demanded from us, they forced us—and poisoned our pleasure in our own selflessness. Apart from this, there was only a certain Bashmakov, editor of the reactionary *Narodny Golos* (People's Voice) and of a French-language diplomatic paper, *Journal de St. Petersbourg*, who failed to show the liberals' general readiness to grin and bear it; he obtained permission from the ministry not to submit proofs of finished copies of his newspapers for censorship, and published the following indignant statement in *Narodny Golos*:

"Committing an infringement of the law under duress," wrote this knight of police legality, "despite my firm conviction that a law, even if it is a bad law, must be observed until the legal authorities have repealed it, I am publishing this issue *against my will* without consulting the censorship, although I have no right to do so. I protest with all my heart against the moral coercion practiced against me and declare that I intend to observe the law as soon as the slightest physical possibility for doing so exists, as I would consider it a dishonor to have my name counted among the strikers at the present turbulent time. Aleksandr Bashmakov."

This statement perfectly characterizes the real correlation of forces between official legality and revolutionary law as it established itself during this period. In the interests of justice we feel we should add that Mr. Bashmakov's action compares very favorably with the behavior of the semi-Octobrist *Slovo* which officially applied for, and obtained, the Soviet's written instructions not to submit its issues to the censorship. Such people needed the new master's permission before they dared to flout the authority of the old regime.

The Union of Print-Workers was on its guard the whole time. Today it puts a stop to a publisher's attempt to circumvent the Soviet's resolution by getting in touch with the idle censorship office. Tomorrow it cuts short a scheme to use an idle printing machine to publish a pogrom proclamation. Cases of this kind become more and more frequent. The struggle with pogrom literature began with the confiscation of an order for 100,000 copies of a proclamation signed by "a group of workers" and calling for a rising against the "new Tsars," i.e., the social-democrats. The original draft of this pogrom proclamation carried the signatures of Count Orlov-Davydov and Countess Musin-Pushkin. The typesetters asked the Soviet for directives; the Executive Committee replied: stop the presses, destroy the stereotypes, confiscate any finished copies. And the Executive Committee published the original proclamation of the nobly-born hooligans, accompanied by its own comments, in the social-democrats' paper.

The general principle adopted both by the Executive Committee and by the Union of Print-Workers was to allow the printing of texts which did not contain direct appeals to violence and pogroms. Thanks to the united efforts of the typesetters, all purely pogrom literature was excluded from the private print shops, so that appeals to violate were now printed only in the department of police and the directorate of the gendarmerie, with the doors and shutters tightly closed, on hand-operated presses previously confiscated from the revolutionaries.

Generally speaking, the reactionary press appeared without any let or hindrance. During the first few days, it is true, there were a small number of exceptions. We know of one attempt by typesetters to publish their comments on a reactionary article and of several protests against crude anti-revolutionary statements. In Moscow, some typesetters refused to publish the program of the Octobrist group which came into being at that time.

"There's freedom of the press for you!" Guchkov, the future head of the Union of October 17, complained at a rural congress. "Why, it's the old regime, only the other way around. All that's left for us is to use the methods used under the old regime: send materials for printing abroad or start an underground print shop."

It goes without saying that the indignation of the pharisees of capitalist freedom knew no bounds. They considered themselves right because they held that the typesetter is not responsible for the text he sets up. But at that exceptional time political passions had reached such a pitch that a worker, even while at work, never for a moment lost the sense of his revolutionary responsibility. Typesetters in certain reactionary publishing houses even went so far as to give up their jobs, thus voluntarily condemning themselves to penury. Of course they were in no sense infringing the freedom of the press by refusing to set reactionary or liberal slanders against their own class. At the worst, they were violating their own contracts.

But capital is so deeply saturated with the brutal metaphysic of "free employment," which compels workers to do the most disgusting kinds of work (building prisons and warships, forging leg-irons, printing sheets of bourgeois lies) that it never tires of branding a morally motivated refusal to perform such work as a physical violation, either of the "freedom of labor," or of the "freedom of the press."

⬦ ⬦ ⬦

October 22 saw the first appearance of Russian newspapers freed from an age-long bondage. Amidst the swarm of old and new bourgeois newspapers for whom the possibility of saying whatever they wanted was not a blessing but a curse, because at that great time they had nothing to say; because their vocabulary did not include the words with which they might have, or should have, addressed the new reader; because the collapse of censorship had left inviolate their inner censor, their cautious habit of always looking over their shoulder at authority; amidst this brotherhood, who now dressed their political inarticulateness in the toga of superior statesmanship, now adorned it with the cap and bells of marketplace radicalism, the clear and virile voice of the socialist press immediately stood out.

"Our newspaper is the organ of the revolutionary proletariat," the social-democratic *Nachalo* declared. "With its self-less struggle, the Russian proletariat has opened to us the freedom of the word. We dedicate our free word to the service of the Russian proletariat." We, the Russian journalists of socialism, who for many years had led, like moles, the life of the revolution's underground, knew the value of open skies, fresh air and the free word. We, who had served our apprenticeships in the dark night of the reaction, when harsh winds blew and owls hooted. We, small in numbers, weak, scattered, lacking experience, almost boys, against the terrible apocalyptic beast. We, armed only with our boundless faith in the gospel of international socialism, against the powerful enemy clad from head to foot in the armor of international militarism. Hiding in the nooks and crannies of "legal" society, we had declared war on the autocracy, a struggle for life or death. What was our weapon? The word. If anyone were to calculate the number of hours of prison and exile our party paid for each revolutionary word, the figures would be horrifying—a gruesome statistic of vital energy and life's blood!

On the long road strewn with traps and pitfalls, there stand between the illegal writer and the illegal reader a number of illegal intermediaries: the typesetter, the carrier, the distributor. What a chain of effort and danger! One false step and the work of all is lost. How many printing presses were confiscated before they were able to commence work! How much literature was burned in the courtyards of gendarmerie offices before it was able to reach the reader! How much work wasted, how many forces paralyzed, how many existences ruined!

Our pathetic clandestine hectographs, our homemade clandestine hand-presses were what we pitted against the rotary presses of lying officialdom and licensed liberalism. Was it not like fighting Krupp's guns with a Stone-Age ax? They had laughed at us. And now, in the October days, the Stone-Age ax had won. The revolutionary word was out in the open, astonished and intoxicated by its own power.

The revolutionary press met with colossal success. Two large social-democratic newspapers were published in Petersburg, each of them with more than 50,000 subscribers from the first days of their existence, as well as a cheaper paper whose circulation rose to 100,000 within two or three weeks. The social-revolutionaries' paper also had a large circulation. At the same time the provinces, which had created their own socialist press within a short time, were also crying out for the capital's revolutionary publications in large and constantly increasing numbers.

Conditions for the press, like all other political conditions, varied between one part of the country and another. Everything depended on whether the reaction or the revolution felt itself to be the stronger in a particular place. In the capital, censorship virtually ceased to exist. In the provinces it maintained itself, but, influenced by the tone of the capital's newspapers, it let the reins hang very loose. The struggle of the police against the revolutionary press lacked any unifying idea. Orders for the confiscation of individual publications were issued, but no one seriously tried to implement them. Issues of social-democratic papers supposed to have been confiscated were sold openly not only in the working-class districts but also in Nevsky Prospect. The provinces devoured the capital's press like manna from heaven. Long queues of newspaper buyers waited at railway stations for the arrival of postal trains. Vendors were practically torn to pieces. People would open a fresh issue of *Russkaya Gazeta* and start reading the main articles out loud. The railway station would become filled to capacity and transformed into a tumultuous auditorium. This happened for two days, three days, and then became part of the system.

But sometimes the total passivity of the police was replaced by unbridled violence. Gendarmerie n.c.o.'s would confiscate the "seditious" Petersburg press before it had time to leave the railway wagons, and destroy it on the spot. The satirical magazines provided a special target for the frenzy of the police. The campaign against them was led by Durnovo, the Home Minister, who later proposed the re-establishment of preliminary censorship of press drawings. He had good cause to dislike them: invoking the authoritative description once made by Alexander III, the cartoonists never failed to depict the Home Minister's stupid head as attached to the body of a pig. But Durnovo was not the only one to hate the satirical magazines; all the Tsar's aides-de-camp, gentlemen in waiting, chamberlains, equerries, and the rest, were united with him in a passion of vindictive rage.

And this gang finally succeeded in tampering with the press law by which the ministry had decided "immediately, prior to legislative sanction by the State Duma, to put into effect the freedom of the press." In other words, they effectively succeeded in curtailing that freedom of the press which, thanks to the Petersburg proletariat, had already been won. The provisional rules of November 24, which put the press back into the hands of the administration, made punishable offenses of any incitement to strike or demonstrate, insults to the armed forces, the dissemination of false information concerning the government's activities, and, finally, the dissemination of false rumors in general. In Russia, "provisional rules" of every kind are usually the most long-lasting form of legislation. This is proving true of the provisional rules governing the press. Issued pending the convening of the State Duma, they were subjected to a general boycott and, like the whole of Witte's ministry, remained suspended in mid-air. But the triumph of the counter-revolution in December cleared the ground for their enforcement. The "provisional rules" came into force and were accompanied by a new clause penalizing the "glorification of crimes" on the one hand and, on the other hand, granting discretionary powers to provincial and town governors. These vicious "rules" have survived the first Duma, the second Duma, and will doubtless safely survive the third.

◇ ◇ ◇

In connection with the history of the struggle for the freedom of the press it still remains for us to tell the story of how the *Izvestia* of the Soviet of Workers' Deputies was published. The history of the publication of these bulletins of the revolution forms an interesting page in the chapter on the Russian proletariat's struggle for the freedom of speech.

The first issue, published before the "constitution," was small both in size and in the number of copies printed. It was printed clandestinely, for money, in a private print shop. The second issue was printed on October 18.* A group of volunteers went to the printing works of the radical *Syn Otechestva* (Son of the Fatherland), which a little later passed into the hands of the socialist revolutionaries. The management hesitated. The situation was still confused and no one could tell what the consequences of printing a revolutionary publication might be.

"Now if you were to arrest us," hazards someone from the management.

"You are under arrest," is the reply.

"By force of arms," adds another volunteer, pulling a revolver out of his pocket.

"You're under arrest! All under arrest!"

"Everybody in, nobody out!"

"Where's your telephone? Take the telephone!"

Work begins. New people keep arriving—journalists, typesetters. The typesetters are invited to go to the workshops and get down to work, the journalists are asked to write news items. The place is a hive of activity.

The *Obshchestvennaya Polza* (The Public Weal) print shop is occupied. Entrances are locked. Sentries are posted.

The foreman comes into the stereotype workshop. The matrices are being knocked out, the furnace is being lit. Unfamiliar faces all around.

* All subsequent episodes, as related by us, are based on notes published by Comrade Simanovsky, chief organizer of the Soviet's "flying print shop" under the title *How We Published the Soviet's Izvestia.* (Author)

"Who are you? Who allowed you to do this?" the new-comer demands, getting excited, and trying to put out the furnace. He is told to keep off, otherwise they'll lock him up in a closet.

"What's going on here?"

He is told that the third issue of the Soviet's *Izvestia* is being printed. "Why didn't you say so to start with? I don't mind . . . I'm always ready . . ." and the experienced craftsman gets down to work.

"How are you proposing to do the printing? The electricity supply is cut off," says the manager who is under arrest.

"Which is your power station? We'll get the current restored within half an hour."

The manager names the power station, but is skeptical. He has been trying in vain for several days to get the current restored, if only to get some light in the private apartments; the power station, where the strikers are being replaced by seamen, is supplying current only to state institutions.

Exactly half an hour later the light comes on, the machines can start working. The management's faces reflect a respectful surprise. A few moments later the worker sent to the power station returns with a note from the officer in charge. At the request of the Soviet of Workers' Deputies the electricity supply to Bolshaya Podyacheskaya, 39, has been restored for the *Obshchestvennay a Polza* print shop. A signature follows.

In harmony and even gaily, the "raiders" and the "arrested" together produce a large number of copies of the third issue.

In the end the police discover where *Izvestia* is being printed. They appear at the print shop, but too late: all copies have been taken away, the galleys have been removed. Not until the night of November 3–4 during the second strike did the police succeed in catching the *Izvestia* "flying squad" in action. This happened in the print shop of *Nasha Zhizn* (Our Life), where work was continuing for the second day running. Meeting with a refusal to unlock the doors, the police broke them open. Simanovsky writes: "Under the protection of a company of rifle-men with rifles at the ready, the police broke into the print shop, revolvers in hand, but were themselves embarrassed by the peaceful picture of the print-workers calmly continuing their business despite the appearance of bayonets."

"We are all here by order of the Soviet of Workers' Deputies," the workers declared, "and we demand the withdrawal of the police, since otherwise we cannot be responsible for the safety of the equipment."

While negotiations were going on with the police, and while the latter were gathering up the originals and proofs and sealing them to the tables and composing frames, the arrested workers wasted no time; they began at once to carry on agitational work among the soldiers and policemen, quietly reading the Soviet's address to them and handing out copies of *Izvestia*. Then the typesetters had their names taken and were released, the doors of the print shop were sealed and a police guard was mounted. But the investigating authorities who arrived on the next day found nothing! The doors were locked, the seals unbroken, but neither composition nor proofs nor originals were to be seen. Everything had been transferred to the print shop of the *Birzhevye Vedomosti* (Stock-Exchange Gazette), where the sixth issue of *Izvestia* was being printed without hindrance.

The evening of November 6 saw the biggest action of this kind: the huge print-works of *Novoye Vremya* were taken over. On the day after, that influential reptile of a newspaper devoted two articles to the event, one of which was headed: *How the official proletarian newspaper is printed.*

This is how the story appeared to the "victim":

At about 6:00 P.M. three young men called at the print-works. The manager happened to come in at the same time. The callers were announced to him and he invited them into the print-works office.

"Send everybody out," one of the three told the manager. "We have to speak to you alone."

"There are three of you and I am alone," said the manager; "I prefer to talk to you in front of witnesses."

"We request you to ask everyone to wait in the next room, we have only a few words to say to you."

The manager agreed. Then the callers told him that they had come by order of the Executive Committee and that they were instructed to seize the print-works of *Novoye Vremya* and print the seventh issue of *Izvestia* there.

"I can't discuss this with you," declared the manager. "The place isn't mine; I must consult the owner."

"You cannot leave the premises; ask the owner to come here if you need him," replied the deputies.

"I can tell him over the telephone."

"No, all you can do over the telephone is ask him to come here."

"Very well."

The manager, accompanied by the deputies, went to the telephone and asked Suvorin (Jr.) to come around. Suvorin declined, saying that he was unwell, and sent Goldstein, a member of the editorial board, instead. Goldstein describes the further course of events fairly accurately except that he emphasizes a few points intended to show up his own civic courage:

When I came to the print-works the gas lighting was off and the street was almost entirely dark. Outside the print-works building and nearby I noticed several small groups of people; on the pavement outside the door there were eight or ten men. Inside the courtyard, directly by the gate, there were three or four more. A foreman met me and took me to the office. There I found the print-works manager and three young men unknown to me, evidently workers. When I entered they rose to their feet.

"What have you to say, gentlemen?" I asked.

Instead of a reply one of the young men handed me a paper with instructions from the Soviet of Workers' Deputies to print the next issue of *Izvestia* at the *Novoye Vremya* print works. The order was written on a scrap of paper and rubber-stamped.

"The turn of your print-works has come," one of the messengers said to me. "What do you mean by that?" I asked.

"We've printed our paper at *Rus, Nasha Zhizn, Syn Otechestva* and *Birzhevye Vedomosti,* and now we're going to print it here.

You must give us your word of honor, on behalf of Suvorin as well, that you won't report us until we have finished our work."

"I can't answer for Suvorin and I don't intend to give my own word of honor."

"In that case we shan't let you out of here."

"I'll force my way out, I warn you I'm armed."

"We're armed just as much as you," said the deputies, pulling out their revolvers.

"Call the watchman and the foreman," they told the manager.

He looked at me inquiringly. I shrugged my shoulders. They called in the watchman and asked him to take off his sheepskin. The foreman, too, was called into the office. We were all arrested. A minute later I could hear a crowd coming up the stairs. In the office door and in the anteroom there were people.

The takeover had taken place.

The three deputies went in and out, behaving in an extremely active manner.

"Do you mind if I ask you," I said to one of the deputies, "which machine you propose to use?"

"The rotary machine."

"And if you damage it?"

"We've got a first-class man to operate it."

"What about paper?"

"We'll take yours."

"But that's plain robbery!"

"Can't be helped . . ."

In the end Mr. Goldstein gave in, promised to keep quiet and was allowed to go:

I went downstairs. The gateway was in total darkness. Directly by the gate, wearing the sheepskin taken from the watchman, a "proletarian" with a revolver was on duty. Another struck a match, a third put the key in the lock. The lock clicked, the gate opened and I went out.

The night passed quietly. The print-works manager, who had been told that he could go if he gave his word of honor not to say anything, refused to leave. The proletarians let him stay on. The work of composing proceeded rather slowly, and copy came in very gradually. The latest materials for printing had not yet come in. When the manager offered advice about speeding up the work, the answer was: "There's no hurry, we've got plenty of time!" The make-up man and the proofreader, both very experienced men, did not turn up until 5:00 A.M.

Typesetting was finished by 6:00 A.M. Then they started knocking out the matrix-molds and pouring off the stereotype. Because of the strike there was no gas to heat the furnaces for the stereotype. Two workers were sent off somewhere and the gas came on. All the shops were shut, but food was obtained without difficulty all through the night. The shops opened up for the proletarians. At 7:00 A.M. the printing of the official proletarian newspaper began. They used the rotary press and they worked efficiently. Printing continued until 11:00 A.M. The print shop was then cleared and bundles of the printed newspaper were carried away and carted off in cabs, a sufficient number of which had been assembled outside. The police learned about all this on the next day and seemed very surprised.

Only an hour after the work was finished, a large police detachment accompanied by a company of infantry, some cossacks and some uniformed janitors, burst into the premises of the Union of Print-Workers to confiscate the seventh issue of *Izvestia*. They met with the most energetic resistance. They were told that the available copies (only 153 out of the 35,000 printed) would not be handed over voluntarily. Workers in many print shops, hearing of the police invasion of their Union's premises, stopped work which they had only just resumed after the November strike, to await further developments. The police suggested a compromise: those present would look away, the police would snatch the copies of *Izvestia*, and the official report would state that the confiscation had been carried out by force. But this compromise was indignantly rejected. The police did not venture to use force, and retreated in full battle order, having failed to seize a single copy of *Izvestia*.

After the takeover of the *Novoye Vremya* print-works, the city governor informed the police administration that all police officers in whose district a similar takeover took place in the future would be severely penalized. The Executive Committee replied by announcing that *Izvestia*, which appeared only during general strikes, would when necessary continue to be printed in the same way. And indeed, during the December strike, the second Soviet of Workers' Deputies (after the arrest of the first) published four more issues of *Izvestia*.

The detailed report of the raid on its print-works published by *Novoye Vremya* had a very unexpected result. Revolutionaries in the provinces took advantage of the model thus provided, and the seizure of print-works for the publication of revolutionary literature thenceforth became widespread throughout Russia. However, the word "seizure" should only be used with considerable reservations. We are not thinking of the print-works of liberal newspapers, where the management wanted only one thing—to evade responsibility—and therefore expressed their full readiness to be arrested. But even in the most publicized episode involving *Novoye Vremya* the takeover would not have been possible without the passive or active sympathy of the entire personnel. Once the leader of the takeover proclaimed a "state of siege," thus removing responsibility from the print-works personnel, the distinction between the besieged and the besiegers disappeared, the "arrested" typesetters were quite willing to set revolutionary manuscripts, the machine operator took his place at the press, and the manager encouraged both his own men and the others to work more quickly. Success was not assured by any carefully prepared takeover plan, and certainly not by physical force, but by that revolutionary atmosphere of unity without which none of the Soviet's activities would have been conceivable.

At first glance it may be difficult to understand why the Soviet chose the risky method of night raids for publishing its paper. The social-democratic press was appearing quite openly at this time. Its tone differed little from that of *Izvestia*. It published the Soviet's decisions and reported its meetings in full. True, *Izvestia* appeared almost exclusively during periods of general strike, when the rest of the press was silent. But would it not have been possible for the Soviet to exempt the legal social-democratic papers from the strike, thus relieving itself of the necessity to raid the print-works of the bourgeois press? Yet it did not do this. Why?

If the question is put in isolation, it cannot be answered. But everything becomes clear if we see the Soviet as a whole, in its origins and in all its tactics, as the organized embodiment of the supreme rights of the revolution at its moment of extreme tension, when it cannot and does not wish to adapt itself to the enemy, when it marches straight ahead, heroically extending its territory and sweeping all obstacles from its path. During general strikes, when all life came to a standstill, the old regime considered it a point of honor to continue printing its Government Gazette without interruption, and it did so under the protection of its troops. To this the Soviet opposed its armed workers' detachments, which ensured the publication of the revolution's own newspaper.

CHAPTER 14

❖◇❖◇❖◇❖◇❖◇❖◇❖

Opposition and Revolution

Far from restoring order, the Tsar's manifesto helped to reveal the full extent of the contradiction between the two poles of Russian society: the reactionary pogrom mentality of the nobility and bureaucracy, and the workers' revolution. During the first days, or rather hours, it looked as though the manifesto had not made any difference to the mood of the most moderate elements of the opposition. But it only looked that way. On October 18 the so-called Ironfounders' Consultative Office, one of capital's most powerful organizations, wrote to Count Witte: "We must say it straight out: Russia believes only in facts; her blood and her poverty will no longer allow her to believe in words." Putting forward the demand for a full amnesty, the Office "noted with especial pleasure" that demonstrative violence on the part of the revolutionary masses had been extremely limited and that they had proceeded with unheard-of discipline.

(157)

Without being, according to its own declaration, a supporter "in theory" of universal franchise, the Office had arrived at the conviction that "the working class, which has demonstrated with such force its political consciousness and party discipline, must participate in popular self-government."

All this was generous and broad-minded, but, alas, extremely short-lived. To say that it was a purely cynical gesture would be too crude. Undoubtedly illusion played an important part in the matter: capital still had some hope that far-reaching political reform might immediately allow the fly-wheel of industry to turn unhindered. This explains the fact that a large part of the entrepreneurs, if not the majority, adopted an attitude of friendly neutrality towards the October strike itself. There was almost no closing down of plants. The owners of engineering works in the Moscow region decided to refuse the services of cossacks. But the most usual expression of sympathy towards the political aims of the struggle was the payment of wages throughout the period of the October strike. While awaiting the flowering of industry under a "rule of law," the liberal entrepreneurs were perfectly prepared to enter this expenditure under the heading of special production costs. However, as capital paid the workers for these strike days it made it abundantly clear that it was doing so for the last time. The power of the workers' action had shown them the necessity of being on guard. Capital's fondest hopes remained unrealized: the movement of the masses did not calm down after the manifesto; on the contrary, with every passing day it displayed more and more clearly its strength, its independence, its socially revolutionary character. While the plantation owners of the sugar industry were threatened with confiscation of their lands, the capitalist bourgeoisie was compelled as a whole to retreat before the workers step by step, raising their wages and shortening the working day.

Besides the fear of the revolutionary proletariat, which reached fever pitch during the two last months of 1905, there were narrower but no less acute interests which drove capital towards an immediate alliance with the government. In the first place there was the prosaic but irresistible need for money, and the object of the entrepreneurs' concupiscence as well as of their attacks was the State Bank. This institution served as the hydraulic press for the autocracy's "economic policy" of which Witte had been the grand master during the decade of his financial rule. On the bank's operations, and together with these, on the minister's views and sympathies, the life and death of the largest industrial undertakings depended. Unconstitutional loans, the discounting of fantastic bills, widespread favoritism in the sphere of economic policy, these and other factors greatly contributed towards turning capital into an oppositional force. But when, under the triple effect of war, revolution, and economic crisis, the bank reduced its operations to a minimum, many capitalists found themselves in a really tight spot. They no longer cared tuppence for general political perspectives; they needed money, at whatever cost. "We don't believe in words," they told Count Witte at 2:00 A.M. on October 19, "give us facts." Count Witte plunged his hand into the cash-box of the State Bank and gave them "facts." A lot of facts.

The volume of discounts rose abruptly—138.5 million roubles in November and December 1905 as against 83.1 million for the same period in 1904. Credits to private banks rose to an even greater extent—148.2 million roubles on December 1, 1905 as against 39 million in 1904. All other operations underwent a similar increase. "Russia's blood and poverty," advanced, as we have seen, as a slogan by a capitalist syndicate, were duly taken into account by Witte's government. The result was the setting up of the "Union of October 17." This party was born not so much from a political maneuver, as from an ordinary bribe. From the first, the Soviet of Workers' Deputies encountered a resolute and conscious enemy in the entrepreneurs organized in their professional or political unions.

But while the Octobrists at least adopted a clearly anti-revolutionary position from the start, the most pathetic political role during those days was played by the party of lower-middle-class and intellectual radicals. Six months later this party was to put on an extraordinary show of false classical pathos on the stage of the Tauride Palace. We have in mind the Kadet Party.

The constituent congress of the Constitutional-Democratic Party (Kadets) was in progress at the very peak of the October strike. Less than half the delegates turned up for the congress; the rest had been immobilized by the railway strike. On October 14 the new party defined its attitude to the events as follows: "In view of our complete agreement with the claims being made, the party considers it its duty to declare its full solidarity with the strike movement. It categorically (categorically!) rejects the notion of achieving its aims by means of negotiations with the representatives of power. It will do everything to prevent a clash, but, should this fail, it declares in advance that its sympathy and its support are on the side of the people." Three days later the Tsar's manifesto was signed. The revolutionary parties at last escaped from the curse of clandestinity and, before they had time to wipe the blood and sweat off their foreheads, plunged headlong among the popular masses, appealing to them and uniting them for the struggle. It was a time of greatness, when the heart of the people was forged anew by the hammer of the revolution.

What were the Kadets, those frock-coated politicians, those tribunes of the rural assemblies, to do in such a situation? They passively waited for the constitutional waters to start flowing. There was a manifesto, but there was no parliament. And they did not know when and how it would come, or whether it would come at all. Their secret dream was to save the revolution from itself, but they could not see any means of doing so. They did not dare to venture forth to the popular meetings. Their press revealed their flabbiness and pusillanimity. It was not widely read. Thus at this most testing period of the Russian revolution the Kadets found themselves outside active political life. A year later, fully admitting this fact, Milyukov tried to justify his party—not for failing to throw its weight into the balance on the side of revolution, but for not attempting to stop the revolution. "Any protest, even by a party such as the Constitutional-Democratic Party," he wrote at the time of elections to the second Duma, "would have been completely impossible during the last months of 1905. Those who now reproach the party for failing to protest at the time, by organizing meetings, against the revolutionary illusions of Trotskyism . . . do not understand, or have forgotten the mood of the democratic audiences who were attending the public meetings." Such is the "popular" party's self-vindication: it did not dare to confront the people, lest the people were put off by its ugly face.

The Union of Unions played a less unworthy role during this period. The radical intelligentsia actively helped to make the October strike general. By organizing strike committees and sending deputations on their behalf, it stopped the activities of establishments outside the workers' direct sphere of influence. In this way work was stopped in rural and town councils, banks, offices, courts, schools, even in the Senate. The financial aid offered by the left wing of the intelligentsia to the Soviet of Workers' Deputies also played a not unimportant role. Nevertheless the picture of the titanic role of the Union of Unions created by the bourgeois press in Russia and the West appears absurd if we consider its activities in the public arena. The Union of Unions took care of the revolution's supplies, and, at best, it acted as an auxiliary fighting unit. It never claimed a leading position.

Indeed, could it have done so? The Union's typical member was and remained the same old educated philistine, his wings clipped by history. The revolution aroused him and raised him higher than himself. It left him without his daily newspaper, put out his electric light, and on the darkened wall it wrote in letters of fire the names of new and great, though vague, ideals. He wanted to have faith, but he did not dare. Perhaps we shall obtain a better insight into the drama of his soul if we look at him, not while he is writing a radical resolution, but while seated at his own tea table.

◇ ◇ ◇

The day after the end of the strike I went to see a family of my acquaintance which lived in the normal urban atmosphere of lower-middle-class radicalism. The program of our party, which had just been printed on large sheets of paper, hung on the dining-room wall; it had appeared as a supplement to the first issue of the social-democrats' newspaper published after the strike. The whole family was in a state of excitement.

"Well, well . . . not bad!"

"What isn't bad?"

"How can you ask? Your own program! Just read what it says here."

"I've had occasion to read it more than once."

"Listen to me then. It literally says: 'The party sets as its immediate political objective the overthrow of the Tsar's autocracy' . . . you hear me, overthrow! . . . 'and its replacement by a democratic republic' . . . a republic! Do you understand what that means?"

"I think I do."

"But this has been printed legally, this is sold openly under the eyes of the police, you can buy it for five kopecks outside the Winter Palace! The overthrow of the Tsar's autocracy, retail price five kopecks! Just try and beat that!"

"And do you like it?"

"What does it matter whether I like it or not, we aren't talking about me. It's *they*, down there in Peterhof, who have to face it now. Let me ask you: do *they* like it?"

"I doubt it."

The *pater familias* was the most excited of all. Only two or three weeks previously he had hated social democracy with the blind hatred of the petty bourgeois steeped in populist prejudices from early youth; today his feelings towards it were entirely different, a mixture of worship and dread.

"This morning we were reading this same program in the office of the Imperial Public Library. The same issue of the paper was delivered there, you know. You should just have seen those gentlemen! The director asked his two deputies and myself into his office, locked the door and read the program out loud to us from A to Z. I give you my word of honor, we all hadn't any breath left. 'What do you say to this?' the director asks me."

" 'What do you say to it, Sir?' I reply."

" 'You know,' he says, 'I've lost the use of my tongue. A little while ago it was a crime to criticize a policeman in a newspaper. Today they're openly telling His Imperial Majesty: get out! These people don't care a hang about etiquette, no, they certainly don't. Whatever they think, they say.' Then one of the deputies said, 'The writing is a bit heavy, isn't it, they want a lighter style.' The director looked at him over the top of his glasses, 'This isn't a Sunday feature, my dear sir, this is the program of a party.' And do you know the last thing they said, these gentlemen in the Public Library? They asked each other: How does one join the social-democratic party? How do you like that?"

"I like it very much."

"Well . . . how does one really join?" my host asks, a little hesitantly.

"Nothing could be simpler. The main condition is that you endorse the program. Then you join your local organization and you pay your dues regularly. You like the program, don't you?"

"Damn it, it's not bad at all, nobody could deny that. But what do you think of the present position? Only mind you, don't speak as the editor of a social-democratic paper, but absolutely frankly. Of course it's a long way yet to a democratic republic, but the constitution's there, isn't it?"

"No, in my view the republic is much closer and the constitution much further away than it seems to you."

"But what have we got now, damn it all? Isn't it a constitution?"

"No, it's merely a prologue to martial law."

"What? Nonsense. That's your newspaperman's jargon. You can't believe what you're saying. It's wild talk."

"No, it's the purest realism. The revolution's strength and boldness are growing. Look at what is happening in the factories, in the streets. Look at the sheet of paper you've pinned to your wall. You wouldn't have put it there a fortnight ago. Now let me ask you what you asked me a moment ago: what do *they* in Peterhof think about it all? They're still alive, you know, and they want to go on living. And they've still got the army. Are you by any chance hoping that they'll surrender without a fight? No, believe me, before they go they'll put all they've got into action, down to the last bayonet."

"And the manifesto? The amnesty? They're facts, aren't they?"

"The manifesto is only the proclamation of a momentary truce, only a breathing space. And the amnesty? From your windows you can see the spire of the Peter and Paul Fortress; it's still standing pretty solidly. And Kresty Prison too. And the Secret Political Police Department. You doubt my frankness, but let me tell you this: I personally am perfectly eligible for amnesty, but I'm in no hurry to resume legal status. Until the whole business is over I'll go on living on my false passport. The manifesto has not changed either my status in law or my tactics."

"But perhaps in that case, you fellows ought to follow a more cautious policy?"

"Such as?"

"Such as refrain from talking about the overthrow of the autocracy."

"Do you mean to say you think that if we use a more polite form of language, Peterhof will agree to a republic and the confiscation of lands?"

"Hmm . . . I think, after all, you're exaggerating."

"We shall see. Good-bye. I'm off to a meeting of the Soviet. But what about joining the party? You need only say the word, we'll sign you up in no time."

"Thank you, thank you . . . there's plenty of time . . . the situation is so uncertain . . . we'll have another talk . . . Good-bye and all the best!"

CHAPTER 15

The November Strike

The October ministry was feeling its way from danger to danger, amidst a thousand underwater reefs. Where to? It did not know itself.

On October 26 and 27 a mutiny flared up in Kronstadt, at a distance of three gunshots from Petersburg. The politically conscious among the soldiers tried to restrain the mass, but a spontaneous fury broke out. Having proved unable to halt the movement, the best elements in the army placed themselves at its head. But they did not succeed in preventing some hooligan pogroms, provoked by the authorities. The major role in this was played by the gangs of the well-known miracle worker Ioann of Kronstadt, who carried with them the most ignorant of the sailors. Martial law was declared in Kronstadt on October 28, and the unfortunate mutiny was crushed. The best of the soldiers and sailors were threatened with execution.

On the day the Kronstadt fortress was captured, the government issued a strong warning to the country by placing the whole of Poland under martial law; this was the first large bone which, on the eleventh day of its existence, the manifesto ministry threw to the Peterhof camarilla. Count Witte assumed entire responsibility for this step; in a government communiqué he lied about the Poles having made an "insolent" (!) attempt at secession, and warned them against entering upon a dangerous path, "not for the first time." The very next day, so as not to find himself Trepov's prisoner, he was obliged to sound the retreat; he admitted that the government was not so much taking into account actual events as anticipating the possible consequences of their development, given the "excessive impressionability of the Poles." Thus martial law was, in a sense, the constitution's tribute to the political temperament of the Polish people.

A number of districts of Chernigov, Saratov, and Tambov provinces, where agrarian unrest had broken out, were placed under martial law on October 29. It appeared that the Tambov muzhiks, too, suffered from "excessive impressionability."

The teeth of liberal society began to rattle with fear. For all the contemptuous grimaces the liberals had made at Witte, they nevertheless in their heart of hearts firmly believed in him. But now Durnovo had stepped out confidently from behind Witte's back; and Durnovo was just intelligent enough to adapt Cavour's aphorism—"the state of siege is the method of government of fools"—into a theory for his own guidance.

The workers' revolutionary instinct told them that to allow the counterrevolution to get away with this open attack was to encourage its insolence. On October 29 and 30 and November 1 mass meetings, held at most of the Petersburg industrial plants, called for drastic protest measures by the Soviet.

At a crowded and tumultuous meeting on November 1, after heated discussion, an overwhelming majority of the Soviet's members adopted the following decision:

The government continues to march on corpses. It is court-martialing the valiant soldiers and sailors of Kronstadt who rose to the defense of their rights and the people's freedom. It has thrown the noose of martial law around the neck of oppressed Poland.

The Soviet of Workers' Deputies calls upon the revolutionary proletariat of Petersburg to manifest its fraternal solidarity with the revolutionary soldiers of Kronstadt and the revolutionary workers of Poland by means of a political general strike, which has already shown its formidable power, and by means of mass protest meetings.

Tomorrow, November 2, at 12:00 noon, the workers of Petersburg will stop work under the following slogans: Down with courts-martial! Down with the death penalty! Down with martial law in Poland and throughout Russia!

The success of the appeal surpassed all expectations. Despite the fact that barely two weeks had passed since the cessation of the October strike which had required so much sacrifice, the workers of Petersburg stopped work with extraordinary unanimity. All large plants and factories represented on the Soviet were on strike before 12:00 noon on the second. Many medium-sized and small industrial undertakings which had not hitherto participated in political struggle now joined the strike, elected deputies and sent them to the Soviet. The regional committee of the Petersburg railway center adopted the Soviet's decision and all railways with the exception of the Finland railway ceased to operate. The absolute number of working-class strikers involved in the November strike exceeded not only that of the January strike but also that of the October strike. The postal and telegraph services, horse-cab drivers, the horse-tramway and the majority of shop assistants did not strike. Among the newspapers, only the *Government Herald*, the *Petersburg City Governor's Gazette* and *Izvestia* were published, the first two under the protection of troops, the third under that of workers' armed detachments.

Count Witte was taken completely unawares. Two weeks previously he had thought that since power was in his hands, all he had to do was to lead, encourage, restrain, threaten, administer. The November strike, the proletariat's indignant protest against the government's hypocrisy, knocked the great statesman sideways. Nothing is so characteristic of his total failure to understand the meaning of revolutionary events, his childish confusion in the face of them, and at the same time his self-opinionated conceit than the telegram with which he hoped to pacify the proletariat. Here is the text in full:

Brother workers, go back to work, abandon sedition, think of your wives and children. Do not heed bad advice. The Tsar has instructed us to pay special attention to the workers' problems. For this purpose His Imperial Majesty has set up a Ministry of Trade and Industry, which is to establish just relations between workers and employers. Give us time and everything possible will be done for you. Listen to the advice of a man who is well disposed towards you and wishes you well. Count Witte.

This shameless telegram, where cowardly hatred, concealing a knife in its pocket, attempted to posture as friendly condescension, was received and made public at the Soviet's meeting on November 3, and provoked a storm of indignation. Immediately, with fervent singlemindedness, the reply proposed by us was adopted and was published in *Izvestia* on the next day. Here is its text:

The Soviet of Workers' Deputies, having taken note of Count Witte's telegram to his "brother-workers," wishes first of all to express its extreme surprise at the Tsar's favorite's extraordinary familiarity in permitting himself to address the workers of Petersburg as his "brothers." There exists no family kinship whatsoever between the proletarians and Count Witte.

On the substance of the matter, the Soviet declares:

1. Count Witte calls upon us to think of our wives and children. In reply, the Soviet of Workers' Deputies calls upon all workers to count how many widows and orphans have been added to the ranks of the working class since the day Count Witte assumed state power.

2. Count Witte draws attention to the Tsar's gracious attention

to the working people. The Soviet of Workers' Deputies reminds the Petersburg proletariat of Bloody Sunday, January 9.

3. Count Witte asks for "time" and promises to do "everything possible" for the workers. The Soviet of Workers' Deputies knows that Witte has already found time to hand Poland over to the military hangmen, and the Soviet of Workers' Deputies does not doubt that Count Witte will do everything possible to strangle the revolutionary proletariat.

4. Count Witte calls himself a man who is well-disposed towards us and wishes us well. The Soviet of Workers' Deputies declares that it has no need of favors from the Tsar's favorites. It demands a people's government on the basis of universal, equal, direct, and secret franchise.

Well-informed persons reported that when the Count received this reply from his striking "brothers" he suffered an attack of asphyxia.

On November 5 the Petersburg telegraph agency reported: "In view of the rumors being spread in the provinces (!) about the use of courts-martial and the execution of other ranks who took part in the Kronstadt disorders, we are authorized to state that all such rumors are premature(?) and unfounded. . . . Participants in the Kronstadt events have not been and will not be judged by court-martial." This categorical statement meant nothing other than the government's capitulation in the face of the strike. The puerile reference to "rumors in the provinces" at a time when the protesting proletariat of Petersburg had brought the capital's commercial and industrial life to a temporary halt could not, of course, disguise this fact. On the Polish question the government began to make concessions even earlier by declaring its intention to lift martial law in the provinces of the Kingdom of Poland as soon as the "excitement" there "died down." *

On the evening of November 5 the Executive Committee, considering that the supreme psychological moment had come, submitted to the Soviet a resolution to end the strike. As a de-

* Martial law was lifted by ukase on November 12.

scription of the political situation at that moment we quote the speech made by the Executive Committee's rapporteur:

A government telegram stating that the Kronstadt sailors are not to be judged by court-martial but by a military district court has just been made public.

This telegram is nothing but a demonstration of the weakness of the Tsarist government, nothing but a demonstration of our strength. Once more we can congratulate the Petersburg proletariat on a tremendous moral victory. But let us say straight out: even if this government telegram had not appeared, we should still have had to call upon the workers of Petersburg to stop the strike. To-day's news shows that the political manifestation all over Russia is on the wane. Our strike, real as it is, is in the nature of a demonstration. Only from this viewpoint can we judge its success or failure. Our direct and immediate aim was to show the awakening army that the working class is on its side, that it will stand up for the army. Have we not achieved this aim? Have we not brought every honest soldier's heart over to our side? Who can deny it? And if that is so, can anyone assert that we have achieved nothing? Can the ending of the strike be viewed as our defeat? Have we not demonstrated to the whole of Russia that only a few days after the ending of the great October struggle, before the workers had had time to wash away their blood and heal their wounds, the discipline of the masses proved to be so great that at a single word from the Soviet they struck again as one man.

Look! this time the strike has been joined even by the most backward factories which had never been on strike before, and their deputies are sitting here in the Soviet with us. Leading elements in the army have organized protest meetings and in that way have taken part in our manifestation. Is that not victory? Is that not a brilliant success? Comrades, we have done all that we had to do. Once more the European stock exchange has saluted our strength. The Soviet's decision to call for a strike was immediately reflected in a considerable drop of our exchange rate abroad. Thus every one of our actions, whether it was our reply to Count Witte or to the government as a whole, struck a decisive blow at absolutism.

Certain comrades are demanding that the strike should continue until the Kronstadt sailors have been placed under trial by jury and martial law in Poland has been lifted. In other words, until the fall

of the present government, for Tsarism will move all its forces
against our strike, comrades, we have got to face that fact. If we
consider that the purpose of our action is the overthrow of the
autocracy, then, of course, we have not attained that aim. From
that point of view we should have concealed our indignation and
refrained from making a demonstration of protest. But our tactics,
comrades, are not at all based on that model. Our actions are a
series of consecutive battles. Their purpose is to disorganize the
enemy and to win new friends. And whose sympathy is more
precious to us than the army's? Understand this: in discussing
whether or not we should continue the strike, we are in substance
discussing whether to retain the demonstrative nature of the strike
or to turn it into a decisive struggle, that is, to continue it to the
point of total victory or defeat. We are not afraid of battles or
defeats. Our defeats are but steps to our victory. But for each battle
we seek the most favorable conditions. The events are working for
us and there is no advantage for us in forcing their progress. I ask
you: to whose advantage is it to put off the decisive clash, ours or
the government's? Ours, comrades! For tomorrow we shall be
stronger than we are today, and the day after tomorrow stronger
than tomorrow.

Do not forget, comrades, that the conditions under which we
can hold meetings of thousands of people, organize the broad masses
of the proletariat and address the entire population through our
revolutionary press were created for us only recently. We must
make the utmost use of these conditions for the widest possible
agitation and organization among the ranks of the proletariat. We
must extend the period of preparation of the masses for decisive
action, extend it out as much as we can, perhaps by a month or
two, in order then to act as an army which is as united and organized
as absolutely possible. Of course the government would prefer to
shoot us to pieces now, when we are less prepared for the final
battle.

Some comrades have the following doubt today, as they did
on the day when the funeral demonstration was canceled: by
beating a retreat today, shall we be able to arouse the masses at
another moment? Will the masses not go back to sleep? My reply
is: do you really think that the present regime can create the conditions for the masses to sleep peacefully? Do we really need to
worry that there will be no future events to rouse them again?
Believe me, there will be all too many such events—Tsarism will

take care of that. Do not forget, too, that the electoral campaign, which must bring the entire revolutionary proletariat to its feet, lies ahead of us. And who knows whether this electoral campaign will not end by blowing the existing regime sky-high? Let us keep cool, let us not anticipate events. Let us have more trust in the revolutionary proletariat. Did it go to sleep after January 9? After Shidlovsky's commission? After the Black Sea events? No, the revolutionary tide is steadily rising, and the moment when it breaks and drowns the whole autocratic regime is not far off.

A decisive and merciless struggle lies ahead. Let us call off the strike now, let us be satisfied with its tremendous moral victory. Let us exert every effort to create and consolidate the thing we need more than anything else: organization, organization and organization. We need only look around us to see that every day is bringing us new conquests in that field.

The railway employees and postal and telegraph officials are organizing. With the steel of their rails and the wires of their telegraph, they will bind into a single whole all the revolutionary centers of our country. They will enable us to bring the whole of Russia to her feet within twenty-four hours when the time comes. We must prepare for that moment and carry discipline and organization to their highest point. Comrades, to work!

We must immediately proceed to organize and arm the workers for battle. You must form "fighting tens" with elected leaders at every plant, "hundreds" with other leaders and a commander over the "hundreds." You must develop discipline in these cells to such a high point that at any given moment the entire plant will march forward at the first call. Remember that at the moment of decision we can count only on ourselves. The liberal bourgeoisie is already beginning to treat us with distrust and hostility. The democratic intelligentsia is vacillating. The Union of Unions, which joined us so readily during the first strike, is far less sympathetic to the second. One of their members told me the other day: "You are turning the public against you with your strikes. Do you really expect to win without help?" I reminded him of a moment in the French Revolution when the Convention decreed that "the French nation will not sign any treaty with the enemy on its territory." One of the members of the Convention called out: "Have you then concluded a treaty with victory?" The answer was: "No, we have concluded a treaty with death."

Comrades, when the liberal bourgeoisie, as though proud of its treachery, asks us: "Do you expect to fight alone, without our help? Have you then concluded a treaty with victory?" we shall hurl into its face the answer: "No, we have concluded a treaty with death."

The Soviet by an overwhelming majority of votes adopted the decision to call off the strike on Monday, November 7, at 12:00 noon. Printed posters of the Soviet's decision were distributed in the plants and factories and posted in the city. On the appointed day, at the appointed hour, the strike ended with the same unity with which it had begun. It had lasted 120 hours, three times less long than martial law in Poland.

The significance of the November strike did not, of course, lie in the fact that it removed the noose from the necks of a few dozen sailors—what do a few lives matter in a revolution that devours tens of thousands? Nor did it lie in the fact that it forced the government hastily to abandon martial law in Poland —what does another month of emergency rule matter in the history of that long-suffering country? The November strike was a cry of warning addressed to the country at large. Who knows if a savage bacchanalia of reaction would not have set in throughout the country if the experiment in Poland had been successful, if the proletariat had not demonstrated that it was "alive and fit and ready to give blow for blow?" *

In a revolution where complete solidarity among the many races of the population made a glorious contrast to the events in Austria in 1848, the Petersburg proletariat, in the name of the revolution itself, could not and dared not hand over its Polish brothers without protest into the impatient hands of the reaction. And, concerned though it was about its own future, it could not and dared not pass the Kronstadt rising in silence. The November strike was a cry of solidarity hurled by the proletariat over the heads of the government and the bourgeois opposition to the prisoners in the barracks. And the cry did not remain unheard.

Reporting on the November strike, the correspondent of the

* A textual quote from a resolution of the Soviet. (Author)

London *Times* quoted a guards colonel who made the following remark: "Unfortunately it cannot be denied that the intervention of the workers on behalf of the Kronstadt mutineers had a regrettable moral influence on our soldiers." It is in this "regrettable moral influence" that the main significance of the November strike must be sought. With a single blow it stirred the consciousness of many circles within the army and, in a matter of a few days, gave rise to a number of political meetings in the barracks of the Petersburg garrison. Not only individual soldiers but also soldiers' delegates began to show up in the Executive Committee and even at meetings of the Soviet itself, making speeches, demanding support; revolutionary liaison among the troops was reinforced; proclamations were widely read.

During those days the agitation within the ranks of the army reached even its aristocratic leadership. During the November strike the author had occasion to participate as a "workers' speaker" at a military gathering which was unique of its kind. It is worthwhile to tell the story here.

Armed with an invitation from Baroness X.,* I arrived at 9:00 P.M. at one of the wealthiest houses in Petersburg. The doorman, looking like a man who has made up his mind to be surprised at nothing in those days, took my overcoat and hung it up in the middle of a long row of officers' greatcoats. A footman stood waiting for me to give him my visiting card. Alas, what kind of a visiting card can an "illegal person" have? To help him out of his difficulty, I handed him the hostess' invitation card. A student, followed by a radical university lecturer and, finally, by the Baroness herself, came out into the hall. Evidently they had expected the "workers' speaker" to have been a more formidable person. I gave my name. They cordially asked me to enter. Lifting aside the door-curtain, I saw a company of sixty or seventy persons. On one side of the aisle, thirty or forty officers, including some elegant guardsmen, were seated on rows of chairs; on the other side were ladies. In the front

* She can now be named: Uexküll von Hildebrandt.

corner there was a group of black-coated journalists and radical lawyers. An old gentleman I had not seen before, seated behind a small table, acted as chairman. At his side I saw Rodichev, the future "tribune" of the Kadets. He was speaking about the establishment of martial law in Poland, and about what ought to be the attitude to the Polish question of the liberal public and of the thinking elements of the army; the speech was dull and limp, the thoughts expressed were short and limp, and the applause at the end was limp too.

After him spoke Peter Struve, yesterday's "exile of Stuttgart," who owed his return to Russia to the October strike and had used the opportunity thus offered in order immediately to occupy a position on the extreme right flank of *zemstvo* liberalism and, from that position, to unleash a violent campaign against the social-democrats. A hopelessly poor speaker, stammering and gasping, he tried to prove that the army should stand on the ground of the manifesto of October 17 and defend it against attacks both from the right and from the left. This conservative piece of poisonous wisdom sounded particularly odd on the lips of a former social-democrat. As I listened to his speech I recalled that seven years previously this man had written: "The further to the east of Europe, the weaker, more cowardly and more low becomes the bourgeoisie," after which he had himself crossed over to the camp of the liberal bourgeoisie on the crutches of German revisionism to prove the truth of his historical generalization by his own example.

After Struve, the radical journalist Prokopovich spoke about the Kronstadt rising; then there was a professor who had fallen into disgrace, and who was hesitating whether to choose liberalism or social democracy and in the meantime talked about everything and nothing; then a well-known lawyer (Sokolov), who invited the officers not to oppose political agitation in the barracks. The speeches became more and more resolute, the atmosphere more heated, the applause more energetic. When my turn came, I pointed out that the workers were unarmed, that, together with them, liberty was unarmed too, that the keys to the nation's arsenals were in the officers' hands, and that at the decisive moment those keys must be handed over to the people, to whom they belonged by right. It was the first, and probably the last time in my life that I had to address an audience of such a kind.

The "regrettable moral influence" of the proletariat on the soldiers led the government to institute a number of repressive measures. Arrests were made in one of the guards regiments; a number of sailors were transferred under escort from Petersburg to Kronstadt. From all sides soldiers were asking the Soviet what they should do. To these inquiries we answered with a proclamation which became known as the *Manifesto to the Soldiers*. Here is its text:

> The Soviet of Workers' Deputies replies to the soldiers:
> Brother soldiers of the army and navy!
> You often turn to us, the Soviet of Workers' Deputies, for advice and support. When soldiers of Preobrazhensky regiment were arrested, you turned to us for help. When students of the army electro-technical school were arrested, you turned to us for support. When naval crews were being sent under escort from Petersburg to Kronstadt, they sought our protection.
> Many regiments are sending deputies to us.
> Brother soldiers, you are right. You have no other protection but the working people. Unless the workers stand up for you, there is no salvation for you. The accursed barracks will strangle you.
> The workers are always on the side of honest soldiers. In Kronstadt and Sevastopol workers fought and died together with sailors. The government set up a court-martial to judge sailors and soldiers in Kronstadt, and immediately the workers of Petersburg went on strike everywhere.
> They are willing to go hungry, but not willing to look on in silence while soldiers are ill-treated.
> We, the Soviet of Workers' Deputies, tell you in the name of all Petersburg workers:
> Your troubles are our troubles, your needs our needs, your struggle our struggle. Our victory will be your victory. We are

bound by the same chains. Only the united efforts of the people and the army will break those chains.

How to free the men of Preobrazhensky regiment? How to save the men of Kronstadt and Sevastopol?

For this it is necessary to clear the country of the Tsar's prisons and courts-martial. We shall not free the men of Preobrazhensky regiment nor save the men of Kronstadt and Sevastopol by a single blow. With a united, mighty thrust we must sweep arbitrary rule and absolutism from the face of our motherland.

Who can perform this great deed?

Only the working people together with their brothers in the armed forces.

Brother soldiers! Awake! Arise! Come over to us! Honest and courageous soldiers, form your unions!

Wake the slumberers! Help the stragglers! Come to agreement with the workers! Establish links with the Soviet of Workers' Deputies!

Forward, for truth, for the people, for freedom, for our wives and children!

The Soviet of Workers' Deputies holds out to you its fraternal hand.

This manifesto was adopted and published during the last days of the Soviet's existence.

CHAPTER 16

◇◇◇◇◇◇◇◇◇◇◇◇◇

Eight Hours and a Gun

In this struggle the proletariat stood alone. No one wanted or was able to help it. The point at issue this time was not the freedom of the press, nor the arbitrary rule of uniformed thugs, nor even universal franchise. The workingman was demanding a guarantee that his muscles, his nerves, his brain should be safeguarded. He had decided to win back for himself a part of his own life. He could not wait any longer—and he did not want to. In the events of the revolution he had sensed his own strength for the first time, and through the same events he had first come to glimpse a different, higher form of life. It was as though he had been born again for the life of the spirit. All his senses were tensed like strings on a musical instrument. New, immeasurable, radiant worlds opened up before him. . . . Will he be born soon, the great poet who is to re-create for us the revolutionary resurrection of the working masses?

(179)

After the October strike which had transformed smoke-grimed factories into temples of revolutionary speech, after a victory which had filled the weariest hearts with pride, the worker found himself once more in the damnable grip of the machine. In the half-sleep of a gray dawn, he plunged into the gaping mouth of the industrial hell; late in the evening, after the placated machine had blown its whistle, again half-asleep, he dragged his weary body to the dark, repellent hole that was his home. Yet all around bright lights were burning, so near and yet so far—lights that he himself had lit. The socialist press, political meetings, the party struggle—a tremendous and beautiful feast of interests and passions. Where was the solution? In the eight-hour working day. This was the program of programs, the precept of precepts. Only the eight-hour day could immediately release the class force of the proletariat for the revolutionary politics of the time. To arms, proletarians of Petersburg! A new chapter opens in the grim book of struggle.

Already during the great strike delegates had often said that, when work was resumed, the masses would on no account agree to work under the old conditions. On October 26 delegates from one of the Petersburg districts decided, without the knowledge of the Soviet, to introduce the eight-hour working day at their factories by revolutionary means. On the twenty-seventh the delegates' proposal was unanimously adopted at several workers' meetings. At the Alexandrovsky mechanical engineering works the question was decided by secret ballot to avoid pressure. The results were 1,668 for, 14 against. As of the twenty-eighth, several major metalworking plants began to work the eight-hour day. An identical movement flared up simultaneously at the other end of Petersburg. On the twenty-ninth the initiator of the campaign reported to the Soviet that the eight-hour day had been introduced "by takeover" means, at three large plants. Thunderous applause. No room for doubts and hesitations. Was it not the takeover that had given us the freedom of assembly and of the press? Was it not by revolutionary initiative that we had harvested the constitutional manifesto? Were the privileges of capital more sacred to us than the privileges of the monarchy? The timid voices of the skeptics were drowned in a wave of universal enthusiasm.

The Soviet adopted a decision of enormous importance: it called on all factories and plants to introduce the eight-hour working day by takeover means on their own initiative. This decision was adopted almost without debate, as though it were a completely natural step. The Soviet gave the workers of Petersburg twenty-four hours for preparatory measures. And the workers found this long enough. "The Soviet's proposal was received with enthusiasm by our workers," wrote my friend Nemtsov, a delegate from a metalworking plant.

In October we fought for the whole country's demands, but now we are putting forward our own proletarian claim, which will clearly show our bourgeois bosses that we never for a moment forget the demands of our class. After discussion, the works committee (an assembly of workshop representatives; the leading role in the works committees was played by delegates from the Soviet) decided unanimously to introduce the eight-hour day as from November 1. On the same day the deputies announced the works committee's decision in all the workshops, suggesting that the workers should bring food to work with them so as not to have to take the usual midday break. On November 1 the workers turned up at the plant at 6:45 A.M. as always. At noon the whistle blew for the midday break; this provoked many jokes among the workers, who had decided to take only thirty minutes off for lunch instead of the prescribed one hour forty-five minutes. At 3:30 P.M. the entire personnel of the plant stopped work, having worked exactly eight hours.

"On Monday October 31," we read in No. 5 of *Izvestia*, "all factory workers in our district, in accordance with the Soviet's decision, having completed eight hours' work, left their workshops and went out into the streets carrying red banners and singing the "Marseillaise." On their way, the demonstrators 'swept up' several smaller enterprises which were still continuing to work." The Soviet's decision was carried through with the same revolutionary unity in other districts. On November 1 the movement spread to almost all metal works and the larger textile factories. Workers at Schlisselburg factories telegraphed the Soviet with the query: "How many hours should we work as of today?" The campaign developed with irresistible unanimity. But the five-day November strike cut into the campaign like a wedge at its very start. The situation became more and more difficult. The reactionary element within the government was making desperate efforts to rise to its feet, not without success. The capitalists were uniting energetically for a counter-blow under Witte's protection. The bourgeois democrats, wearied by the strikes, longed only for peace and quiet.

Until the November strike the capitalists had reacted to workers reducing the duration of the working day in different ways: some threatened immediately to close down their plants, others merely deducted the corresponding amounts from wages. At a number of plants and factories the management made concessions, agreeing to reduce the working day to nine and one-half and even to nine hours. The print-workers' union, for example, accepted such an offer. The employers' mood was generally uncertain. But by the end of the November strike, united capital had had time to recover its forces and adopted a completely intransigent position: there would be a universal lockout. The government, clearing the way for the employers, was the first to close the state plants. Meetings were more and more frequently dispersed by armed forces in order to demoralize the workers. The situation became increasingly acute. After the state-operated enterprises, a number of private ones were closed down. Several tens of thousands of workers were thrown into the streets. The proletariat was up against the wall. A retreat became unavoidable. But the working masses persisted in their claim, refusing even to hear of a return to work under the old conditions.

On November 6 the Soviet adopted a compromise solution by declaring that the claim was no longer universal and calling for a continuance of the struggle only in those enterprises where there was some hope of success. The solution was clearly an unsatisfactory one because it failed to provide a clear-cut slogan and so threatened to break up the movement into a series of dissociated struggles. In the meantime the situation continued to deteriorate. While the state-operated plants were re-opened, at the delegates' insistence, for work under the old conditions, the gates of thirteen more factories and plants were closed by private employers. An additional 19,000 people were left without work. Concern with re-opening of the plants, even under the old conditions, pushed the question of the forcible introduction of the eight-hour day more and more into the background.

Drastic steps were required, and on November 12 the Soviet decided to sound the retreat. This was the most dramatic of all the meetings of the workers' parliament. The vote was divided. Two leading metalworking plants insisted on continuing the struggle. They were supported by representatives of several textile, glassmaking, and tobacco factories. The Putilov works were definitely against. A middle-aged woman weaver from Maxwell's factory rose to speak. She had a fine, open face; she wore a faded cotton dress although it was late autumn. Her hand trembled with excitement as she nervously fingered her collar. Her voice had a ringing, inspired, unforgettable quality. "You've let your wives get accustomed to sleeping in soft beds and eating sweet food," she hurled at the Putilov delegates. "That's why you are afraid of losing your jobs. But we aren't afraid. We're prepared to die, but we'll get the eight-hour day. We'll fight to the end. Victory or death! Long live the eight-hour day!"

To this day, thirty months later, this voice of hope, despair, and passion is still ringing in my ears, a lasting reproach, an indomitable call to action. Where are you now, heroic comrade in faded cotton? Ah, you were accustomed to sleep in a soft bed and eat sweet food . . .

The ringing voice came to a halt. There was a moment of painful silence. Then a storm of passionate applause. At that moment the delegates, who had been bowed down by an oppressive sense of helplessness under the capitalist yoke, rose high above their everyday cares. They were applauding their future victory over cruelty and inhumanity.

After a debate lasting four hours, the Soviet by an overwhelming majority adopted a resolution to retreat. After pointing out that the coalition between united capital and the government had transformed the question of an eight-hour working day in Petersburg into a state problem, and that the workers of Petersburg could not therefore achieve victory in isolation from those of the country at large, the resolution stated: "For this reason, the Soviet of Workers' Deputies considers it necessary temporarily to halt the immediate and universal introduction of the eight-hour working day by takeover methods." To carry out the retreat in an organized fashion required a great deal of effort. Many workers preferred the course indicated by the woman weaver from Maxwell's. "Comrade workers from other factories and plants," the workers of a large factory who had decided to continue the struggle for a nine-and-a-half-hour working day wrote to the Soviet, "forgive us for doing this, but we have no strength left to suffer this gradual exhaustion of ourselves both physical and moral. We shall fight to the last drop of our blood. . . ."

When the campaign for an eight-hour working day was opened, the capitalist press naturally screamed that the Soviet was out to ruin the country's industry. The liberal-democratic press, which during this period went in fear and trembling of its master on the left, was silent, as though struck dumb. Only when the December defeat of the revolution had freed it from its bonds did it begin to translate all the reaction's charges against the Soviet into its own liberal jargon. The struggle for the eight-hour day was the action the liberal democrats most strongly condemned in retrospect. But it should be borne in mind that the

idea of reduction of the working day by takeover methods—
that is, by de facto stoppage of work without previous agreement
with the employers—was not born in October, nor within the
Soviet. Attempts of this kind were made many times in the course
of the strikes of 1905; and they were not always unsuccessful.
Thus at the state-operated works, where political motives are
stronger than economic ones, the workers obtained a nine-hour
day by such action. Nevertheless the idea of introducing a normal
working day by revolutionary means in Petersburg alone, after
a preparation of only twenty-four hours, may appear utterly
fantastic. The respectable treasurer of a respectable trade union,
for instance, might find it downright lunatic. And indeed it was
lunatic—from the viewpoint of normal "rational" times. But
under the conditions of revolutionary "madness" it had its own
"rationale." Of course a normal working day in Petersburg alone
makes no sense. But the Soviet believed that the Petersburg campaign would bring the proletariat of the entire country to its feet.
Of course the eight-hour working day can only be introduced
with the cooperation of state power. But state power is precisely
what the proletariat was fighting for at that moment. Had it won
a political victory, the introduction of the eight-hour day would
have been no more than a natural consequence of the "fantastic
experiment." But it failed to win; and therein, of course, lay its
gravest "fault."

And yet we believe even now that the Soviet acted as it was
entitled to do and as it should have done. In effect, it had no
choice. If, guided by "realistic" considerations of expediency, it
had begun calling on the masses to turn back, the masses would
simply not have obeyed it. The struggle would have flared up all
the same, but without leadership. Strikes would have occurred,
but in an isolated manner. Under such conditions a defeat would
have led to total demoralization. The Soviet took a different view
of its task. Its leading elements by no means counted on immediate and full success for the campaign; but they saw the mighty,
spontaneous movement as an incontrovertible fact, and they de-

cided to transform it into a majestic demonstration, such as had never yet been seen in any socialist movement, in favor of the eight-hour working day.

The practical fruits of this campaign, namely considerable reductions of working hours in a number of enterprises, were promptly snatched back again by the employers. But the political results left an indelible mark on the consciousness of the masses. Henceforth the idea of an eight-hour working day achieved a popularity among even the most backward strata of the working class that many years of laborious propaganda could not have ensured. At the same time this claim became organically united with the fundamental slogans of political democracy. Having met with the organized resistance of capital, the working masses again returned to the basic issue of revolution, the inevitability of an uprising, the essential need for arms.

Defending the resolution to drop the campaign in the Soviet, the rapporteur of the Executive Committee summed up the campaign in the following words: "We may not have won the eight-hour day for the masses, but we have certainly won the masses for the eight-hour day. Henceforth the war-cry: *Eight hours and a gun!* shall live in the heart of every Petersburg worker."

CHAPTER 17

◇◇◇◇◇◇◇◇◇◇◇◇

The Peasant Riots

The decisive events of the revolution took place in the towns. But the countryside was not quiet either. It began to stir noisily, clumsily, stumbling as though awakened from a long sleep; but even its first, uncertain movements made the ruling classes' hair stand on end.

During the two or three years preceding the revolution, relations between peasants and landowners had become extremely exacerbated. "Misunderstandings" were constantly flaring up, now here, now there. From the spring of 1905 the ferment in the countryside grew in a menacing way, assuming different forms in different parts of the country. In rough outline there were three principal areas of the peasant "revolution": 1) the north, which was distinguished by considerable development of the processing industries; 2) the southeast, relatively rich in land; and 3) the center, where land penury was further aggravated by

(187)

the piteous state of industry. The peasant movement, in turn, developed four main types of struggle: takeover of landowners' lands accompanied by eviction of the landowners and wrecking of their estates, with the object of extending the lands available to peasants for their own use; seizure of grain, cattle, and hay and felling of forests, for the immediate satisfaction of the needs of famine-stricken villages; a strike and boycott movement aimed either at reduction in land rents or wage increases and, finally, refusal to supply recruits or pay taxes and debts. These forms of struggle, in different combinations, spread over the country, being adapted to the economic conditions of each region. The peasant movement was at its most violent in the underprivileged central region; here, the wrecking of landowners' homes and property was devastating. Strikes and boycotts were practiced principally in the south; and in the north, where the movement was weakest, the felling of forests was its most common form of expression. Wherever economic discontent began to be mixed with radical political demands, the peasant refused to recognize the administrative authorities and to pay taxes. Let us take a closer look at the peasants' way of making revolution.

In Samara province the disorders spread to four districts. At first, the peasants would come to farms owned by landowners and take away nothing but cattle food, making a precise count of the cattle belonging to each farm, leaving the exact amount of food necessary to feed it, and removing the rest in their carts. The peasants acted quietly, without violence, trying to reach agreement so that there might be "no unpleasantness." They explained to the owner that these were new times and people had to live in a new way, more fairly; those who owned a lot should share with those who owned nothing, etc.

Later, groups of "delegates" would appear at the railway stations where large quantities of landowners' grain were stored. They would ascertain whose grain it was and announce that "by common decision" they were going to take it away with them.

"How do you mean, take it away, brothers?" the stationmaster would protest, and then continue: "I shall be held responsible you know . . . have pity on me . . ." "That's true," the terrible "expropriators" then agreed, "we've no wish to get you into trouble. The point is, the railway station's nearer, we didn't want to go all the way to the farm, it's so far. But there's nothing for it, we'll have to go to 'Himself' and take the grain straight out of his barn." The grain stored at the station would remain untouched, the peasants would go off to the farm and share out the grain stored there in a fair manner. But soon the arguments about the "new times" began to lose their effect on the landowner; he plucked up courage and tried to send the peasants packing. Then the good-natured peasants reared up—and not a stone would be left standing on the master's property.

In Kherson province large crowds of peasants walked from one estate to another with carts for taking away "shared-out" property. There was no violence and no killing because the frightened landowners and their stewards fled, opening all bolts and shutters at the first demand from the peasants. In the same province an energetic battle was fought for the lowering of land rent. The prices were fixed by the peasants' associations on the basis of "justice." From Bezyukov Monastery alone 15,000 *dessyatins* were taken without payment on the ground that "monks ought to pray to God, not buy and sell land for profit."

The most stormy events, however, occurred in Saratov province at the end of 1905. Not a single passive peasant was left in the villages which were drawn into the movement; all were involved in the rising. The landowners and their families were expelled from their homes, all movable property was shared out, the cattle were led away, the laborers and house servants were paid off and, finally, the "red cockerel" was set on the buildings (that is, they were set on fire). Armed detachments headed the peasant "columns" carrying out these raids. The village police and watchmen made themselves scarce, and in certain places were arrested by the armed peasants. The landlord's buildings were set on fire to make it impossible for the landlord to return to his lands after a certain time; but there was no violence.

Having destroyed the entire property the peasants would compose a "verdict" stating that from the following spring the lands would pass to the peasant community. Moneys seized in farm offices, state-owned liquor shops and from collectors of payments for liquor were immediately made communal property; local peasants' committees or "brotherhoods" were in charge of sharing out the expropriated goods. Estates were sacked almost regardless of the existing relations between peasants and individual landowners: if the estates of reactionary landlords were wrecked, so were those of liberals; political nuances were washed away by the wave of class hatred. The homes of local liberal *zemtsy* were razed to the ground, old country houses with their valuable libraries and picture galleries were burned down leaving no trace. In certain districts, the landowners' houses that were left standing could be counted on one's fingers. The story of this peasants' crusade was the same everywhere.

A newspaper wrote: "It begins, and the sky is lit up by fires all night long. It is a terrible picture. In the morning you see long lines of horse carriages filled with people fleeing from the estates; as soon as night falls, it is as though the horizon wore a necklace of fires. Some nights you could count up to sixteen fires. . . . The landowners flee in panic, and panic spreads everywhere along their path."

Within a short time more than 2,000 landowners' estates were wrecked and burned all over the country, including 272 in Saratov province alone. The landowners' losses, according to official data for the ten worst-hit provinces, amounted to 29 million roubles, including approximately 10 million for Saratov province.

If it is generally true that the course of class struggle is not determined by political ideology, this truth applies three times over to the peasantry. The Saratov muzhik must of course have had weighty reasons—concrete ones within his own homestead, his threshing-floor and village—for throwing a lighted bundle of straw on the landowner's roof. Yet it would be a mistake to ignore completely the effect of political agitation. Confused and chaotic as the peasant rising was, it nevertheless contained the unmistakable elements of an attempt at political generalization; and these elements had been introduced by the work of the parties. In 1905 even the liberal *zemtsy* tried to bring oppositional enlightenment to the peasants. Semi-official peasant representation was introduced in a number of rural councils, and questions of a general nature were put up for discussion. The employees of the rural councils—statisticians, teachers, agronomists, nurses—were incomparably more active than the landed liberals. Many of these people belonged to the social democrats or social revolutionaries; the majority were non-party radicals, for whom private land ownership was by no means a sacred institution.

For a number of years prior to 1905 the socialist parties had organized, through rural employees, revolutionary groups among the peasants and had disseminated illegal political literature. In 1905 the political agitation assumed mass proportions and emerged from underground. The absurd ukase of February 18, which established something like the right of petitioning, played an important role in this development. Taking advantage of this right, or rather of the confusion among local authorities created by the ukase, political agitators organized village meetings and encouraged the peasants to adopt resolutions on the abolition of private ownership of the land and the introduction of popular representation. In many places, peasants who had signed such a resolution regarded themselves as members of a "peasants' union" and elected committees from among their own ranks, who in many cases completely thrust aside the legal village authorities.

This is what happened, for example, among the cossack population of the Don region. Meetings of 600 or 700 people assembled in the cossack villages. "A curious gathering," one of the agitators wrote. "Behind the table sits the cossack *ataman* (head-man), fully armed. Men with and without sabers are standing and sitting everywhere. We have become accustomed to seeing such men as a somewhat disagreeable climax to our meetings and as-semblies; now, it is strange to look into their eyes as they slowly light up with anger against the landlords and officials. What an incredible difference there is between the cossack on military duty and the cossack at the plow!" Agitators were enthusiastically welcomed, parties of cossacks rode to fetch them over distances of dozens of miles and carefully guarded them from the police. But many peasants in the remoter areas had only a confused idea of their own role. "These are kind gentlemen," many a muzhik would say after signing his name under a resolution, "they'll get us a bit of land of our own."

The first peasants' congress took place near Moscow in August 1905. More than 100 representatives from twenty-two provinces met for two days in a large old barn well off the road. At this congress the idea of the All-Russian Peasants' Union, which was to unite many party and non-party peasants and in-tellectuals, first took shape.

The Manifesto of October 17 opened up still wider horizons for political agitation in the countryside. Even Count Hezden, now deceased, an extremely moderate member of the *zemstvo* of Pskov province, began organizing local meetings to explain the "new system." At first the peasants took little interest, but eventually they were aroused and decided that it was time to pass from words to deeds; for a start, they would "strike" a privately owned forest.* The liberal Count had not reckoned with anything like that. Thus the landed liberals only burned their fingers in their attempts to establish class harmony on the

---

* The term "striker" came to be synonymous with "revolutionary" among the peasants and the broad masses of the population. "To strike" meant to perform any revolutionary action. "To strike the district police officer" meant to arrest or kill him. This curious use of the word testifies to the tremendous revolutonary influence of the workers and their methods of struggle.

basis of the Tsar's manifesto; but the revolutionary intelligentsia enjoyed a tremendous success.

Peasant congresses were held in individual provinces, political agitation became feverish, mountains of revolutionary literature were deposited in the villages, the peasants' union grew in strength and size. A congress of 200 peasants' deputies was held in remote Vyatka province; three companies of the local army battalion also sent their delegates, expressing sympathy and promising support. A similar declaration was made by the representatives of local workers. The authorities, taken by surprise, gave permission to the congress to organize meetings in the towns and villages. Meetings went on continuously for a fortnight, and a congress resolution to refuse to pay taxes was energetically followed.

For all the diversity of its forms, the peasant movement produced mass phenomena throughout the country. Near the frontiers it immediately assumed a clearly defined revolutionary character. The Lithuanian peasantry, acting in accordance with a decision adopted by a congress at Vilno attended by more than 2,000 representatives, used revolutionary means to replace village clerks, elders, and elementary-school teachers, sacked gendarmes and rural district commandants, and introduced elective courts and district executive committees. The Georgian peasantry in the Caucasus took even more drastic forms of action.

The second congress of the peasants' union opened in Moscow on November 6 without any attempt at secrecy. It was attended by 187 delegates from twenty-seven provinces, 105 of whom were accredited by village and district communities and the rest by provincial and area committees and local groups of the union. The delegates included 145 peasants, the remainder being intellectuals closely associated with the peasantry, such as men and women schoolteachers, rural council employees, doctors, etc. In a folkloric sense this was one of the revolution's most interesting gatherings; one saw many picturesque characters, provincial "naturals," spontaneous revolutionaries who had "thought it all out for themselves," village politicians with passionate temperaments and even more passionate hopes, but with rather confused ideas.

Here are a few profile sketches drawn by one of the participants in the congress:

Anton Shcherbak, a cossack "father," tall, gray-haired, with a short mustache and piercing eyes, looking as if he had walked straight out of the canvas of Repin's *Zaporozhtsy*; he described himself, however, as a farmer from both hemispheres, having spent twenty years in America and owning a well-equipped farm with his Russian family in California. . . . The priest Miretsky, a delegate from Voronezh province, submitted five "verdicts" passed by district communities. In one of his speeches Father Miretsky described Jesus Christ as the first socialist. "If Christ were alive today, he would be on our side." . . . Two peasant women wearing cotton blouses, woolen shawls and goatskin shoes attended as delegates from the women of a village in the same Voronezh province. . . . Captain Pereleshin came as delegate from the cottage craftsmen of the same province. He turned up in uniform and carrying a saber, and caused quite a stir. Someone in the hall shouted: "Out with the police!" Then the captain rose to his feet and declared, to universal applause: "I'm Captain Pereleshin from Voronezh province, I've never concealed my convictions and have acted completely openly, that's why I'm wearing my uniform."

The central discussion was about tactics. Some of the delegates were in favor of peaceful struggle—meetings, "verdicts," "peaceful" boycotting of authorities, creation of revolutionary self-government, "peaceful" takeover of arable land, "peaceful" refusal to pay taxes and supply recruits. Others, especially those from Saratov province, called for armed struggle and immediate support of any uprisings wherever they flared up. In the end a compromise decision was adopted.

"The people's grievous troubles due to land penury," the resolution read, "can only be ended by the transfer of all land into the communal property of the entire people, on condition that land is used only by those who work it themselves, assisted only by their families or in free association with others." The establishment of a just agrarian system was entrusted to the Constituent Assembly, which was to be convened on the basis of the purest democratic principles "not later than in February next (!)." To achieve this end, "the peasants' union will enter into agreement with its brother workers, with municipal, factory, works, and railway unions etc., and also with all other organizations defending the interests of working people. . . . In the event that the people's demands are not satisfied, the peasants' union will resort to a general agrarian (!) strike, that is, it will withhold its labor from the owners of agrarian enterprises of all descriptions and will thus close down those enterprises. As for the organization of a general strike, this will be decided by agreement with the working class."

Having further resolved to discontinue the consumption of liquor, the resolution finally stated "on the basis of information received from all corners of the Russian countryside that failure to satisfy the people's demands would cause great troubles in our country and inevitably lead to a universal peasant uprising, for the cup of the peasants' patience has spilled over." Naïve though this resolution was in certain of its passages, it nevertheless showed that the progressive peasantry was adopting a revolutionary course. From the meetings of this peasants' parliament the specter of land expropriation rose before the eyes of the government and the nobility in all its cruel reality. The reaction sounded the alarm—and it had every reason to do so.

On November 3, that is, only a few days before the congress, the government published a manifesto proclaiming the gradual abolition of redemption payments for land allocations and the enlargement of the peasant bank funds. The manifesto expressed the hope that the government, in alliance with the Duma, would succeed in satisfying the essential needs of the peasants—"without detriment to any other owners of land." The resolution of the peasants' congress did not appear to correspond with these hopes. But the actual local practice of the "peasant population so dear to Our heart" was even less satisfactory. Wreckings and burnings, "peaceful" takeovers of private arable land, the unilateral fixing of wage rates and land rents caused the landowners to exert furious pressure on the government. Demands for the sending of troops came from all corners of the land. The government shook itself awake and realized that the time for sentimental effusions was past and the moment had come for "business."

The peasants' congress closed on November 12; on the fourteenth the Moscow officers of the union were already under arrest. That was the beginning. Two or three weeks later, in reply to inquiries concerning further peasant unrest, the Minister for Home Affairs issued the following instructions, which we reproduce verbatim: "Rioters to be exterminated immediately by force of arms, their dwellings to be burned down in the event of resistance. Arbitrary self-rule must be eradicated once and for all—now. Arrests would not serve any purpose at present and anyway it is impossible to try hundreds and thousands of persons. It is essential that the troops should fully understand the above instructions. P. Durnovo."

This cannibalistic order opened a new phase in the counter-revolution's infernal saturnalia. This new phase first developed in the towns, and only then spread to the countryside.

CHAPTER 18

◇◆◇◆◇◆◇◆◇◆◇◆◇

The Red Fleet

"Revolution," old Suvorin, that arch-reptile of the Russian bureaucracy, wrote at the end of November, "gives an extraordinary élan to men and gains a multitude of devoted, fanatical adherents who are prepared to sacrifice their lives. The struggle against revolution is so difficult precisely because it has so much fervor, courage, sincere eloquence, and ardent enthusiasm to contend with. The stronger the enemy, the more resolute and courageous revolution becomes, and with every victory it attracts a swarm of admirers. Anyone who does not know this, who does not know that revolution is attractive like a young, passionate woman with arms flung wide, showering avid kisses on you with hot, feverish lips, has never been young."

The spirit of mutiny swept the land. A tremendous, mysterious process was taking place in countless hearts: bonds of fear were being broken, the individual personality, having hardly

had time to become conscious of itself, became dissolved in the
mass, and the mass itself became dissolved in the revolutionary
élan. Having freed itself from inherited fears and imaginary
obstacles, the mass did not want to, and could not, see the real
obstacles in its path. Therein lay its weakness, and also its
strength. It rushed forward like the ocean tide whipped by a
storm. Every day brought new strata of the population to their
feet and gave birth to new possibilities. It was as though someone were stirring the social cauldron, right to its very bottom,
with a gigantic spoon. While liberal officials were cutting and
re-cutting the as yet unworn robe of Bulygin's Duma, the country did not know a moment of quiet. Workers' strikes, incessant
meetings, street processions, wreckings of country estates, strikes
of policemen and janitors, and finally unrest and mutiny among
the soldiers and sailors. Everything disintegrated, everything
turned to chaos.

Yet at the same time within this chaos there arose a need
for a new order, and elements of that order began to crystallize.
Regularly recurring meetings in themselves introduced the principle of organization. The meetings elected deputations, the
deputations grew into representative assemblies. But just as spontaneous indignation outpaced the work of political consciousness, so the desire for action left the feverish attempts at
organization far behind.

Therein lies the weakness of the revolution—*any* revolution
—but therein also lies its strength. Anyone who wants to play
an influential part in a revolution must grasp the whole of it.
Those wise tacticians who think that revolution can be treated
like a stick of asparagus, the edible part being separated at will
from the useless part, are condemned to play the sterile role of
mere reasoners. Since *no* revolutionary event creates "rational"
conditions for the application of their "rational" tactics, such
reasoners are fatally doomed to remain outside and behind *all*
events. In the end nothing is left for them but to repeat Figaro's
words: "Alas, there will not be a second performance in which

we can give you reason to forget the shortcomings of the first."

Our aim is not to describe nor even to list all the events of 1905. We are drawing a very general sketch of the progress of the revolution and, moreover, if we may so express ourselves, on the scale of Petersburg although from the viewpoint of the nation as a whole. But even within our chosen framework we cannot leave aside one of the most important events of the fateful year which took place between the October strike and the December barricades: the military rising in Sevastopol. It began on November 11, and on the seventeenth Chukhnin was already reporting to the Tsar: "The military storm has abated, not so the revolutionary storm."

The traditions of the *Potemkin* were still alive in Sevastopol. Chukhnin had dealt cruelly with the sailors of the Red Battleship: four were shot, two hanged, several dozen were sent to hard labor, and finally the *Potemkin* itself was renamed *Panteleimon*. But he failed to instill terror in anyone, and succeeded only in intensifying the mutinous feelings within the navy. The October strike started a phase of colossal street meetings, with sailors and infantry soldiers acting not only as constant participants but also as speakers. A sailors' orchestra played the "Marseillaise" at the head of a revolutionary demonstration: in short, total "demoralization" reigned. An order forbidding military personnel to attend popular meetings led to special military meetings being held in the courtyards of naval and army barracks. The officers did not dare to protest, and the doors of the barracks were open day and night for the representatives of our party's Sevastopol committee. The committee had continuously to contend with the impatience of the sailors, who demanded "action."

The *Prout*, transformed into a hard-labor prison ship, which was cruising nearby, served as a constant reminder that the victims of the June rising were still suffering for their part in the *Potemkin* affair. The *Potemkin's* new crew declared their readiness to take the battleship to Batum in support of the Caucasian rising. The recently built cruiser *Ochakov* showed equal readiness to fight. But the social-democratic organization insisted on wait-and-see tactics, and suggested the creation of a Soviet of soldiers' and sailors' deputies in close liaison with the workers' organization, and a naval rising in support of the imminent political strike of the proletariat. The sailors' revolutionary organization accepted this plan. But the revolution went beyond it.

Meetings continually became larger and more frequent. They began to take place in the square lying between the naval barracks and those of the Brest infantry regiment. Since the military were not allowed to attend workers' meetings, workers in the thousands began coming to the soldiers' meetings. The gatherings included tens of thousands of people. The idea of joint action was enthusiastically received. The most progressive companies elected deputies. The military authorities decided to take measures. Officers' attempts to make "patriotic" speeches at the meetings yielded lamentable results. The sailors, well-versed in the art of discussion, put their superiors to shameful flight.

Then it was decided to ban all political meetings. An armed company was posted at the gate of the naval barracks on November 11. Rear Admiral Pisarevsky, in everyone's hearing, issued the following order: "No one to be let out of the barracks; in the event of insubordination, fire." Petrov, a sailor in the company which had just received this order, stepped forward, charged his rifle in sight of everyone and, with one shot, killed Major Stein of the Brest regiment, and with a second shot wounded Pisarevsky. An officer immediately ordered "Arrest him!" No one moved. Petrov threw down his rifle. "What are you waiting for? Take me." Petrov was arrested. Sailors came running from all sides, demanding his release and offering to stand surety for him. The excitement reached a peak.

An officer, trying to find a solution, questioned Petrov: "Petrov, did you fire accidentally?"

"How, accidentally? I stepped forward, I charged my rifle, I took aim. What's accidental about that?"

"But they're asking for your release . . ."

And Petrov was released. The sailors were eager to go into action at once. All officers on duty were arrested, disarmed, and locked in the office. In the end, influenced by a social-democrat speaker, the sailors decided to await the next morning's meeting of deputies. About forty sailors' representatives met all night. They decided to release the officers from arrest but not to allow them to enter the barracks. They also decided to continue carrying out the duties they considered essential. A gala procession with bands was to go to the infantry barracks to involve the soldiers in the movement. In the morning a workers' deputation arrived for consultation. A few hours later the entire port was at a standstill; the railways also stopped operating. The situation was developing fast. Semi-official telegrams reported: "Inside the naval barracks, perfect order reigns. The sailors' conduct is extremely correct. No drunkenness." All sailors, without arms, were divided into companies. Only one company left behind to protect the barracks against sudden attack was armed. Petrov was elected its commander.

Some of the sailors, led by two social-democrat speakers, went off to the neighboring barracks of the Brest regiment. The soldiers' mood was far less certain. Only under strong pressure from the sailors was the decision taken to disarm the officers and remove them from the barracks. The officers of Mukden surrendered their sabers and revolvers without any resistance and, saying: "We're unarmed, you aren't going to touch us," passed through the soldiers' ranks. But the soldiers were hesitant from the start and it was at their insistence that a few duty officers were allowed to remain in the barracks. This had a tremendous influence on the subsequent course of events.

The soldiers began to form ranks, intending to march through the town together with the sailors to the barracks of

the Belostok regiment. As they formed ranks, they made sure
that any "freemen" (civilians) should march separately and not
join them. At the peak of these preparations, the fortress commandant Neplyuev, together with General Sedelnikov, a di-
visional commandant, drove up in his carriage. He was asked to
remove the machine guns which had been placed on Istorichesky
Boulevard since morning. Neplyuev replied that this did not
depend on him but on Chukhnin. Then he was asked to give his
word of honor that, as fortress commandant, he would not make
use of the machine guns. The general showed sufficient courage
to refuse. It was decided to disarm and arrest him. He refused to
hand over his arms, and the soldiers could not make up their
minds to use force. Finally a few sailors had to jump into the
carriage and drive the generals across to their own naval barracks. There they were disarmed immediately, *sans phrases,** and
placed under arrest in the office. Later, however, they were
released.

The soldiers, with bands playing, marched out of their barracks. The sailors, in strict marching order, came out of theirs.
Masses of workers were already waiting in the square. What a
moment! The encounter was enthusiastic. Handshakes, embraces. The air was filled with fraternal greetings and solemn
promises to support one another to the end. After re-forming
ranks, the procession set out right across the town to the barracks of the Belostok regiment. The soldiers and sailors carried
St. George's banners, the workers those of the social-democratic
party. The semi-official agency reports: "The demonstrators
held a march through the town in exemplary order, with a band
at the head of the procession and with red banners." The way
lay along Istorichesky Boulevard, where the machine guns were.
The sailors appealed to the machine-gunners' company to remove the machine guns. They did. (Later, however, the machine
guns reappeared.)

"Armed companies of the Belostok regiment," the agency

* In French in the original.

reports, "in the presence of their officers, presented arms and allowed the demonstrators to pass." A grandiose meeting was held outside the barracks of the Belostok regiment. The success, however, was incomplete; the soldiers vacillated; some expressed solidarity with the sailors, others merely promised not to fire. In the end the officers actually succeeded in marching the Belostok regiment out of the barracks. The procession did not return to the naval barracks until evening.

Meanwhile the social-democratic banner had been run up on the *Potemkin*. The *Rostislav* signaled back: "I see you." Other warships failed to respond. Reactionary elements among the sailors protested because the revolutionary banner had been placed above the St. Andrew's flag. The red banner had to be taken down. The situation still remained uncertain. But already there was no turning back.

A commission made up of sailor and soldier delegates from different units, including seven warships, and of several representatives of the social-democratic organization who had been invited by the sailors, was in constant session in the offices of the naval barracks. A social-democrat was elected its permanent chairman. Here all information was collected, and from here all decisions came. Here, too, the special demands of the sailors and soldiers were formulated and combined with general political demands. For the broad masses these special demands took first place. The commission's chief worry was its shortage of ammunition; the number of rifles was adequate, but cartridges were very scarce. "The lack of a leader well versed in military matters," writes an active participant in the events, "was also acutely apparent."

The deputies' commission urgently insisted that the naval units should disarm their officers and remove them from the ships and barracks. This was an essential measure. Those officers of the Brest regiment who had remained in the barracks were having a very disruptive effect on the soldiers. They made active propaganda against the sailors, the "freemen," and the "yids," and they added ample supplies of alcohol to their rations. At night, led by these officers, the soldiers shamefully fled to a camp—not through the main gate but through a hole in the wall. Next morning they once more returned to barracks, but took no further active part in the struggle. The indecision of the Brest regiment was bound to affect the mood of the sailors.

On the next day, however, success returned like the sun: the sappers had joined the rising. They arrived at the naval barracks in marching order and bearing arms. They were enthusiastically received and quartered in the barracks. The mood rose once more. Deputations came from all sides: the fortress artillery, the Belostok regiment and the frontier guards undertook not to fire. The authorities, no longer relying on the local regiments, began to draw in troops from the neighboring towns: Simferopol, Odessa, Feodosia. Active and successful revolutionary agitation was carried on among these newcomers. The commission's communications with the naval ships met with many difficulties, especially because the sailors were unable to read signals. Even so, assurances of complete solidarity were received from the cruiser *Ochakov*, the battleship *Potemkin*, the torpedo-boats *Volny* and *Zavetny* and, later, from several other torpedo-boats. The other vessels hesitated and, in their turn, merely promised not to fire.

On the thirteenth a naval officer came to the barracks with a telegram: the Tsar demanded that the mutineers should lay down their arms within twenty-four hours. The officer was jeered at and driven outside the gates. To protect the town against a possible pogrom, sailors formed patrols. This measure immediately reassured the population and won their sympathy. The sailors themselves guarded the liquor shops to prevent drunkenness. Throughout the rising, exemplary order reigned in the town.

The evening of November 13 was a decisive moment: the deputies' commission invited Lieutenant Schmidt, a retired naval officer, who had gained great popularity at the time of the October meetings, to take over military command of the operations. He courageously accepted the invitation and from that day stood at the head of the movement. By the following evening Schmidt had taken up quarters on the cruiser *Ochakov*, where he remained until the last. He raised the admiral's flag on the *Ochakov* and sent out a signal: "Am in command of fleet, Schmidt," hoping thereby to draw the entire squadron into the rising. Then he sailed his cruiser to the *Prout* to release the "*Potemkin* men." No resistance was offered. The *Ochakov* took the prisoners on board and sailed with them around the whole squadron. Shouts of "Hurrah" were heard from every ship. Some vessels, including the battleships *Potemkin* and *Rostislav*, ran up the red banner; but on the latter it remained up only for a few minutes.

Having taken over the leadership of the rising, Schmidt announced his course of action by the following declaration:

To the Mayor of Sevastopol.
I have today dispatched the following telegram to the Tsar Emperor:
"The glorious Black Sea Fleet, holding sacred its allegiance to the people, calls upon you, Sire, immediately to convene a Constituent Assembly, and ceases to obey your ministers.
Citizen Schmidt
Commander of the Fleet."

The order to suppress the rising was telegraphed from Petersburg. Chukhnin was replaced by the hangman Meller-Zakomelsky, soon to acquire his sinister fame. The town and fortress were placed under martial law and all streets were occupied by troops. The decisive hour had come. The mutineers were counting on the troops' refusal to fire and on the remaining vessels of the squadron joining them. And indeed the officers on several vessels were arrested and placed at Schmidt's disposal on the *Ochakov*; among other things, it was hoped that this measure would protect the flag cruiser from enemy fire. Large crowds waited on shore for the salute which was to announce

the squadron joining the movement. But this hope was not fulfilled.

The "pacifiers" did not let the *Ochakov* cruise around the
squadron for a second time; they opened fire. The crowds mis-
took the first salvo for the salute, but soon realized what was
happening and fled from the harbor in terror. Firing began on
all sides. Firing from the ships, firing from the fortress and field
artillery guns, firing by the machine guns on Istorichesky Boulevard. One of the first salvos destroyed the electrical engine of
the *Ochakov*. Having fired only six times, the *Ochakov* fell
silent and had to raise the white flag. Despite this, firing against
the cruiser continued until a fire broke out on board. The fate
of the *Potemkin* was still worse. Here the gun crews did not
have time to place the firing pins and locks in position, and so
were completely helpless when fired upon. The *Potemkin* raised
the white flag without firing a single shot. The sailors' shore
units held out longest, and surrendered only when they had not
a single cartridge left. The red banner flew over the mutinous
barracks until the end. The barracks were finally occupied by
government troops at about 6:00 A.M.

When the first fear caused by the firing had passed, part of
the crowd returned to the harbor. "The picture before our eyes
was truly dreadful," writes the participant in the rising whom
we have quoted before. "Several torpedo boats and sloops were
immediately sunk by artillery crossfire. Soon flames appeared
on the *Ochakov*. Sailors were trying to swim to safety and calling for help. They were shot dead in the water. Boats which
went to their rescue were also fired upon. Sailors who managed
to swim to the shore where troops were standing were killed
on the spot. Only those who swam ashore where there was a
sympathetic crowd were saved." Schmidt attempted to escape
dressed as a common sailor, but was captured.

The bloody work of the hangmen of "pacification" was done
by 3:00 A.M. Now they had to transform themselves into the
hangmen of "justice."

The victors reported: "More than 2,000 men have been captured and arrested . . . 19 officers and civilians arrested by the revolutionaries have been released; 4 banners, money safes, and a large quantity of state property, cartridges, arms and equipment, as well as 12 machine guns, have been seized." Admiral Chukhnin telegraphed to Tsarskoye Selo: "The military storm has abated, not so the revolutionary storm."

What a tremendous step forward compared with the Kronstadt mutiny! There, a spontaneous flare-up that ended in savage excesses. Here, a rising that developed according to plan and consciously sought to achieve order and unity of action. "In the rebellious town," the social-democratic paper *Nachalo* wrote at the height of the Sevastopol events, "nothing is heard of hooligans and looters, and the number of cases of simple theft is less than normal for the simple reason that the embezzlers of state property in army and navy uniform have left this happy place. . . . You want to know, citizens, what is democracy backed by an armed population? Look at Sevastopol. Look at republican Sevastopol whose only authorities are elected and responsible ones."

And yet this revolutionary Sevastopol held out for only four or five days and surrendered long before it had exhausted all its reserves of military force. Strategic errors? Indecision on the part of the leaders? Neither the one nor the other can be denied. But the final result was due to deeper causes.

The rising was led by sailors. The very nature of their activities demands from sailors a greater degree of independence and resourcefulness, makes them more self-reliant than land soldiers. The antagonism between common sailors and the closed upper-class caste of naval officers is even deeper than it is in the army, where half the officers are plebeians. Lastly, the disgrace of the Russo-Japanese war, the onus of which had been borne by the navy, destroyed any last vestiges of respect the sailors might still have had for their grasping and cowardly captains and admirals.

As we have seen, it was the sappers who were most resolute

in joining the sailors; they came armed, and took up quarters in the naval barracks. The same fact can be observed in all revolutionary movements in our army: the most revolutionary are sappers, engineers, gunners, in short, not the gray illiterates of the infantry, but skilled, highly literate, technically trained soldiers. To this difference at the intellectual level corresponds one of social origin: the vast majority of infantry soldiers are young peasants, whereas the engineers and gunners are recruited chiefly from among industrial workers.

We have seen the indecision shown by the Brest and Belostok regiments throughout the days of the rising. They decided to remove all their officers. At first they joined the sailors, then they fell away. They promised not to fire, and then, in the end, they were completely dominated by their superiors and shamefully agreed to fire on the naval barracks. Later we were to observe the same revolutionary instability among the peasant-bred infantry, both on the Siberian Railway and in the Sveaborg Fortress.

But it was not only in the army that the technically trained, that is, proletarian elements played the principal revolutionary role. The same also happened within the navy. Who were the men who led the sailors' "mutinies"? Who raised the red banner on the battleship? The technicians, the engine men. These industrial workers in sailors' uniforms who form a minority among the crew nevertheless dominate the crew because they control the engine, the heart of the battleship.

Friction between the proletarian minority and the peasant majority in the armed forces is a characteristic of all our military risings, and it paralyzes them and robs them of power. The workers carry their class advantages with them to the barracks: intelligence, technical training, resoluteness, an ability for concerted action. The peasants contribute their overwhelming numerical strength. The army, by universal conscription, overcomes the muzhik's lack of productive coordination in a mechanical way, and his passivity, his chief political fault, is transformed into an irreplaceable virtue. Even when the peasant regiments are drawn into the revolutionary movement on the ground of their immediate needs, they are always inclined to adopt wait-and-see tactics, and at the enemy's first decisive attack they abandon the "mutineers" and allow themselves to be placed once more under the disciplinary yoke. It follows from this that attack is the only proper method for military risings: attack without any interruptions that might engender hesitation and disorder. But it also follows that the tactics of revolutionary attack encounter their greatest obstacle in the backwardness and distrustful passivity of the muzhik-soldier.

This contradiction was shortly to reveal itself with full force in the suppression of the December rising, which closed the first chapter of the Russian revolution.

CHAPTER 19

❖❖❖❖❖❖❖

On the Threshold
of Counter-Revolution

"For a bad government," writes that shrewd conservative, de Tocqueville, "the most dangerous moment is usually the one when it begins to change." Events were furnishing more and more decisive proof of this truth to Count Witte each day. The revolution was resolutely and mercilessly against him. The liberal opposition did not dare to support him openly. The court camarilla was against him. The government apparatus was crumbling in his hands. And, finally, he was his own enemy—understanding nothing of the events, lacking any plan, relying upon intrigue instead of on a program for action. And while he fussed and fidgeted, revolution and reaction were moving inexorably against each other.

We read in a secret memorandum against "Trepov's men" written in November 1905 on Count Witte's instructions:

(210)

. . . Facts, including some taken from the files of the Police Department, clearly demonstrate that a significant part of the serious charges leveled at the government by the public and the people during the days directly following the manifesto were well-founded. Parties were created by some of the highest government officials to offer "organized resistance to extreme elements"; patriotic manifestations were organized by the government, while other demonstrations were dispersed; peaceful demonstrators were fired upon, people were beaten up and the offices of a provincial rural council were set on fire in full view of the police and troops; pogromists were left untouched while salvos were fired at people who ventured to defend themselves against them; the crowd was egged on to violence, consciously or unconsciously (?), by means of official announcements signed by the highest representative of the state power in a large town, and when, following this, disorders occurred, no measures were taken to suppress them. All these facts took place within three or four days in widely separated parts of Russia and provoked a storm of indignation among the population which completely canceled out the initial enthusiastic welcome accorded to the manifesto of October 17.

The population became firmly convinced that all these pogroms which so unexpectedly and yet simultaneously swept Russia had been provoked and direrted by the same hand, which, moreover, was a very powerful hand indeed. Unfortunately the population had very serious grounds for believing this.

When the governor-general of Kurlandia sent a telegram supporting the demand by a meeting of twenty thousand persons that martial law be lifted and expressing the view that "martial law is incompatible with the new circumstances," Trepov confidently wired back the following text: "Re your telegram of October 20. Disagree your conclusion martial law incompatible new situation." Witte silently accepted his subordinate's barefaced statement that martial law in no way ran contrary to the manifesto of October 17, and even tried to convince a workers' deputation that "Trepov isn't at all the monster he's said to be." True, Trepov was obliged to resign from his post under the pressure of universal indignation. But Durnovo, who replaced him as Minister of Home Affairs, was no better. Besides, Trepov himself, being appointed palace commandant, retained all his influence on the running of affairs. The behavior of the provincial bureaucracy depended far more on him than on Witte.

"The extreme parties," the same November memorandum states, "have gained strength because, in sharply criticizing all the government's actions, they all too often proved to be right. These parties would have lost much of their prestige if the masses had seen, immediately after the publication of the manifesto, that the government had really decided to follow the new path outlined in the manifesto, and that it was in fact following that path. Unfortunately the exact opposite happened, and the extreme parties had yet another occasion—the importance of which can hardly be appreciated—of priding themselves on the fact that they, and they alone, had correctly estimated the value of the government's promises." In November, as the memorandum shows, Witte began to understand this. But he was deprived of the possibility of applying his understanding in practice. The memorandum to the Tsar, written on his instructions, remained a dead letter.*

Floundering helplessly, Witte was henceforth merely towed along by the counter-revolution.

A congress of *zemtsy* met in Moscow on November 6 to determine the liberal opposition's attitude towards the government. Its mood was one of vacillation, but with an undoubted bias to the right. True, some radical voices were heard. It was said that "the bureaucracy is incapable of creative action but only of destruction"; that any creative force must be sought "in the mighty workers' movement which produced the manifesto of October 17"; that "we do not want a constitution granted as a favor, and will accept it only from the hands of the Russian

---

* This interesting memorandum was published in a collection of documents (which, needless to say, was confiscated) entitled *Materials for a History of the Russian Counter-Revolution* (St. Petersburg: 1908).

people." Rodichev, who had an irresistible fondness for the pseudo-classical style, exclaimed: "Either there will be universal direct franchise, or there will be no Duma!" But at the same congress it was also stated: "Agrarian disturbances and strikes all create fear; capital has taken fright, and so have men of property who are taking their money out of the banks and going abroad." Cautious landowners asked: "The institution of satrapies as a means of fighting agrarian disorders is sneered at, but who can suggest a more constitutional means of fighting them?" "It is better to accept no matter what compromise than to make the struggle more acute." "The time has come to call a halt," cried Guchkov, here appearing on the political arena for the first time, "we are only adding fuel to a fire that will consume us all."

Early news of the rising of the Sevastopol fleet put the oppositional courage of the *zemtsy* to an impossible test. "What we have here," said Petrunkevich, that Nestor of *zemstvo* liberalism, "is not revolution but anarchy." Under the direct impact of the Sevastopol events the argument for immediate agreement with Witte's ministry prevailed. Milyukov made an attempt to restrain the congress from taking any obviously compromising steps. He reassured the *zemtsy* by saying that "the insurrection in Sevastopol is ending, the chief mutineers have been arrested, and any fears would seem to be premature." In vain! The congress decided to send a deputation to Witte with a resolution of conditional confidence couched in oppositional-democratic phrases.

Meanwhile the Council of Ministers, with the participation of several "public figures" from the liberal right wing, was discussing the system of elections to the State Duma. These so-called "public figures" defended universal franchise as a regrettable necessity. Witte tried to prove the advantages of gradually perfecting Bulygin's brilliant system. No results were reached, and from November 21 the Council of Ministers proceeded without the assistance of the "public figures." On November 22 the *zemtsy* deputation, composed of Messrs. Petrunkevich, Muromtsev, and Kokoshkin, handed the *zemstvo* resolution to Count Witte and, having received no answer at the end of seven days, returned in shame to Moscow.

The Count's reply, couched in a tone of high-ranking bureaucratic arrogance, followed on their heels. The Council of Ministers' task, the reply stated, consisted first and foremost in executing His Imperial Majesty's will; anything that went beyond the limits of the manifesto of October 17 must be swept aside; the prevailing unrest made it impossible to abandon the manifesto's restrictive clauses; as for those social groups which were unwilling to support the government, the government's only concern was that such groups should realize the consequences of their conduct.

As a counterweight to the *zemstvo* congress, which, for all its flaccid pusillanimity, still undoubtedly stood far to the left of the *zemstvos'* and provincial dumas' real mood, a deputation from the Tula provincial *zemstvo* was taken to Tsarskoye Selo on November 24. The head of the deputation, Count Bobrinsky, in a speech of unparalleled Byzantine servility, said *inter alia:* "We do not ask for many rights, because our own good demands that the Tsar's power be great and effective . . . Sire, it is not from single voices raised in clamor that you will learn the truth about the people's needs, but only from the State Duma, lawfully convened by you. We beseech you not to tarry in convening it. The nation has already taken to its bosom the decree for the holding of elections on August 6 . . ."

Events seemed to conspire to force the property-owning classes into the camp of order. A postal and telegraph strike flared up spontaneously and unexpectedly in the middle of November. It was the response of the awakening helots of the postal administration to a circular issued by Durnovo forbidding officials to form unions. The postal and telegraph union addressed an ultimatum to Count Witte asking for the withdrawal of Durnovo's circular and the reinstatement of officials dismissed for belonging to the union. On November 15 a congress of 73 delegates of the union meeting in Moscow unanimously decided that the following telegram be dispatched on all lines: "No reply received from Witte. Strike." Tension was so great that in Siberia the strike began before the time limit indicated in the ultimatum had expired. By the next day the strike, applauded by wide circles of progressive officials, had spread to the whole of Russia. Witte sagely explained to various deputations that the government "had not expected" such a turn of events. The liberals, worried by the harm to "culture" caused by the interruption in postal communications, began with furrowed brows to study "the limits of the freedom of professional associations in Germany and France."

The Petersburg Soviet of Workers' Deputies did not hesitate for a single moment. And, although the postal and telegraph strike had certainly not broken out at the Soviet's initiative, it continued in Petersburg with its active support. A sum of 2,000 roubles was issued to the strikers from the Soviet's treasury. The Executive Committee sent speakers to their meetings, printed their proclamations, and organized pickets. It is hard to assess the effect of these tactics on "culture"; but there can be no doubt that it made the postal officials sympathetic towards the proletariat. At the very beginning of the strike the postal and telegraph congress sent five delegates to the Soviet.

The interruption of postal communications certainly caused great harm to trade, if not to culture. The merchants and stockbrokers ran backwards and forwards from the strike committee to the ministry, now imploring the postal officials to end the strike, now demanding repressive measures against the strikers. As a result of ever new threats to their pockets, the capitalist classes became more reactionary day by day. The reactionary insolence of the conspirators of Tsarskoye Selo also increased continually. If anything still restrained the onslaught of reaction, it was only fear of the revolution's inevitable response. This is graphically demonstrated by an incident which occurred in connection with a verdict passed on some railway officials by a court-martial at the Central Asian fortress of Kushka. The incident is so striking that we must report it here, however briefly.

On November 23, at the height of the postal and telegraph strike, the committee of the Petersburg railway center received a telegraphic message from Kushka saying that an Engineer Sokolov and several other officials had been court-martialed on a charge of revolutionary agitation and had been condemned to death, the sentence to be carried out at midnight on the twenty-third. Despite the strike, all railway centers were put in telegraphic contact with one another within a few hours. The railway army wanted an urgent ultimatum to be issued to the government. And an ultimatum was issued. Acting in agreement with the Executive Committee of the Soviet of Deputies, the railwaymen's union told the ministry that unless the death sentence were rescinded by 8:00 P.M. all traffic on the railways would be brought to a halt.

The author has a vivid recollection of the memorable meeting of the Executive Committee at which a plan of action was drawn up while waiting for the government's reply. Everyone's eyes were on the clock. Representatives of different railway lines came one after the other to report that more and more lines had sent messages by telegraph associating themselves with the ultimatum. It was clear that unless the government gave in, a desperate struggle would begin. What happened? At five minutes past eight—the Tsarist government had lingered for only three hundred seconds to save face—the Minister of Communications informed the railwaymen's committee by urgent telegram that execution of the sentence would be halted.

On the next day the ministry itself made its capitulation public in a government communiqué saying that it had received a "request" (!) to repeal the sentence, accompanied by an expression of the "intention" (!), failing such a step, to declare a strike. The government was not in receipt of any reports from the local military authorities, which was "probably due to the fact that the state telegraph is on strike." At all events, "immediately upon receiving these telegraphic messages," the Minister of War had sent orders "to defer the execution of the sentence, if sentence had been passed, pending elucidation of the facts of the case." The official communiqué fails to mention that the Minister of War was obliged to send his orders through the railwaymen's union, since the telegraph, being on strike, was not accessible to government agencies.

This handsome victory was, however, the revolution's last. After this it suffered only defeats. At first its organizations were under intermittent attack. It became evident that a ruthless assault was being prepared. As early as November 14, the officers of the peasants' union were arrested in Moscow on the strength of a government decree instituting reinforced security measures. At about the same time the arrest of the chairman of the Petersburg Soviet was decided upon in Tsarskoye Selo. But the administration delayed carrying out this decision. It did not yet feel completely confident; it tested the ground and hesitated.

The Minister of Justice opposed the Tsarskoye Selo plot, arguing that the Soviet could not be considered a secret association because it acted absolutely openly, announced its meetings, printed reports of its proceedings in the newspapers and even entered into contact with persons within the administration. "The fact that neither the government nor the administration," the well-informed press wrote in summing up the Minister's viewpoint, "took any measures to stop activities designed to overthrow the existing order; that the administration, on a number of occasions, actually sent patrols to the Soviet's meetings to preserve order; and that the Petersburg city governor himself received Khrustalev, the chairman of the Soviet, knowing who he was and in what capacity he appeared—all this entitles the members of the Soviet of Workers' Deputies to regard their activities as by no means contradictory to the policies being followed in government spheres, and, therefore, as not criminal."

However, in the end the Minister of Justice found ways of

overcoming his legalistic scruples, and on November 26 Khrustalev was arrested at the premises of the Executive Committee.

A word concerning the significance of this arrest. At the second meeting of the Soviet on October 14, the young lawyer Georgiy Nosar, later to acquire great popularity under the name of Khrustalev, was elected chairman at the proposal of the representative of the social-democratic organization. He remained chairman of the Soviet until the day of his arrest on November 26, and all the organizational threads of the Soviet's practical activities were gathered in his hands. Within a few weeks the cheap radical press on the one hand, and the reactionary police press on the other, had created a historical legend around Khrustalev's personality. Just as, on an earlier occasion, January 9 had seemed to them the fruit of Georgiy Gapon's inspired thinking and demagogical genius, so the Soviet of Workers' Deputies appeared to them as a pawn in the titanic hands of Georgiy Khrustalev-Nosar.

The error in the second case was even more flagrant and absurd than in the first. Although the work done by Khrustalev as chairman was immeasurably richer in content than Gapon's adventurist activities, the personal influence exerted by the chairman of the Soviet on the course and the end result of events was incomparably smaller than the influence gained by the mutinous priest from the Department of Police. That is not Khrustalev's fault: it is the revolution's merit. Between January and October it had put the proletariat through an intensive political school. The notions of "hero" and "crowd" were no longer applicable in the revolutionary practice of the working masses. The leaders' personality became dissolved in the organization; and, at the same time, the united mass itself became a political entity.

A man of practical ability and resourcefulness, an energetic and skillful chairman although only a mediocre orator, an impulsive character without any political past nor any clearly-defined political face, Khrustalev was made for the role he was to play at the end of 1905. The working masses, although in a revolutionary mood and possessed of a strong class sense, were on the whole without any definite party allegiance. Everything we have said about the Soviet itself can be applied to Khrustalev. All the socialists with a political past were party men, and the candidature of a party man would have introduced friction into the Soviet from the moment it came into existence. Furthermore, Khrustalev's lack of political allegiance facilitated the Soviet's relations with the non-proletarian world and especially with the organizations of the intelligentsia, from which it received considerable material assistance. In entrusting the chairmanship to a non-party man, the social-democrats counted on having political control of the Soviet. They were not mistaken. After a mere three or four weeks, the colossal growth of their influence and power could be judged, *inter alia*, by the fact that Khrustalev publicly announced that he was joining the social-democrats (Mensheviks).

What did the government hope to achieve by arresting Khrustalev? Did it think that by removing the chairman it would destroy the organization? Surely that would have been too stupid, even for a Durnovo. But it is difficult to give a precise answer as to motives, if only because their own motives were probably unclear to the reactionary conspirators who met in Tsarskoye Selo to discuss the destinies of the revolution, and yet who could do no more than resort to a police measure. In any case, the chairman's arrest under the circumstances in which it was carried out assumed tremendous symptomatic significance for the Soviet. It became crystal clear to anyone who might have doubted it only a day earlier that neither side could retreat, that a decisive clash was inevitable, and that this clash lay, not months or weeks ahead, but days.

CHAPTER 20

❖❖❖❖❖❖❖❖❖❖❖

The Last Days
of the Soviet

To abandon the public arena after Khrustalev's arrest was something the Soviet could not do: a freely elected parliament of the working class, it owed its strength precisely to the public character of its activities. To dissolve its organization would have meant deliberately giving an opening to the enemy. Only one solution remained: to continue along the same path as before, heading towards a conflict. At a meeting of the Executive Committee on November 26 the representative of the socialist-revolutionary party (Chernov "himself") proposed issuing a declaration to the effect that the Soviet would reply by a terrorist *coup* to every repressive measure of the government. We came out against this proposal. During the brief period that remained before the opening of military operations, the Soviet had to establish the closest possible liaison with other towns, with the peasants' union, the railwaymen's union, the Postal and

Telegraph Union and the army (two delegates had been sent off for this purpose in the middle of November, one to the Volga and the other to the south); terrorist attacks on individual ministers would certainly have absorbed the Executive Committee's entire energy and attention.

Instead, we proposed that the following resolution be submitted to the next meeting of the Soviet: "On November 26 the Tsarist government arrested the chairman of the Soviet of Workers' Deputies, Comrade Khrustalev-Nosar. The Soviet is electing a temporary presidium and is continuing to prepare for armed insurrection." Three persons were selected as candidates for the presidium: Yanovsky, the rapporteur of the Executive Committee (that was the name under which the author of this book was active in the Soviet), the treasurer Vvedensky (Sverchkov) and Zlydnev, a worker deputy from the Obukhov plant.

The general meeting of the Soviet took place on the next day, openly as always, with 302 deputies present. The atmosphere was highly charged; many members of the Soviet wanted an immediate and direct response to the Ministry's guerrilla raid. But after a short debate the meeting unanimously adopted the Executive Committee's resolution and, by a secret ballot, elected the proposed candidates to the presidium.

The chairman of the Main Committee of the peasants' union, who was present at the meeting, spoke about the decision taken at the union's November congress not to supply recruits to the government, not to pay taxes, and to withdraw deposits from state banks and savings banks. As the Executive Committee had already on November 23 adopted a resolution inviting workers, "in view of the government's imminent bankruptcy," to accept payment of wages only in gold and to withdraw their deposits from savings banks, a decision was taken to amalgamate these financial boycott measures and to announce them in a manifesto addressed to the people in the name of the Soviet, the peasants' union and the socialist parties.

Would it be possible to hold further general meetings of the proletarian parliament? There could be no certainty about this. The meeting decided that, in the event of it being impossible to convene the Soviet, its functions should be transferred to the Executive Committee with an enlarged membership. It was on the basis of this decision, that, after the Soviet's arrest on December 3, its powers passed into the hands of the second Soviet's Executive Committee.

The meeting then received warm greetings on behalf of the politically conscious soldiers of the Finland battalions and also from the Polish Socialist party and the All-Russian Peasants' Union. The delegate from the revolutionary peasantry promised fraternal support at the decisive hour. To the indescribable enthusiasm of deputies and guests and to the sound of thunderous applause, the representative of the peasants' union and the chairman of the Soviet shook hands. The meeting dispersed late at night. The last to leave were the members of the police duty patrol who, as always, had been guarding the entrance to the meeting on the city governor's orders. It is an interesting sidelight on the situation that on the same night a minor police official, acting under the instructions of the same city governor, stopped a lawful and peaceful meeting of bourgeois voters headed by Milyukov.

Most Petersburg plants associated themselves with the Soviet's resolution, which also found a sympathetic echo in resolutions adopted by the Moscow and Samara Soviets, the railwaymen's and postal and telegraph unions, and a number of local organizations. Even the Central Bureau of the "Union of Unions" endorsed the Soviet's decision and published an appeal "to the country's vital elements" to prepare themselves actively for an imminent political strike and for "the last armed clash with the enemies of popular freedom."

However, the sympathy which the liberal and radical bourgeoisie had towards the proletariat in October was by now cooling off. The situation became more and more acute, and liberalism, frustrated by its own inaction, was becoming increasingly surly towards the Soviet. The man in the street, knowing little of politics, had a semi-benevolent, semi-subservient attitude toward the Soviet. If he feared that a railway strike might break out while he was on a journey, he would call at the Soviet's office for information. He came there, too, in the hope of dispatching his telegrams during the postal and telegraph strike; and if the telegram was considered sufficiently important, it was duly dispatched. (For example, the widow of Senator B., after many fruitless visits to various ministries, finally appealed to the Soviet to enable her to send a telegram on an important family matter.) The Soviet's written orders exempted townspeople from having to observe the law; for example, an engraver's workshop, on receiving written "permission" from the Soviet, agreed to make a seal for the illegal Postal and Telegraph Union. The Northern Bank credited the Soviet for an out-of-date check. The print shop of the naval ministry asked the Soviet for instructions as to whether or not it should go on strike.

All kinds of people and organizations appealed to the Soviet in moments of danger, seeking help against individuals, officials, and the government itself. When martial law was proclaimed in Lifland province, the Latvian section of the population of Petersburg appealed to the Soviet to "make a stand" against this latest instance of arbitrary Tsarist rule. On November 30 the stretcher-bearers' union appealed to the Soviet on behalf of its members whom by false promises the Red Cross had enticed to join the Russo-Japanese war and had then sent home unrewarded; the Soviet's arrest put an end to its lively correspondence on this subject with the Central Directorate of the Red Cross.

The Soviet's premises were always crowded with petitioners and plaintiffs of all kinds—mostly workers, domestic servants, shop assistants, peasants, soldiers, and sailors. Some had an absolutely phantasmagorical idea of the Soviet's power and its methods. There was one blind veteran of the Russo-Turkish war, covered with crosses and decorations, who complained of dire poverty and begged the Soviet to "put a bit of pressure on Number One" (that is, the Tsar). Applications and petitions arrived from remote parts of the country. After the November strike the inhabitants of one district of a Polish province sent a telegram of thanks to the Soviet. An old cossack from Poltava province complained of unjust treatment by the Princes Repnin who had exploited him as a clerk for twenty-eight years and then dismissed him without cause; the old man was asking the Soviet to negotiate with the Princes' on his behalf. The envelope containing this curious petition was addressed simply to The Workers' Government, Petersburg, yet it was promptly delivered by the revolutionary postal service.

A special deputy from a team of navvies in Minsk province came to the Soviet; a landlord wanted to pay his debt of 3,000 roubles to the team in some kind of shares. "What should we do?" the deputy asked, "we'd like to take the shares, yet we're afraid: we've heard a rumor that your government wants us workers to accept payment in gold or silver only . . ." The case was investigated and it was found that the landowner's shares were almost valueless.

News of the Soviet began reaching the countryside only towards the end of its activity, and requests from peasants became more and more frequent. Peasants from Chernigov province wanted to be put in touch with the local socialist organization, peasants from Mogilev province sent messengers with "verdicts" from several villages who undertook to act together with the town workers and the Soviet.

A tremendous field of action was opening up before the Soviet. Everywhere a vast expanse of new political ground was waiting for the deep plowshare of revolution. But time was short. The reaction was feverishly forging its weapons, and the blow was expected from hour to hour. Amid the mass of day-to-day business the Executive Committee hurried to put the Soviet's resolution of November 27 into action. It issued a proclamation addressed to the troops (see *The November Strike*) and, at a joint meeting with representatives of the revolutionary parties, approved the text of a "financial" manifesto submitted by Parvus. On December 2 the Manifesto was published in eight Petersburg newspapers, four socialist ones and four liberal ones. Here is the text of this historic document:

"MANIFESTO"

The government is on the brink of bankruptcy. It has reduced the country to ruins and scattered it with corpses. The peasants, worn out by suffering and hunger, are incapable of paying taxes. The government gave credits to the landowners out of the people's money. Now it is at a loss as to what to do with the landowners' mortgaged estates. Factories and plants are at a standstill. There is unemployment and a general stagnation of trade. The government has used the capital obtained by foreign loans to build railways, warships, and fortresses and to store up arms. Foreign sources have now been exhausted, and state orders have also come to an end. The merchant, the supplier, the contractor, the factory owner, accustomed to enriching themselves at the treasury's expense, find themselves without new profits and are closing down their offices and plants. One bankruptcy follows another. Banks are failing. All trade exchanges have been reduced to the barest minimum. The government's struggle against revolution is causing daily unrest. No one is any longer sure what the morrow will bring.

Foreign capital is going back home. "Purely Russian" capital is also seeping away into foreign banks. The rich are selling their property and going abroad in search of safety. The birds of prey are fleeing the country and taking the people's property with them.

For many years the government has spent all its state revenue on the army and navy. There is a shortage of schools. Roads have been neglected. In spite of this, there is not enough money even to keep the troops supplied with food. The war was lost partly because military supplies were inadequate. Mutinies of the poverty-stricken, hungry troops are flaring up all over the country.

The railways are economically sick through the government's fault. Many millions of roubles are needed to restore the railway economy.

The government has pilfered the savings banks, and handed out deposits to support private banks and industrial enterprises, often entirely fictitious ones. It is using the small saver's capital to play the stock exchange, where that capital is exposed to risk daily.

The gold reserves of the state bank are negligible compared with the existing claims of government loans and the demands of trade turnover. It will be reduced to nothing if gold coin is demanded for every transaction.

Taking advantage of the absence of any control of the state finances, the government has long been issuing loans which far exceed the country's means of payment. With these new loans it is covering the interest on old ones.

Year after year the government issues false accounts of expenditure and revenue, showing both to be less than they are in reality and robbing indiscriminately to show a surplus instead of an annual deficit. Officials are free to rob the treasury which in any case is already exhausted.

Only the Constituent Assembly, after the overthrow of the autocracy, can halt this financial ruin. It will carry out a close investigation of the state finances and will draw up a detailed, clear, accurate, and certified balance sheet of state revenue and expenditure (budget).

Fear of popular control which would reveal to all the world the government's financial insolvency is forcing it to keep putting off the convening of the people's representative assembly.

In order to safeguard its rapacious activities the government forces the people to fight unto death. Hundreds of thousands of citizens perish and are ruined in this fight, and industry, trade, and means of communication are destroyed at their very foundations.

There is only one way out: to overthrow the government, to deprive it of its last strength. It is necessary to cut the government off from the last source of its existence: financial revenue. This is necessary not only for the country's political and economic liberation, but also, more particularly, in order to restore the financial equilibrium of the state.

We have therefore decided:

To refuse to make land redemption payments and all other payments to the treasury. In all transactions and in the payment of wages and salaries, to demand gold, and in the case of sums of less than five roubles, full-weight hard cash (coinage).

To withdraw deposits from savings banks and from the state bank, demanding payment of the entire sum in gold.

The autocracy has never enjoyed the people's confidence and has never received any authority from the people.

At the present time the government is behaving within the

frontiers of its own country as though it were ruling conquered territory.

We have therefore decided not to allow the repayment of loans which the government contracted while it was clearly and openly waging war against the entire people.

Signed: The Soviet of Workers' Deputies.

The Main Committee of the All-Russian Peasants' Union.

The Central Committee and the Organization Committee of the Russian Social-Democratic Workers' party.

The Central Committee of the party of Socialist Revolutionaries.

The Central Committee of the Polish Socialist party.

It goes without saying that this manifesto could not, in itself, overthrow Tsarism and its finances. It was the first State Duma that, six months later, expected such a miracle to be wrought by its Vyborg declaration, which called on the population "peacefully, on the English model," to refuse to pay taxes. The Soviet's financial manifesto was nothing other than an overture to the December rising. Reinforced by a strike and by fighting on the barricades, it produced a powerful echo throughout the country. Whereas during the month of December in the previous three years deposits in savings banks had exceeded payments by 4 million roubles, in December 1905 the excess of payments over deposits equaled 90 million: during a single month the manifesto extracted 94 million roubles from government reserves! When the insurrection had been crushed by the Tsarist hordes, equilibrium in the savings banks was once more restored.

◇ ◇ ◇

In the last ten days of November martial law was proclaimed in Kiev and its administrative district and in Lifland, Chernigov, Saratov, Penza, and Simbirsk provinces, the chief centers of rural disturbances.

On November 24, on the day of the introduction of the "temporary" press regulations, the rights of provincial governors and town governors were widely extended.

On the twenty-eighth the post of "temporary" governor-general of the Baltic Lands was created. On the twenty-ninth the local satraps were empowered, in the event of railway or postal and telegraph strikes, to introduce emergency rule in their provinces without reference to the central authorities.

On December 1 Nicholas II granted an audience to a hastily made up, motley deputation of frightened landowners, monks, and urban pogromists. This deputation demanded merciless punishment of the revolutionary malefactors and, at the same time, of those persons in high places who abetted the revolution; not satisfied with this hint towards Witte, the deputation added: "by autocratic command, be pleased to recall certain servants of thy monarchic will." "I receive you in the certainty," Nicholas replied to this dirty gang of serf-traders and money-loving thugs, "that I see before me true sons of Russia, devoted with all their hearts to myself and the fatherland." At a signal from Petersburg, the provincial administrations dispatched a large number of messages of gratitude to the Tsar Emperor purporting to come from members of the peasantry and lower middle class. The "Union of the Russian People," which, as we understand, received its first large subsidy at this time, organized a number of meetings and distributed pogromist-patriotic literature.

On December 2 the eight newspapers which had printed the Soviet's Financial Manifesto were confiscated and their publication interrupted. On the same day drastic new regulations were issued making it illegal for employees of the railways and the postal, telegraph, and telephone services to strike or form unions under threat of sentences of up to four years' imprisonment. The revolutionary papers made public the following order by the governor of Voronezh province based on a secret circular by Durnovo: "*Top secret.* Immediately identify all ringleaders of the antigovernment and agrarian movement and incarcerate them in local prisons pending further action in accordance with the Minister for Home Affairs' instructions." The government published its first threatening declaration. The extreme parties, it said, had adopted as their aim the disruption of the country's economic, social, and political structure; the social-democrats and socialist-revolutionaries were, in essence, anarchists: they declared war on the government, vilified their opponents, prevented society from enjoying the benefits of the new regime: they provoked strikes in order to turn the workers into raw material for revolution. "The shedding of the workers' blood (by the government!) is incapable of causing them (the revolutionaries!) any pangs of conscience." If ordinary measures proved of no avail against these phenomena, then "the necessity would undoubtedly arise to adopt measures of an entirely exceptional nature."

The caste interests of the privileged and the frightened, the vindictive rage of the bureaucrats, the servility of the bought, the dull hatred of the fooled, all these mingled together to form a single repulsive, bloody, dirty block of reaction. Tsarskoye Selo issued supplies of gold, Durnovo's ministry wove a furtive fabric of conspiracy, the hired assassins whetted their knives.

Meanwhile the revolution grew irresistibly. New forces kept joining its main army, the industrial proletariat. In the towns there were meetings of janitors, doormen, cooks, domestic servants, floor-polishers, waiters, public bath attendants, laundresses. Astonishing characters appeared at public meetings and came to the offices of the revolutionary press: "politically conscious" combatant cossacks, railway policemen, ordinary policemen and police officers, even some repentant police detectives. From some mysterious, unknown depths, the social earthquake kept throwing up new strata whose very existence is unsuspected in times of peace. Petty officials, prison warders, army clerks waited in the offices of the revolutionary newspapers for their turn to be heard.

The November strike had a tremendous effect on the army. A wave of army meetings swept the entire country. The barracks were filled with the spirit of mutiny. Here discontent generally arises on the ground of the soldiers' immediate needs, then develops rapidly and assumes a political orientation. From the last third of November on, military disturbances of extreme gravity occurred in Petersburg (among sailors), Kiev, Yekaterinodar, Yelisavetpol, Proskurovo, Kursk, and Lomzha. In Warsaw, guardsmen demanded the release of their arrested officers. Messages came in from all sides indicating that the entire Manchurian army was aflame with revolution. A meeting held at Irkutsk on November 28 was attended by the entire garrison—some 4,000 men. Under the chairmanship of a non-commissioned officer the meeting decided to endorse the demand for a Constituent Assembly. In many towns soldiers fraternized with workers at meetings. On December 2 and 3 rioting began among troops of the Moscow garrison. There were meetings in which even cossacks took part, street processions were held to the strains of the "Marseillaise," officers of certain regiments were forcibly removed from their posts . . .

And finally, as a revolutionary background to the towns which were seething like cauldrons, came the flames of peasant risings in the countryside. At the end of November and the beginning of December agrarian disorders spread to a large number of rural areas: in the center near Moscow, on the Volga, on the Don, and in the Kingdom of Poland there were incessant peasants' strikes, wreckings of state-owned liquor shops, arson on country estates, seizures of property and land. The whole of Kovno province was in the grip of the Lithuanian peasants' rising. Messages of ever-increasing alarm arrived from Lifland. Landowners were fleeing from their estates, provincial administrators were abandoning their posts.

With a clear image of Russia at that time one realizes how inevitable was the December conflict. "The showdown should have been avoided," say certain men wise in their hindsight (Plekhanov). As though it were a matter of a chess game, not of the elemental movement of millions!

❖ ❖ ❖

"The Soviet of Workers' Deputies," wrote *Novoye Vremya*, "is not discouraged. It continues to act energetically and publishes its decisions in a pure, Spartan language, brief, clear and understandable to all. The same cannot by any means be said of Count Witte's government, which prefers the long-winded and tedious language of a melancholy maiden." On December 3 Witte's government in its turn adopted a language that was "brief, clear and understandable to all." It surrounded the building of the Free Economic Association with troops drawn from every arm of the services, and arrested the Soviet.

The Executive Committee met at 4:00 P.M. The agenda for the meeting had been determined in advance by the confiscation of the eight newspapers, the draconian new rules concerning strikes and Durnovo's conspiratorial telegram. The representative of the Central Committee of the social-democratic party (Bolsheviks) submitted his party's proposal to accept the challenge to establish contact immediately with all revolutionary organizations throughout the country, to appoint a date for the commencement of a political general strike, to mobilize all forces and all reserves and, supported by the agrarian movements and soldiers' riots, to go forward towards a decisive solution.

The delegate from the railwaymen's union said that it was certain that the railwaymen's congress convened for December 6 would decide in favor of a strike.

The representative of the Postal and Telegraph Union spoke in favor of the party's proposal and expressed the hope that a general strike movement would instill new life into the postal and telegraph strike, which was beginning to peter out. The debate was interrupted by the news that the Soviet was to be arrested that day. Confirmation arrived half an hour later. By that time the large assembly hall on the ground floor had filled with delegates, party representatives, press correspondents, and guests. The Executive Committee, which was meeting upstairs, decided that some of its members should withdraw so as to ensure continuity in case of arrest. But it was already too late. The building was surrounded by soldiers of the Izmailovsky guards regiment, mounted cossacks, policemen, and gendarmes. The whole place was filled with the noise of trampling feet, the ringing of spurs, the clatter of arms. Delegates were heard protesting vociferously downstairs. The chairman opened a first-floor window, leaned out and called: "Comrades, don't offer resistance! We declare in advance that if any shots are fired, they will have to come from the police or an *agent provocateur.*" A few minutes later the soldiers climbed the stairs to the first floor and took up a position at the door of the room in which the Executive Committee was meeting.

The chairman (addressing an officer): "I suggest you close the door and do not disturb our business."

The soldiers remain in the passage but do not close the door.

The chairman: "The meeting continues. Who wants to take the floor?"

The Representative of the Office Workers' Union: "By today's act of brute force the government has reinforced the arguments in favor of a general strike. It has determined the strike in advance. The outcome of the proletariat's new and decisive action depends on the troops. Let them come out in defense of the motherland!" (The officer hastily shuts the door. The speaker raises his voice.) "Even through closed doors the fraternal call of the workers, the voice of their tormented country will reach the soldiers!"

The door opens and a company commander of the gendarmerie, pale as death, creeps in (he was afraid of a bullet), followed by a couple of dozen policemen who place themselves behind the delegates' chairs.

The chairman: "I declare the meeting of the Executive Committee closed."

The sound of loud metallic banging came from downstairs. It was as though a dozen blacksmiths were working at their anvils. The delegates were smashing their Brownings so as to prevent them falling into the hands of the police!

A search began. Everyone refused to give their names. Searched, their descriptions noted and a number allocated to each, the members of the Executive Committee were escorted away by the half-drunken guardsmen.

The Petersburg Soviet of Workers' Deputies was in the hands of the Tsarskoye Selo conspirators.

CHAPTER 21

December

On December 4 the Moscow Soviet endorsed the "financial manifesto"; on December 6, directly influenced by major disturbances in the Moscow garrison, the Soviet, which by this time represented 100,000 workers, decided, together with the revolutionary parties, to proclaim a political general strike in Moscow on the next day, December 7, and to do its best to transform the strike into armed insurrection. A conference of deputies from twenty-nine railways, which was meeting in Moscow on December 5 and 6, decided to join the Soviet in carrying out this plan. The postal and telegraph congress adopted a similar decision.

The strike in Petersburg started on the eighth, reached its climax the following day and began to collapse after the twelfth. It was far less unanimous than the November strike, and involved not more than two-thirds of the workers. This indecision can be explained by the fact that the Petersburg workers realized very clearly that this time it was not a matter of a strike demonstration but of a life-or-death struggle. January 9 had left an indelible mark on the consciousness of the masses. Faced with a garrison of monstrous size with guards regiments as its backbone, the Petersburg workers could not themselves take the initiative of a revolutionary rising; their mission, as the October strike had shown, was to deliver the final blow to absolutism once it was already weakened by insurrection in the rest of the country. Major victory in the provinces was the essential psychological precondition for decisive action in Petersburg. But no victory came, and indecision was followed by retreat.

Besides the passivity of Petersburg, the fact that the Nikolayevskaya Railway (Petersburg-Moscow) continued to run had a fatal effect on the further progress of events. The general mood of wait-and-see prevailing in the capital influenced the Petersburg committee of the railwaymen's union. The government, its attention centered wholly on the Nikolayevskaya line, took advantage of the delay and sent troops to occupy the line. Some of the workshops struck, but the railway telegraph was operated by the authorities and the line itself by a railway battalion. Attempts to stop the traffic were made repeatedly but without success. On December 16 workers from Tver destroyed part of the track to prevent the transfer of troops from Petersburg to Moscow, but it was too late. Trains had already transported the Semyonovsky guards regiment to Moscow. Generally speaking, however, the railway strike began very unitedly. Most lines had struck by the tenth, and the rest joined them during the following days.

In opening the strike, the conference of the railwaymen's union declared: "We undertake to bring back the troops from Manchuria much sooner than the government would have done. . . . We shall adopt every measure to convey grain supplies to the starving peasants and provisions to our comrades on the railway lines." This is not the first time that we encounter a phenomenon whose meaning should be pondered by those anarchists who are still capable of thought: in paralyzing state power, a general strike imposes extremely important state functions on its own organization. And it must be admitted that, on the whole, the railwaymen's union functioned very well indeed. Trains carrying reserve supplies, revolutionary armed detachments, and members of revolutionary organizations traveled with remarkable regularity and speed despite the proximity of government troops in many places. Many stations were run by elected commandants. Red flags were raised over railway buildings. The first city to strike was Moscow (on the seventh). On the next day it was joined by Petersburg, Minsk, and Taganrog, on the tenth by Tiflis, on the eleventh, Vilna, on the twelfth, Kharkov, Kiev, and Nizhny Novgorod, on the thirteenth, Odessa and Riga, on the fourteenth, Lodz, and on the fifteenth, Warsaw, to mention only the largest centers. In all, the strike was joined by thirty-three towns as against thirty-nine in October.

Moscow stood at the center of the December movement.

From the first days of December some of the regiments of the Moscow garrison were in a state of revolutionary upsurge. Despite all the efforts made by the social-democrats to prevent isolated flare-ups, the ferment kept breaking through into the open. Among the workers, voices were raised demanding immediate support for the soldiers; it would be wrong, they argued, to let the favorable moment slip by. The soldiers guarding the factories came wholly under the influence of the workers; many of them said: "As soon as you rise, we'll rise too; we'll open up the arsenal for you." It was not uncommon for soldiers and officers to speak at meetings. On December 4 a Soviet of Soldiers' Deputies was formed within the army, and soldiers' representatives joined the workers' Soviet. Vague but persistent rumors of the army joining the workers came from other towns. Such was the atmosphere in which the Moscow strike began.

Some 100,000 men stopped work on the first day. Two engine-drivers who tried to drive trains out of one of the stations were killed. Minor clashes took place in several parts of the town. A workers' detachment raided and emptied a gun shop. From that day on, ordinary policemen on the beat vanished from the Moscow streets; the police now appeared only in groups. On the second day the number of strikers increased to 150,000; the strike in Moscow became general and spread to factories in the countryside around Moscow. Huge meetings were held everywhere. At the railway terminal where trains from the Far East arrived, the crowd disarmed officers returning from Manchuria. Workers took several dozen *pouds* of cartridges from a railway wagon; later, others seized another wagon-load of arms.

On December 8, the second day of the strike, the Executive Committee decided: "Wherever troops appear, try to enter into conversation with the soldiers and to influence them with comradely words. . . . For the time being, avoid open clashes; offer armed resistance only if the troops behave in an exceptionally challenging manner." Everyone understood that the decisive word would be spoken by the army. The smallest encouraging rumor about the mood of the garrison was passed from mouth to mouth. All the time the revolutionary crowd was fighting an incessant battle with the Moscow authorities over the army.

For example: having heard that infantrymen were marching down the street to the strains of the "Marseillaise," some print-workers sent a deputation to meet them. But it was too late. The military authorities had the excited soldiers surrounded by cossacks and dragoons, marched them back to their barracks, then accepted their demands. On the same day 500 cossacks under the command of a police officer received orders to fire on demonstrators. The cossacks refused to obey, entered into conversations with the crowd, and then, at a command issued by one of their non-commissioned officers, turned their horses around and slowly rode away, accompanied by friendly cries from the crowd.

On another occasion, a ten-thousand-strong workers' demonstration came face to face with a detachment of cossacks. Two working women carrying red flags step out of the crowd and hurl themselves at the cossacks. "Go ahead, fire at us," they shout, "we shan't surrender the flags alive." The cossacks are surprised and embarrassed. The moment is decisive. The crowd, sensing their hesitation, immediately challenges the cossacks: "Our hands are empty, are you really going to fire at us?" "Don't you fire at us, then we shan't either," the cossacks reply. Their officer, frightened and angry, bursts into a flood of invective. But too late. His voice is drowned in indignant cries from the crowd. Somebody makes a short speech; the crowd cheers. Another minute, and the cossacks turn their horses around and gallop away, their rifles slung across their shoulders.

Eventually, after troops had broken up a popular meeting and beaten up the unarmed crowd, the mood in the city became more tense. The crowds in the streets swelled, rumors of all kinds sprang up and died again every hour. Every face bore the imprint of happy excitement mixed with fear. Gorky, who was in Moscow at the time, wrote:

Many believe that it was the revolutionaries who began building the barricades; this, of course, is very flattering, but it is not quite correct. It was the man in the street, the non-party man, who began building the barricades, and therein lies the special nature of the event. The first barricades on the Tverskaya were built gaily, with jokes and laughter, and the widest possible variety of people took part in this cheerful labor, from the respectable gentleman wearing an expensive overcoat to the cook-general and the janitor who until recently had been a traditional prop of "stable authority." The dragoons fired a salvo at the barricade, several people were wounded, two or three killed—there was a howl of indignation, a unanimous cry for revenge, and everything changed at once. After that salvo the man-in-the-street started building barricades not in play but in earnest, meaning to defend his life against Mr. Dubasov and his dragoons.

The *druzhinniki*, that is to say, the militarily organized armed detachments from the revolutionary organizations, became more active. They systematically disarmed every policeman they came across. It was then that the order "Hands up!", the purpose of which was to ensure the safety of the attackers, first began to be issued. Whoever disobeyed the order was killed. Soldiers were not touched for fear of alienating them. One meeting went so far as to decide that anyone who opened fire without orders from the commander of the detachment should be executed. Workers at factory gates carried on agitational work among the soldiers.

But by the third day of the strike bloody clashes with the army began to occur. For example: a squadron of dragoons disperses an evening meeting in a city square plunged into darkness by the strike. "Brothers, don't touch us, we're with you!" The soldiers ride off. But a quarter of an hour later they return in larger numbers and attack the crowd. Darkness, panic, shouts, curses; part of the crowd seek safety in a railway pavilion. The dragoons call for surrender. The crowd refuses. Several salvos are fired; a schoolboy is killed, a number of people wounded. Driven by conscience or by fear of revenge, the dragoons gallop off. "Murderers!" The crowd stands around the bodies of the first victims, fists furiously clenched. "Murderers!" Another moment, and the blood-spattered pavilion is in flames. "Murderers!" The crowd seeks an outlet for its emotions. In the darkness, surrounded by danger, it moves forward, runs into obstacles, presses on. More shots are fired. "Murderers!" The crowd builds barricades. Because it is inexperienced, it works clumsily, without any system. Right there, in the darkness, a group of thirty or forty sing the revolutionary funeral song: "You have fallen victim . . ." More salvos, more wounded and killed. The adjoining courtyards are transformed into first-aid posts, people living in nearby houses act as stretcher-bearers and guard the gates.

As military operations began, the Social-Democratic Fighting Organization posted a proclamation on the walls of Moscow in which it gave the following technical instructions to insurgents:

1. The first rule: do not act as a crowd. Act in small groups of three or four, not more. But let the number of such groups be as large as possible and let each one of them learn to attack quickly and to disappear as quickly. The police are trying to use units of a hundred cossacks to fire on crowds of several thousands. What you must do is to put one or two marksmen against a hundred cossacks. It is easier to hit a hundred men than a single man, especially if this single man fires without warning and disappears, no one knows where.

2. Also, comrades, do not occupy fortified buildings. The troops will always recapture them or simply destroy them by artillery fire. Let our fortresses be courtyards with entrances front and back, and all places from which it is easy to fire and easy to withdraw. Even if they capture such a place, they will find no one in it, yet it will cost them dear.

The revolutionaries' tactics were promptly determined by the situation itself. In contrast to this, the government troops showed themselves totally unable, for a whole five days, to adapt themselves to the opponents' tactics, combining bloodthirsty barbarity with bewilderment and confusion.

Here is a typical example of a battle. Twenty-four men who make up one of the most recklessly courageous Georgian *druzhiny*, are marching along quite openly, in twos. The crowd warns them that sixteen dragoons with their officer are riding towards them. The *druzhina* stops, forms ranks, pulls out its Mausers, and prepares to fire. As soon as the mounted unit appears, the *druzhina* fires. The officer is wounded, the horses in the front rank, wounded, rear up, the dragoons are taken unawares and cannot fire back. This enables the *druzhina* to fire up to 100 rounds and the dragoons flee in disorder leaving behind several killed and wounded. "Now see that you get away," the crowd urges, "the artillery are coming." They are right; the artillery promptly appears on the scene, causing several dozen killed and wounded among the unarmed crowd which never expected to be fired on. Meanwhile the Georgians have started another shooting match with the troops in another place. The *druzhina* is almost invulnerable because it is clad in the armor of popular sympathy.

Here is another example, one of many. A group of thirteen *druzhinniki* occupying a building withstood, for four hours, the fire of 500 or 600 soldiers with 3 guns and 2 machine guns at their disposal. When they had used up all their ammunition and inflicted great losses on the troops, the *druzhinniki* withdrew without a single wound; whereas the soldiers destroyed several city blocks with artillery fire, set a number of wooden houses on fire and killed more than a few terrified citizens, all in order to put a dozen revolutionaries to flight.

The barricades were not defended. They served only as obstacles to the movement of troops, especially dragoons. Houses in the barricaded areas were outside the reach of artillery fire. After a heavy barrage, the troops would "take" the barricades to make sure there was no one behind them; but as soon as the troops had gone the barricades were rebuilt. On December 10, Dubasov's artillery began its work in earnest. Guns and machine guns fired without cease, clearing one street after another. The victims were no longer counted in single numbers but in dozens. The crowds, angry and distraught, rushed from place to place, unable to believe that what was happening before their eyes was real. The soldiers were firing, not at single revolutionaries, but at that vague enemy whose name was Moscow: Moscow's houses with their children and old men, Moscow's unarmed street crowds. "Murderers! Cowards! Is that how you hope to restore your Manchurian glory?"

After the first barrages, the building of barricades became feverish. The rhythm of work became broader, the methods bolder. The crowd overturned a large fruit stand, a newspaper kiosk, tore down shop signs, smashed cast-iron railings, took down overhead tramway wires.

"In defiance of the police order that all gates should be kept bolted," the reactionary newspapers reported, "many house gates have been taken off their hinges and used in building barricades." By December 11 all the most important points throughout the city were surrounded by a network of barricades. Whole streets were wrapped in a cobweb of barbed wire.

Dubasov announced that any crowd "of more than three persons" would be fired upon. But the dragoons fired at single individuals as well. They would first search them; failing to find any arms, they would let them go, and then send a bullet after them. They even fired at people reading Dubasov's proclamation. It was enough for a single shot to be fired from a window —often clearly by an *agent provocateur*—for the artillery guns to be immediately turned on the house. Pools of blood and blobs of brain and hair sticking to shop signs revealed where shrapnel had passed through. Many houses had gaping holes in them. Outside a damaged building—hideous publicity of insurrection! —a plate with a lump of human flesh and an inscription: "Give money for the wounded."

After two or three days the mood of the Moscow garrison became distinctly unfavorable to the insurgents. From the beginning of the disturbances, the military authorities had taken certain measures in the barracks: they had sent away the reserve troops, the volunteers, and those considered unreliable, and had provided better meals for the rest. Only the most dependable units were used at first in suppressing the insurrection. The more doubtful regiments, their most politically conscious elements removed, were confined to barracks and were sent into action only during the second phase. At first these troops acted unwillingly and without confidence. But a random bullet or an officer's words playing on their weariness or hunger could drive them to terrible excesses of cruelty. Dubasov reinforced all these factors by plentiful issues of free vodka; the dragoons were half-drunk all the time.

However, guerrilla attacks cause not only anger but also fatigue; the general hostility of the population had a demoralizing effect on the soldiers. December 13 and 14 were the days of crisis. The troops, deadly tired, refused to fight an enemy they could not see and whose forces were fantastically exaggerated by rumors. During those days there were several cases of suicide among officers.

Dubasov reported to Petersburg that only 5,000 of the 15,000 men of the Moscow garrison could be put into action, as the others were unreliable, and called for reinforcements. He was told that part of the Petersburg garrison had been sent to the Baltic lands, another part was unreliable, and the rest were needed on the spot. These exchanges became known in the town through documents stolen from army headquarters and acted as a powerful injection of courage and hope. But Dubasov won. He insisted on being put in touch with Tsarskoye Selo by telephone and declared that he could not guarantee that "the autocracy would remain intact." The order was given at once to dispatch the Semyonovsky guards regiment to Moscow.

On December 15 the situation changed abruptly. Hope of the guardsmen's arrival quickly restored the spirits of reactionary groups in Moscow. An armed "militia" assembled from the slums by the Union of Russian People appeared in the streets. The government's active forces were enlarged by troops transferred from nearby towns. The *druzhinniki* were exhausted. The man-in-the-street had had enough of uncertainty and fear. The morale of the working masses was falling, hopes of victory vanished. The shops, banks, offices and stock exchange reopened. Traffic in the streets became more animated. One of the newspapers came out. Everyone felt that the life of the barricades was over. Firing died down in most parts of the town. On the sixteenth, with the arrival of the troops from Petersburg and Warsaw, Dubasov became complete master of the situation. He passed to the offensive and completely cleared the center of the city of barricades. Recognizing the hopelessness of the situation, the Soviet and the party decided on that day to end the strike on December 19.

Throughout the insurrection the Presnya district, Moscow's Montmartre, had led a life of its own. On December 10, when gunfire was already heard in the center of the city, Presnya was still calm. Political meetings were held, but they no longer satisfied the masses. The people wanted action and made their will clearly known to the deputies. At last, at 4:00 P.M. the order to build barricades was received from the center. Presnya came to life. Here there was none of the disorganization which reigned in the rest of the town. The workers formed groups of ten, elected team leaders, armed themselves with shovels, picks, and axes, and marched into the streets in orderly formation, like regular road-making gangs. No one was left without a job. The women carried sledges, gates, logs of firewood into the streets. Workmen cut down and sawed up telegraph poles and lamp posts. The whole Presnya rang with the sound of axes: it was like the felling of a forest.

Cut off from the city by troops, solidly traversed by a network of barricades, Presnya became a proletarian encampment. *Druzhinniki* were on duty everywhere; at night armed sentries paced between the barricades and demanded the password from passers-by. Girl workers showed the greatest enthusiasm. They went out on reconnaissance, started conversations with policemen and in that way obtained useful information.

How many active *druzhinniki* were there in Presnya? About 200, not more. They had some eighty Mauser revolvers and rifles at their disposal. Despite these small numbers, clashes with the troops occurred incessantly. Soldiers were disarmed, those offering resistance were killed. Workers restored the destroyed barricades. The *druzhinniki* strictly observed guerrilla tactics: they formed groups of two or three, fired at the cossacks and artillerymen from houses, timber depots, empty railway wagons, moved quickly from place to place and again showered bullets on the enemy. On December 12 the *druzhinniki* captured a gun. For a quarter of an hour they milled around not knowing what to do with it. The dilemma was solved by the arrival of a large detachment of dragoons and cossacks, who recaptured the gun.

On the evening of December 13 the Presnya *druzhinniki* captured six artillerymen and brought them to a factory. They were given a meal at the communal table. During the meal speeches of a political nature were made. The soldiers listened attentively and with sympathy. After supper they were allowed to go back without being searched or disarmed; the workers were anxious to stay friends.

On the night of December 15 in the street, the *druzhinniki* arrested Voyloshnikov, the chief of the secret police, searched his apartment and confiscated photographs of persons under police surveillance and 600 roubles of public money. Voyloshnikov was immediately condemned to death and was shot in the courtyard of the Prokhorov factory. He heard the verdict calmly and met his death with courage, dying more nobly than he had lived.

Trial shelling of Presnya began on the sixteenth. The *druzhinniki* responded with energetic fire and forced the artillery to retreat. But on the same day it became known that Dubasov had received large reinforcements from Petersburg and Warsaw, and spirits began to fall. The exodus of weavers to the country-side began. The roads were filled with refugees on foot, carrying white shoulder bags.

On the night of the sixteenth Presnya was encircled in an iron ring of government troops. Soon after 6:00 A.M. on the seventeenth these troops opened a remorseless cannonade. Guns were fired as much as seven times a minute. This continued, with an hour's respite, until 4:00 P.M. Many factories and houses were destroyed and set on fire. The barrage was conducted from two sides. Houses and barricades were in flames, women and children darted about the streets in clouds of black smoke, the air was filled with the roar and clatter of firing. The glow was such that miles away it was possible to read in the streets late at night, as though it were day. Until noon the *druzhiny* conducted successful operations against the troops, but continuous enemy fire forced them to stop. Only a small group of *druzhinniki* remained under arms on their own initiative and at their own risk.

By the morning of the eighteenth Presnya had been cleared of barricades. The "peaceful" population were allowed to leave Presnya; the troops were careless enough to allow people to leave without searching them. The *druzhinniki* were the first to leave, some of them still with arms. Later, there were shootings and other violence by the soldiers, but by then not a single *druzhinnik* remained in the area.

The "pacification troops" of the Semyonovsky regiment, who were sent to "pacify" the railway, were ordered not to make arrests and to proceed without mercy. They met with no resistance anywhere. Not a single shot was fired against them, yet they killed approximately 150 persons on the railway line. The shootings were carried out without investigation or trial. Wounded men were taken from ambulance wagons and finished off. Corpses lay around without anyone daring to carry them away. One of those shot by the Petersburg guards was the engine-driver Ukhtomsky, who saved the lives of a group of *druzhinniki* by driving them away on his engine at colossal speed under machine-gun fire. Before they shot him, he told his executioners what he had done: "All are safe," he concluded with calm pride, "you'll never get them now."

The rising in Moscow lasted for nine days, from December ninth to the seventeenth. How large, in reality, were the fighting forces of the insurrection? They were negligible. The party *druzhiny* comprised between 700 and 800 men—500 social-democrats and 250 to 300 socialist revolutionaries. Approximately 500 railwaymen equipped with firearms operated at the stations and along the lines. Approximately 400 armed men from among the print-shop operatives and shop assistants made up the auxiliary units. There were also some groups of unattached sharpshooters. Speaking of these, mention must be made of four volunteers from Montenegro. Splendid marksmen, fearless and tireless, they worked as a group, killing only policemen and officers. Two of them were killed, a third wounded, the Winchester rifle of the fourth was destroyed. He was given a new rifle and pursued his terrible sport alone. Every morning he was issued with 50 cartridges, but he complained that it was too little. He seemed in a daze, weeping for his lost comrades and seeking a dreadful vengeance for their loss.

How, then, could so small a number of *druzhinniki* offer battle for a week and a half to a garrison consisting of several thousand men? The answer to this riddle of the revolution lies in the mood of the popular masses. The whole city with its streets, houses, walls, and gates entered into a conspiracy against the government troops. The million-strong population formed a living wall between the guerrillas and the government troops. There were only a few hundred *druzhinniki*. But the barricades were built and rebuilt by the masses. The people surrounded the armed revolutionaries with an atmosphere of active sympathy, foiling the government's plans wherever they could. Who were they, these sympathetic hundreds of thousands? The intelligentsia, the petty bourgeoisie and, above all, the workers. Apart from the mercenary mob, only the uppermost capitalist stratum was on the government's side. The Moscow city duma, which only two months before the rising had proudly exhibited its radicalism, now hastily placd itself behind Dubasov. Not only the Octobrist Guchkov but also Golovin, the future Kadet chairman of the second Duma, joined the governor-general's council.

What was the number of victims of the Moscow insurrection? The exact figure is unknown and will never be ascertained. Data supplied by 47 hospitals and clinics indicate 885 wounded, 174 mortally wounded or killed. But those killed were only rarely taken to the hospital; in most cases they lay at the police stations and were then taken secretly to the cemetery. During those days, 454 persons killed or mortally wounded were buried at the cemetery. Yet many bodies were taken outside the city in railway wagons. It would not be far wrong to suppose that the toll of the Moscow rising was about 1,000 dead and about the same number wounded. These figures included 86 children, of whom some were infants in arms. The significance of these figures becomes vividly clear if we remember that as a result of the March 1848 rising in Berlin, which dealt an irreparable blow to Prussian absolutism, the number killed was only 183. The government never announced the exact number of losses on either side; an official report speaks only of "several tens" of soldiers killed and wounded. In reality there were several hundred. The price was not too high, for what was at stake was Moscow, "the heart of Russia."

Leaving aside the border regions (the Caucasus and the Baltic lands), the December insurrectionary wave reached its maximum height in Moscow. Nevertheless there were barricades and exchanges of fire with the troops in several other towns, such as Kharkov, Alexandrovsk, Nizhny Novgorod, Rostov and Tver.

Once the insurrection was broken everywhere, the era of punitive expeditions began. As their official designation shows, their purpose was not to combat an enemy but to wreak vengeance on the defeated. In the Baltic lands, where the insurrection flared up a fortnight earlier than in Moscow, the punitive expeditions were divided up into small detachments which carried out the bloodthirsty instructions of the Baltic barons, that dirty caste from which the Russian bureaucracy drew its most brutish representatives. Latvian workers and peasants were shot, hanged, flogged to death with rods and stocks, made to run the gauntlet, executed to the strains of the Tsarist anthem. According to highly incomplete information, 749 persons were executed, more than 100 farms were burned down, and many people were flogged to death in the Baltic lands within the space of two months.

Thus it was that absolutism by the grace of God struggled

for its existence. Between January 9 and the convening of the first State Duma on April 27, 1906, according to approximate but certainly not exaggerated figures, the Tsarist government killed more than 14,000 persons, executed more than 1,000, wounded more than 20,000 (many of these died of their wounds), and arrested, exiled, and imprisoned 70,000 persons. The price was not excessive, for what was at stake was the very existence of Tsarism.

CHAPTER 22

Summing Up

The history of the Petersburg Soviet of Workers' Deputies is the history of fifty days. The constituent meeting of the Soviet was held on October 13. On December 3 a meeting of the Soviet was closed down by government troops.

The first meeting was attended by a few dozen persons; by the second half of November the number of deputies had grown to 562, including 6 women. These persons represented 147 factories and plants, 34 workshops and 16 trade unions. The main mass of the deputies—351 persons—belonged to the metalworkers; these played the decisive role in the Soviet. There were 57 deputies from the textile industry, 32 from the printing and paper industries, 12 from the shop-workers and 7 from office workers and the pharmaceutical trade. The Executive Committee acted as the Soviet's ministry. It was formed on October 17 and consisted of 31 persons—22 deputies and 9 representatives of parties (6 from the two social-democrat factions and 3 from the socialist revolutionaries).

What was the essential nature of this institution which within a short time assumed such an important place within the revolution and marked the period of its maximum power?

The Soviet organized the working masses, directed the political strikes and demonstrations, armed the workers, and protected the population against pogroms. Similar work was also done by other revolutionary organizations before the Soviet came into existence, concurrently with it, and after it. Yet this did not endow them with the influence that was concentrated in the hands of the Soviet. The secret of this influence lay in the fact that the Soviet grew as the natural organ of the proletariat in its immediate struggle for power as determined by the actual course of events. The name of "workers' government" which the workers themselves on the one hand, and the reactionary press on the other, gave to the Soviet was an expression of the fact that the Soviet really was a workers' government in embryo. The Soviet represented power insofar as power was assured by the revolutionary strength of the working-class districts; it struggled for power insofar as power still remained in the hands of the military-political monarchy.

Prior to the Soviet we find among the industrial workers a multitude of revolutionary organizations directed, in the main, by the social-democratic party. But these were organizations *within the proletariat*, and their immediate aim was to achieve influence over the masses. The Soviet was, from the start, the organization *of the proletariat*, and its aim was the struggle for revolutionary power.

As it became the focus of all the country's revolutionary forces, the Soviet did not allow its class nature to be dissolved in revolutionary democracy: it was and remained the organized expression of the class will of the proletariat. In the struggle for power it applied methods which were naturally determined by the nature of the proletariat as a class: its role in production, its vast numbers, its social homogeneity. More than that, the Soviet combined its struggle for power as the head of all the revolutionary forces with directing independent class activity by the working masses in many different ways; it not only encouraged the organization of trade unions, but actually intervened in disputes between individual workers and their employees. It was precisely because the Soviet, the democratic representative body of the proletariat at a time of revolution, stood at the meeting-point of all its class interests, that it immediately came under the all-determining influence of the social-democratic party. The party now had its chance to make use of all the tremendous advantages of its Marxist training, and because it was able to see its political way clear in the great "chaos," it succeeded almost without effort in transforming the Soviet—formally a non-party organization—into the organizational instrument of its own influence.

The principal method of struggle used by the Soviet was the political general strike. The revolutionary strength of such strikes consists in the fact that, acting over the head of capital, they disorganize state power. The greater, the more complete the "anarchy" caused by a strike, the nearer the strike is to victory. But on one condition only: the anarchy must not be created by anarchic means. The class which, by simultaneous cessation of work, paralyzes the production apparatus and with it the centralized apparatus of power, isolating parts of the country from one another and sowing general confusion, must itself be sufficiently organized not to become the first victim of the anarchy it has created. The more completely a strike renders the state organization obsolete, the more the organization of the strike itself is obliged to assume state functions. These conditions for a general strike as a proletarian method of struggle were, at the same time, the conditions for the immense significance of the Soviet of Workers' Deputies.

By the pressure of strikes, the Soviet won the freedom of the press. It organized regular street patrols to ensure the safety of citizens. To a greater or lesser extent, it took the postal and telegraph services and the railways into its hands. It intervened authoritatively in economic disputes between workers and capitalists. It made an attempt to introduce the eight-hour working day by direct revolutionary pressure. Paralyzing the activity of the autocratic state by means of the insurrectionary strike, it introduced its own free democratic order into the life of the laboring urban population.

After January 9 the revolution showed that it controlled the consciousness of the working masses. On June 14, by the rising on board the *Potemkin Tavrichesky*, the revolution showed that it could become a material force. By the October strike it showed that it could disorganize the enemy, paralyze his will, and reduce him to complete humiliation. Finally, by organizing workers' Soviets throughout the country, the revolution showed that it was able to create organs of power. Revolutionary power can rest only on active revolutionary strength. Whatever one's views on the further development of the Russian revolution may be, the fact is that no social class except the proletariat has hitherto shown itself capable and ready to support revolutionary power.

The revolution's first act was the attempted dialogue between the proletariat and the monarchy in the city streets; the revolution's first important victory was achieved by a purely class weapon of the proletariat, the political strike; finally, the representative body of the proletariat assumed the role of the first embryonic organ of revolutionary power. With the Soviet we have the first appearance of democratic power in modern Russian history. The Soviet is the organized power of the mass itself over its separate parts. It constitutes authentic democracy, without a lower and an upper chamber, without a professional bureaucracy, but with the voters' right to recall their deputies at any moment. Through its members—deputies directly elected by the workers—the Soviet exercises direct leadership over all social manifestations of the proletariat as a whole and of its individual groups, organizes its actions and provides them with a slogan and a banner.

According to the census of 1897, there were approximately 820,000 "actively employed" persons living in Petersburg, including 433,000 workers and domestic servants. In other words, the proletarian population of the capital amounted to 53 per cent. If we include the non-employed population, we obtain a somewhat lower figure (50.8 per cent) owing to the relatively small size of proletarian families. But in any event the proletariat represented more than half the population of Petersburg.

The Soviet of Workers' Deputies was not the official representative of the capital's entire half-million-strong proletarian population; organizationally speaking, it represented approximately 200,000 persons, principally factory and plant workers, and although its political influence, both direct and indirect, extended to a wider circle, very important strata of the proletariat (building workers, domestic servants, unskilled laborers, cab drivers) were scarcely or not at all represented. It cannot be doubted, however, that the Soviet represented the interests of the whole proletarian mass. Even where so-called "Black Hundreds" groups existed in factories, their numbers shriveled day by day and hour by hour. Among the proletarian masses, the political dominance of the Soviet in Petersburg found no opponents but only supporters. The only exceptions might have been among the privileged domestic servants—lackeys of the high-ranking lackeys of the bureaucracy, of ministers, stock-exchange operators and high-class tarts, people with whom conservatism and monarchism is an occupational disease.

Among the intelligentsia, which is so numerous in Petersburg, the Soviet had many more friends than enemies. Thousands of students recognized the political leadership of the Soviet and ardently supported its measures. The professional and civil service intelligentsia, with the exception of those grown hopelessly fat at their desks, was on its side—at least for the time being.

The Soviet's energetic support of the postal and telegraph strike attracted the sympathetic attention of the lower strata of the civil service. All who were oppressed, dispossessed, honest, life-affirming in the city were consciously or instinctively drawn towards the Soviet.

Who was against it? The representatives of predatory capitalism, stock-exchange operators speculating on rising prices, contractors, merchants, and exporters ruined by the strikes, suppliers of bullion, the gang ensconced in the Petersburg duma (that householders' syndicate), the higher bureaucracy, *poules de luxe* whose keep formed part of the state budget, highly paid, highly decorated public men, the secret police—all that was coarse, dissolute, and doomed to death.

Between the Soviet's supporters and its enemies stood the politically indeterminate, hesitant, or unreliable elements. The most backward groups of the petty bourgeoisie, not yet drawn into politics, had not had time to grasp the role and significance of the Soviet. The labor-employing craftsmen were frightened and alarmed: in them, the petty property-owner's detestation of strikes fought with vague expectations of a better future.

The unsettled professional politicians from intellectual circles, radical journalists who did not know what they wanted, democrats riddled with skepticism, were peevishly condescending towards the Soviet, counted its mistakes on their fingers and generally made it understood that if only it was they who stood at the head of the Soviet, the proletariat's happiness would be assured forevermore. Such gentlemen's excuse is their impotence.

In any case the Soviet was, actually or potentially, the organ representing the overwhelming majority of the population. Its enemies among the population would have been no threat to its dominance had they not been supported by absolutism, still alive and supported in its turn by the most backward elements of the *muzhik* army. The Soviet's weakness was not its own weakness but that of any purely urban revolution.

The period of the fifty days was the time of the revolution's greatest power. The Soviet was its organ of struggle for power. The class character of the Soviet was determined by the sharp class division of the urban population and the profound political antagonism between the proletariat and the capitalist bourgeoisie, even within the historically limited framework of the struggle against absolutism. After the October strike the capitalist bourgeoisie consciously attempted to slow down the revolution; the petty bourgeoisie proved too weak to play an independent part; the proletariat had unchallenged hegemony over the urban revolution, and its own class organization was its weapon in the struggle for power.

The strength of the Soviet grew as the government became increasingly demoralized. Non-proletarian circles became more and more sympathetic towards it as the old state power showed itself to be by comparison more and more helpless and confused.

The mass political strike was the Soviet's principal weapon. Because it established direct revolutionary links between all groups of the proletariat and supported the workers of all enterprises with the authority and force of the entire working class, it gained the power of stopping the country's economic life. Although ownership of the means of production continued to remain in the hands of the capitalists and the state, and although state power continued to remain in the hands of the bureaucracy, the actual running of the national means of production and communication—at least so far as the possibility to interrupt the regular functioning of economic and state life was concerned—lay in the hands of the Soviet. It was precisely this ability of the Soviet, an ability proved in practice, to paralyze the economy and to introduce anarchy into the life of the state, that made the Soviet what it was. Given these facts, to seek ways of ensuring the peaceful coexistence of the Soviet and the old regime would have been hopelessly utopian. Yet all criticisms of the Soviet's tactics, if we lay bare their real content, proceed from just this fantastic idea: after October, the Soviet should have refrained

from all offensive action and should have concentrated on organizing the masses on the ground won from absolutism.

But what was the nature of the October victory?

It cannot be disputed that as a result of the October campaign absolutism repudiated itself "in principle." But it had not
really lost the battle; it merely refused to engage. It made no
serious attempt to use its rural army against the mutinous, striking towns. Naturally it was not for reasons of humanity that it
refrained from making such an attempt; quite simply, it was
deeply discouraged and robbed of its composure. The liberal
elements in the bureaucracy, awaiting their chance, achieved
preponderance at a moment when the strike was already on the
wane, and published the manifesto of October 17, that abdica-
tion "in principle" of absolutism. But the whole material organization of the state—the civil service hierarchy, the police, the
courts of law, the army—still remained the undivided property
of the monarchy. What could, what should the Soviet's tactics
have been under such conditions? Its strength consisted in the
fact that, supported by the productive proletariat, it was able
(insofar as it *was* able) to deprive absolutism of the possibility
of operating the material apparatus of its power. From this viewpoint the Soviet's activity meant the organizing of "anarchy."
Its continuing existence and development meant the consolidat-
ing of "anarchy." Prolonged coexistence was an impossibility.
The future conflict was, from the very start, the material core of
the half-victory of October.

What was there left for the Soviet to do? Pretend that it did
not see the conflict as inevitable? Make believe that it was organizing the masses for the future joys of a constitutional regime?
Who would have believed it? Certainly not absolutism, and certainly not the working class.

The example of the two Dumas was to show us later how
useless outwardly correct conduct—empty forms of loyalty—are
in the struggle against absolutism. In order to anticipate the tactics of "constitutional" hypocrisy in an autocratic country, the

(257)

Soviet would have had to be made of different stuff. But where would that have led? To the same end as that of the two Dumas: to bankruptcy.

There was nothing left for the Soviet to do but recognize that a clash in the immediate future was inevitable; it could choose no other tactics but those of preparing for insurrection.

What could have been the nature of such preparations, if not to develop and consolidate precisely those of the Soviet's qualities which enabled it to paralyze the life of the state and which made up its strength? Yet the Soviet's natural efforts to strengthen and develop those qualities brought the conflict inevitably nearer.

The Soviet was increasingly concerned with extending its influence over the army and the peasantry. In November the Soviet called upon the workers to express actively their fraternal solidarity with the awakening army as personified by the Kronstadt sailors. Not to do this would have been to refuse to extend the Soviet's strength. To do it was a step towards the coming conflict.

Or was there perhaps a third way? Perhaps the Soviet, together with the liberals, could have appealed to the so-called "statesmanship" of the authorities? Perhaps it could and should have found the line that divided the rights of the people from the prerogatives of the monarchy, and stopped this side of that sacred boundary? But who could have guaranteed that the monarchy, too, would stop on its side of the demarcation line? Who would have undertaken to organize peace, or even a temporary truce, between the two sides? Liberalism? On October 18 one of the Soviet's deputations proposed to Count Witte that, as a sign of reconciliation with the people, the troops might be withdrawn from the capital. "It is better to stay without electricity and water than without troops," the Minister replied. Obviously the government had no intention of disarming.

What was the Soviet to do? Either it had to withdraw, leaving the matter in the hands of the chamber of conciliation, the future State Duma, which is what the liberals really wanted; or it had to prepare to hold on with armed power to everything that had been won in October, and, if possible, to launch a further offensive. We now know only too well that the chamber of conciliation was transformed into an arena of new revolutionary conflict. Consequently the objective role played by the first two Dumas only confirmed the truth of the political forecast on which the proletariat constructed its tactics. But we need not look so far ahead. We can ask: who or what was to guarantee the very coming into existence of that "chamber of conciliation," whose destiny was never to conciliate anyone? The same "statesmanship" of the monarchy? Its solemn promises? Count Witte's word of honor? The *zemtsy*'s visit to Peterhof, where they were received at the back door? The warning voice of Mr. Mendelssohn? Or, finally, the so-called "natural course of events" on whose shoulders liberalism piles all the tasks that history would impose on the initiative, intelligence, and strength of liberalism itself?

But if the December clash was inevitable, did not the reason for December's defeat lie in the composition of the Soviet? It has been said that the Soviet's fundamental flaw was its class nature. In order to become the organ of "national" revolution, the Soviet should have broadened its structure, so that representatives of all the strata of the population might find their place within it. This would have then stabilized the Soviet's authority and increased its strength. But is that really so?

The Soviet's strength was determined by the role of the proletariat in a capitalist society. The Soviet's task was not to transform itself into a parody of parliament, not to organize equal representation of the interests of different social groups, but to give unity to the revolutionary struggle of the proletariat. The principal weapon in the Soviet's hands was the political strike—a method unique to the proletariat, which is the class of wage labor. The homogeneity of its class composition eliminated internal friction within the Soviet and rendered it capable of revolutionary initiative.

By what means could the Soviet's composition have been broadened? The representatives of the liberal unions might have been invited to join; this would have enriched the Soviet with the presence of twenty or so intellectuals. Their influence in the Soviet would have been proportional to the role played by the Union of Unions in the revolution, that is, it would have been infinitely small.

What other social groups might have been represented in the Soviet? The *zemstvo* congress? The trade and industrial organizations?

The *zemstvo* congress met in Moscow in November; it discussed the question of its relations with Witte's ministry, but the question of relations with the workers' Soviet never even entered its head.

The Sevastopol rising occurred when the *zemstvo* congress was in session. As we have seen, this immediately caused the *zemtsy* to swerve to the right, so that Mr. Milyukov was obliged to reassure them with a speech roughly to the effect that the insurrection, God be thanked, had already been suppressed. What could have been the form of any revolutionary cooperation between these counter-revolutionary gentlemen and the workers' deputies who saluted and supported the Sevastopol insurgents? No one has yet given an answer to this question. One of the half-sincere, half-hypocritical tenets of liberalism is the demand that the army should remain outside politics. In contrast to this, the Soviet employed tremendous energy in trying to draw the army into revolutionary politics. Or should the Soviet perhaps have had such infinite trust in the Tsar's manifesto that it left the army entirely in Trepov's hands? And, if not, where was the program on whose basis cooperation with the liberals might have been conceivable in this vitally important field? What could have been these gentlemen's contribution to the Soviet's activities, if not one of systematic opposition, endless debate, and internal demoralization? What could they have given us other than their advice, which we knew anyway by reading the liberal press? It may be that "statesmanship" really was the prerogative of the Kadets and the Octobrists; nevertheless the Soviet could not transform itself into a club for political polemics and mutual indoctrination. It had to be, and remained, an organ of struggle.

What could the representatives of bourgeois liberalism and bourgeois democracy have added to the Soviet's strength? How could they have enriched its methods of struggle? It is enough to recall the role they played in October, November, and December, enough to know how little resistance these elements were to offer to the dissolution of *their own* Duma, to understand that the Soviet was entitled to, that it was duty bound to remain a class organization, that is, an organ of struggle. Bourgeois deputies might have made the Soviet more numerous, but they were absolutely incapable of making it stronger.

By the same token we reject those purely rationalist, unhistorical accusations which argue that the Soviet's irreconcilable class tactics hurled the bourgeoisie back into the camp of order. The labor strike, which showed itself to be a mighty weapon of revolution, also introduced "anarchy" into industry. This was enough in itself to make oppositional capital put the slogan of public order and continuing capitalist exploitation above all the slogans of liberalism.

The employers decided that the "glorious" (as they called it) October strike had to be the last—and organized the anti-revolutionary Union of October 17. They had sufficient reason for doing so. Each of them had ample opportunity to discover in his own factory that the political gains of the revolution go hand in hand with the consolidation of the workers' stand against capital. Certain politicians think that the main trouble with the struggle for the eight-hour day was that it caused the final split in the opposition and turned capital into a counter-revolutionary force. These critics would like to put the class energy of the proletariat at the disposal of history without accepting the consequences of the class struggle. It goes without saying that the unilateral introduction of the eight-hour day was bound to produce a violent reaction on the part of the employers. But it is puerile to believe that without this particular campaign the capitalists' rapprochement with Witte's capitalist stock-exchange government would not have taken place. The unification of the proletariat as an independent revolutionary force placing itself at the head of the popular masses and offering a constant threat to "public order" was argument enough in favor of a coalition between capital and the authorities.

True, during the first phase of the revolution, when it manifested itself in spontaneous scattered outbursts, the liberals tolerated it. They clearly saw that the revolutionary movement shook the foundations of absolutism and forced it towards a constitutional agreement with the ruling classes. They put up with strikes and demonstrations, adopted a friendly attitude towards revolutionaries, and criticized them only mildly and cautiously. After October 17, when the conditions for the constitutional deal were already written down, and it seemed that all that was left was to put them into effect, the revolution's further work obviously undermined the very possibility of such a deal between the liberals and the authorities. From then on the proletarian masses, united by the October strike and organized within themselves, put the liberals against the revolution by the very fact of their existence. The liberals felt that the Moor had done his work* and should now quietly go back to his lathe. The Soviet, on the contrary, believed that the main struggle lay ahead. Under such circumstances any revolutionary cooperation between the capitalist bourgeoisie and the proletariat was out of the question.

December follows from October as a conclusion follows

---

* A reference to a line in Schiller's play *The Conspiracy of Fiesco in Genoa:* "The Moor has done his work, the Moor may go." (Trans.)

from a premise. The outcome of the December clash is to be explained, not by isolated tactical errors, but by the decisive fact that the mechanical forces of reaction proved greater than that of the revolution. The proletariat was defeated in the insurrection of December and January, not by its own mistakes, but by a more real quantity: the bayonets of the peasant army.

Liberalism, it is true, is of the opinion that deficiency of fire power should in all circumstances be answered by speed of leg power: it regards retreat at the moment of decision as the most truly courageous, mature, pondered and effective tactic. This liberal philosophy of desertion made an impression on certain *littérateurs* in the ranks of social-democracy itself, who, in retrospect, posed the question: if the proletariat's defeat in December was due to the insufficiency of its forces, did not its error consist precisely in the fact that, not being sufficiently strong for victory, it accepted battle? To this we can reply: if battles were engaged only in the certainty of victory, there would be no battles fought in this world. A preliminary calculation of forces cannot determine in advance the outcome of revolutionary conflicts. If it could, the class struggle should have long since been replaced by bookkeeping. That is what, a little while ago, the treasurers of certain trade unions were dreaming of. But it turned out that even with the most modern system of accounting it is impossible to convince capitalists by evidence extracted from a ledger, and that arguments based on figures must, in the end, be supported by the argument of a strike.

And however well everything is calculated in advance, every strike gives rise to a whole series of new facts, material and moral, which cannot be foreseen and which eventually decide the outcome of the struggle. Now imagine that such a trade union, with its precise accounting methods, has been swept aside; extend the strike over the entire country and give it a great political aim; put state power and the proletariat face to face as immediate enemies; surround both with allies—real, potential, or imaginary; add the indifferent strata of the population, ruthlessly fought for by both sides; add the army, whose revolutionary elements emerge only in the turmoil of events; add exaggerated hopes on the one hand and exaggerated fears on the other, both being very real factors; add the paroxysms of the stock exchange and all the complex effects of international relations—and you will obtain the climate of the revolution. Under such circumstances the subjective will of a party, even a "dominant" party, is only one of the factors involved, and not by any means the most important one.

In revolution, even more than in war, the moment of battle is determined less by calculations on either side than by the respective position of both the opposition armies. It is true that in war, owing to the mechanical discipline of armies, it is sometimes possible to lead an entire army away from the field of battle without any engagement taking place; yet in such cases the military commander must still ask himself whether the strategy of retreat will not demoralize his troops and whether, by avoiding today's battle, he is not preparing the ground for a more disastrous one tomorrow. General Kuropatkin might have a great deal to say on that point. But in a developing revolutionary situation a planned retreat is, from the start, unthinkable. A party may have the masses behind it while it is attacking, but that does not mean that it will be able to lead them away at will in the midst of the attack. It is not only the party that leads the masses: the masses, in turn, sweep the party forward. And this will happen in any revolution, however powerful its organization. Given such conditions, to retreat without battle may mean the party abandoning the masses under enemy fire.

Of course the social democrats, being the "dominant" party, might have refused to accept the reaction's challenge in December and, to use the same Kuropatkin's happy expression, might have "withdrawn to previously prepared positions," that is, into clandestinity. But by doing so it would merely have enabled the government, in the absence of any generalized resistance, to smash the legal and semi-legal workers' organizations (which the party itself had helped to create), one by one. That would have been the price paid by social democracy for the doubtful privilege of being able to stand aside from the revolution, philosophize about its mistakes, and work out faultless plans whose only disadvantage is that they are produced at a moment when no one any longer wants them. It is easy to imagine how this would have assisted the consolidation of links between the party and the masses!

No one can assert that the social democrats speeded up the conflict. On the contrary, it was on their initiative that the Petersburg Soviet, on October 22, canceled the funeral procession so as not to provoke a clash without first trying to make use of the confused and hesitant "new regime" for widespread agitational and organizational work among the masses. When the government made its over-hasty attempt to re-establish control over the country and, as a first step, proclaimed martial law in Poland, the Soviet maintained purely defensive tactics and did nothing to carry the November strike to the stage of open conflict; instead, it turned the strike into a protest movement and contented itself with the tremendous moral effect of this on the army and the Polish workers.

But if the party, because of its awareness of the need for organizational preparedness, evaded battle in October and November, in December this consideration no longer applied. Not (needless to say) because such preparedness had already been achieved, but because the government—which also had no choice—had opened the battle by destroying all the revolutionary organizations created in October and November. If, under those conditions, the party had decided to refuse to give battle once again, and even if it had been able to withdraw the revolutionary masses from the open arena, it would only have been preparing the ground for insurrection under still less favorable conditions: namely the absence of a sympathetic press and all mass organizations, and in the demoralized atmosphere which inevitably follows a retreat.

(265)

Marx wrote:*

> In revolution as in war it is absolutely necessary at the decisive moment to stake everything, whatever the chances of the struggle. History does not know a single successful revolution that does not testify to the correctness of this proposition. . . . Defeat after persistent struggle is a fact of no less revolutionary significance than an easily snatched victory. . . . In any struggle it is absolutely inevitable that he who throws down the glove runs the risk of being defeated; but is that a reason to declare oneself defeated from the start and to submit without drawing the sword?
>
> Anyone who commands a decisive position in a revolution and surrenders it instead of forcing the enemy to venture an attack deserves to be regarded as a traitor. (*Karl Marx, Revolution and Counter-Revolution in Germany.*)

In his well-known Introduction to Marx's *The Class Struggles in France*, Engels left a way open for serious misunderstandings when he balanced the new possibilities of victory arising from the evolution of the class composition of the army against the military-technological difficulties of insurrection (rapid railway transport of troops, the destructive power of modern artillery, the broad streets of modern towns). On the one hand Engels made a very one-sided assessment of the significance of modern techniques in revolutionary risings and, on the other hand, he did not consider it necessary or convenient to explain that the evolution of the class composition of the army can become politically significant only when there is a direct confrontation between the army and the people.

A word on both sides of the question.* The decentralized nature of revolution necessitates the continual transfer of troops. Engels says that, thanks to the railways, garrisons can be more

---

* In point of fact this text was written by Engels in Marx's name. (Author)

* It should be stated very clearly, however, that Engels in his Introduction had in mind only German affairs, whereas our considerations are based on the experience of the Russian revolution. (This not very convincing note was inserted in the German text purely for censorship reasons. Author)

than doubled within twenty-four hours. But he overlooks the fact that a genuine mass rising inevitably presupposes a railway strike. Before the government can begin to transfer its armed forces, it must—in ruthless combat with the striking personnel —seize the railway line and rolling stock, organize traffic, and re-store the destroyed track and blown-up bridges. The best rifles and sharpest bayonets are not enough for all this; and the experience of the Russian revolution shows that even minimal success in this direction requires incomparably more than twenty-four hours.

Further, before proceeding to the transfer of armed forces, the government must know the state of affairs in the country. Telegraph speeds up information to an even greater extent than the railways speed up transport. But, here again, a rising both presupposes and engenders a postal and telegraph strike. If the insurrection is unable to bring the postal and telegraph personnel over to its side—a fact that would bear witness to the weakness of the revolutionary movement!—it can still overturn the tel-egraph poles and cut the wires. Although this is detrimental to both sides, the revolution, whose principal strength by no means resides in an automatically functioning organization, stands to lose far less than the state.

The telegraph and the railways are, without any question, powerful weapons in the hands of the modern centralized state. But they are double-edged weapons. And while the ex-istence of society and the state as a whole depend on the con-tinuance of proletarian labor, this dependence is most obvious in the case of the railways and the postal and telegraph service. As soon as the rails and wires refuse to serve, the government apparatus is fragmented into separate parts without any means of transport or communication (not even the most primitive ones) between them. That being so, matters may go a very long way before the authorities succeed in "doubling" a local garrison.

Side by side with the transfer of troops, an insurrection

confronts the government with the problem of transport for military supplies. We already know the difficulties which a general strike creates in this respect; but to these should be added the further risk that military supplies may be intercepted by the insurgents. This risk becomes the more real, the more decentralized the character of the revolution and the larger the masses drawn into it. We have seen workers at Moscow stations seize weapons being transported to some distant theater of operations. Similar actions occurred in many places. In the Kuban region insurgent cossacks intercepted a transport of rifles. Revolutionary soldiers handed ammunition over to insurgents, etc.

Of course, when all is said and done, there can be no question of a purely military victory by the insurgents over the government troops. The latter are bound to be physically stronger, and the problem must always be reduced to the mood and behavior of the troops. Without class kinship between the forces on both sides of the barricades, the triumph of the revolution, given the military technology of today, would be impossible indeed. But on the other hand it would be a most dangerous illusion to believe that the army's "crossing over to the side of the people" can take the form of a peaceful, spontaneous manifestation. The ruling classes, confronted with the question of their own life or death, never willingly surrender their positions because of theoretical considerations concerning the class composition of the army.

The army's political mood, that great unknown of every revolution, can be determined only in the process of a clash between the soldiers and the people. The army's crossing over to the camp of the revolution is a moral process; but it cannot be brought about by moral means alone. Different motives and attitudes combine and intersect within the army; only a minority is consciously revolutionary, while the majority hesitates and awaits an impulse from outside. This majority is capable of laying down its arms or, eventually, of pointing its bayonets at the reaction only if it begins to believe in the possibility of a people's victory. Such a belief is not created by political agitation alone. Only when the soldiers become convinced that the people have come out into the streets for a life-and-death struggle—not to demonstrate against the government but to overthrow it—does it become psychologically possible for them to "cross over to the side of the people."

Thus an insurrection is, in essence, not so much a struggle against the army as a struggle *for* the army. The more stubborn, far-reaching, and successful the insurrection, the more probable —indeed inevitable—is a fundamental change in the attitude of the troops. Guerrilla fighting on the basis of a revolutionary strike cannot in itself, as we saw in Moscow, lead to victory. But it creates the possibility of sounding the mood of the army, and after a first important victory—that is, once a part of the garrison has joined the insurrection—the guerrilla struggle can be transformed into a mass struggle in which a part of the troops, supported by the armed and unarmed population, will fight another part, which will find itself in a ring of universal hatred. We have seen in the Black Sea Fleet, in Kronstadt, in Siberia, in the Kuban region, later in Sveaborg and in many other places that when the class, moral, and political heterogeneity of the army causes troops to cross over to the side of the people, this must, in the first instance, mean a struggle between two opposing camps within the army. In all these cases, the most modern weapons of militarism—rifles, machine guns, fortress and field artillery, battleships—were found not only in the hands of the government but also in the service of the revolution.

On the basis of the experience of Bloody Sunday, January 9, 1905, a certain English journalist, Mr. Arnold White, arrived at the brilliant conclusion that if Louis XVI had had a few batteries of Maxim guns at his disposal, the French Revolution would not have taken place. What pathetic superstition to believe that the historical chances of revolutions can be measured by the caliber of rifles or the diameter of guns! The Russian revolution showed once more that people are not ruled by rifles, guns, and battle-

ships: in the final analysis, rifles, guns, and battleships are controlled by people.

On December 11, the Witte-Durnovo ministry, which by that
time had become the Durnovo-Witte ministry, published an
electoral law. At a time when Dubasov, the dry-land admiral,
was restoring the honor of St. Andrew's flag in the streets of
Presnya, the government hastened to open up a legal path for
reconciliation between the property-owning public on the one
hand and the monarchy and bureaucracy on the other. From
that moment on, the struggle for power, though revolutionary
in essence, developed under the guise of constitutionalism.

In the first Duma the Kadets passed themselves off as the
leaders of the people. Since the popular masses, with the exception of the urban proletariat, were still in a chaotically oppositional mood, and since the elections were boycotted by
the parties of the extreme left, the Kadets found themselves masters of the situation in the Duma. They "represented" the whole
of Russia: the liberal landowners, the liberal merchants, the lawyers, doctors, civil servants, shopkeepers, shop assistants, partly
even the peasants. Although the Kadet leadership remained, as
before, in the hands of landowners, professors, and lawyers, the
party, under pressure from the interests and needs of the countryside which relegated all other problems to the background,
turned to the left. Thus we come to the dissolution of the Duma
and the Vyborg manifesto, which was later to cause so many
sleepless nights to the liberal windbags.

The Kadets were returned to the second Duma in smaller
numbers but, as Milyukov admitted, they now had the advantage of being backed, not merely by the discontented man-in-
the-street, but by the voter who wanted to dissociate himself
from the left, that is, to give his vote more consciously to the
antirevolutionary platform. Whereas the main mass of landowners and representatives of large capital had crossed over
into the camp of active reaction, the urban petty bourgeoisie,
the commercial proletariat, and the rank-and-file intelligentsia

now voted for the left-wing parties. A part of the landowners and the middle layers of the urban population followed the Kadets. The representatives of the peasants and workers stood to the left of them.

The Kadets voted for the government plan for army recruitment, and promised to vote for the budget. In exactly the same way they would have voted for new loans to cover the state deficit and, without hesitation, would have assumed responsibility for the autocracy's old debts. Golovin, that pathetic figure in the speaker's chair, embodying all the impotence and insignificance of liberalism, said after the Duma had been dissolved that the government ought to interpret the Kadets' behavior as its own victory over the opposition. He was perfectly right. Under such circumstances one might have thought there were no grounds for dissolving the Duma; yet it was dissolved. This proves that there exists a stronger force than the political arguments of liberalism. That force is the inner logic of revolution.

In the struggle with the Kadet-dominated Duma the government was filled more and more with a sense of its own power. It saw this pseudo-parliament, not as a historical challenge that demanded a solution, but as an assembly of political opponents who had to be rendered harmless. A handful of lawyers for whom politics was rather like making a plea before a high court appeared to be rivals of the government and claimants to power. Their political eloquence oscillated between legal syllogisms and pseudo-classical phrase-mongering. In the debate on the subject of courts-martial the two parties were brought face to face. The Moscow lawyer Maklakov, in whom the liberals saw the man of the future, applied annihilating legal criticism to martial justice and, with it, to the government's entire policy. "But courts-martial are not a legal institution," Stolypin replied. "They are a weapon of struggle. You want to prove that this weapon is not consistent with the law? Well, it is consistent with expediency. Law is not an aim in itself. When the existence of the state is threatened, the government is not only entitled but is duty bound to leave legal considerations aside and to make use of the material weapons of its power."

This reply, which expresses not only the philosophy of the government *coup* but also that of the popular rising, caused extreme embarrassment to the liberals. "What an unheard-of admission!" cried the liberal journalists, vowing for the thousand and first time that right is stronger than might.

Yet their entire policy was designed to convince the government of the contrary. They retreated again and again. In order to save the Duma from dissolution they abdicated all their rights, thus proving beyond dispute that might is stronger than right. Under such conditions the government was bound to feel tempted to continue using its weapons of power to the end.

The second Duma was dissolved. Now conservative national-liberalism, personified by the Union of October 17, appears as the successor of the revolution. The Kadets see themselves as the heirs to the revolution's tasks. The Octobrists were in actual fact the heirs of the Kadets' appeasement tactics. However furtively contemptuous the Kadets were to the Octobrists, the latter drew the only logical conclusions from the Kadets' own premise: if you do not get your support from the revolution, you have to get it from Stolypin's constitutionalism.

The third Duma gave the Tsarist government 456,535 army recruits, although the promised reforms in Kuropatkin's and Stessel's Department of Defense amounted to no more than new epaulettes, collar-tabs, and shakos. It approved the budget of the Ministry of Home Affairs which handed 70 per cent of the country over to the satraps who used the emergency laws like a hangman's noose, and left the remaining 30 per cent free to be hanged and garrotted on the basis of "normal" laws. It accepted all the basic provisions of the famous ukase of November 9, 1906, issued by the government on the basis of Paragraph 87. Its purpose was to skim off a layer of solid property owners from the peasantry, and to leave all the rest to the process of natural selection in the biological sense of that term. In place of the expropriation of landowners' lands for the benefit of the peasantry, the reaction put the expropriation of community-owned peasant lands for the benefit of the kulaks. "The law of November 9," said one of the extreme reactionaries of the third Duma, "has enough explosive gas in it to blow up the whole of Russia."

Driven into a historical cul-de-sac by the irreconcilable attitudes of the nobility and the bureaucracy, who once more emerged as the unlimited masters of the situation, the bourgeois parties are looking for a way out of the economic and political contradictions of their position—in imperialism. They seek compensation for their domestic defeats in foreign affairs—in the Far East (the Amur railway), Persia, and the Balkans. The so-called "annexation" of Bosnia and Herzegovina was greeted in Petersburg and Moscow with the deafening clatter of all the old ironware of patriotism. And the Kadet party, which, of all the bourgeois parties, claimed to be the most opposed to the old order, now stands at the head of militant "neo-Slavism"; the Kadets are hoping that capitalist imperialism will solve the problems left unsolved by revolution. Driven to de facto abandonment of any idea of confiscating the landowners' lands and of any democratization of the social system—which means the abandonment of any hope of creating, by means of a farming peasantry, a stable domestic market for capitalist development —the Kadets transfer their hopes to foreign markets. For success to be achieved in that direction, strong state power is needed; and the liberals find themselves compelled to give active support to Tsarism as the actual holder of such power. The oppositionally-tinted imperialism of the Milyukovs merely serves as a kind of ideological cosmetic for that revolting mixture of autocratic bureaucracy, brutal landlordism and parasitic capitalism that is at the very core of the third Duma.

The situation which has arisen as a result of all this may yet lead to the most unexpected consequences. The same government that buried the reputation of its strength in the waters of Tsushima and the battlefields of Mukden; the same government that suffered the terrible sequel of its adventurist policies, now unexpectedly finds itself patriotically trusted by the "nation's" representatives. It acquires, without difficulty, half a million new soldiers and half a billion roubles for its current military expenditure; and, in addition, it receives the Duma's support for its new adventures in the Far East. More than that: by right and left, by the Black Hundreds and the Kadets, it is actually reproached because its foreign policy is not active enough! The logic of events thus drives the government on to the hazardous path of fighting for the restoration of its world prestige. Who knows? Perhaps, before the fate of the autocracy is finally and irrevocably decided in the streets of Petersburg and Warsaw, it will be put to the test once more on the banks of the Amur or the coast of the Black Sea.

CHAPTER 23

◇◈◇◈◇◈◇◈◇◈◇

Annexes

The Party of the Proletariat
and the Bourgeois Parties in the Revolution*

You know, comrades, that I radically disagree with what our party's official view was during the period of our revolution now ending and with the role played in it by the bourgeois parties.

To the Menshevik comrades their own views appear extraordinarily complex. I have often heard them accuse me of having an over-simplified idea of the Russian revolution. And yet, despite extreme formlessness which is disguised as complexity —or, perhaps, precisely because of this formlessness—the Mensheviks' views boil down to a very simple formula, which even Mr. Milyukov could understand. In his postscript to a recently published book, *The Elections to the Second State Duma*, the ideological leader of the Kadet party writes:

* From a speech made at the London congress of the Russian Social-Democratic Revolutionary Party, 12–25 May 1907.

As for the left-wing groups in the narrow sense, that is, the socialist and revolutionary groups, it will be more difficult to reach an
understanding with them. But here again, although there may not
be any definite positive factors, there exist very strong negative ones
which will, to some extent, assist a rapprochement between us. Their
aim is to criticize and discredit us, and for this purpose, if for no
other, we have to exist and be active. We know that for all socialists,
not only in Russia but throughout the world, the revolution now
taking place is a bourgeois revolution, not a socialist revolution, and
has to be carried out by a democratic bourgeoisie. No socialists anywhere in the world . . . would be prepared to run for such a
democracy, and if the people returned them to the Duma in large
numbers, it was surely not to establish socialism today or for them
to carry through any preparatory "bourgeois" reforms. . . . Therefore it will be far more advantageous to them to concede the role
of parliamentarians to us rather than compromise themselves by
playing that role.

As you see, Milyukov goes straight to the heart of the matter. The passage I have just quoted contains all the principal
elements of the Mensheviks' view of the revolution and of the
relationship between bourgeois and social democracy. "The revolution now taking place is a bourgeois, not a socialist one."
That is the first point. The bourgeois revolution has to be made
"by democratic bourgeoisie." That's the second point. Social
democracy cannot carry through bourgeois reforms with its
own hands; its role is purely oppositional, and consists of "criticizing and discrediting." Lastly and fourthly, to enable the
socialists to remain in opposition, "we (that is, the democratic
bourgeoisie) have to be in existence and active."

And what if "we" are not in existence? What if there is
no bourgeois democracy capable of marching at the head of the
bourgeois revolution? Then it has got to be invented. And that
is precisely what the Mensheviks are doing. They are constructing a bourgeois democracy, its qualities and its history, out of
the rich fund of their own imagination.

As materialists, we must first of all ask ourselves the question of the social foundations of a bourgeois democracy. In

what classes, what strata of the population, can it find support?

We are all agreed that the capitalist bourgeoisie is simply not in question as a revolutionary force. Certain industrialists in Lyons played a counter-revolutionary role even at the time of the great French Revolution, which was a national revolution in the broadest sense of the word. But we are always being told about the middle, and especially the petty bourgeoisie, as the guiding force of the bourgeois revolution. What exactly does this petty bourgeoisie represent?

The Jacobins were supported by an urban bourgeoisie which had come out of craft workshops. Small craftsmen, apprentices, the whole petty urban population closely connected with them, formed the army of the revolutionary sans-culottes, the principal support of the leading party of the Montagnards. This compact mass of the urban population, which had gone through the long historical school of artisanal trade, carried the revolution forward. The objective result of the revolution was the creation of "normal" conditions for capitalist exploitation. But the social mechanism of the historical process decreed that these conditions for the bourgeoisie's rule must be created by the mob, the democracy of the streets, the sans-culottes. It was their dictatorship of terror that cleansed bourgeois society of the useless rubbish that encumbered it, after which the bourgeoisie achieved domination by overthrowing the dictatorship of the petty-bourgeois democracy.

I ask—alas, not for the first time: where is the social class in Russia that could raise up a revolutionary bourgeoisie on its shoulders, could put it in power and give it the possibility of performing such a tremendous task in opposition to the proletariat? That is the central question, and once more I put it to the Mensheviks.

It is true that we have enormous masses of revolutionary peasantry. But the comrades from the Minority know as well as I that the peasantry, however revolutionary it may be, is not capable of playing an independent, still less a leading, political role. Undoubtedly the peasantry can prove to be a tremendous force in the service of the revolution, but it would be unworthy of a Marxist to believe that a party of mużhiks can place itself at the head of a bourgeois revolution and, by its own initiative, liberate the nation's productive forces from their archaic shackles. The town leads in modern society, and it alone is capable of leading a bourgeois revolution. Where then, is our urban bourgeoisie which might be capable of leading the nation?

Comrade Martynov has searched for it many a time, magnifying glass in hand. He has found schoolteachers in Saratov, lawyers in Petersburg, and statisticians in Moscow. He and all those who think like him, refuse to admit that in the Russian revolution it is the industrial proletariat which occupies the position once occupied by the artisanal semi-proletarian bourgeoisie of the sans-culottes at the end of the eighteenth century. I want to draw your attention, comrades, to this fundamental fact.

Our large industry did not grow naturally out of artisanal trade. The economic history of our towns never went through a craft period. In Russia, capitalist industry came into being under direct and immediate pressure from European capital. It took possession of what was, in essence, primitive virgin soil without encountering any resistance from artisanal culture. Foreign capital flowed into Russia through the channel of state loans and the pipeline of private enterprise. It gathered around itself an army of the industrial proletariat without allowing artisanal trade to develop, nor even to come into being. As a result of this process, the principal force in our towns at the moment of bourgeois revolution consisted of an industrial proletariat of an extremely highly developed social type. That is a fact which cannot be refuted and which must be placed at the very foundation of all our conclusions concerning the tactics of revolution.

If the comrades from the Minority believe in the victory of the revolution, or even if they merely admit the possibility of such a victory, they will not be able to deny that, apart from the proletariat, we can have no claim to revolutionary power. Just as the petty-bourgeois urban democracy of the French Revolution placed itself at the head of the revolutionary nation, so the proletariat, that sole revolutionary democracy of our towns, must seek support among the peasant masses and must take power if the revolution is to be victorious. A government supported directly by the proletariat and, through it, by the revolutionary peasantry does not yet mean a socialist dictatorship. I am not now touching upon the further prospects for a proletarian government. Perhaps the proletariat is destined to fall, as the Jacobin democracy fell, to clear a space for the rule of the bourgeoisie. I want to establish only one thing: if, as Plekhanov predicted, the revolutionary movement in Russia triumphs as a workers' movement, then the victory of the proletariat in Russia is possible only as a revolutionary victory of the proletariat—or else it is not possible at all.

On this conclusion I insist most adamantly. If we are forced to admit that the social contradictions between the proletariat and the peasant masses will not allow the proletariat to become the leader of the peasantry, and that the proletariat itself is not strong enough for victory, then we must reach the conclusion that our revolution is not destined to win at all. If that is so, then the natural finale of the revolution must be a deal between the liberal bourgeoisie and the old power. We must certainly face the possibility of such an outcome. But that way lies the defeat of the revolution, a defeat due to its internal weakness.

In essence, the Mensheviks' analysis—and, first and foremost, their evaluation of the proletariat and its possible relations with the peasantry—leads them inexorably towards revolutionary pessimism. Yet they persist in ignoring this logic and, instead, base their revolutionary optimism on . . . bourgeois democracy. Hence their attitude towards the Kadets. For them the Kadets are the symbol of bourgeois democracy, and bourgeois democracy is the natural claimant to revolutionary power.

From this viewpoint Comrade Martynov has constructed a whole philosophy of the history of the constitutional-democratic party. The Kadets, he explains, swing to the right in periods of revolutionary lull and to the left in periods of revolutionary ascendancy; and therefore they will inherit the revolutionary future. I must point out, however, that here the history of the Kadets is tendentiously made to fit a preconceived notion. Martynov reminds us that in October 1905 the Kadets declared their sympathy for the strikes. That is an incontrovertible fact. But what lay hidden behind their platonic sympathy? The most vulgar bourgeois fear of street terror. As soon as the revolutionary movement grew stronger, the Kadets disappeared completely from the political arena. Milyukov explains the reasons for this disappearance with utter frankness in the brochure I have already quoted:

When, after October 17, free political assemblies first appeared in Russia, their mood was unquestionably left-wing. . . . During the last months of 1905 it was absolutely impossible to resist this trend, even for a party like the Kadets, which was then in the first months of its existence and was preparing for parliamentary struggle. Those who now reproach the Kadets with failure to protest at that time, by organizing meetings, against the "revolutionary illusions" of Trotskyism and the relapse into Blanquism, simply do not understand—or have forgotten—the mood of the democratic public at meetings during that period. (*The Elections to the Second State Duma*, pp. 91 and 92.)

As you see, Mr. Milyukov does me too much honor by connecting my name with the period when the revolution reached its highest point. But that is not why the quotation is interesting. The important point for us is that in October and November the only work that the Kadets might have done would have consisted in fighting revolutionary "illusions," that is to say, in substance, opposing the revolutionary movement of the masses—and the only reason why they failed to do that work was that they were afraid of the democratic public which attended popular meetings at the time. And this in the very honeymoon of their existence! This at the climax of our revolution!

Comrade Martynov remembers the Kadets' platonic greetings to the strikers. But, being the tendentious historian that he is, he forgets to mention the November congress of the *zemtsy*, at the head of which stood the Kadets. Did the congress discuss the question of its participation in the popular movement? No, it discussed the terms of its deal with Witte's ministry. When news came of the Sevastopol rising, the congress immediately and decisively swung to the right—the right, not the left. And only Mr. Milyukov's speech which boiled down to saying that, thank heaven, the rising had already been suppressed—only this speech succeeded in putting the Kadet *zemtsy* back on the constitutional track. You see that Martynov's general thesis is open to very serious reservations.

Next we come to the Kadets in the first Duma. Without doubt that is the most "brilliant" page in the history of the liberal party. But what explained this temporary success? We can differ in our evaluations of the boycott tactic. But we must all agree that it was this tactic which, artificially and for that reason only temporarily, propelled large democratic strata towards the Kadets, forced many radicals to consider themselves represented by the Kadet party, and thus transformed the Kadets into the organ of "national" opposition; it was this exceptional situation that drove the Kadets to issue the Vyborg declaration, which Comrade Martynov has also mentioned. But by the time of the elections to the second Duma the Kadets were already back in their more natural position of fighting "revolutionary illusions." Mr. Alexey Smirnov, the historiographer of the Kadet party, has this to say about the election campaign in the towns where the Kadets' influence was at its greatest: "No supporters of the government were found among the urban voters. . . . The focal point of the struggle at election meetings therefore shifted . . . to the debate between the People's Freedom party and the left socialist parties" (*The Elections to the Second State Duma*, p. 90).

The oppositional chaos of the first election was replaced, in the second campaign, by a fight over the issue of revolutionary democracy. The Kadets mobilized their voters against the slogans of democracy, revolution, and the proletariat. That is a cardinal fact. The Kadets' social basis became narrower and less democratic. And this was not a temporary, accidental, transitory circumstance. It indicated a truly serious division between liberalism and revolutionary democracy. Milyukov has no illusions concerning this result of the second election. After pointing out that in the first Duma the Kadets had a majority— "perhaps because they had no competitors"—and that in the second election they lost that majority, the leader of the Kadet party says: "But instead we have the support of a considerable part of the country which has declared itself in favor of our tactics against the tactics of revolution." (*Ibid*., p. 286.)

We cannot but wish that those of our comrades who constitute the Minority were equally clear-sighted and definite in their assessment of events. Do you believe that things will happen differently in the future? That the Kadets will once more inscribe democracy on their banners, and become more revolutionary? Or do you think that, on the contrary, the further development of the revolution will lead to a final break between the democrats and the liberals, and will throw the latter back into the camp of reaction? Are not the tactics of the Kadets in the second Duma leading to that? Do not your own tactics lead to that? Your speeches in the Duma? Your accusations at public meetings and in the press? On what, then, do you base your belief that the Kadets will see the light, will change their ways? On the facts of political development? No, on your own schema. To "carry the revolution to its conclusion" you need an urban bourgeoisie. You look for it everywhere, and you can find nothing but the Kadets. And so you wax wonderfully optimistic about them, you dress them up, you want to force them to play a historical role which they cannot, will not, do not want to play.

I have not had an answer to my central question, though I have asked it many times. You have no prognosis for revolution. Your policy lacks perspective.

And that is why your attitude towards the bourgeois parties is formulated in words which the congress would do well to remember: "As each case arises." The proletariat, according to you, does not conduct a systematic struggle to gain influence over the popular masses; it does not check every one of its tactical steps from the viewpoint of a single guiding idea: that of rallying the oppressed working people, of becoming their herald and their leader; no, it conducts its policy "as each case arises." It loses the possibility of giving up temporary gains for the sake of more profound victories; it weighs and measures everything empirically, it plans all its political actions "as each case arises." Why must I prefer blondes to brunettes? Comrade Plekhanov has asked. Well, I must admit that if we are talking about blondes and brunettes, that's a matter of what the Germans call *Privatsache*, of free personal choice. I do not suppose that even Aleksinsky, well known as he is for his high principles, will insist that the congress must arrive at a "unity of ideas" about the color of their hair, as a precondition for unity of action. (Applause).*

* "The London Congress of the Russian Social-Democratic Revolutionary Party." Full text of the debates. Published by the Central Committee, 1909, p. 295.

CHAPTER 24

The Proletariat
and the Russian Revolution

On the Menshevist Theory
of the Russian Revolution*

Every good European, and, not least, every European socialist thinks of Russia as the land of the unexpected, for the simple reason that results always seem unexpected when you do not know their causes. French travelers in the eighteenth century reported that the Russians heated their streets with bonfires. European socialists in the twentieth century naturally disbelieved this, but nevertheless considered the Russian climate too severe to admit of the development of social democracy. The opposite also is true. A certain French novelist, I forget whether it was Eugène Sue or Dumas *père*, makes his hero drink tea in Russia, *sous l'ombre d'une kljukwa*, in the shadow of a kliukva, kliukva being the Russian word for cranberry. Of course any educated European today knows that for a man and a samovar to find

* A. Tscherewanin. *Das Proletariat und die russische Revolution*. [Stutt-gart: Verlag Dietz, 1908.]

(284)

room under a cranberry plant is almost as difficult as it is for a camel to pass through the eye of a needle. But the colossal events of the Russian revolution, by their utter unexpectedness, have driven many Western socialists to believe that the Russian climate, so recently in need of street heating, has suddenly become capable of transforming frail arctic plants into giant baobabs. And this is why, when the first mighty impact of the revolution was crushed by the military forces of Tsarism, many hastened to cross from the shadow of the kliukva into the shadow of disillusionment.

Fortunately the Russian revolution has provoked in the socialist West a genuine desire to make sense of Russian society. I would find it hard, however, to say which is more valuable—this intellectual interest or the third state Duma, which, after all, is also a gift of the revolution, at least in the sense that a dog's corpse washed up by the tide on a sandbank is a "gift" of the ocean.

Thanks are certainly due to the publishing house of Dietz in Stuttgart which has produced three volumes to meet the interest aroused by the revolution.* We must point out, however, that the three books are by no means of equal value. Maslow's work is a major study of Russia's agrarian relations. Its scientific value is so great that the author may be forgiven, not only the extreme formal weakness of the book, but even his far from sound version of Marx's theory of land rent. Paschitnow's book, while in no sense an independent study, offers a certain amount of useful material concerning the Russian worker's position—in the factory or mine, at home, in hospital, to some extent in his trade union, but not within the country's social organism. But then the author never set out to do this. Consequently his work is of very little help in understanding the revolutionary role of the Russian proletariat.

* Peter Maslow. *Die Agrarfrage in Russland.* Paschitnow. *Lage der arbeitenden Klasse in Russland.* A. Tscherewanin. *Das Proletariat und die russische Revolution.*

That is the important question which Tscherewanin's brochure, recently published in a German translation, attempts to illuminate; and it is this brochure which we wish to discuss in the following pages.

I

Tscherewanin begins by analyzing the general causes of the revolution. He sees it as the product of a clash between the irresistible demands of the country's capitalist development and the feudal forms of the Russian state and its laws. "The inexorable logic of economic development," he writes, "created a situation where all strata of the population, with the exception of the feudal nobility, were finally compelled to adopt a position hostile to the government." (p. 10.)

In this line-up of oppositional and revolutionary forces "the proletariat undoubtedly played a central role." (*Ibid.*) But the proletariat only had significance as part of the oppositional whole. It could be effective within the historical framework of a general struggle for the creation of the new bourgeois society only to the extent that it was supported by the bourgeois opposition, or rather to the extent that the proletariat itself, by its revolutionary actions, supported the bourgeois opposition. And vice versa: each time that the proletariat by its immoderate actions (or, if you wish, its historically premature actions), isolated itself from bourgeois democracy, it suffered defeats and slowed down the development of the revolution. That is the substance of Tscherewanin's historical theory.*

Throughout the whole brochure he is an indefatigable opponent of any overestimation of the Russian proletariat's revolutionary strength or political role.

He analyzes the great drama of January 9 and arrives at the

* F. Dan develops the same notion in his recent article in No. 2 of *Neue Ziet*. But his conclusions, at any rate those relating to the past, are less bold than Tscherewanin's.

following conclusion: "Trotsky is wrong when he writes that the workers marched to the Winter Palace on January 9, not with humble pleas, but with a demand." (p. 27.) He accuses the party organization of overestimating the maturity shown by the Petersburg proletariat in February 1905 in the matter of Senator Shidlovsky's commission, when the elected representatives of the masses demanded public and legal guarantees for themselves and, on being refused them, walked out, and when the workers responded to the arrest of their representatives by going on strike. He gives a brief historical sketch of the great October strike and formulates his conclusions as follows: "We have seen the elements that went into the making of the October strike and the role played in it by the bourgeoisie and the intelligentsia. We have clearly established that the proletariat did not deal this serious and possibly mortal blow to absolutism by itself nor by its own forces alone." (p. 56.) After the issuing of the manifesto of October 17 the whole of bourgeois society wanted the restoration of calm. Therefore it was "madness" on the part of the proletariat to choose the path of revolutionary insurrection. The proletariat's energies should have been channeled into elections to the Duma.

Tscherewanin attacks those who pointed out that, at that moment, the Duma was only a promise and that no one knew when and how the elections would take place or whether they would take place at all. Quoting an article written by me on the day when the manifesto was issued, he says: "The victory just won was quite wrongly minimized in *Izvestia*, the paper of the Soviet Workers' Deputies, which wrote soon after the manifesto: 'A constitution has been given, but the autocracy remains. Everything has been given, and nothing has been given.'"

Thereafter, according to Tscherewanin, things went from bad to worse. Instead of supporting the congress of the *zemtsy*, which was demanding universal franchise for elections to the Duma, the proletariat provoked a brutal break with liberalism and bourgeois democracy by choosing two new and "doubtful" allies: the peasantry and the army. The introduction of the eight-hour day by revolutionary means, the November strike as a response to martial law in Poland—mistake followed mistake, and the path led to the fatal debacle of December, which, in turn, together with further errors on the part of the social-democrats, prepared the ground for the collapse of the first Duma and the triumph of counter-revolution.

Such is Tscherewanin's view of history. The German translator has done everything in his power to tone down the author's accusations and diatribes, but even in this softened form Tscherewanin's work reads far more like an indictment of the proletariat's revolutionary crimes than a proper description of the proletariat's revolutionary role.

Tscherewanin replaces any materialist analysis of social relations by a formalist deduction along the following lines: our revolution is a bourgeois revolution; a victorious bourgeois revolution must transfer power to the bourgeoisie; the proletariat must collaborate in the bourgeois revolution; consequently it must collaborate in transferring power into the hands of the bourgeoisie; hence the idea of power being taken over by the proletariat is incompatible with good tactics by the proletariat in an era of bourgeois revolution; the actual tactics pursued by the proletariat led it into a struggle for state power, and were therefore bad.

Such a handsome logical construction, which the scholasticists called, I believe, *sorites*, leaves aside the most important question; the question of the actual inner social forces and class mechanism of a bourgeois revolution. We know the classical example. In the French Revolution the conditions for the hegemony of a capitalist bourgeoisie were prepared by the terrorist dictatorship of the victorious sans-culottes. This happened at a time when the main mass of the urban population was composed of a petty bourgeoisie of craftsmen and shopkeepers. This mass was led by the Jacobins. In Russia today the main mass of the urban populations is composed of the industrial proletariat. Is this analogy enough to suggest a potential historical situation in which the victory of a "bourgeois" revolution is rendered possible only by the proletariat gaining revolutionary power? Or does the revolution therefore stop being a bourgeois one? Yes and no. The answer does not depend on formal definitions but on the further progress of events. If the proletariat is overthrown by a coalition of bourgeois classes, including the peasantry whom the proletariat itself has liberated, then the revolution will retain its limited bourgeois character. But if the proletariat succeeds in using all means to achieve its own political hegemony and thereby breaks out of the national confines of the Russian revolution, then that revolution could become the prologue to a world socialist revolution.

The question as to what stage the Russian revolution will reach can, of course, be answered only conditionally. But one thing is unconditional and certain: the mere definition of the Russian revolution as a bourgeois revolution says nothing about its inner development, and certainly does not mean that the proletariat must adapt its tactics to bourgeois democracy because the latter is the only legitimate claimant to state power.

II

First of all: what kind of a political body are they, these "bourgeois democrats"? In speaking of the liberals, people usually identify them with the popular masses, that is, above all with the peasantry. But in reality, and therein lies the root of the matter, such an identification has not occurred and cannot occur.

The Kadets—the party which has set the tone in liberal circles during the last two years—were formed in 1905 by the amalgamation of the *zemstvo* constitutionalists and the "League of Liberation." The liberal *fronde* of the *zemtsy* was the expression, on the one hand, of the landowners' envy and discontent with the monstrous industrial protectionism of the state and, on the other, of the opposition of the more progressive landowners, who saw that the barbaric backwardness of Russia's agrarian relations was an obstacle to their putting their economy on a cap-

italist footing. The League of Liberation united under its banner
those sections of the intelligentsia who were prevented by their
"decent" social standing and their resulting prosperity from
taking the revolutionary path. Many of these gentlemen had
previously gone through the school of "legal" Marxism. The
zemstvo opposition was always distinguished for its cowardly
impotence, and our Most August dimwit was merely stating a
bitter truth when, in 1894, he called their political aspirations
"senseless dreams." But, on the other hand, neither were the
members of the privileged intelligentsia, who carry no social
weight of their own and are directly or indirectly dependent on
the state, on state-protected large capital or on liberal landowners, capable of forming an even moderately impressive political
opposition.

Thus the Kadet party was a combination of the *zemtsy's* oppositional impotence with the all around impotence of the diploma-carrying intelligentsia. The real face of *zemtsy* liberalism was
fully revealed by the end of 1905 when the landowners, startled
by the agrarian disorders, swung sharply around to support the
old regime. The liberal intelligentsia was forced, with tears in its
eyes, to forsake the country estate where, when all is said and
done, it had been no more than a foster child and to seek ac-
knowledgment in its historic home—the city. If we sum up the
results of the three electoral campaigns, we see that Petersburg
and Moscow, with her special population breakdowns, were the
Kadets' citadels. Yet Russian liberalism, as we can see from all its
pathetic behavior, never succeeded in overcoming its total insignificance. Why? The explanation is not to be sought in the revolutionary excesses of the proletariat but in far deeper historical
causes.

The social basis of bourgeois democracy and the driving
force of the European revolution was the third estate whose
nucleus was composed of the urban petty bourgeoisie—craftsmen, merchants, and intellectuals. The second half of the nineteenth century was a period of its complete decay. Capitalist

development not only crushed artisanal democracy in the West, but also prevented it from ever forming in the East.

When European capital arrived in the Russia of the cottage craftsman, it gave him no time to separate himself from the peasant or to become an urban artisan, but put him directly into the bondage of the factory. At the same time it transformed Russia's old, archaic towns—including Moscow, the "large village"—into centers of modern industry. The proletariat, without any artisanal past, without craft traditions or prejudices, found itself concentrated in vast masses from the start. In all the principal branches of industry large capital effortlessly snatched the ground from under the feet of medium and small capital. Petersburg and Moscow cannot be compared with the Berlin or Vienna of 1848, still less with the Paris of 1789, which had not even dreamed of railways or the telegraph and regarded a workshop employing 300 workers as the largest conceivable enterprise. But it is very noticeable that Russian industry, so far as its degree of concentration is concerned, can not only bear comparison with other European states but actually leaves them all far behind. The small table which follows serves to illustrate this:

	GERMAN EMPIRE,[1] CENSUS OF 1895		AUSTRIAN EMPIRE,[2] CENSUS OF 1902		RUSSIA,[3] CENSUS OF 1902	
	No. of enterprises	*No. of workers*	*No. of enterprises*	*No. of workers*	*No. of enterprises*	*No. of workers*
Enterprises employing 51–1,000 workers	18,698	2,595,536	6,334	993,000	6,334	1,202,800
Enterprises employing more than 1,000 workers	255	448,731	115	179,876	458	1,155,000

[1] *Remeslo i torgovlya v Germanskoy imperii*, p. 42.
[2] Austrian statistical yearbook, 1907, p. 229.
[3] A. V. Polezhayev. *Uchyot chislennisti i sostava rabochikh v Rossii.* (Petersburg), p. 46 ff.

We have not included enterprises employing less than 50 workers because the data available for these in Russia are very incomplete. But even these two rows of figures show the colossal pre-eminence of Russian over Austrian industry from the point of view of concentration of production. Whereas the total number of medium- and large-sized enterprises happens, purely accidentally, to be the same (6,334), that of giant-size enterprises (more than 1,000 workers) is four times higher in Russia than in Austria. We get a similar result if, instead of backward Austria, we base the comparison on such advanced capitalist countries as Germany and Belgium. Germany has 255 gigantic enterprises with a total number of workers slightly below 1 million; Russia has 458 with a total number of workers exceeding 1 million. The same point is vividly illuminated by comparing the profits derived from different categories of commercial and industrial enterprises in Russia.

	No. of enterprises	*Profits in 1,000,000 roubles*
Profits from 1,000 to 2,000 roubles	37,000 or 44.5 per cent	56 or 8.6 per cent
Profits of over 50,000 roubles	1,400 or 1.7 per cent	291 or 45.0 per cent

In other words, roughly one-half of all enterprises receives less than one-tenth of total profits, whereas one-sixtieth of all enterprises accounts for almost half of all surplus value.

These few figures bear eloquent testimony to the fact that the late arrival of capitalism in Russia has rendered the contradictions between the capitalists and the workers—those twin poles of bourgeois society—exceptionally acute. Workers in Russia occupy the place which, at the corresponding period, was occupied in Western Europe by artisanal and commercial democracy emerging from corporations and guilds—not only in the public economy, not only in the composition of the urban population, but also in the economics of revolutionary struggle.

In Russia there is no trace of that sturdy petty bourgeoisie which, hand in hand with the young proletariat that had not yet had time to form itself as a class, took the Bastilles of feudalism by assault.

It is true that the petty bourgeoisie has always and everywhere been politically a somewhat amorphous body; yet in its best historical days it developed tremendous political activity. But when, as in Russia, one finds a hopelessly retarded bourgeois-democratic intelligentsia suspended over an abyss of class contradictions, caught in a web of feudal traditions and academic prejudices, born to the accompaniment of socialist imprecations, not daring even to think of influencing the workers, and incapable of placing itself, instead of the proletariat, at the head of the peasantry by fighting the interests of the landlords—then this miserable democracy-without-a-backbone becomes the Kadet party.

Indeed, without giving way to feelings of national pride, we can assert that the brief history of Russian liberalism was unparalleled in the history of the bourgeois countries for its intrinsic shoddiness and concentrated imbecility. But, of course, it cannot be denied that no previous revolution ever absorbed so much popular energy while yielding such negligible objective results. From whatever angle we consider the events, the intimate connection between the utter insignificance of the bourgeois-democrats and the revolution's lack of results leaps to the eye. The connection is undeniable, but it does not mean that our conclusions have to be negative. The Russian revolution's lack of results is only the obverse of its profound and enduring quality.

Our revolution is a bourgeois revolution in terms of the immediate problems which engendered it; but, because of the extreme class differentiation of our trading and industrial population, there exists no bourgeois class that can place itself at the head of the popular masses and combine its social weight and political experience with their revolutionary energy. The oppressed workers and the peasant masses must learn by themselves, in the harsh school of merciless conflicts and cruel defeats, to create the political and organizational conditions necessary for their own victory. No other way is open to them.

III

When it took over the industrial functions of an artisanal democracy, the Russian proletariat also had to take over its tasks, but not its methods or its means.

Bourgeois democracy has at its service the entire apparatus of official public institutions—the schools and universities, municipal establishments, the press, the theater. That this is an immense advantage was demonstrated by the fact that even our rickety liberalism found itself automatically organized and equipped when the moment came for those actions of which it proved capable: namely, resolutions, petitions and electioneering.

The proletariat received no cultural or political heritage from bourgeois society other than the internal cohesion which results from the production process itself. On this basis it had to create its political organization in the gunfire and smoke of revolutionary battles. It came out of this difficulty with flying colors: the period of the maximum tension of its revolutionary energy, the end of 1905, was at the same time the period of the creation of a remarkable class organization, the Soviet of Workers' Deputies. But that was only the smaller half of the problem. The workers had to defeat, not only their own disorganization, but also the organized force of the enemy.

The general strike emerged as the method of revolutionary struggle most appropriate to the proletariat. Despite its relatively small numbers, the Russian proletariat controls the centralized machine of state power and the colossal mass of the country's concentrated productive forces. This is what made the striking proletariat so powerful that absolutism itself, in

October 1905, was forced to stand to attention before it. Soon after, however, it was seen that a general strike only poses the problem of revolution, but does not solve it.

Revolution is first and foremost a struggle for state power. But a strike, as analysis suggests and as events have shown, is a revolutionary means of exerting pressure on the existing power. That, by the way, is precisely why the Kadet liberals, whose demands never went beyond the granting of a constitution, sanctioned the general strike as a means of struggle; but they did so only momentarily and in retrospect, at a moment when the proletariat had already recognized the limitations of the strike and realized that its limits must inevitably be transcended.

The hegemony of the town over the countryside, of industry over agriculture, and at the same time the modern nature of Russian industry, the absence of a strong petty bourgeoisie for whom the workers might have acted as auxiliary troops, all these factors made the Russian proletariat into the principal revolutionary force and confronted it with the problem of capturing state power. The scholasticists who regard themselves as Marxists only because they look at the world through the paper on which Marx's works are printed can quote as many texts as they like to prove the "untimeliness" of the political hegemony of the proletariat: the Russian working class, the class which, under the leadership of a purely class organization, fought a duel with absolutism at the end of 1905 while large capital and the intelligentsia acted as seconds on either side, the Russian proletariat, by virtue of its whole revolutionary development, was brought face to face with the problem of capturing state power. A confrontation between the proletariat and the army became unavoidable. The result of the confrontation depended on the behavior of the army, and the behavior of the army, on its composition.

The political role of the workers in Russia is infinitely greater than their number. This was shown by events and, later, by the elections to the second Duma. The workers carried their class advantages—technical expertise, intelligence, a capacity for concerted action—with them into the barracks.

In all revolutionary movements within the army the principal part has been played by skilled soldiers—gunners and sappers—whose home is the town, the factory suburb. In naval risings, engine crews were always to the fore; these proletarians, even though they represented a minority within the ship's crew as a whole, were able to control it because they controlled the engine, the warship's heart. But the colossal numerical preponderance of the peasantry is bound to tell in the army, which is based on universal conscription. The army mechanically overcomes the muzhik's lack of productive coordination, and transforms his chief political vice, his passivity, into a major advantage for itself. In most of its actions in 1905 the proletariat alternated between ignoring the passivity of the countryside and relying on its instinctive discontent. But when the struggle for state power became the immediate issue, the solution was found to lie in the hands of the armed muzhik, the nucleus of the Russian infantry. The Russian proletariat in December 1905 foundered, not on its own mistakes, but on a more real force: the bayonets of the peasant army.

I V

This short analysis largely relieves us of the necessity to answer Tscherewanin's indictment point by point. Behind a mass of separate actions, statements, and "mistakes," Tscherewanin fails to see *the proletariat itself*, its social relations and revolutionary growth. If he rejects the proposition that on January 9 the workers came out, not to plead, but to demand, it is because he cannot see the substance of the event behind its outward form. When he is so anxious to emphasize the role of the intelligentsia in the October strike, it in no way alters the fact that it was the proletariat, by its revolutionary action, that transformed the left democrats from the *zemtsy's* appendage into a contemporary auxiliary unit of the revolution, forced a purely proletarian method of struggle—the general strike—upon them and made them dependent on a purely proletarian organization, the Soviet of Deputies.

According to Tscherewanin, the proletariat after the manifesto should have concentrated all its energies on elections to the Duma. But, remember, at that time there were no elections; no one knew when or how they would be held, and no guarantee was offered that they would be held at all.

What did exist side by side with the manifesto of October 1905 was the great all-Russian pogrom. How could anyone be confident that, instead of a Duma, there might have been just another pogrom? What could the proletariat have done under such circumstances, having once broken down the old barriers of the police state? Only what it in fact did. Quite naturally, it seized new positions and dug itself into them: it demolished censorship, created a revolutionary press, won the freedom of assembly, protected the population against hooligans (whether uniformed or in rags), built up militant trade unions, rallied around its class representative body, established links with the revolutionary peasantry and the army. At a time when the liberal public was babbling about the army "remaining outside politics," the social democrats tirelessly carried on agitation in the barracks. Were they right or not?

At a time when the November congress of the *zemtsy* (which Tscherewanin believes in retrospect we should have supported) rushed headlong towards the right at the first news of the Sevastopol rising and regained its equanimity only on being informed that the rising was already crushed, the Soviet of Deputies, by contrast, enthusiastically saluted the insurgents. Was it right or not? Where, along what road, were guarantees of victory to be sought: in the peace of mind of the *zemtsy*, or in the fraternal union of the proletariat with the armed forces?

Of course the program of land confiscation proposed by the workers pushed the landowners over to the right. But then it also pushed the peasants over to the left. Of course the ruthless industrial struggle thrust the capitalists back into the camp of order. But then it also aroused the political consciousness of the most ignorant and intimidated among the workers. Of course agitation within the armed forces brought the inevitable conflict closer. But what else was there to be done? Should Trepov have been left in sole command of the soldiers—those same soldiers who, even during the honeymoon of the new freedoms, had abetted the pogromists and fired on workers? Tscherewanin himself senses that nothing could have been done other than what was in fact done.

"The tactics were wrong all the way through," he says in concluding one of his analyses, and immediately adds: "Suppose even that they were unavoidable and that no other tactics were possible at that moment. But this is quite immaterial, and does not alter the final objective conclusion that the social-democrats' tactics were wrong all the way through." (p. 92.) Tscherewanin constructs his tactics as Spinoza did his ethics, that is to say, geometrically. He admits that under the existing conditions there was no room for the application of his tactics—and that, of course, is precisely why men who thought like him played no role whatever in the revolution. But what is there to be said of "realistic" tactics whose only shortcoming is that they cannot be applied? Let us say of them, in Luther's words: "Theology is concerned with life, and should not consist of mere meditation and reflection on the affairs of God according to the laws of reason. . . .

"Every art, whether it be intended for domestic usage or for the world, is rendered null and worthless (*ist verloren und taugt nichts*) if it becomes mere speculation and cannot be applied in practice."

CHAPTER 25

◇◇◇◇◇◇◇◇◇◇◇

Our Differences*

The Year 1905, the Reaction,
and Revolutionary Prospects

"You are perfectly right in saying," Lassalle wrote to Marx in 1854, at a time of extreme world reaction, "that the present

* This article was published in the Polish journal *Przeglad social-demokratyczny* in the period of blackest reaction in Russia, almost a total standstill in the working-class movement, and the Mensheviks' renegade disavowal of the revolution and its methods.

The article also criticizes the official position of Bolshevism at that time on the question of the revolution's character and the proletariat's tasks within it.

The criticisms addressed to Menshevism remain valid to this day: Russian Menshevism is reaping the fruits of its fatal errors in the years 1903–1905, its formative years; world Menshevism is today repeating the mistakes of Russian Menshevism.

The critique of the Bolshevik position of the time (democratic dictatorship of the proletariat and peasantry) is today of historic interest only. Past differences have long been resolved.

In the first edition of this book the chapter was printed in an incomplete form because neither the full Russian manuscript nor the Polish review in which the article was printed were available at that time. In the present edition all gaps have been filled by following the Polish text.

(299)

apathy cannot be overcome by theoretical means. I would go so far in extrapolating this thought as to say that apathy has *never* been overcome by purely theoretical means, that is, the theoretical overcoming of political apathy produced disciples, sects or *unsuccessful* practical movements, but has never yet produced either a real world movement or a universal mass movement of minds. The masses are drawn into the current of a movement, not only practically but also intellectually, by the dynamic force of real events alone."

Opportunism cannot understand this. It may seem paradoxical to say that the principal psychological feature of opportunism is its *inability to wait*. But that is undoubtedly true. In periods when friendly and hostile social forces, by virtue of their antagonism and their interaction, create a total political standstill; when the molecular process of economic growth, by intensifying the contradictions, not only fails to disturb the political balance but actually strengthens it and, as it were, makes it permanent—in such periods opportunism, devoured by impatience, looks around for "new" ways and means of putting into effect what history is not yet ready for in practice. Tired of its own inadequacy and unreliability, it goes in search of "allies." It hurls itself avidly upon the dung-heap of liberalism. It implores it, it appeals to it, it invents special formulae for how it could act. In reply, liberalism merely contaminates it with its own political putrefaction. Opportunism then begins to pick out isolated pearls of democracy from the dung-heap. It needs allies. It rushes from place to place, grabbing possible allies by their coattails. It harangues its own adherents, admonishing them to be considerate towards all potential allies. "Tact, more tact, still more tact!" It is gripped by a special disease, the mania of caution in respect to liberalism, the sickness of tact; and, driven berserk by its sickness, it attacks and wounds its own party.

Opportunism builds on relations which are not yet ripe. It wants immediate "success." When oppositional allies fail to be of use, it rushes to the government, pleading, arguing, threatening. In the end it finds a place for itself inside the government (this is called ministerialism), achieving nothing thereby except to show that history cannot be overtaken by administrative means any more than it can by theory.

Opportunism does not know how to wait. And that is precisely why great events always catch it unawares. They knock it off its feet, whiz it around like a chip of wood in a whirlpool and sweep it forward, knocking its head now against one bank, now against the other. It tries to resist, but in vain. Then it submits to its fate, pretends to be happy, waves its arms to show that it is swimming, and shouts louder than anyone else. And when the hurricane has passed, it creeps ashore, shakes itself, complains of headache and painful limbs and, in the wretched hangover following its euphoria, spares no harsh words for revolutionary "dreamers."

I

In a recently published book entitled *The Present Situation and the Possible Future*, the well-known Moscow Menshevik Cherevanin writes: "In November and December (1905) it was not even Bolshevist tactics that triumphed, but those of Parvus and Trotsky." (p. 200.) Martynov, the semi-official philosopher of Menshevist tactics writing in the last issue of the *Golos Sozial-Demokrata* speaks of "the fantastic theory of Parvus and Trotsky . . . which enjoyed momentary success among us in the October days, in the period of the Soviet of Workers' Deputies." (No. 4–5, p. 17.) The inconsistency in the months referred to is due simply to the fact that Martynov is not too sure of the chronology of events and by "October days" means the months of October, November, and December. Philosophers who deal with large historical epochs are well-known to be careless about dates. But what *was* the "fantastic theory"?

Cherevanin speaks of "Parvus' and Trotsky's clearly unreasonable view according to which Russia could be carried from a semi-savage state straight into socialism." (p. 177.) Cherevanin has no difficulty in exposing the unreasonableness of this view in a few pages. What is the Russian proletariat? By the most generous estimate, it represents 27.6 per cent of the population. But agricultural laborers cannot be included in the revolutionary balance sheet because they are too ignorant and backward, servants and day laborers because they are scattered and unorganized; and so we are left with a mere 3.2 million souls of the trading and industrial proletariat. "Thus 5 to 11 per cent of the entire population is the basis on which Trotsky and Parvus meant to build a socialist system! And all the while they naïvely believed that they were applying Marxism to reality." (p. 179.) Cherevanin wins hands down, of that there can be no doubt. The trouble is only that he has borrowed his image of the men he opposes from those newspaper hacks, mostly renegades of Marxism, who insist on painting the devil of permanent revolution as luridly and crudely as possible.

The question for us was never whether Russia can be "carried straight into socialism." Even to pose the question in such a way demands a very special type of brain.

The question for us concerned the *class dynamics* of the Russian revolution—not the "permanent revolution," not the "socialist revolution," but the one that is going on in Russia at the present time.

These quotations are in themselves enough to show how opportunists write history in a state of revolutionary hangover. But perhaps it is still more interesting to show how they *make* history. We cannot, alas, say anything about Cherevanin in this context, as we have not the least idea of the role he played in the events of the revolution. But we do have documentary evidence of the views (if not the activities) of some of his confederates. "You ask," one of them wrote, "what our demands in the Constituent Assembly are going to be? Our clear and categorical reply is this: we shall demand, not 'socialization,' but socialism, not equal shares of the land, but public ownership of *all* (italics in the original) means of production." True, "vulgar Marxists" might object that "a socialist revolution in Russia is technically impossible in the near future." But the author triumphantly demolishes their objections and concludes: "The social-democrats alone . . . have boldly raised the slogan of permanent revolution at the present time, they alone will lead the masses to the last and decisive victory." Who wrote this? A distinguished Menshevik.

It is true that Martynov tells us of the "momentary success" of the views of Parvus and Trotsky in the "October days." But then the same Martynov talks about "the warning voice of the Mensheviks, whose heads were not turned so quickly (?) and who continued steadfastly (steadfastly!), sometimes against the tide of events, to preserve the legacy of Russian social democracy." (*Golos Sozial-Demokrata*, No. 4–5, p. 16.) Such valor is beyond praise, who shall deny it? And yet, and yet the article we have quoted, which vulgarizes the idea of permanent revolution, was written by a Menshevik (cf. *Nachalo*, Nos. 7 and 11, leading articles). Perhaps this Menshevik who suffered such a violent attack of revolutionary vertigo was not a "reliable," not a "real" Menshevik? But no. It was the St. Peter of Menshevism, its very cornerstone. It was Comrade Martynov.

Here you have a page from a textbook on the political physiology of opportunism. Is it to be wondered at if men who, at the most important and responsible moment in our history lost every notion of their fundamental premises, are today raging against the "unreasonableness" of the unrepentant and . . . against the insanity of revolution itself?

II

Social democracy was born of revolution and is heading towards revolution. All its tactics, in periods of so-called peaceful devel-

opment, can be ultimately reduced to the policy of accumulating
forces which can only be fully realized in periods of open revolutionary conflict. "Normal," "peaceful" periods are those in
which the ruling classes impose on the proletariat their own
legality and their forms of political resistance (courts of law,
police-supervised political assemblies, parliamentarianism). Revolutionary periods are those in which the proletariat pours its
political indignation into the molds best suited to express its
revolutionary nature (free assemblies, free press, general strikes,
insurrection). "But in the fever of revolution (!), when revolutionary aims seem so close to fulfillment, it is difficult for sensible
Menshevik tactics to find the right path." (Cherevanin, p. 209.)
Social-democratic tactics which cannot be applied because of the
"fever of revolution"? The fever of revolution, what terminol-
ogy! In the end it turns out that "sensible Menshevik tactics"
consisted in "demanding a temporary concerted effort" with the
Kadet party—and this policy, which would, of course, have
saved the revolution, was prevented by the madness of revolution.

When you re-read the correspondence between the great
founders of Marxism, as they mounted guard so vigilantly in
their watchtowers—one, the youngest, in Berlin, the other two,
the stronger ones, in London, the center of world capitalism—
and intently scanned the political horizon, noting every phenomenon that might indicate the approach of revolution; when you
re-read those letters and hear bubbling in them the lava of revolution on the point of eruption; when you breathe that atmosphere of an impatient and yet tireless anticipation of revolution
—then you begin to hate the cruel dialectic of history which,
for its momentary purpose, associates with Marxism these barren
reasoners who lack both theoretical and psychological insight,
and who set their tactical wisdom against the "fever" of revolution!

Lassalle wrote to Marx in 1859:

The instinct of the masses in revolution is generally much surer than the good sense of intellectuals. . . . It is precisely the masses' lack of education that protects them from the underwater reefs of "sensible" behavior. . . . In the last analysis, revolution can only be made with the help of the masses and their passionate self-sacrifice. But the masses, just because they are "gray," just because they lack education, are quite unable to understand possibilism, and—since an undeveloped mind recognizes only extremes, knows only yea and nay with nothing between the two—because of this they are interested only in extremes, in what is immediate and whole. In the end this is bound to mean that the (sensible and intelligent) book-keepers of revolution, instead of having their outwitted enemies before them and their friends behind them, are, on the contrary, con-fronted only with enemies and have no one behind them at all. Thus what seemed to be higher reason turns out in practice to be the height of foolishness.

Lassalle is perfectly right when he opposes the revolutionary instinct of the uneducated masses to the "sensible and intelli-gent" tactics of the "bookkeepers of revolution." But he does not, of course, take crude instinct as his ultimate criterion. There is a higher one: "the perfect knowledge of the laws of history and movement of peoples. Only realistic wisdom," he con-cludes, "can naturally transcend realistic common sense and rise above it." Realistic wisdom, which in Lassalle is still covered with a film of idealism, appears in Marx as materialist dialectics. Its whole force consists in the fact that it does not oppose its "sensible tactics" to the real movement of the masses, but only formulates, purifies and generalizes that movement. Just because revolution tears the veil of mystery from the true face of the so-cial structure, just because it brings the classes into conflict in the broad political arena, the Marxist politician feels that revolution is his natural element. What, then, are these "sensible" Men-shevik tactics that cannot be implemented, or, worse still, that ascribe their own failure to the "fever" of revolution and delib-erately wait for that fever to pass, that is to say, for the revolu-tionary energy of the masses to be exhausted or mechanically crushed?

III

Plekhanov was the first to have the melancholy courage of viewing the events of the revolution as a series of errors. He has given us an extraordinarily vivid example of how a man can, for twenty-five years, tirelessly defend materialist dialectics against all forms of dogmatist reasoning and rationalist utopianism, only to prove himself a dogmatist-utopian of the purest water in real revolutionary politics. In all his writings of the revolutionary period you will look in vain for the thing that matters most: the immanent mechanism of class relationships, the inner logic of the revolutionary development of the masses.

Instead, Plekhanov indulges in endless variations on the theme of that empty syllogism whose chief premise is that *our revolution is a bourgeois revolution*, and whose conclusion is that *we must show tact in our dealings with the Kadets*. He gives us neither theoretical analysis nor revolutionary policy, only a tedious reasoner's notes in the margin of the great book of events. The highest attainment of his critique is a pedagogical moral: if the Russian social-democrats were Marxists rather than metaphysicians, then our tactics at the end of 1905 would have been entirely different.

Astonishingly, Plekhanov absolutely fails to ask himself how it happened that he preached the purest Marxism for twenty-five years and succeeded only in creating a party of revolutionary "metaphysicians"; or, more important still, how these "metaphysicians" managed to carry the working masses with them in their error, while the "true" Marxists found themselves in the position of solitary reasoners. One of two things must be true: either Plekhanov does not possess the secret of passing from Marxism as a doctrine to revolutionary action, or the "metaphysicians," in conditions of actual revolution, have some mysterious advantage over the "real" Marxists. But if the latter were the case, it would not help if all Russian social-democrats adopted

Plekhanov's tactics, since they would anyway be put in the shade by "metaphysicians" of non-Marxist origin. Plekhanov is careful to avoid this fatal dilemma. But Cherevanin, that honest Sancho Panza of Plekhanov's theorizing, takes the bull by the horns— or, to keep closer to Cervantes, takes the ass by the ears—and manfully proclaims: the fever of revolution leaves no room for true Marxist tactics!

Cherevanin was forced to reach this conclusion because he faced the problem which his master so carefully avoided: the problem of giving a general picture of the progress of the revolution and of the proletariat's role within it. While Plekhanov carefully confined himself to partisan criticisms of specific actions and statements and completely ignored the inner dynamic of events, Cherevanin asked himself: what would our history look like today if it had developed in accordance with "true Menshevik tactics"? He answered the question in a brochure, *The Proletariat in Revolution* (Moscow, 1907), which offers a rare example of the courage of which a limited intelligence can be capable. Then, having corrected every error and rearranged all events in the Menshevist order, so that they were logically bound to lead the proletariat to victory, he asked himself: why, then, did history take the wrong path? And he answered this question in his book *The Present Situation and the Possible Future*, which, once again, proves that the tireless courage of a limited intelligence is sometimes, although not always, capable of revealing part of the truth.

"The revolution's defeat is so profound," Cherevanin says, "that to reduce the causes for it to any errors on the part of the proletariat would be *quite impossible*. Obviously it is not a matter of errors," he reasons, "but of other, deeper causes." (p. 174.) The fatal role in the revolution was played by the return of the big bourgeoisie to its alliance with Tsarism and the nobility. In the process of the unification of these forces into a single counter-revolutionary whole, "the proletariat played a major, *determining* role. And, looking back, we can now say that this was its *inevitable* role." (p. 175, italics mine throughout. L.T.) In his earlier brochure he followed Plekhanov's line and ascribed all our troubles to the Blanquism of the social-democrats. Now his honest, though limited, intelligence rebels against this and he says: "Let us imagine that the proletariat had been under the leadership of true Mensheviks all the time and had acted according to Menshevik principles.* The proletariat's tactics would then have been better, but its fundamental aspirations would not have changed and these would inevitably have led to defeat" (p. 176). In other words, the proletariat as a class would not have been capable of imposing on itself the Menshevist self-denying ordinance. By carrying on its class struggle, it inevitably pushed the bourgeoisie into the camp of reaction. Tactical errors merely "reinforced the proletariat's melancholy (!) role in the revolution, but did not play a decisive part." Thus the "melancholy role of the proletariat" was determined by the nature of its class interests.

A shameful conclusion, tantamount to complete surrender in the face of all the accusations addressed by liberal cretinism to the proletariat's class party! And yet this shameful conclusion contains a particle of the historical truth: collaboration between the proletariat and the bourgeoisie proved impossible, not because the social-democrats' thinking was faulty, but because of the profound dismemberment of the bourgeois "nation." Given its clearly defined social type and its level of political consciousness, the Russian proletariat could give free rein to its revolutionary energy only under the banner of its own interests. But the radicalism of its interests, even the most immediate ones, inevitably pushed the bourgeoisie over to the right.

Cherevanin has understood this. But, he says, that was precisely the cause of our defeat. Very well. But what is the conclusion to be drawn? What was there left for the social-

---

* Please note the method of thinking. The Mensheviks do not express the class struggle of the proletariat, but the proletariat acts in accordance with Menshevik principles. It might be still better to say: let us assume that history behaves in accordance with Cherevanin's principles . . . etc.

democrats to do? Try to deceive the bourgeoisie with algebraic formulae à la Plekhanov? Fold their arms and leave the proletariat to their inevitable fate? Or on the contrary, to recognize that any hope of an enduring alliance with the bourgeoisie was vain, to base its tactics on tapping the full class force of the proletariat to awaken the deepest social interests of the peasant masses, to appeal to the proletarian and peasant army—and seek victory along this path? In the first place, no one could tell in advance whether victory was possible or not and, secondly, regardless of whether victory was probable or not, this was the only path upon which the party of the revolution could enter unless it preferred immediate suicide to the mere possibility of defeat.

That inner logic of the revolution which Cherevanin is only now, in retrospect, beginning to sense, was clear to those whom he now dismisses as "unreasonable" even before the start of the decisive revolutionary events.

We wrote in July 1905:

Initiative and resolution can be expected from the bourgeoisie even less today than in 1848. On the one hand, the obstacles are much greater, and on the other hand the social and political dismemberment of the nation has gone infinitely further. A silent national and world conspiracy of the bourgeoisie is putting terrible obstacles in the path of the harsh process of liberation, trying to stop it from going any further than a deal between the property-owning classes and the representatives of the old order—a deal aimed at holding down the popular masses. Under such conditions, democratic tactics can develop only in the process of struggle against the liberal bourgeoisie. We must be clearly aware of this. Not the fictitious "unity" of the nation against its enemies (Tsarism), but a profound development of the class struggle within the nation: that is our path. . . . Undoubtedly the class struggle alone can do this. And, on the other hand, there can be no doubt that the proletariat, having by its pressure released the bourgeoisie from stagnation, must nevertheless, at a certain moment, enter into conflict with it as with a direct obstacle, however regular and logical the progress of events.

The class which is capable of winning this battle will have to

fight it, and will then have to assume the role of a leading class
—if Russia is to be truly re-born as a democratic state. These conditions, then, lead to the hegemony of the "fourth estate." It goes without saving that the proletariat must fulfill its mission, just as the
bourgeoisie did in its own time, with the help of the peasantry and
the petty bourgeoisie. It must lead the countryside, draw it into the
movement, make it vitally interested in the success of its plans. But,
inevitably, the proletariat remains the leader. This is not the "dictatorship of the proletariat and the peasantry," it is the dictatorship
of the proletariat supported by the peasantry. And the proletariat's
work will not, of course, be confined within the limits of a single
state. The very logic of its position will immediately throw it into
the world arena.*

IV

Despite their differences, the various factions in the party all
agreed on one issue: everyone counted on total victory, that is,
on the revolution seizing state power. Cherevanin now pulls out
his abacus to calculate the respective forces of the revolution
and the reaction and, after adding up the grand total, comes to
the conclusion that "all the revolution's successes contained in
embryo the inevitable defeat to come." (p. 198.) On what does
he base his calculations? On the extent of various strikes, on the
nature and forms of peasant unrest, on figures of elections to the
three Dumas. In other words he deduces the progress and outcome of the battle not directly from economic relations, but
from the forms and episodes of the revolutionary struggle. His
conclusion that the Russian revolution was doomed to failure
from the start is not based on the economic characteristics and
statistics of the classes, but on a study of the active struggle between those classes, their clashes, the open trial of their respective forces.

Of course Cherevanin's method is an ignorant one. But even

* Preface to Lassalle's "*Speech before a Jury.*" A certain international
vagueness of expression can be explained by the fact that the article was
written for legal publication in the "pre-constitutional" era, more precisely in July 1905.

this ignorant method is only possible because the strike spread over the entire country, insurrection flared up, the muzhiks wrecked and burned several provinces and, in the end, elections to the State Duma were held. And how could it be otherwise? You could not, for example, in the case of a revolution in Persia, imagine a Persian Cherevanin predicting to his compatriots the fatal effect of an alliance between Tsarism (a Tsarism strengthened by domestic events) and England's liberal government. And even if such a prophet were to be found, even if, on the grounds of his calculations, he tried to restrain the popular masses from risings which ultimately led to defeat, the Persian revolutionaries would be quite right to advise this sage to take up temporary residence in a lunatic asylum.

The Russian revolution occurred before Cherevanin had a chance to calculate its debit and credit. Revolution was the ready-made arena in which we had to act. We did not create the events, but we had to adapt our tactics to them. Once we were engaged in the struggle, we had, by that very fact, to count on victory. But a revolution is a struggle for state power. Being the party of the revolution, we have the task of making the masses conscious of the need to seize state power.

V

The Mensheviks' view on the Russian revolution was never distinguished by great clarity. Together with the Bolsheviks they spoke of "carrying the revolution to the end," but both sides interpreted this in a purely formal sense, that is, in the sense that we had to achieve our *minimum program*, after which would come an era of "normal" capitalism in a democratic setting. However, "carrying the revolution to the end" presupposed the overthrow of Tsarism and the transfer of state power into the hands of a revolutionary public force. What force? The Mensheviks said: bourgeois democracy. The Bolsheviks said: the proletariat and the peasantry.

But what is the bourgeois democracy of the Mensheviks? It it not a definite, tangible social force having concrete existence, it is an extra-historical category created by journalistic analogy and deduction. Because the revolution has to be "carried to the end," because it is a bourgeois revolution, because, in France, the Revolution was carried to the end by democratic revolutionaries —the Jacobins—therefore the Russian revolution can transfer power only into the hands of a revolutionary bourgeois democracy.

Having thus erected an unshakable algebraic formula of revolution, the Mensheviks then try to insert into it arithmetical values which do not in fact exist. While reproaching others with exaggerating the strength of the proletariat, they themselves placed limitless hopes in the Union of Unions and the Kadet party. Martov greeted the formation of the "people's socialism" group with the greatest enthusiasm, while Martynov picked on the "Folk Teachers" of Kursk. The Mensheviks realized that in a capitalist country where wealth, population, energy, knowledge, public life, and political experience were becoming increasingly concentrated in the towns, the peasantry cannot play a leading revolutionary role. History cannot entrust the muzhik with the task of liberating a bourgeois nation from its bonds. Because of its dispersion, political backwardness, and especially of its deep inner contradictions which cannot be resolved within the framework of a capitalist system, the peasantry can only deal the old order some powerful blows from the rear, by spontaneous risings in the countryside, on the one hand, and by creating discontent within the army on the other.

But in the capitalist towns, those centers of modern history, there has to be a decisive party, based upon the revolutionary urban masses, and capable of utilizing the peasant risings and the discontent in the army to deal a final ruthless blow to the enemy, displacing him from all positions and seizing state power. The Mensheviks were unable to find such a party. That is why their abstract "carrying the revolution to the end" turned, in practice, into "supporting the Kadets *quand même,** while the most logical among them, as we have already seen, came to the conclusion that the climate of revolution is, in any case, too harsh for the exotic tactics of Menshevism.

The contradictions of Menshevism are a caricatured mirror-image of the contradictions of history itself—history which has set our country an immense revolutionary task, but which first swept away bourgeois democracy, as a political and economic force in any part of the world, with the iron broom of large-scale industry.

In contrast to the populists, our Marxists have refused to recognize Russia's "special nature" for so long that they have come, in principle, to equate Russia's political and economic development with that of Western Europe. From this to the most absurd conclusions there is only one step.

When Dan, following Martynov's example, complains that the weakness of the urban bourgeois democracy is "our greatest misfortune," we can really do no more than shrug our shoulders sympathetically. Do these people really understand what they are bewailing? Let us try to explain it to them. They are aggrieved because large capital now reigns in the economic sphere internationally, and has not allowed a strong artisanal and commercial petty bourgeoisie to come into being in Russia. They are aggrieved because the leading role of the petty bourgeoisie in political and economic life has passed to the modern proletariat. The Mensheviks fail to understand that the social causes of the weakness of bourgeois democracy are, at the same time, the source of social democracy's strength and influence. And then they believe this to be the principal cause of the revolution's weakness. We shall not point out how pathetic this attitude is from the viewpoint of international social-democracy as the party of world socialist revolution. It is enough for us that the conditions of our revolution are as they are. The third estate cannot be brought back to life by weeping and wailing. The con-

* In French in the original.

clusion remains that only the proletariat in its class struggle, placing the peasant masses under its revolutionary leadership, can "carry the revolution to the end."

VI

Agreed, say the Bolsheviks. For our revolution to be victorious, the proletariat and the peasantry must fight side by side. But, writes Lenin in the second issue of *Przeglad,* "the coalition of the proletariat and the peasantry which gains victory in a bourgeois revolution is nothing other than the revolutionary-democratic dictatorship of the proletariat and the peasantry." Its purpose will be to democratize economic and political relations within the limits of private ownership of the means of production. Lenin draws a distinction of principle between the socialist dictatorship of the proletariat and the democratic (that is, bourgeois-democratic) dictatorship of the proletariat and the peasantry. He believes that this logical, purely formal operation can act as a perfect protection against the contradiction between the low level of productive forces and the hegemony of the working classes. If we thought that we could achieve a socialist revolution, he says, we would be inviting complete political defeat. But all is saved if the proletariat, having achieved power together with the peasantry, is firmly aware that its dictatorship is merely "democratic." Lenin has never tired of repeating this idea ever since 1904. But that does not make it any more correct.

Because Russia's social conditions are not ripe for a socialist revolution, political power would be the greatest misfortune for the proletariat. So say the Mensheviks. They would be right, says Lenin, if the proletariat were not aware that the point at issue is only a *democratic* revolution. In other words, Lenin believes that the contradiction between the proletariat's class interests and objective conditions will be resolved by the proletariat imposing a political limitation upon itself, and that this self-limitation will be the result of the proletariat's theoretical awareness that the revolution in which it is playing a leading role is a bour-geois revolution. Lenin transfers the objective contradiction into the proletariat's consciousness and resolves it by means of a class asceticism which is rooted, not in religious faith, but in a "scien-tific" schema. It is enough to see this intellectual construct clearly to realize how hopelessly idealistic it is.

I have demonstrated in detail elsewhere* that twenty-four hours after the establishment of a "democratic dictatorship" this idyll of quasi-Marxist asceticism is bound to collapse utterly. Whatever the theoretical auspices under which the proletariat seizes power, it is bound immediately, on the very first day, to be confronted with the problem of unemployment. An explana-tion of the difference between socialist and democratic dictator-ship is not likely to be of much help here. In one form or another (public works, etc.) the proletariat in power will im-mediately have to undertake the maintenance of the unemployed at the state's expense. This in turn will immediately provoke a powerful intensification of the economic struggle and a whole series of strikes.

We saw all this on a small scale at the end of 1905. And the capitalists' reply will be the same as their reply to the demand for the eight-hour day: the shutting down of factories and plants. They will put large padlocks on the gates and will tell themselves: "There is no threat to our property because it has been established that the proletariat is at present in a position of democratic, not socialist, dictatorship." What can the workers' government do when faced with closed factories and plants? It must re-open them and resume production at the government's expense. But is that not the way to socialism? Of course it is. What other way do you suggest?

The objection might be raised that I am imagining a situation in which the dictatorship of the workers is unlimited, whereas in fact what we are talking about is the dictatorship of a coalition between the proletariat and the peasantry. Very well, let us take

* *Our Revolution*, pp. 249–259.

this objection into account. We have just seen how the proletariat, despite the best intentions of its theoreticians, must in practice ignore the logical boundary line which should confine it to a democratic dictatorship. Lenin now proposes that the proletariat's political self-limitation should be supplemented with an objective antisocialist "safeguard" in the form of the muzhik as collaborator or co-dictator. If this means that the peasant party, which shares power with the social-democrats, will not allow the unemployed and the strikers to be maintained at state cost and will oppose the state's opening of factories and plants closed down by the capitalists, then it also means that on the first day of the coalition, that is, long before the fulfillment of its tasks, the proletariat will enter into conflict with the revolutionary government. This conflict can end either in the repression of the workers by the peasant party, or in the removal of that party from power. Neither solution has much to do with a "democratic" dictatorship by a coalition.

The snag is that the Bolsheviks visualize the class struggle of the proletariat only until the moment of the revolution's triumph, after which they see it as temporarily dissolved in the "democratic" coalition, reappearing in its pure form—this time as a direct struggle for socialism—only after the definitive establishment of a republican system. Whereas the Mensheviks, proceeding from the abstract notion that "our revolution is a bourgeois revolution," arrive at the idea that the proletariat must adapt all its tactics to the behavior of the liberal bourgeoisie in order to ensure the transfer of state power to that bourgeoisie, the Bolsheviks proceed from an equally abstract notion—"democratic dictatorship, not socialist dictatorship"—and arrive at the idea of a proletariat in possession of state power imposing a bourgeois-democratic limitation upon itself. It is true that the difference between them in this matter is very considerable: while the anti-revolutionary aspects of Menshevism have already become fully apparent, those of Bolshevism are likely to become a serious threat only in the event of victory.* Of course the fact that both Mensheviks and Bolsheviks invariably talk about the "independent" policy of the proletariat (the former in relation to the liberal bourgeoisie, the latter to the peasantry) in no way alters the fact that both, at different stages of the development of events, become scared of the consequences of the class struggle and hope to limit it by their metaphysical constructs.

VII

The victory of the revolution can transfer power only into the hands of a party that enjoys the support of the armed urban population, that is, of the proletarian militia. Once it achieves power, the social-democratic party will be faced with a profound contradiction which cannot be resolved by naïve references to "democratic dictatorship." "Self-limitation" by a workers' government would mean nothing other than the betrayal of the interests of the unemployed and strikers—more, of the whole proletariat—in the name of the establishment of a republic. The revolutionary authorities will be confronted with the objective problems of socialism, but the solution of these problems will, at a certain stage, be prevented by the country's economic backwardness. There is no way out from this contradiction within the framework of a national revolution.

The workers' government will from the start be faced with the task of uniting its forces with those of the socialist proletariat of Western Europe. Only in this way will its temporary revolutionary hegemony become the prologue to a socialist dictatorship. Thus permanent revolution will become, for the Russian proletariat, a matter of class self-preservation. If the workers' party cannot show sufficient initiative for aggressive revolu-

---

* *Note to the present edition.* This threat, as we know, never materialized because, under the leadership of Comrade Lenin, the Bolsheviks changed their policy line on this most important matter (not without inner struggle) in the spring of 1917, that is, before the seizure of power. (Author)

tionary tactics, if it limits itself to the frugal diet of a dictatorship that is merely national and merely democratic, the united
reactionary forces of Europe will waste no time in making it
clear that a working class, if it happens to be in power, must
throw the whole of its strength into the struggle for a socialist
revolution.

CHAPTER 26

◇◆◇◆◇◆◇◆◇◆◇◆◇

The Struggle for Power*

We have before us a sheet inscribed with a program and a tactical plan for action. It is entitled *The Task of the Russian Proletariat. A Letter to Comrades in Russia,* and it bears the signatures of P. Akselrod, Astrov, A. Martynov, L. Martov and S. Semkovsky.

The *Letter* poses the problem of revolution in a highly generalized way. As the authors stop describing the situation brought about by the war and try to discuss political prospects and tactical conclusions, so their analysis becomes less definite and clear-cut; even the actual terms used become vague and the social definitions ambiguous.

---

* From the newspaper *Nashe Slovo*, Paris, 17 October 1915. We reprint this article, written at a later period, because it offers a concise description of the conditions pertaining to the period of transition from the first revolution of 1905 to the second of 1917. (Author)

(319)

Russia's condition today, as visible to an outsider, appears at first glance to be dominated by two principal moods or outlooks: on the one hand, a concern with national defense (apparently shared by everyone from Romanov to Plekhanov), and, on the other hand, a universal discontent, also exhibited by almost everyone, from the oppositional-bureaucratic *fronde* all the way to the participants in spontaneous street clashes. These two dominant moods create the illusion that the popular revolution to come will grow directly out of the cause of national defense. But the same two moods also largely determine the vagueness with which the question of the "popular revolution" is posed, even when, as in Martov *et al.*, it is formally opposed to the cause of "national defense."

The war and its defeats have created neither the problem of revolution nor the revolutionary forces for resolving it. History does not begin, for us, with the surrender of Warsaw to the Bavarian prince. Both the revolutionary contradictions and the social forces today are the same as those with which we first came properly face to face in 1905—with the very significant changes introduced by the intervening ten years. All that the war has done is to reveal, with mechanical clarity, the objective nonviability of the regime. At the same time it has caused great confusion in the public mind so that "everybody" seems equally imbued with the desire to resist Hindenburg and, at the same time, with detestation of the regime of June 3. But just as the very first steps towards organizing a "people's war" are bound immediately to run into the Tsar's police, making it obvious that the Russia of June 3 is fact and the "people's war" is fiction, so the approach to a "popular revolution" is barred at the very threshold by the attitude of Plekhanov, who, it is true, might also be regarded as fiction together with all his disciples, were he not backed by Kerensky, Milyukov, and Guchkov and nonrevolutionary and antirevolutionary national-democracy and national-liberalism in general.

The *Letter* cannot, of course, ignore the class dismemberment of our nation which is expected to save itself from the consequences of the war and of the present regime by means of revolution. "The nationalists and the Octobrists, the progressives, the Kadets, the industrialists and even part (!) of the radical intelligentsia, screaming in unison that the bureaucracy is incapable of defending the country, demand the mobilization of public forces for national defense." The *Letter* concludes, perfectly rightly, that this attitude, which presupposes "an alliance in the cause of national defense with Russia's present rulers, her bureaucrats, noblemen and generals," is antirevolutionary. And it points out, again quite rightly, that antirevolutionary attitudes are characteristic of "bourgeois patriots of every hue"—as well as of the social-patriots, whom the *Letter* does not mention.

It follows from this that the social-democratic party is not only the most consistent party of revolution, but in fact the only revolutionary party in the land; and that all the other parties are not simply less committed to using revolutionary methods, but are actually nonrevolutionary. In other words, the social-democratic party, in seeing the problem in terms of revolution, is completely isolated in the open political arena, and this despite the "universal discontent." That is the first conclusion about which we must be perfectly clear.

But, of course, parties are not identical with classes. The attitude of a political party and the interests of the social stratum which it represents may not completely overlap, and this may eventually develop into a profound contradiction. Again, the behavior of parties may be influenced by the mood of the popular masses. That is certainly true. But that makes it all the more essential for us, in making our calculations, to take less account of the less permanent and reliable factors, such as party slogans and party tactics, and concentrate on the more enduring historical factors, such as the social structure of the nation, the correlation of class forces, and established trends of development.

Yet the authors of the *Letter* completely avoid these questions. All they tell us about the nature of "popular revolution" in the Russia of 1915 is that it "must be made" by the proletariat and the democracy. We know what the proletariat is, but what is the "democracy"? A political party? It follows from the foregoing that this is not so. The popular masses, then? Which ones? What is meant is doubtless the petty bourgeoisie of industry and trade, the intelligentsia, and the peasantry.

In a series of articles entitled *The Military Crisis and Political Prospects* we have given a general assessment of the potential revolutionary significance of these social forces. Proceeding from the experience of the revolution of 1905, we have studied the question of how the past decade has modified the correlation of forces and asked ourselves whether these modifications are for democracy (bourgeois) or against it. The question is a central one when discussing revolutionary perspectives and the proletariat's tactics. Has bourgeois democracy grown stronger in Russia since 1905, or has it become still weaker than before? The question of our bourgeois democracy has been argued over many times, and anyone who does not yet know the answer to it is bound to be in the dark. We have supplied the answer. *A national bourgeois revolution in Russia is impossible because of the absence of a genuinely revolutionary bourgeois democracy.* The time for national revolutions is past, in Europe anyway, and so is the time for national wars. There is a deep inner connection between the two. We are living in the era of imperialism, which means not only a system of colonial expansion but also a very distinctive type of domestic regime. It is no longer a matter of a bourgeois nation opposing an old regime, but of the proletariat opposing the bourgeois nation.

The role of the artisanal and commercial petty bourgeoisie was negligible even in the revolution of 1905. In the ten years which have elapsed, the social significance of this class has unquestionably diminished still further. Capitalism in Russia has an incomparably more cruel and more drastic way of dealing with the intermediate classes than in the countries of the old economic culture.

The intelligentsia has, of course, expanded numerically, and its economic role has become more significant. But its former illusory "independence" has finally vanished at the same time. The social significance of the intelligentsia is wholly determined by its role in the organization of the capitalist economy and of bourgeois public opinion. Its material connection with capitalism has permeated it through and through with imperialist tendencies. We have already quoted the *Letter* as saying that "even part of the radical intelligentsia . . . demands the mobilization of public forces for national defense." That is quite incorrect. Not "part" of the radical intelligentsia, but the *whole* of it demands such mobilization; and not only the whole of the radical intelligentsia, but also a large, if not the major, part of the socialist intelligentsia. By making the intelligentsia out to be better than it really is we shall hardly swell the ranks of "democracy."

The petty bourgeoisie of industry and trade, then, is weaker than ever, and the intelligentsia has abandoned its revolutionary positions. Urban democracy as a revolutionary factor scarcely deserves a mention. There remains the peasantry. But, so far as we know, neither Akselrod nor Martov ever cherished any exaggerated hopes of the peasantry's independent revolutionary role. Have they reached the conclusion that, in the past ten years of a continually increasing differentiation within the peasant class, this role has become stronger? Such a supposition would be clearly inconsistent both with theoretical considerations and with the whole of our historical experience.

But then, what "democracy" does the *Letter* have in mind? And what does it mean by popular revolution?

The slogan of a Constituent Assembly presupposes a revolutionary situation. Does such a situation exist? Yes, it does. But the question of whether Russia has at last produced a bourgeois democracy able and willing to settle accounts with Tsarism is quite irrelevant to it. On the contrary, if there is something the war has made absolutely clear, it is the absence of a revolutionary democracy in Russia.

The attempt of the Russia of June 3 to settle the revolutionary problem at home by imperialist actions abroad has obviously failed. But that does not mean that the responsible or semi-responsible parties of the June 3 regime will now take to the revolutionary path. What it does mean is that the revolutionary problem revealed by the military catastrophe, while continuing to drive the country's rulers on to the path of imperialism, redoubles the importance of the only revolutionary class in the land.

The bloc of June 3 has been fragmented. Within it there is friction and struggle. That does not mean that the Octobrists and the Kadets are ready to adopt a revolutionary view of power, or ready to storm the fortress of the bureaucracy and the united nobility. But it does mean that the regime's ability to resist a revolutionary attack has undoubtedly, for a certain period, been weakened.

The monarchy and the bureaucracy have been compromised. That does not mean that they will surrender power without a fight. They have made it clear, by the dissolution of the Duma and by the latest ministerial changes, how far they are from giving in. But bureaucratic instability, which is bound to increase, will greatly assist the social-democrats in their work of revolutionary mobilization of the proletariat.

The lowest strata of the urban and rural population will become more and more impoverished, ill-used, discontented, embittered. That does not mean that an independent force of revolutionary democracy will fight side by side with the proletariat. Neither the social material nor the leading personnel for such a force exists. But it does mean that the climate of profound discontent among the lowest strata of the population will assist the revolutionary onslaught of the working class. The less the proletariat reckons on the emergence of a bourgeois democracy, the less it tries to adapt itself to the passivity and narrow-mindedness of the petty bourgeoisie and the peasantry, the more resolute and irreconcilable it becomes, the more clearly it manifests its determination to fight "to the end"—that is to say, until it has seized power—the greater chance it will have of carrying the nonproletarian popular masses with it at the moment of decision. Slogans, such as confiscation of lands, etc., are useless in themselves. And that is even more true of the army, by which state power stands or falls. The mass of the army will be swayed in favor of the revolutionary class only when it is convinced that this class is not merely demonstrating or protesting, but is actually fighting for power and has a chance of winning.

In Russia there exists an objective revolutionary problem—the problem of state power—which the war and its defeats have revealed more sharply than ever. There exists the ever increasing disorganization of the rulers. There exists the growing discontent of the urban and rural masses. But the proletariat alone, and to an incomparably greater degree than in 1905, is the only revolutionary factor that can exploit this situation.

There is one sentence in the *Letter* which seems to touch upon this central element in the entire problem. Russia's social-democratic workers, it says, must place themselves "at the head of the all-national struggle for the overthrow of the monarchy of June 3." We have just explained what "all-national" must mean. But if the words "at the head" do not simply mean that the politically conscious workers must shed their blood more freely than anyone else without understanding exactly what they will achieve by so doing, but that they must assume *political leadership* in a struggle which will, above all, be the struggle of the proletariat itself, then it is clear that *victory in this struggle must transfer power to those who have led it, that is to say, to the social-democratic proletariat.*

Hence what we are talking about is not a "provisional revolutionary government" (an empty formula which history is supposed to fill with a content as yet unknown) but a *revolu-*

tionary workers' government—the seizure of power by the Russian proletariat.

The all-national Constituent Assembly, the republic, the eight-hour working day, the confiscation of landowners' lands, all these are slogans which, together with the slogans of the immediate cessation of the war, the right of nations to self-determination, and a United States of Europe, will play a tremendous part in the agitational work of the social-democratic party. Yet revolution is first and foremost a problem of power—not of the political *form* (Constituent Assembly, republic, European federation), but of the *social content* of power. Under existing conditions, the slogan of a Constituent Assembly or of the confiscation of landowners' lands loses all direct meaning unless it is backed by the proletariat's immediate readiness to fight for the seizure of power. For unless the proletariat seizes power from the monarchy, no one else will do so.

The tempo at which the revolutionary process will unfold is another matter. It depends on many factors, military, political, national, and international. These factors may speed up the development or slow it down, ensure the revolution's victory or lead to another defeat. But, whatever the conditions, the proletariat must see its path clearly and tread it in full consciousness. Above all else, it must be free from illusions. And the worst illusion of the proletariat throughout its history has always been reliance on others.

CHAPTER 27

On the Special Features
of Russia's
Historical Development

A Reply to M. N. Pokrovsky

I

In No. 3 of *Krasnaya Nov'* (May–June 1922) Comrade Pokrovsky has published an article devoted to my book *1905*. This article demonstrates—negatively, alas!—what a complicated business it is trying to apply the methods of historical materialism to living human history, to what clichés even extremely well-informed people like Comrade Pokrovsky are sometimes liable to reduce history.

The doubts aroused by Comrade Pokrovsky's article start with the title: *Is It True that Absolutism in Russia "Existed in Defiance of Social Development?"* The words "existed in defiance of social development" appear in quotation marks, so that it looks as if I asserted that Russian absolutism "existed in defiance of social development" *at all times*, leaving to Comrade Pokrovsky the rewarding and not very difficult task of pointing out that such a statement is against common sense. But in reality my thought, thus misquoted, was that Tsarism, having entered into complete contradiction with the demands of Russia's social development, continued to exist thanks to the power of its organization, the political nullity of the Russian bourgeoisie and its growing fear of the proletariat. Within the spirit and the meaning of the same historical dialectic it is quite right to say —as we have said in the Manifesto of the Communist International—that capitalism today exists, not only in defiance of the demands of historical development, but also of the elementary demands of human life.

Further, while admitting the usefulness of the publication of my book as a whole, Comrade Pokrovsky energetically objects to the re-issue of its introductory chapter *Russia's Social Development and Tsarism*. What was useful and even indispensable, he says, in 1908–09 to a foreign public profoundly ignorant of Russia's past, is of no use whatever to our young people today, who by now have learned a thing or two. Comrade Pokrovsky goes on to say that in this introductory chapter I put forward liberal, "Mliyukovite" (sic) views on Tsarism as an absolutely self-contained state organization not connected with the exploiting classes. "This schema (of Trotsky's) is in the first place incompatible with our outlook, and, in the second place, objectively incorrect." And it is necessary to fight this incorrect and incompatible schema "just as energetically as we are fighting religious prejudice (!!!)." No more and no less.

But if it is true that in my German book I expounded such monstrous anti-Marxist views—unnoticed, one might add, by all the German Marxist reviewers of the book at the time—how could these views have been "useful" and even "indispensable" for a foreign public in 1908–09, however profound its ignorance? Unless we believe, as the popular proverb has it, that "what's good for a Russian is death to a German," it is quite impossible to understand why the liberal fatuities which Comrade Pokrovsky so kindly ascribes to me should have been good for the German workers twelve years ago. Yet even I, conscious as I am of the very special and peculiar nature of Russia's historical development, cannot subscribe to the proverb; still less should Comrade Pokrovsky subscribe to it, since it is clear from his article that he denies the existence of any such special features.

Comrade Pokrovsky makes confusion more confounded when he asserts that my false theory "is already associated with another name in the past, that of Plekhanov who followed the same path (and went much further along it)." (p. 146.) What are we to make of that? True, the article does not indicate precisely where it is that my path has taken me, but since "Plekhanov went much further along it" (the path of liberalism), that is quite enough to prepare the reader for the conclusion, already familiar to us, that my views of Russian history must be fought "just as energetically as we are fighting religious prejudice." What a fearful dream! But mark well that it is a dream, for here we have entered the sphere of theoretical and even chronological fancy. The story seems to be that, first of all, Plekhanov adopted the liberal theory of special historical development (in advocating a common bloc with the Kadets); that I then developed the same liberal theory in 1908 and 1909 (for the benefit of the Germans); that this was not actually harmful but in fact even useful (serve the Germans right); but that, since I have now taken to presenting Plekhanov's views to our young workers, for whom Comrade Pokrovsky is personally responsible, he now practically equates me with the Patriarch Tikhon and offers to fight me "just as energetically" as the latter.

All this is a great muddle, above all chronologically. My introductory chapter on the special features of Russia's historical development was not written for the German public at all, but first appeared in Russian in my book *Our Revolution* published in Petersburg in 1907 (p. 224). I did the preparatory work for this chapter in 1905 and, later, in 1906 (in prison). The direct motive for writing it was a desire to provide historical and theoretical justification for the slogan of the seizure of power by the proletariat as opposed both to the slogan of a bourgeois-democratic republic and to that of democratic government by the proletariat and the peasantry. As we see, Plekhanov's Kadeto-philia does not come into it. In my preface to Marx's *The Paris Commune* (1906) I formulated the view that the experience of the Commune was of direct importance for the Russian working class because, as a result of the whole preceding historical development, it was directly faced with the problem of seizing power.* This line of thought provoked extreme theoretical indignation among many comrades, indeed among the overwhelming majority. That indignation was expressed not only by the Mensheviks but also by Comrades Kamenev and Rozhkov (then a Bolshevik). Their point of view could be summed up as follows: the political hegemony of the proletariat must be preceded by the political hegemony of the bourgeoisie; a bourgeois democratic republic must serve as a long historical school for the proletariat; any attempt to skip this phase is adventurism; if the working class in the West has not seized power, how can the Russian proletariat set itself such a task, etc., etc.

* "Social democracy," the *Preface* states, "must be, and wishes to be, the conscious expression of an objective development. But since, at a certain moment of the revolution, the objective development of the class struggle confronts the (Russian) proletariat with the alternative between assuming the rights and obligations of state power and surrendering its class position, the social-democratic party regards the seizure of state power as its next immediate task. In doing so it by no means ignores the objective processes of development of a deeper nature, processes of growth and concentration of production; but it says that, since the logic of the class struggle, which in the last analysis is based on the progress of economic development, is pressing for the dictatorship of the proletariat before the bourgeoisie has 'completed' its economic mission (it has hardly begun on its historical mission), this means only that history is placing colossally difficult tasks on the proletariat's shoulders. It may even be that the proletariat will be worn out by the struggle and will fall under the weight of its tasks; this may happen. But it cannot refuse those tasks for fear of class disintegration or of the whole country falling into barbarism." (Marx: *The Paris Commune*. 1906 Edition. Preface, pp. X–XI.)

Such were the conclusions we drew 16 years ago from the "special features" of Russia's historical development. And here comes Comrade Pokrovsky, after a delay of a decade and a half, worrying that our views mean . . . a denial of the class struggle. No more and no less!

From the viewpoint of that spurious Marxism which nour-
ishes itself on historical clichés and formal analogies and transforms historical epochs into a logical succession of inflexible
social categories (feudalism, capitalism, socialism, autocracy,
bourgeois republic, dictatorship of the proletariat), the slogan
of the seizure of power by the Russian working class was bound
to appear as a monstrous denial of Marxism. Yet any serious
empirical evaluation of the social forces as manifested in the
years 1903 and 1905 had to show that the Russian working class
struggle for the seizure of power was very much alive.

Is that a special feature of the Russian situation or is it not?
Does it presuppose profound differences between the whole of
Russia's development, and that of other European countries,
or does it not? How did it come about that it was the Russian
proletariat, that is to say, the proletariat of the most backward
(with Comrade Pokrovsky's permission) country in Europe,
which was faced with such a task? And what does Russia's backwardness consist in? Merely in the fact that Russia is belatedly
repeating the history of the countries of Western Europe? But
if that is so, are we entitled to speak of the Russian proletariat
seizing state power? Yet (we venture to remind our critics) that
is precisely what the Russian proletariat has done. What, then,
is the real substance of the problem? Russia's incontestably and
incontrovertibly backward development, under the influence
and pressure of the higher culture of the West, leads not to a
simple repetition of the Western European historical process
but to a set of fundamentally new features which require independent study. That is how the problem was posed—and, whatever Comrade Pokrovsky may say, it is entirely compatible with
our outlook.

It is perfectly true that a few years later (in 1914) Plekhanov
formulated a view of the peculiar features of Russia's historical
development which was very close to the one put forward in
the above-mentioned chapter of the book *Our Revolution*.
Plekhanov quite rightly dismisses the schematic theories of both

the doctrinaire "Westerners" and the Slavophil Narodniks on this subject, and, instead, reduces Russia's "special nature" to the concrete, materially determined peculiarities of her historical development. It is radically false to claim that Plekhanov drew any compromising conclusions from this (in the sense of forming a bloc with the Kadets, etc.), or that he could have done so with any semblance of logic.

The weakness of the Russian bourgeoisie and the illusory nature of Russia's bourgeois democracy undoubtedly represent very important features of Russia's historical development. But it is precisely from this, given all other existing conditions, that the possibility and the historical necessity of the proletariat's seizure of power arises. True, Plekhanov never arrived at this conclusion. But then neither did he draw any conclusion from another of his unquestionably correct propositions, namely: "The Russian revolutionary movement will triumph as a working class movement or it will not triumph at all." If we mix up everything Plekhanov said against the Narodniks and the vulgar Marxists with his Kadetophilia and his patriotism, there will be nothing left of Plekhanov. Yet in reality a good deal is left of Plekhanov, and it does no harm to learn from him now and again.

That the historical life of every society is founded on production; that production gives rise to classes and to groupings of classes; that the state is formed on the foundations of class struggle, and that the state is an organ of class oppression—these notions were not a mystery either for me or for my opponents in 1905. Within these limits the history of Russia obeys the same laws as the history of France, England, or any other country. This does not touch upon the peculiarities of Russia's historical development. Tsarism was the weapon of the property-owning, exploiting classes and in this sense it did not differ from any other state organization, but this does not mean that the correlation of forces between the autocratic power (the monarchy, the bureaucracy, the army, and all the other organs of oppression) on the one hand, and the nobility and bourgeoisie on the other, was the same in Russia as in France, Germany, and England.

The unique nature of our political situation, which finally led to the triumph of the October Revolution before the proletarian revolution in Europe had even begun, depended upon the special correlation of forces between the various classes and the state power. When Comrades Pokrovsky or Rozhkov argued with the Narodniks or the liberals, saying that the organization and policies of Tsarism were determined by the economic development and interests of the property-owning classes, they were basically right. But when Comrade Pokrovsky tries to repeat the same argument against me, he simply misses the mark.

Comrade Pokrovsky's thought is gripped in a vice of rigid social categories which he puts in place of live historical forces. He substitutes for the relative, that is, historically conditioned and socially limited independence of the autocracy from the ruling classes, some kind of absolute independence, thus transforming Tsarism into a mere form without content. And then, after ascribing this view of Tsarism to myself, he writes: "But how can this be brought into line with our call to the proletariat to struggle for power against the bourgeoisie? How can we seize from the bourgeoisie something that it has never had," etc. For Comrade Pokrovsky the question is a simple one: either the bourgeoisie was in possession of all power, or it had none at all. If it had no power, then what did we mean by talking of "taking power from the bourgeoisie"? And if we have taken power from the bourgeoisie, then how can we say that it did not have power? This way of posing the problem is neither historical, nor materialist, nor dialectical. It will not do even from the point of view of purely formal logic. Even if the bourgeoisie in Russia had had no power at all, the proletariat might still have fought for power, precisely so as not to allow it to fall into the bourgeoisie's hands.

But, of course, the problem was not as formal as that. The

bourgeoisie did not possess the whole of power but was only gradually becoming associated with it. That association was not complete. The course of events, that is to say, above all, military defeat and pressure from below, caused the gap between the autocracy and the bourgeoisie to widen. The monarchy fell into this gap. The bourgeoisie, in March 1917, tried to assume power wholly and immediately. But the working class, supported by the peasant army, snatched the power from its hands in October 1917. In this way our belated historical development against the background of full-blooded imperialism in Europe resulted in the fact that by the time our bourgeoisie was strong enough to push Tsarism off its pedestal, the proletariat had already become an independent revolutionary force.

But the very question which, for us, is the central topic for investigation does not exist for Comrade Pokrovsky. In his review of a book by Vipper (in the same issue of *Krasnaya Nov'*) he writes: "To set sixteenth century Muscovite Russia against a background of the general European relations of the time is a highly tempting task. There is no better way of refuting the prejudice, prevalent to this day even in Marxist circles, concerning the alleged 'primitiveness' of the economic foundation on which the Russian autocracy grew up." And again: "To show the autocracy in its true historical context as an aspect of commercial and capitalist Europe . . . the task is not only of the highest interest to the historian, it is also pedagogically very important for the reading public; there is no more radical means of putting an end to the legend of the 'uniqueness' of the Russian historical process." Every word here is a dig at ourselves. We see that Comrade Pokrovsky baldly denies the primitive and backward nature of our economic development and dismisses as a "legend" the uniqueness of the Russian historical process. The trouble is that Comrade Pokrovsky is completely hypnotized by the relatively lively development of Russian trade in the sixteenth century, a fact which both he and Rozhkov have noticed.

It is difficult to understand how Comrade Pokrovsky could have fallen into such an error. Anyone might think that trade is the foundation and the infallible criterion of economic life. A good twenty years ago the German economist Karl Bücher tried to establish trade (the path from producer to consumer) as the criterion of all economic development. Struve naturally hastened to transplant this "discovery" into Russian economic "science." Bücher's theory was, quite naturally, energetically refuted by Marxists at the time. We seek the criteria of economic development in production—in technology and the social organization of labor—and we regard the path traveled by the product from the producer to the consumer as a secondary phenomenon whose roots are to be found, once more, in production.

Paradoxical though this may seem from the viewpoint of the Büchers and the Struves, the great (at least in the spatial sense) upsurge of Russian trade in the sixteenth century was due precisely to the extremely primitive and backward nature of the Russian economy. The West European town was dominated by artisanal corporations and trade guilds. Our towns, by contrast, were administrative and military centers, i.e., centers of consumption rather than of production. The artisanal guild life of the West was formed at a relatively high level of economic development, when all the basic processing industries had separated themselves from agriculture, transformed themselves into independent trades, created their own organizations, their centers (the towns) and their own, initially limited (local, regional), but nevertheless stable markets. Thus the medieval European town was based on a relatively advanced differentiation of the economy which engendered correct relations between the town (the center) and its agricultural periphery. Russia's economic backwardness, on the other hand, found expression first and foremost in the fact that artisanal trade failed to separate itself from agriculture and retained the characteristics of a home industry. In this respect we are closer to India than to Europe, just as our medieval towns were closer to Asia than to Europe and our autocracy, placed between European absolutism and Asian despotism, had many features resembling the latter.

Given the enormous expanse of our territory and the sparseness of the population (surely another fairly objective criterion of backwardness?), the exchange of goods presupposed the intermediary role of commercial capital at a very high level of intensity. Such intensity was possible precisely because the West was far more developed than ourselves, had a wide variety of complex needs, sent us its merchants and its goods and by so doing advanced the exchange of goods in Russia itself on the basis of Russia's extremely primitive and in many respects barbarian economic relations. Not to understand this, the greatest peculiarity of our historical development, is to fail to see our history as such.

My Siberian employer (in whose office ledger I entered *pouds* and *arshins* for a period of two months), Yakov Andreyevich Chernykh—this happened at the beginning of the twentieth century, not in the sixteenth—was in practically unlimited control of economic life in the Kirensk district by virtue of his trade operations. He bought furs from the Tungus natives, he bought church lands from priests in remote districts, and he sold them cotton and, especially, vodka (at that time the vodka monopoly had not yet been introduced in Irkutsk province). He was illiterate, but a millionaire (in the currency of the time). His dictatorship as the representative of trade capital was unquestioned; he even spoke of the local indigenous population as "my little Tungus folk." The town of Kirensk, like Verkholensk and Nizhne-Ilimsk, was a place of residence for police officers of various rank, kulaks in a state of hierarchical dependence on one another, a variety of petty government officials, and a handful of wretched artisans. I never found any organized artisanal trade there as a basis of urban economic life—no corporations, no guilds, although Yakov Andreyevich was officially listed as a "merchant of the second guild."

Believe me, this slice of real Siberian life takes us much further towards an understanding of the historical peculiarities of Russia's development than what Comrade Pokrovsky has to say on the subject. That is really the truth. Yakov Andreyevich's trade operations spread from the middle reaches of the Lena and its eastern tributaries to Nizhny Novgorod and even Moscow. Few Western European firms can mark up similar distances on their business maps. Yet this merchant dictator was the most perfect and convincing expression of our economic backwardness, our barbarity and primitiveness, our illiteracy, the sparseness of our population, the dispersion of our peasant villages and our dirt roads which form blockades of impassable bog for two months every spring and autumn in our remoter districts, etc., etc. How did Chernykh acquire so much economic power on the basis of this Siberian, middle-Lena backwardness? Because the West—"Mother Russia," "Moscow"—was dragging Siberia towards an odd marriage: a marriage between a primitive nomadic economy and a shiny brand-new alarm clock made in Warsaw.

II

Craft corporations formed the foundation of medieval urban culture which spread also to the countryside. Medieval science, scholasticism, the Reformation all grew out of the artisanal trades. Nothing like this existed in Russia. Symptoms and embryonic traces of it can, of course, be found, but they appear quite insignificant when compared with the powerful economic and cultural formation which existed in the West. On this foundation the medieval European town came into being, grew, and struggled with the Church; it was from the same town that monarchy challenged the feudal lords. It was the town which, by manufacturing firearms, created the technical preconditions for the existence of permanent armies. Can it be said—but perhaps this contradicts the class theory of the state?—that the monarchy in Western Europe became increasingly independent of the first estate as the towns grew and their antagonism with the feudal lords increased?

In the last analysis, royal power of course remains an organization for the oppression of the working masses and especially the peasant serfs. But surely there is a difference between a state power which amalgamates with the landowning class, and a state power which dissociates itself from that class, creates its own bureaucratic apparatus, and acquires its own enormous power, i.e., a state power which, while protecting the interests of the exploiters against the exploited, becomes a relatively independent force—and the primary one—among other dominant forces.

Where were Russia's craft-corporation towns which even remotely resembled those of Western Europe? Where was their struggle with feudal power? Did any struggle between the town and the feudal landlord provide the foundation for the development of Russian autocracy? Because of the very nature of our towns, no such struggle ever took place, any more than did a religious reformation. Is that a peculiar feature of our historical development, or is it not? Our crafts remained at the home industries stage, which is to say that they never dissociated themselves from peasant agriculture. Our reformation, receiving no leadership from the towns, remained at the stage of peasant sects. Here is primitiveness, here is backwardness crying to high heaven, yet Comrade Pokrovsky does not wish to notice them. And Tsarism, too, arose as an independent state organization (again, independent only relatively, within the limits of a conflict between actual historical economic forces), not as a result of the struggle of powerful towns against powerful feudal lords, but because of the complete industrial anemia of our towns and the anemia of our feudal landowners.

Poland, as regards its social structure, stood between Russia and the West just as Russia stood between Europe and Asia. The Polish towns knew corporate artisanal trade to a far greater extent than did the Russian ones. But they never developed enough to help the royal power to break feudal power. State power remained directly in the hands of the nobility. The result was the total impotence and eventual collapse of the state. Where there are no "special features," there is no history, but only a sort of pseudo-materialistic geometry. Instead of studying the living and changing matter of economic development it is enough to notice a few outward symptoms and adapt them to a few ready-made clichés. This primitive method of historical investigation is adequate for fighting liberal or Narodnik prejudices, not to mention sentimental Slavophilism, but quite inadequate for understanding the real paths of Russia's historical development.

What I have said of Tsarism applies likewise to capitalism and the proletariat, and I find it difficult to understand why Comrade Pokrovsky's wrath is directed only at the first chapter which speaks of Tsarism. Russian capitalism did not develop from artisanal trade via the manufacturing workshop to the factory for the reason that European capital, first in the form of trade capital and later in the form of financial and industrial capital, flooded the country at a time when most Russian artisanal trade had not yet separated itself from agriculture. Hence the appearance in Russia of modern capitalist industry in a completely primitive economic environment: for instance, a huge Belgian or American industrial plant surrounded by dirt roads and villages built of straw and wood, which burn down every year, etc. The most primitive beginnings and the most modern European endings. Hence the tremendous role of Western European capital in Russia's economy. Hence the political weakness of the Russian bourgeoisie. Hence the ease with which we were able to defeat the Russian bourgeoisie. Hence the difficulties which followed when the European bourgeoisie intervened in the affair and when the former owners of factories and plants tried talking to us, through Lloyd George and Barthou, in Genoa and at The Hague.

And our proletariat? Did it ever pass through the school of

the medieval apprentice fraternities? Does it have the age-old traditions of the guilds? Nothing of the kind. It was snatched from the plow and hurled straight into the factory furnace. I remember an old friend, Korotkov, a cabinetmaker from Nikolayev, who wrote a song back in 1897. It was called *The Proletarians' March* and it began with the words: "We are the alpha and the omega, we are the beginning and the end . . ." And that's the plain truth. The first letter is there and so is the last, but all the middle of the alphabet is missing. Hence the absence of conservative traditions, the absence of castes within the proletariat, hence its revolutionary freshness, hence, as well as for other reasons, the October Revolution and the first workers' government in the world. But hence also the illiteracy, the absence of organizational know-how, the lack of system, of cultural and technical education. All these are shortcomings which we feel at every step of our economic and cultural efforts to build.

European communism has to overcome an infinitely more conservative medium, both external, in the state, and internal, within the proletariat itself. But when it achieves victory it will have infinitely more powerful objective and subjective resources for building a new society. Is that a peculiar feature or is it not? The very necessity for asking such a question in the summer of 1922 strikes me as a . . . rather excessive "peculiarity," but this too is undoubtedly a consequence of our historical development: we were the first to seize power, our tasks are colossal, our cultural forces are few, every man has to split himself into a hundred parts, there is no time to think. And that is why Comrade Pokrovsky, in talking about new and highly complex problems, produces old arguments which were of value in another context and at another logical level, but which become the very opposite of Marxism when endowed with the qualities of a universally applicable cliché.

I have pointed out how much our entire development has

been influenced by the fact that on our western frontiers we constantly came into contact with states that were more developed, better organized and technically better armed than ourselves. Under this pressure the autocracy restructured itself, first by creating marksmen's regiments and later a cavalry and an infantry. Comrade Pokrovsky remarks in this connection: "This would seem to be the point at which one should say that the fundamental interests were not political but economic: the Muscovite autocracy corresponded to somebody's class interests." It is hard to understand here what he means by opposing military and political interests to economic ones. When economic interests are defended by the state they always assume the nature of political aims and tasks; and when they have to be defended, not by diplomatic means, but by the force of arms, they become military tasks.

Comrade Pokrovsky tries to prove that the interests which dominated the autocracy's policies in the sixteenth century were the interests of trade capital. The way he represents this question seems to me to be caricatural. But we hope to return to this narrower and more specialized issue on a later occasion. Here suffice it to say that in constructing a trade-capitalist Russia in the sixteenth century Comrade Pokrovsky falls into the error of the German professor Eduard Meyer who discovered capitalism in ancient Greece and Rome. Meyer was undoubtedly right in noticing that previous views of the economic structure of Greece and Rome (those of Rodbertus and others) as a series of self-contained natural-economic cells (*oikos*) was a schematic and over-simplified one. He showed that these basic cells were connected with one another and with other countries by a fairly well developed system of commodity exchange. At the same time, in certain spheres and branches there was also mass production. Utilizing modern economic relations and concepts, Meyer retrospectively constructed a Greco-Roman capitalism. His error consisted in the fact that he failed to appreciate the quantitative, and therefore also qualitative, differences between various types of economies—*oikos*, simple commodity, and capitalist.

Comrade Pokrovsky's error, we repeat, is basically the same. But the crux of the matter for us at this moment is elsewhere. Let us assume that the interests of trade capital were really dominant in the autocracy's policies in the sixteenth century and that the autocracy itself was a "dictatorship of trade capital." But the autocracy had commercial aims, which of course corresponded to economic interests, in Persia, in Turkey, in the Baltic lands, in Poland, and in the more distant countries of the West. The struggle for these aims led to military conflicts. It is quite irrelevant who was the attacker and who the defender (a question which Comrade Pokrovsky brings in for no good reason when he ascribes to me the notion that the autocracy merely "defended" Russia from foreign attacks). And it was in these *military* conflicts, which of course meant the accomplishment of *political* tasks deriving from *economic* interests, that the Russian state came into contact with the military organizations of the Western nations which were founded on a higher economic, political, and cultural basis.

Thus Russian capital immediately after its birth came into contact with the more developed and powerful capital of the West and fell under its dominance. Thus, too, the Russian working class, as soon as it came into being, found itself equipped with ready-made weapons created by the experience of the Western European proletariat: Marxist theory, trade unions, political parties. Anyone who explains the nature and the policy of our autocracy only by the interests of the Russian property-owning classes forgets that apart from the more backward, poorer, more ignorant Russian exploiters there existed also the richer and more powerful European exploiters. The property-owning classes of Russia came up against the hostile or partially hostile property-owning classes of Europe. These contacts took place through the mediation of the state organization. The autocracy was that state organization. The whole structure and the whole history of the Russian autocracy would have been different if there had been no European towns, European gunpowder (or if we had invented it) and the European stock exchange.

In the last period of its existence the autocracy was not only the organ of the property-owning classes in Russia but also of the European stock exchange as organized for the exploitation of Russia. This dual role in turn afforded it a considerable degree of independence. A telling example of this independence was the fact that the French stock exchange, in order to support the Russian autocracy, granted it a loan in 1905 against the will of the Russian bourgeois parties.

In reality there is just one small fact which totally demolishes Comrade Pokrovsky's historical concept. That fact is the last imperialist war and the role played in it by Tsarism.

From Comrade Pokrovsky's point of view everything is very simple. Tsarism was the state form of the ruling bourgeoisie which had entered the imperialist phase of development. In that sense Tsarism did not differ from the republican-parliamentary regime in France, the imperialist-parliamentary monarchy in England, etc. And that is quite true. But it is true within the limits of the most general approach to the question—within the limits of a struggle with social-patriotic and pacifist prejudices, with the criteria of defense and attack, etc. It is absolutely inadequate (and therefore untrue) when it comes to assessing the respective roles of Russia, England, Germany, and each individual country in the war; of the internal changes which each of them underwent in the war; of the revolutionary perspectives which opened up before each one, and of the tactics which we should consequently adopt in them.

Although Tsarism revealed that it was not viable as far back as 1904–05, in the Russo-Japanese war, the bourgeoisie struck a bargain with it because it feared the proletariat.

The independence of Tsarism at its most insolent, as during

the Rasputin era, by no means contradicts the class theory of
the state but can be explained by it. The theory, however, must
not be applied mechanically; it must be applied dialectically.
But that is not the end of it; Tsarism was actually smashed in
the imperialist war. Why? Because its productive basis was too
low (Russian primitiveness). In matters of military technology
Tsarism tried to live up to the most advanced models, and in
this it was helped in every way by its wealthier and more enlightened allies. Thanks to them, Tsarism had the most highly
perfected instruments of war at its disposal. But it had not and
could not have the means of reproducing these instruments, nor
did it have the means of transporting them (as well as troops)
with sufficient speed by rail or waterway. In other words, Tsarism, in defending the interests of Russia's property-owning
classes in the international struggle, was operating from a more
primitive base than its enemies or allies.

During the war Tsarism ruthlessly exploited that base, that
is, it absorbed a much higher percentage of the national product
than its powerful enemies and allies. This fact was confirmed,
firstly by the system of war debts, and secondly by Russia's
complete economic ruin. Or does Comrade Pokrovsky doubt
either of these facts?

All these circumstances, which directly predetermined the
October Revolution, the triumph of the proletariat and its subsequent difficulties, cannot be explained away by Comrade Pokrovsky's commonplaces to the effect that no such thing as a
supra-class state exists and that the exploiting classes express their
will through the state power, and have always done so. That
is hardly Marxism; it is only the first letter of Marxism. And
that is where Comrade Pokrovsky would have us stop.

What followed the peculiarities of our historical development, which Comrade Pokrovsky refuses to admit, was not the
denial (in retrospect?) of the class war, but the seizure of state
power by the proletariat and its struggle to keep it in its own
hands. The same peculiarities have also given rise to enormous

international and internal economic difficulties after the seizure of state power. An understanding of these peculiarities is the best insurance for the young generation of workers against passivity in the face of difficulties, against pessimism and skepticism. Meanwhile clichés about historical development can teach nothing to anybody.

28 June 1922.

PART
TWO

CHAPTER 28

◇◈◇◈◇◈◇◈◇◈◇◈◇

Instead of a Preface
to the Second Part

Some curious statistical data on the conditions in which the party of the proletariat in Russia pursues its activities were published at the congress of the social-democratic party held in Stockholm.

The 140 members of the congress had spent, in all, 138 years and 3½ months in jail.

They had spent 148 years and 6½ months in exile.

Eighteen members had escaped from prison once and 4 members twice.

Twenty-three members had escaped from exile once, 5 twice and 1 three times.

If we take into account the fact that the 140 members had spent a total of 942 years in the social-democratic movement, we shall see that the periods spent in prison and exile represented about one-third of the time spent actively in the party. But these figures are, if anything, over-optimistic. To say that the 140 members of the congress engaged in party work for a total of 942 years means only that the political activities of the congress members took place during that period of time; it certainly does not mean that these 942 man-years were completely filled with political work. It may well be that actual, direct political activities, given the conditions of clandestinity, covered only one-fifth or one-tenth of that time. On the other hand, periods spent in prison or exile were exactly as indicated by the figures: the congress members had spent more than 50,000 days and nights behind bars and a still longer period in remote, barbaric regions of the country.

Perhaps we may be allowed to add some statistics from our own past. The author of these lines, arrested for the first time in January 1898 after ten months of activity in workers' circles in the town of Nikolayev, spent two years in jail and escaped from Siberia after serving two years of his total sentence of four years' exile.

The second time the author was arrested on December 3, 1905 as a member of the Soviet of Workers' Deputies. The activities of the Soviet continued over seven weeks. Those sentenced for being members of the Soviet were kept in prison for fifty-seven weeks, after which they were conveyed to Obdorsk for "settlement in perpetuity." . . . Any Russian social-democrat who has worked in the party for ten years or so can supply more or less similar information about himself.

The extraordinarily confused regime which came into being in Russia after October 17, 1905 and which the Almanach de Gotha, with the unconscious humor of legal pedantry, describes as "a constitutional monarchy with an autocratic Tsar," in no way changed these conditions of our political work. We obtained fifty days of freedom, and we enjoyed them to the full. During those glorious days Tsarism realized something we had already known for a long time: namely, that the two of us could not exist side by side. Then came the terrible months of reckoning. After October 17, Tsarism changed Dumas as a boa constrictor sloughs off its skins, but no matter what skin it happened to be wearing, its nature as a boa constrictor remained intact. Those simpletons and liberal hypocrites who, during the past two years, have so often appealed to us to embrace legality are like Marie-Antoinette who recommended to the starving peasants that they should eat cake. Anyone might think that we suffer from some kind of organic revulsion from cake. Anyone might think that our lungs have been infected by some insatiable craving to breathe the air of the dungeons used for solitary confinement in the Peter and Paul Fortress! Anyone might think that we cannot or do not want to find a different employment for those endless hours which the jailer confiscates from our lives.

We are as little enamored of our underground as the drowned man is of the sea bottom. But—let us say it straight—we have no more choice in the matter than our enemy, absolutism. Our clear awareness of this fact allows us to remain optimistic even when the underground mercilessly tightens its ring around our throats. It will not strangle us, of that we are certain. We shall survive everyone. When the bones of the present princes of the earth, their servants and their servants' servants, have turned to dust, when no one is able to find the graves in which many of today's parties and their activities are buried, then the cause we serve will rule the world, then our party, today struggling for breath underground, will become absorbed without trace in a humanity which, for the first time in history, will be master of its own fate.

The whole of history is an enormous machine in the service of our ideals. It works with barbarous slowness, with insensitive cruelty, but it works. We are sure of it. But when its omnivorous mechanism swallows up our life's blood for fuel, we feel like calling out to it with all the strength we still possess:
"Faster! Do it faster!"

Oglby (near Helsingfors)
8–21 April 1907.

CHAPTER 29

The Trial of the Soviet of Workers' Deputies

The era of counter-revolutionary conspiracy opened on December 3, 1905, with the arrest of the Soviet of Workers' Deputies. The December strike in Petersburg and the December risings in various parts of the country were a heroic effort on the part of the revolution to maintain the position it had won in October. During that time the leadership of the working masses of Petersburg passed to the second Soviet, formed from the remnants of the first together with some newly elected deputies. Approximately three hundred members of the first Soviet were confined in three Petersburg prisons. Their future fate was for a long time a mystery, not only to themselves, but also to the ruling bureaucracy. The well-informed press declared that the Minister of Justice absolutely rejected the possibility of the workers' deputies being tried by a court of law. If their perfectly open activities were criminal, then the role of the higher administration, which not only connived with the Soviet but also entered into direct relations with it, was also, in the Minister's opinion, a crime. The ministers argued among themselves, the gendarmes carried on interrogations, the deputies sat in their solitary cells. At the time of the punitive expeditions of December and January there was every reason to think that the Soviet would end up in the noose of a court-martial. At the end of April, in the early days of the first Duma, the workers' deputies, like the country at large, expected an amnesty. Thus their prospects swung between the death penalty and going scot-free.

At last the movement of the pendulum met with a counterforce. The government of Goremykin's Duma (or rather anti-Duma) passed the Soviet's case for examination to the Chamber of Justice assisted by representatives of the estates.*

The indictment, a pathetic concoction cooked up between gendarmes and prosecutors, is of interest as a document of that wonderful era. It reflects the revolution in the same way as a dirty puddle in a police station yard reflects the sun. The members of the Soviet were accused of preparing armed insurrection under two articles, one of which carried a maximum of eight years and the other of twelve years with forced labor. The author of these lines has analyzed the legal basis for that accusation, or rather, the absolute nonexistence of such a basis, in a small essay** which he sent from the House of Preliminary Confinement to the social-democratic faction within the first Duma with a view to a parliamentary question being asked on the subject of the Soviet's trial. The question was never asked because the first Duma was dissolved and the social-democratic faction found itself under trial.

---

* Seven persons: four crown judges; Count Gudovich, representative of the nobility of Petersburg district; Troynitsky, representative of the Petersburg duma, a former provincial governor sacked from the service for embezzlement, a member of the Black Hundreds; and, lastly, a representative of one of the administrative subdistricts of Petersburg province, if I remember rightly a "progressive."
** See chapter entitled *The Soviet and the Prosecution*, below.

The date fixed for the trial, which was to be held in public, was June 20. A wave of protest meetings swept all Petersburg factories and plants. If the prosecution pretended that the Soviet's Executive Committee was a group of conspirators who had sought to impose its own decisions on the masses; if the liberal press after the December events repeated day after day that the Soviet's "naïve revolutionary methods" had long lost their appeal for the masses, who wanted only to lead a quiet life under the new "constitutional" law—then what a splendid refutation of these police slanders and liberal ineptitudes were the June meetings and resolutions of the workers of Petersburg, who, in their factories, declared their solidarity with their imprisoned representatives, who demanded to be put under trial as active participators in the revolutionary events, who insisted that the Soviet had merely executed their collective will, who swore to carry the Soviet's work to its conclusion!

The courtyard of the law courts and the adjoining streets were turned into a military encampment. All Petersburg's police forces were mobilized. Despite these colossal preparations, the trial failed to take place. The president of the Chamber of Justice, against the wishes of both the prosecution and the defense and even, as became known later, of the ministry, postponed the hearing for three months, until September 19, on a formal pretext. This was a subtle political move. At the end of June the situation was full of "unlimited possibilities": a Kadet ministry seemed as likely as the restoration of absolutism. Yet the Soviet's trial demanded a fully confident policy on the part of the president of the court. Therefore the gentleman in question chose to grant history a further three months for reflection. Alas, this diplomatic cunctator was obliged to leave his post only a few days later. The line to be taken was fully defined at Peterhof. The Tsar and his henchmen insisted on utter ruthlessness.

The trial opened under a new president on September 19 and lasted for a month during the most critical phase of the first inter-Duma period, the honeymoon of the era of courts-martial.

Yet, nevertheless, the court examination of many, if not of all the questions involved was conducted with a freedom that would have been completely incomprehensible if, behind it, one could not glimpse the workings of bureaucratic chicanery: this was, apparently, the way in which Stolypin's ministry had chosen to parry Count Witte's attacks. Stolypin's calculation was faultlessly correct: the more true facts the trial revealed, the more graphically it reproduced the picture of the government's humiliation at the end of 1905. Witte's connivance, his two-faced intrigues, his false assurances to Peterhof, his crude attempts to ingratiate himself with the revolution—this was the evidence that the higher bureaucratic interests extracted from the Soviet's trial. All that the defendants could do was to exploit the favorable situation for political ends and to broaden the framework of the trial to the maximum possible extent.

Some 400 witnesses were called, of whom more than 200 appeared and testified before the court.* Workers, factory owners, gendarmes, engineers, domestic servants, ordinary citizens, journalists, post office officials, schoolboys, members of the duma, janitors, senators, hooligans, deputies, professors, and soldiers passed in review before the court throughout the month and under the cross fire of questions from the court, the prosecution, the defense and the defendants—especially the defendants—they reconstituted line by line, brushstroke by brushstroke the picture of the period of activities, so rich in events, of the workers' Soviet.

Before the court's eyes passed the all-Russian October strike which had put Bulygin's Duma to rest; the November strike manifestation in Petersburg, that noble and majestic protest by the proletariat against the court-martialing of the Kronstadt sailors and the rape of Poland; the Petersburg workers' heroic struggle for the eight-hour day; finally, the rising, led by the Soviet, of the long-suffering slaves of the postal and telegraph administration. The minutes of meetings of the Soviet and its Executive

* Many witnesses at the time of the trial were "of unknown address" or in Siberia.

Committee, made public for the first time before the court, revealed to the country the colossal day-to-day work accomplished by the representative body of the proletariat in organizing aid for the unemployed, settling disputes between workers and employers and supervising economic strike action.

The shorthand record of the trial, which is to fill several large volumes, has not been published to date. Only a change in political conditions in Russia can release this invaluable historical document. A German judge and a German-democrat would have been equally astounded if they could have been present in the courtroom during the trial. Exaggerated severity and unbounded license combined here into a bizarre whole, both illuminating, from different aspects, the extraordinary confusion which still reigned in governmental spheres as a legacy of the October strike.

The court building was placed under martial law and virtually transformed into a military encampment. In the courtyard, at the gates, in the adjoining streets were several companies of soldiers and cossacks. Along the entire length of the underground corridor connecting the prison with the law courts, in every room of the law courts building, at the backs of the defendants, at every corner, probably even inside the chimney stack, were gendarmes with drawn sabers: they were meant to form a living wall between the defendants and the outside world, including the public admitted to the court (about 100–120 persons). But thirty or forty lawyers' frock-coats were constantly piercing the wall of blue uniforms. Newspapers, letters, sweets and flowers —infinite quantities of flowers!—appeared in the dock. There were flowers in buttonholes, flowers held in hands and on laps, finally flowers simply lying on the benches. The president of the court did not dare to remove these fragrant intruders. In the end, even gendarmerie officers and officers of the court, totally "demoralized" by the prevailing atmosphere, were handing flowers to the defendants.

And then the workers were called as witnesses! They gathered in dozens in the witness room, and when the court officer opened the door to the courtroom, a wave of revolutionary song would reach the president's chair. These worker witnesses made an astonishing impression. They brought with them the revolutionary atmosphere of the factory suburbs, and such was the divine contempt with which they ignored the mystic solemnity of court ritual that the president, yellow as parchment, could only spread his hands helplessly, while witnesses drawn from "respectable" society and liberal journalists stared at them with envy and respect, as the weak always stare at the strong.

The very first day of the trial was marked by an extraordinary demonstration. Of the fifty-two defendants, the president of the court called only fifty-one. He left out the name of Ter-Mkrchtiants.

"Where is the defendent Ter-Mkrchtiants?" asked Sokolov, one of the defense lawyers.

"His name has been expurged from the list of defendants."

"Why?"

"He . . . er . . . he has been executed."

Yes, in the interval between June 20 and September 19, Ter-Mkrchtiants, released on bail, had been executed on the ramparts of the fortress of Kronstadt for being a participant in the military rising.

The defendants, the witnesses, the defending counsel, members of the public—all rose in silence to honor the memory of the fallen victim. Police and gendarmerie officers, in utter confusion, rose to their feet with the rest.

Witnesses were brought in to take the oath in groups of twenty or thirty. Many came in working clothes, their hands still dirty from their work, carrying their caps in their hands. They would give a brief glance at the judges, then find the defendants with their eyes, bow energetically in the two directions where our benches were placed and say loudly, "Good-day, Comrades!" It was as though they had come for information to a meeting of the Executive Committee. The president hastily took the roll call and invited the witnesses to take the oath. An aged priest placed himself at a portable altar and spread out the instruments of his trade. But the witnesses did not budge. The president repeated his invitation.

"No, we're not going to take any oath," a few voices would reply together, "We don't believe in all that."

"But aren't you members of the orthodox faith?"

"That's what it says in the police books, but we don't hold with that kind of thing."

"In that case, Father, you may go, your services will not be wanted today."

Apart from policemen, the only people who took the oath read by the orthodox priest were Lutheran and Catholic workers. The "orthodox" ones all refused to take the oath and merely undertook to tell the truth.

This procedure was repeated monotonously for every new group. Only sometimes did the heterogeneous composition of a group of witnesses introduce a new and unexpected element.

"Those taking the oath," the president addressed a new group of witnesses, "go forward and face the priest. Those not taking the oath, stand back."

A small, elderly gendarme detached himself from the group and marched smartly towards the portable altar. The workers, exchanging remarks and thumping heavily with their boots, retired by a few steps. Between them and the elderly gendarme remained the witness O., a well-known Petersburg lawyer, householder, liberal and member of the Duma.

"Are you taking the oath, witness O.?" asked the president.

"I . . . I . . . well, yes . . ."

"In that case, kindly step forward and face the priest."

Hesitantly, his face contorted, the witness advanced towards the portable altar. He glanced back over his shoulder; there was no one behind him. In front of him stood the little old man in a gendarme's uniform.

"Raise your hand!"

The old gendarme raised three fingers high above his head.

O., the lawyer, slightly raised his hand, looked around once again and stopped.

"Witness O.," the president asked in an irritated voice, "are you taking the oath or are you not?"

"Why yes, yes, of course."

And the liberal witness, overcoming his scruples, raised his hand almost as high as the gendarme. Together with the gendarme he repeated the childish words of the oath after the priest. If a painter painted such a scene, no one would believe him! The profound social symbolism of this small courtroom event was felt by everyone. The working-class witnesses exchanged ironical glances with the accused, those from "respectable" society lowered their gaze in embarrassment. The jesuitical president was gloating openly. A tense silence fell upon the courtroom.

Another scene: the interrogation of Count Tiesenhausen, a member of the Petersburg duma. He had been present at that meeting of the Duma to which the Soviet's deputation had submitted a number of demands.

"Mr. Witness," asked defense counsel, "what was your personal attitude to the demand for the creation of an armed militia?"

"I consider the question irrelevant," the Count replied.

"Counsel's question is legitimate within the framework in which I am conducting the trial," ruled the president.

"In that case I wish to say that at the time I was sympathetic to the idea of an armed militia, but since then I have completely changed my mind."

Ah, how many of them had changed minds on that issue, and on many others, during the past year! The liberal press, while expressing "complete sympathy" with the accused personally, could not find strong enough words to dismiss their tactics. The radical newspapers, with regretful smiles, spoke of the Soviet's "illusions." Only the workers remained loyal without any reservations.

Many industrial plants presented their collective written

testimony through individual witnesses called by the court. The accused insisted that such statements should be attached to the court file and read out during the hearings.

One such document, selected at random, states:

We the undersigned, workers at the Obukhov plant, convinced that the government intends the trial of the Soviet of Workers' Deputies to be a travesty of justice, and profoundly shocked by the government's intention to represent the Soviet as a handful of conspirators pursuing aims alien to the working class, hereby declare that the Soviet is not composed of a handful of conspirators but of the true representatives of the entire Petersburg proletariat. We protest against the government's unjust treatment of the Soviet and particularly against the charges made against our comrades, who merely fulfilled our demands within the Soviet; and we declare to the government that if our comrade, P. A. Zlydnev, whom we all respect, is guilty, then we are guilty likewise, to which we testify with our signatures.

The resolution was accompanied by several sheets of paper covered with more than 2,000 signatures. The papers were dirty and crumpled; they had been passed from hand to hand in all the workshops of the plant. The Obukhov resolution was by no means the most sharply worded. There were some which the president refused to render publicly because of their "extremely improper" tone in respect to the government and the court.

The signatures attached to these resolutions totaled tens of thousands. The testimony of witnesses, many of whom, on leaving the courtroom, fell directly into the hands of the police, supplied an excellent commentary to these documents. The conspirators whom the prosecutor's office was so determined to find were completely swallowed up by the heroic and nameless mass. In the end, the prosecutor, who carried out his shameful role while maintaining the standards of outwardly correct behavior, was obliged to admit two facts in his accusatory speech: first, that at a certain level of political development the proletariat tends to "gravitate" towards socialism and, second, that the mood of the working masses during the period of the Soviet's activities had been revolutionary.

There was another important position which the prosecution was forced to surrender. "Preparing armed insurrection" was, of course, the hub of the entire trial.

"Did the Soviet call for armed insurrection?"

"As a matter of fact, it didn't," the witnesses replied. "All the Soviet did was to formulate everybody's conviction that an armed rising was inevitable."

"The Soviet called for a Constituent Assembly. Who was to establish it?"

"The people itself!"

"How?"

"By force, of course. You don't get anywhere by persuasion."

"So the Soviet did arm the workers for insurrection?"

"No, for self-defense."

The president shrugged his shoulders ironically. But in the end the testimony of witnesses and accused forced the court to accept this "contradiction." The workers had armed themselves directly for the purpose of self-defense. But their action had, at the same time, been taken for the purpose of insurrection—to the extent that the state power had become the chief instigator of the pogroms. It was to this question that the author devoted his speech before the court.*

The trial reached its climax when the defense put before the court the "Lopukhin Letter" which was to become so celebrated.

The accused and their defense counsel said:

Gentlemen of the court! You seem to disbelieve our claim that the organs of state power played a leading role in preparing and organizing pogroms. Perhaps the evidence produced by witnesses in this trial is not sufficient to convince you. Perhaps you have already

* The text of the speech, transcribed from the shorthand record as yet unpublished in Russia, is reproduced below.

forgotten the revelations made by Prince Urusov, former Deputy Minister of Internal Affairs, in the State Duma. Perhaps you were convinced by General Ivanov of the gendarmerie who told you under oath that the talk of pogroms was a mere pretext for arming the masses. Perhaps you believed the witness Statkovsky, an official of the secret police, who declared under oath that he had not seen a single pogrom proclamation in Petersburg. Then look at this! Here is a certified copy of a letter from Lopukhin, the former director of the police department, to Stolypin, the Minister of Internal Affairs.* On the basis of investigations he carried out personally on Count Witte's special instructions, Mr. Lopukhin states that pogrom proclamations, which Witness Statkovsky alleges never to have seen, were actually printed at the print-works of the secret police, where Statkovsky is employed; that these proclamations were distributed all over Russia by secret police agents and members of the monarchist parties; that close organizational links exist between the department of police and the Black Hundreds gangs; that General Trepov who, at the time of the Soviet, headed this criminal organization and who, in his capacity as palace commandant, possessed enormous power, reported personally to the Tsar on the activities of the police and disposed of immense state funds, outside any ministerial control, for the express purpose of organizing pogroms.

And another fact, gentlemen of the court! Numerous Black Hundreds leaflets—you have them on the preliminary investigation file!—accused the members of the Soviet of appropriating money belonging to the workers. On the strength of the information contained in these leaflets, the gendarmerie general Ivanov conducted a special investigation (which of course yielded no results) at a number of Petersburg factories and plants. We revolutionaries are accustomed to the authorities' use of such methods. But even we, though far from idealizing the gendarmerie, did not realize how far that service was prepared to go. It now transpires that the proclamations which accused the Soviet of appropriating the workers' funds were composed and secretly printed by the self-same gendarmerie to which General Ivanov belongs. This fact is likewise attested by Mr. Lopukhin. Gentlemen of the court! Here is a copy of the letter duly signed by its author. We demand that this valuable document be read out in its entirety before the court. We demand, in addition, that Active State Councillor Lopukhin be called as a witness to testify at this trial.

* Stolypin was Minister of Internal Affairs in Goremykin's cabinet.

The declaration produced the effect of a thunderbolt. The trial was drawing to a close and the president was beginning to feel that, after a rough crossing, he had almost reached a quiet haven, when suddenly he was hurled back into the raging sea.

Lopukhin's letter hinted at the nature of the mysterious reports which Trepov had submitted to the Tsar. Who could tell how the former police chief, who had now turned his back on his policeman's past, would develop these hints under cross-examination by the accused? The court, in holy dread, retreated before the possibility of further revelations. After prolonged debate it refused to take cognizance of the letter or to call Lopukhin as a witness.

The accused then declared that there was nothing further for them to do in the courtroom and categorically insisted on being returned to solitary confinement.

We were removed from the courtroom and our defense counsel withdrew at the same time. In the absence of the accused, the defense and the general public, the prosecutor pronounced his dry and "correct" accusatory speech. In an almost empty courtroom the Chamber pronounced its verdict. The Soviet was found not guilty of supplying arms to the workers for the purpose of insurrection. Fifteen of the accused, including the author of these lines, were nevertheless condemned to loss of all civil rights and lifelong exile to Siberia. Two received short prison sentences. The rest were acquitted.

The trial of the Soviet of Deputies made a tremendous impression upon the country. It can be said with confidence that the social-democratic party owed much of its enormous success in the elections to the second Duma to the agitational effect of this trial of the Petersburg proletariat's revolutionary parliament.

The trial gave rise to an episode which deserves to be mentioned here.

On November 2, the day on which the verdict was made public in its final form, a letter from Count Witte, who had just returned from abroad, was published in *Novoye Vremya*. In this letter the Count, defending himself against the attacks of the right-wing bureaucracy, not only declined the honor of being the chief instigator of the Russian revolution—wherein he was not too far wrong—but also absolutely denied having had any personal dealings with the Soviet. He confidently dismissed the evidence of witnesses and defendants in the trial as "invented for purposes of the defense," evidently not expecting any refutation from behind prison walls. But he was mistaken.

Here is the text of a collective reply from the defendants, published by us in the newspaper *Tovarishch* on November 5:

We are too clearly aware of the difference between our political physiognomy and Count Witte's to explain to the former Prime Minister the motives which oblige us, the representatives of the proletariat, to speak the truth at every stage of our political activity. But we do not think it out of place to refer to the public prosecutor's speech. This professional accuser, paid official of a government which is intrinsically hostile to us, admitted that our statements and speeches had given him all the materials he needed for the prosecution—the prosecution, not the defense!—and described our testimony before the court as truthful and sincere.

Truthfulness and sincerity are qualities which not only his political enemies, but even his professional admirers have never ascribed to Count Witte.

The collective answer then produced documentary evidence to show the rashness of Count Witte's denials* and ended with this summing up of the trial:

Whatever the aims and motives of Count Witte's denial, and however incautious it may seem, its publication has been most timely. It is the final brushstroke to complete the picture of that state power with which the Soviet was confronted. We wish to take the liberty of discussing that picture in a few lines.

Count Witte emphasizes the fact that it was he who placed us in the hands of justice. The date of that historic feat, as we already

---

* Witte was obliged to admit that he had had contacts with the Soviet, but he "explained" that he had chosen to see the Soviet's deputations simply as "workers' representatives."

state above, was December 3, 1905. After that we passed through the hands of the secret police, then of the gendarmerie, and finally we came before the court. Two officials of the secret police department appeared as witnesses in the trial. To the question of whether a pogrom was being prepared in Petersburg in the autumn of last year they replied with a most resolute "No!" adding that they had not seen a single leaflet calling for pogroms. Yet Active State Councillor Lopukhin, former director of the department of police, testifies that pogrom proclamations were printed at that time, precisely, by the secret police administration. So much for the first stage of the "justice" in whose hands Count Witte placed us.

Further, gendarmerie officers who had conducted the investigation into the Soviet's case also appeared before the court. According to their own testimony, their investigation into the matter of the Soviet's alleged appropriation of certain moneys was based on anonymous Black Hundreds leaflets, which the public prosecutor described as "lying and slanderous." What do we find? Active State Councillor Lopukhin affirms that these lying and slanderous leaflets were printed in the self-same gendarmerie department which conducted the investigation into the Soviet's case. So much for the second stage of justice.

And when, ten months later, we found ourselves facing the court, we were permitted to say all the things which, in broad outline, had been known before the trial began; but as soon as we made an attempt to show and prove that, at the time of the Soviet's activities, there was no state power properly speaking; that its most active organs had become transformed into counter-revolutionary associations which flouted not only the written laws but all laws of human morality; that government officials holding the most confidential posts formed a centralized organization for all-Russian pogroms; that the Soviet of Deputies was, in substance, carrying out tasks of national defense—when, in order to show and prove these facts, we asked that Lopukhin's letter, which had been rendered public thanks to our trial, be placed on the court file and, more especially, that Lopukhin himself be cross-examined as a witness, the court, in defiance of the demands of justice, stretched out its powerful hand and closed our lips. Such was the third stage of justice.

And, last of all, when the affair is at an end, when the verdict has been pronounced, Count Witte arrives upon the scene with an attempt to blacken his political adversaries whom, apparently, he regards as finally vanquished. Just as positively as those secret police officials who stated that they never saw a pogrom leaflet, Count Witte asserts that he never had any dealings with the Soviet of Workers' Deputies. Just as positively—and just as truthfully!

We look back calmly upon these four stages of official justice through which we have passed. The representatives of power have deprived us of "all rights" and are sending us into exile. But they cannot deprive us of the right to the confidence of the proletariat and of all our honorable fellow citizens. The last word in our case, as in every other question of our national life, will be spoken by the people. With full confidence we appeal to the people's conscience.

4 November 1906.
House of Preliminary Confinement.

CHAPTER 30

❖❖❖❖❖❖❖❖❖❖❖

The Soviet
and the Prosecution

The trial of the Soviet of Workers' Deputies is only one episode in the revolution's struggle with the government of the conspirators of Peterhof. Hardly anyone, even among the police representatives of the prosecution, can really believe that the trial of the Soviet's members is a legally sound act—that it was begun and was conducted on the independent initiative of the legal authorities in the interests of the "inner logic" of the law. Anyone and everyone knows that the arrest of the Soviet was not a legal, but a military-political act, one of many incidents in the murderous campaign being waged by a power rejected and disowned by the people.

We will not go here into the question of why, of all the possible methods of dealing with the workers' representatives, the authorities chose the relatively complicated one of having them tried by the Chamber of Justice assisted by representatives of the estates. They could have picked any one among a number of other means, which would have been no less effective but simpler. Besides the rich arsenal of administrative measures, there is, for example, the court-martial or that form of justice which, it is true, is not listed in any legal textbook but which has been used successfully in numerous instances. It consists of inviting the accused to take a few steps away from their judges and to turn their backs on them. When the accused have complied with this procedure, a volley of shots is fired to signify a court sentence against which there is no appeal.

But the fact is that the government, instead of dealing with the fifty-two persons singled out by its agents by the torture-chamber method, has organized a legal trial which, moreover, is not simply a trial of fifty-two persons but a trial of the Soviet of Workers' Deputies. By so doing it forces us to make a critique of the legal position it has adopted.

The indictment states that the fifty-two persons named in it are accused of "joining an association . . . which, to their knowledge, aimed at changing the system of government established by fundamental laws in Russia, and replacing it by a democratic republic." Therein lies the substance of the charge, which is supposed to come under Articles 101 and 102 of the Criminal Code.

Thus the indictment depicts the Soviet of Workers' Deputies as a revolutionary "association" formed on the basis of a previously formulated political aim—as an organization whose every member, by the very fact of joining it, subscribed to a definite, previously outlined political program. Such a definition of the Soviet is in profound contradiction with the picture presented by the indictment itself, of the circumstances in which the association came into being. On the first page we read that the initiators of the future Soviet called for the "election of deputies to a Workers' Committee which would put organization, unity, and strength into the working-class movement" and would act as "the spokesman of the needs of Petersburg workers before the rest of society. Elections of deputies were carried out forthwith at a number of factories," the indictment continues. What, then, was the political program of the Soviet while it was being formed? There wasn't one; indeed, there couldn't have been one, for the Soviet, as we have seen, was not formed on the basis of a group of persons holding the same political opinions (like a political party or conspiratorial organization), but on the basis of electoral representation (like a duma or *zemstvo*). It follows beyond any doubt from the very conditions under which the Soviet was formed that the persons named in the indictment, like all other members of the Soviet, were not joining a conspiratorial association which, to their knowledge, aimed at the forcible overthrow of the existing system of government and the establishment of a democratic republic, but a representative body whose further activities were to be determined by the subsequent collective decisions of its members.

If the Soviet is an association as provided in Articles 101 and 102, then where are the limits of that association? Deputies do not sit on the Soviet because they choose to do so, as do the members of an association, but because they are sent there by their electors. Moreover, the electoral body is never dissolved; it always remains in existence at the plant, the deputy accounts to it for his actions and, through its deputy, it most definitely influences the direction of the Soviet's activities. The initiative on all the most important issues—strikes, the struggle for the eighthour day, the arming of the workers—did not come from the Soviet but from the most progressive plants. The workers, that is to say, the electors, held meetings and adopted resolutions which were then submitted to the Soviet by their deputies. Hence the Soviet's organization was, both formally and actually, the organization of the vast majority of the Petersburg workers. It was based on an aggregate of electoral bodies in relation to which the Soviet, in a certain sense, played the same part as the Executive Committee did in relation to the Soviet itself. In one instance the indictment categorically admits this. "The aspiration of the Workers' Committee* to achieve the arming of all citizens," it reads, "was expressed . . . in the decisions and resolutions of individual *organizations forming part of the Workers' Committee*"; and the indictment goes on to quote the relevant decision adopted by a meeting of print-workers. But if the Union of Print-workers, in the opinion of the prosecution, "formed part" of the Soviet (or rather, of the Soviet's organization), then it is evident that every member of the Union was, by that token, a member of an association aiming at the forcible overthrow of the existing system. And not only the Union of Print-workers, but workers in every factory and every plant, by sending their deputies to the Soviet, thereby entered the organization of the Petersburg proletariat as an electoral body. So that if the prosecution intended to apply Articles 101 and 102 fully and consistently in accordance with their precise meaning and spirit, not less than 200,000 Petersburg workers should actually appear in the dock: which is, in fact, the viewpoint of those workers themselves, as witness a number of the strongly worded resolutions they adopted in June demanding to be brought to trial. And this demand is not merely a political demonstration; it is a reminder to the prosecution of its elementary legal obligations.

But legal obligations are the last things that interest the prosecution. It knows that the authorities want a few dozen victims to complete its "victory," and so it limits the number of defendants by means of a series of inconsistencies and crude sophisms.

1. It completely shuts its eyes to the *elective* nature of the Soviet and persists in regarding it as a league of likeminded revolutionaries.
2. Because the total number of the Soviet's members—500 to 600 persons—is too high for the purposes of a tendentious trial of supposed conspirators manipulating the mass of the working class, the prosecution quite artificially singles out the Executive Committee. It deliberately ignores the elec-

* The name sometimes given to the Soviet in the early stages.

tive nature of the Executive Committee and the fact that its composition was fluid and variable and, taking no account of documentary evidence, ascribes to the Executive Committee decisions which were in fact adopted by the Soviet in plenary session.

3. Out of the Soviet's membership, in addition to members of the Executive Committee, the prosecution brings to justice only those deputies who "took an active and (?) personal part in the Soviet's activities." Such a selection is purely arbitrary. The Criminal Code condemns not only "active and personal" participation but any form of participation in a criminal association. The *nature* of the participation determines only the *degree* of punishment.

But in what area is the prosecution's criteria? In its eyes, such facts as checking entrance tickets, taking part in a strike picket or even simply admitting that one belonged to the Soviet are proof of active and personal participation in an association aiming at the forcible overthrow of the government. For example, in respect to the defendants Krasin, Lukanin, Ivanov, and Marlotov, the prosecution quotes only their own admission of participation in the Soviet and from that admission it somehow deduces that their participation was "active and personal."

4. If we add the handful of "outsiders" who were arrested on December 3 purely accidentally as the Soviet's guests, and who had no relation whatsoever to the Soviet and had never opened their mouths at any of its meetings, we obtain a still clearer picture of the indecently arbitrary manner in which the choice of defendants was made.

5. But even that is not all. After December 3 new members joined what was left of the Soviet. The Executive Committee was reconstituted, *Izvestia* went on being published (No. 8 appeared on the day following the Soviet's arrest), and the reconstituted Soviet issued the December strike call. After a certain time the Executive Committee of the new Soviet was arrested. And what happened? Despite the

fact that it was merely continuing the work of the old Soviet and in no way differed from it in its aims or methods of struggle, the case of the new Soviet is not, for some reason, pursued legally but is dealt with by administrative measures.

Did the Soviet stand on legal ground? No, it did not, because no such ground existed.

Even had it wanted to, the Soviet could not have been formed on the basis of the manifesto of October 17 for the simple reason that it was formed before the manifesto: in fact it was thrown up by the revolutionary movement which also gave rise to the manifesto.

The whole indictment is constructed on the crude fiction that legality in Russia during the last year was continuous. The prosecution proceeds from the absurd assumption that all the articles of the Criminal Code remained in force all the time, and that they were applied all the time and were never abolished —neither de jure, nor even de facto.

What actually happened was that a whole number of articles were ripped out of the Code by the hand of the revolution, with the authorities' tacit consent.

Did the *zemstvo* congresses take place on legal ground? Were all the banquets and demonstrations consistent with the Criminal Code? Did the press observe the censorship rules? Did not various associations of the intelligentsia come into being with impunity and "without preliminary permission," as the phrase goes?

But let us stick to the fate of the Soviet itself. In supposing that Articles 101 and 102 of the Criminal Code remained in force without interruption, the prosecution regards the Soviet as a consciously criminal organization from the day of its birth, and therefore sees the very act of joining the Soviet as a crime. But, from this standpoint, how to explain the fact that the supreme representative of power entered into negotiations with a criminal association aiming at the establishment of a republic by revolutionary means? From the standpoint of legal continuity, Count Witte's parleying with the Soviet was a criminal act.

The incident with Count Witte demonstrates to what absurdities the prosecution is reduced by insisting that legality in Russia remained continuous throughout 1905.

In quoting the debate which took place in connection with the sending of the deputation to Witte to demand the release of three members of the Soviet arrested at a street meeting outside Kazansky Cathedral, the indictment speaks of this appeal to Witte as "a legitimate attempt to obtain the release of the arrested persons." (p. 6.)

Thus the prosecution considers it "legitimate" for Count Witte, the supreme representative of the state executive, to negotiate with a revolutionary association which was aiming at the overthrow of the state system Count Witte was meant to defend.

What was the result of this "legitimate attempt"?

The indictment quite correctly records that the chairman of the Committee of Ministers, "after discussion with the city governor, ordered the release of the arrested persons." (p. 6.) In other words, the state power met the demand of a criminal association whose members, according to Articles 101 and 102, should not have been in the Prime Minister's ante-room but at hard labor.

Where, then, was "legitimacy"? Was the street meeting held outside Kazansky Cathedral on October 18 legitimate? Apparently not, since the Soviet's members who conducted the meeting were arrested. Was the sending of a deputation to the government from an anti-government association legitimate? The prosecution replies in the affirmative. It would appear that "legitimacy" demanded, not the release of the arrested persons, but the arrest of their confederates still at liberty. Or did Count Witte grant an amnesty to the criminals? But who gave him the right to grant amnesties?

The Soviet of Workers' Deputies did not stand on legal ground. But neither did the government. Legal ground did not exist.

The October and November days set vast masses of the population in motion, revealed a multitude of profound interests, created a multitude of new organizations and new forms of political life. The old system solemnly liquidated itself by the manifesto of October 17. But no new system as yet existed. Old laws patently at variance with the manifesto had not been abolished; but in fact they were infringed upon at every step. The authorities not only tolerated thousands of such infringements but, in some measure, openly encouraged them. The manifesto of October 17 not only rendered a whole series of existing laws logically null and void—it liquidated the actual legislative apparatus of absolutism.

New forms of public life came into being and existed outside the limits of any legal definition. The Soviet was one of these forms.

The caricatural inconsistency between the definition in Article 101 and the real physiognomy of the Soviet is due to the fact that the Soviet was an institution absolutely not provided for in the laws of old Russia. It came into being at a moment when the old, rotten garment of legality was bursting at every seam and its ragged scraps fell to the ground to be trampled upon by the revolutionary nation. The Soviet did not come into being because it was legally justifiable but because it was factually necessary.

When, after the first battles, the ruling reactionary forces began to regain their strength, they started invoking laws which had in fact been abolished, just as those involved in a street brawl will make use of the first stone that comes into their hands. Article 101 of the Criminal Code was the stone they picked up, and the Chamber of Justice, by imposing a certain penalty on the persons presented by an ignorant gendarmerie and a servile prosecution, was obliged to play the role of catapult.

The question of the participation of official party representatives in the Soviet's decisions reveals more clearly than anything else the hopelessness of the prosecution's legal position.

Anyone who had anything at all to do with the Soviet knows that the representatives of parties had no voting rights either in the Soviet or in the Executive Committee; they took part in the debates but not in the voting. This was due to the fact that the Soviet was organized on the principle of representation of workers by enterprises and trades but not by party groupings. Party representatives were entitled to make their political experience and their knowledge available to the Soviet, and this they did; but they could not enjoy voting rights without violating the principle of representation of the working masses. They were, so to speak, political experts within the Soviet's membership.

This simple fact could have been established without difficulty, yet it presented the greatest difficulties to the investigating and prosecuting authorities.

The first difficulty was of a purely legal nature. If the Soviet is a criminal association having certain previously established aims, if the defendants are members of this criminal association and have to appear as such before the court, what is to be done with those defendants who belonged to the Soviet merely in a consultative capacity and were entitled only to expound their point of view but not to take part in the voting, that is, in the direct and immediate determining of the criminal association's collective will? Just as an expert's statements in court may exercise an important influence on the verdict, without, however, making the expert responsible for that verdict, so the statements of party representatives, however great their influence on the Soviet's actions, cannot make them legally responsible for those actions. They told the Soviet: here is our opinion, here is the opinion of our party, but the decision must depend on you. It goes without saying that the party representatives have no intention of hiding from the prosecution behind this argument. After all, the prosecution is not defending any "articles," any "legality" or "law" but the interests of a certain caste. And since the party representatives by their work dealt as many blows to that caste as did any other members of the Soviet, it is quite natural that the government's vengeance, in the form of the verdict of the Chamber of Justice, should strike them in the same measure as it strikes the representatives of factories and plants.

But one thing is certain: whereas, by a crass distortion of the facts and of their legal meaning, it may be just possible to qualify the deputies as members of a criminal association, the application of Article 101 to the representatives of political parties in the Soviet is the very embodiment of legal absurdity. That, at least, is what human logic tells us; and legal logic cannot be anything other than the application of universal human logic to a specific sphere of phenomena.

The second difficulty facing the prosecution in connection with the status of party delegates in the Soviet was of a political nature. The task set before General Ivanov of the gendarmerie and, later, Assistant Prosecutor Baltz, or whoever was lurking behind him, was simple indeed: they had to represent the Soviet as a conspiratorial organization which, under pressure from a group of energetic revolutionaries, controlled the terrorized masses. Everything speaks against this Jacobin parody of the Soviet as seen by the police: the Soviet's membership, the open character of its activities, its method of discussing and settling all questions, finally the absence of voting rights for party representatives. What, then, does the investigating authority do? If the facts speak against it, too bad for the facts: it disposes of them "by administrative means." From the minutes and the vote counting, indeed from the testimony of its own agents, the gendarmerie could easily discover that the party representatives enjoyed only consultative rights in the Soviet. The gendarmerie knew this; but because this fact would have reduced the scope of its lofty considerations and plans, it did everything in its power to mislead the prosecution on this point. Despite the importance of the question of the legal status of party representatives with the Soviet, the gendarmerie quite systematically and deliberately avoided this question at interrogations. The gendarmerie were very interested in knowing in what places individual members of the Executive Committee sat and how they entered and left the committee room, but they did not in the least want to know whether the 70 social-democrats and 35 socialist revolutionaries, a total of 105 men, had the right of vote on such issues as the general strike, the eight-hour working day, etc. They refrained from putting certain questions to the defendants and the witnesses solely in order to avoid establishing certain facts.* This is perfectly obvious and no one can dispute it.

We have said that the investigating authority was thus misleading the prosecuting authority. But is that so? The prosecution, in the person of its representative, is present at interrogations or, at least, signs the records of interrogations. Thus it is never lacking an opportunity to manifest its interest in the truth; all that is wanted is such an interest. Of course, no trace of such an interest exists. The prosecution not only covered up the "blunders" of the preliminary investigation but actually made use of them to draw conclusions which it knew to be false.

This is most blatantly obvious in that part of the indictment which deals with the Soviet's activity in arming the workers.

We do not propose to discuss here the question of an armed rising and of the Soviet's attitude toward it. This topic has been

* Only in one passage does the indictment state that, according to Rastorguyev, "the representatives of parties did not, allegedly, have voting rights during ballots." (p. 39.) But the prosecution has taken no trouble whatever to clarify the matter for itself, or rather it has deliberately avoided doing so.

considered in other articles. Here it is quite enough for us to say that the armed rising as a revolutionary idea inspiring the masses and guiding their elective organization differs from the prosecution's and the police's "idea" of an armed rising as much as the Soviet of Workers' Deputies differs from the association envisaged in Article 101. But the authorities' hopeless failure to understand the meaning and spirit of the Soviet, their hopeless confusion regarding its political ideas, is directly proportional to their desire to base their accusations on a perfectly simple mechanical object: a Browning revolver.

Although, as we shall see, the police investigation yielded very scant materials on this matter, the author of the indictment makes an attempt—remarkable for its audacity—to prove as a fact that the Executive Committee armed the workers on a mass scale for the purpose of an armed rising. We are obliged to quote the relevant passage of the indictment and examine it in its separate parts.

"It would appear," the prosecution reasons, "that the actual putting into effect of *all the above-mentioned intentions* of the Executive Committee as regards arming the Petersburg workers belonged to the same period (i.e., the second half of November), since, according to the deposition of Grigory Levkin, a deputy from Bogdanov's tobacco factory, it was decided (by whom?) at one of the meetings around the middle of November, to form armed 'tens' and 'hundreds' for the support of demonstrations, and at precisely the same period the deputy Nikolai Nemtsov pointed out that the workers lacked arms and a collection of money for arms was held among the assembled persons (where?)." Thus we learn that in the middle of November the Executive Committee put into effect "all" its intentions with regard to the arming of the proletariat. What proof is there of this? Two unchallengeable pieces of evidence. First, Grigory Levkin testifies that around this time it was decided (presumably by the Soviet) to form armed "tens" and "hundreds." Thus, obviously, the Soviet in the middle of November *put into effect* its intention to arm the workers by, at precisely that time, expressing . . . the intention (or adopting a decision) to arm them! Yet is it even true that the Soviet adopted such a decision? Nothing of the kind. In this instance the indictment is not referring to a decision of the Soviet, which never existed, but to a speech by one of the members of the Soviet (myself), quoted previously on page 17 of the same indictment.

Thus, as proof of the putting into effect of "intentions," the prosecution produces a resolution which, even had it been adopted, would only have been the expression of one such intention.

The second proof of the arming of the Petersburg workers in the middle of November is supplied by Nikolai Nemtsov who "precisely at that time" (!) drew attention to the fact that the workers had no arms. It is not easy to understand why Nemtsov's testimony concerning the *absence* of arms should prove the *presence* of arms. But after this it is stated that "a collection of money for arms was held among the assembled persons." The fact that money for arms was collected among the workers is not in doubt. Let us assume that, in particular, such a collection was also made on the occasion to which the prosecution is referring. But why should it follow from this that "the actual putting into effect of all the above-mentioned intentions of the Executive Committee to arm the Petersburg workers belonged to the same period?" Further: to whom did Nikolai Nemtsov point out that arms were lacking? Evidently to a meeting of the Soviet or the Executive Committee. Therefore we must assume that funds for arming the workers were collected from amidst a few dozen or hundred deputies; and this fact, fairly unlikely in itself, serves as proof that at this time the masses were already armed!

And so the arming of the workers has been proved; now for revealing the purpose of this action. Here is what the indictment has to say on this issue: "The pretext for such arming, according to the testimony of deputy Alexey Shishkin, was the possible occurrence of pogroms, but Shishkin says that this was only a pretext and that, in reality, an armed rising was allegedly being prepared for January 9. *In reality,*" the indictment continues, "the distribution of arms, according to Mikhail Khakharev, a deputy from Odner's plant, was begun by Khrustalev-Nosar as far back as October, and he, Khakharev, received a Browning from Khrustalev 'for protection against the Black Hundreds.' However, this defensive purpose of the distribution of arms is disproved, apart from all the above-mentioned decisions of the Soviet, also by the contents of certain documents found among Georgy Nosar's papers. For example, these papers contain the original copy of a Soviet resolution, without any indication of the date on which it was drafted, which contains an appeal to arms and to the forming of armed detachments and a workers' army 'prepared to repulse the Black Hundreds government which is ravaging the Russian land.' "

Let us stop there for the moment. Resisting the Black Hundreds is only a pretext; the real object of the Soviet's universal arming of the population, carried out in the middle of November, was an armed rising on January 9. This real aim was unknown not only to those who were being armed but also to those who did the arming, so that, but for Alexey Shishkin's testimony, it would never have transpired that the organization of the working masses had fixed a definite date for an armed rising. Another proof that it was precisely in the middle of November that the Executive Committee armed the masses for a rising in January is the fact that, in October, Khakharev received a Browning from Khrustalev "for protection against the Black Hundreds."

But, in the prosecutor's opinion, the defensive purpose of the arming is further disproved by certain documents found among Nosar's papers, e.g., the original copy (?) of a resolution appealing to the workers to arm themselves in order to "repulse the Black Hundreds government which is ravaging the

Russian land." That the Soviet pointed out to the masses the necessity of arming themselves and the inevitability of a rising is clear from many of the Soviet's decisions; no one can dispute it; the prosecution does not have to find proofs of it. What it does want to prove is that the Executive Committee in the middle of November put into effect "all its intentions" as regards the arming of the masses, and that this arming was actually carried out and had the direct and immediate aim of an armed rising; and, to prove this point, the prosecution adduces yet another resolution which differs from the others by the fact that its date cannot be ascertained and it is impossible to tell whether in fact it was adopted by the Soviet at any time. And, finally, it is precisely this doubtful resolution, meant to disprove the defensive nature of the arming, which speaks clearly and unequivocally of *repulsing* the Black Hundreds government which is ravaging the country.

However, the prosecution's long misadventure in the matter of the Brownings does not end there. "Further," the prosecution continues in order to refute the defensive object of the operation, "in Nosar's papers there was found a note from an unknown person pointing out that Khrustalev had promised to hand out several Browning or Smith & Wesson revolvers at the organization's price, and the writer, whose address is at Kolpino, asks that the promised arms be handed to him."

To understand why the author of the note, "whose address is at Kolpino," could not have obtained the revolvers "at the organization's price" *for purposes of self-defense* rather than of an armed rising is as difficult as all the rest. Another note containing a request for revolvers adds nothing new.

In the end the prosecution's data on the question of the arming of the Petersburg workers turn out to be absolutely negligible. "Very insignificant expenses on the acquisition of arms were found in Nosar's documents," the indictment plaintively states, "*since* (!) his papers included a notebook and a separate sheet containing notes on the distribution of revolvers of various makes and boxes of cartridges to the workers, and, *according to these notes*, only sixty-four revolvers were thus distributed."

These sixty-four revolvers as proof of the putting into effect of "all" the Executive Committee's "intentions" concerning an armed rising in January are evidently an embarrassment to the prosecution. It therefore decides upon a bold step: if it cannot be proved that the revolvers *were bought*, it must be proved that they *might have been bought*. With this end in view, the prosecution prefaces the sorry total of sixty-four revolvers with impressive suppositions of a financial nature. After pointing out that a collection of funds for arms was carried out at the plant of the *Compagnie des Wagons-Lits*, the indictment states: "Subscriptions of this kind offered an opportunity of acquiring arms, the Soviet of Workers' Deputies being able, in case of need, to obtain arms in large quantities because it disposed of large sums of money. . . . The total receipts of the Executive Committee amounted to 30,063 roubles 52 kopecks."

Here we have the tone and manner of a newspaper feature which spurns even the outward semblance of proof. First you quote certain notes and "original copies" of resolutions, then you dismiss their testimony with a bold and simple conjecture: the Executive Committee had a lot of money, therefore it had a lot of arms.

If we were to arrive at conclusions by the prosecution's method, we might say: the secret police departments have a lot of money, therefore the pogromists have a lot of arms. But such a conclusion would only superficially resemble that offered in the indictment, for whereas every kopeck in the Soviet's hands was accounted for, which makes it easy to dismiss the prosecution's bold guess as pure nonsense, the cash outgoings of the Secret Police belong to a realm of total mystery which has long awaited criminal investigation.

To finish once and for all with the arguments and conclusions of the indictment concerning the arming of the population, let us try to present them in strictly logical form,

THESIS

Around the middle of November the Executive Committee armed the Petersburg proletariat for the purpose of an armed rising.

PROOFS

(a) One of the Soviet's members at the meeting of November 6 advocated the organizing of the workers in armed units of 10 and 100.

(b) In the middle of November Nikolai Nemtsov referred to the lack of arms.

(c) Alexey Shishkin knew that a rising was fixed for January 9.

(d) As far back as October, Khakharev received a revolver for self-defense against the Black Hundreds.

(e) An undated resolution refers to the necessity for arms.

(f) An unknown person "whose address is at Kolpino" asked for revolvers "at the organization's price."

(g) Although the distribution of only sixty-four revolvers has been established, the Soviet had money, and since money is a universal equivalent, it might have been exchanged for revolvers.

These conclusions are not good enough even to serve as examples of elementary sophisms in secondary-school textbooks of logic. They are so crude that their crudeness is an insult to any normally constituted intelligence.

It is on these materials and on this legal construction that the Chamber of Justice will have to base its verdict.

CHAPTER 31

◇◇◇◇◇◇◇◇◇◇◇◇

My Speech Before the Court

Meeting of October 4 (17) 1907

Gentlemen of the bench, gentlemen representatives of the estates!

The question of an armed rising—a question which, however strange this may seem to the Special Court, occupied no place whatever on the agenda of the meetings of the Soviet of Workers' Deputies throughout the fifty days of its existence—is the principal object of this court inquiry, as it was of the preliminary investigation. The subject of an armed rising as such was not raised or discussed at any of our meetings; more than that, neither was the question of a Constituent Assembly, nor of a democratic republic, nor even of a general strike as such or its fundamental significance as a method of revolutionary struggle, discussed at any meeting. These central issues, which for a number of years were debated first in the revolutionary press and later at various meetings and assemblies, were on no occasion

(384)

considered by the Soviet. Later I shall explain why this was so, and define the Soviet's attitude to an armed rising.

But before passing to this matter, which from the court's viewpoint is the central one, I will permit myself to draw the attention of the Chamber to another question which, compared with the first, is more general but less acute—namely, the question of the Soviet's use of force in general. Did the Soviet consider itself entitled through the agency of one or another of its organs to use force or repressive measures in certain cases? My answer to this question put in such general terms is: Yes! I know as well as the representative of the prosecution that in any "normally" functioning state, whatever its form, the monopoly of brute force and repression belongs to the state power. That is its "inalienable" right, and of this right it takes the most jealous care, ever watchful lest any private body encroach upon its monopoly of violence. In this way the state organization fights for its existence. It is enough to have a concrete picture of modern society, that complex and contradictory cooperative system —for example in a country as vast as Russia—for it to become immediately clear that, given the existing social structure with all its antagonisms, repression is quite inevitable.

We are not anarchists, we are socialists. The anarchists call us "Statists," because we recognize the historical necessity of the state and hence the historical necessity of state repression. But under the conditions created by a political general strike, whose nature consists in the fact that it paralyzes the state mechanism—under such conditions the old power which had long outlived its day and against which, precisely, the political strike was directed, found itself ultimately incapable of action, quite unable to regulate and maintain public order, even by the barbaric means which were the only ones at its disposal. Meanwhile, the strike had thrown hundreds of thousands of workers from the factories into the streets, and had freed these workers for public and political life. Who could direct them, who could bring discipline into their ranks? What organ of the old state power? The police? The gendarmerie? The secret police? I ask myself: who? and I can find no answer. No one, except the Soviet of Workers' Deputies. No one!

The Soviet, which directed this colossal elemental force, saw its immediate task in reducing internal friction to a minimum, preventing excesses and making sure that the inevitable victims of the struggle were as few as possible. And, that being so, the Soviet, in the political strike which had created it, became nothing other than the organ of self-government of the revolutionary masses: an *organ of power*. It ruled the parts of the whole by the will of the whole. It was a democratic power and it was voluntarily obeyed. But inasmuch as the Soviet was the organized power of the overwhelming majority, it was inevitably compelled to use repressive measures against those elements among the masses who brought anarchy into its united ranks. The Soviet, as a new historical power, as the sole power at a time of total moral, political, and technical bankruptcy of the old apparatus, as the sole guarantee of personal immunity and public order in the best sense of that term, considered itself entitled to oppose its force to such elements. The representatives of the old power, which is wholly based on murderous repression, has no right to speak with moral indignation of the Soviet's violent methods. The historical power which the prosecutor represents in this court is the organized violence of a minority over the majority. The new power, whose precursor was the Soviet, is the organized will of the majority calling the minority to order. In this distinction lies the Soviet's revolutionary right to existence, a right that stands above any legal or moral doubt.

The Soviet recognized its right to use repressive measures. But in what cases, and to what degree? We have heard a hundred witnesses on this point. Before passing to repressive measures the Soviet used words of persuasion. That was its true method, and the Soviet was tireless in applying it. By revolutionary agitation, by the weapon of the spoken word, the Soviet continually brought new masses to their feet and subordinated them to its authority. If it met with resistance on the part of ignorant or corrupted groups within the proletariat, it said to itself that the time to render them harmless by physical force would always come soon enough. As you have seen from the testimony of witnesses, it sought other ways. It appealed to the good sense of factory administrations in calling upon them to stop work, it brought influence to bear on ignorant workers through technicians and engineers who were sympathetic to the general strike. It sent deputies to the workers to "bring them out," and only in the most extreme cases did it threaten strike-breakers with the use of force. But did it ever actually use force? Gentlemen of the bench, you have not seen any examples of this in the materials of the preliminary investigation and it proved impossible, despite all efforts, to establish such examples during the court investigation. Even if we were to take seriously those examples of "violence," comic rather than tragic, that did pass in review before the court (so-and-so entered someone's apartment without removing his cap, so-and-so arrested someone else by mutual consent . . .) we need only compare this cap which somebody forgot to remove with the hundreds of *heads* which the old power so often "removes" by mistake, for the Soviet's violent actions to assume their proper proportions in our eyes. And that is all we want. To reconstruct the events of that time in their true form is our task, and for its sake we, the defendants, have taken an active part in this trial.

Let me pose another question which is of importance to this court. Did the actions and declarations of the Soviet of Workers' Deputies possess a legal basis, in the manifesto of October 17 (30)? What was the relationship between the Soviet's resolutions on the Constituent Assembly and the creation of a democratic republic and the October manifesto? The question—let me state it bluntly—simply did not occur to us at the time, but today it is undoubtedly of major importance to this court. We have heard here, gentlemen of the court, the testimony of the witness Luchinin, which struck me personally as extremely interesting and, in some of its conclusions, both pertinent and profound. Among other things, Lukanin said that the Soviet of Workers' Deputies, being a republican body in its slogans, its principles and its political ideals, did actually, directly, and concretely put into effect those freedoms which were proclaimed in principle by the Tsar's manifesto of October 17 and which those responsible for the manifesto actually fought against with all their strength. Yes, gentlemen of the bench and gentlemen representatives of the estates! We, the revolutionary, proletarian Soviet, actually put into effect and implemented the freedom of speech, the freedom of assembly and personal immunity—all those things that had been promised to the Russian people under pressure of the October strike. Whereas all that the apparatus of the old power could do was to tear these lawful attainments of the people into pieces. Gentlemen of the bench, that is an indubitable, objective fact that has already become part of history. It cannot be disputed because it is indisputable.

If I am asked, however—and if my comrades are asked—whether we *subjectively* based our actions and declarations on the manifesto of October 17, we must categorically answer: No. Why? Because we were deeply convinced—and we were not mistaken—that the manifesto of October 17 created no new legal basis whatever, that it did not create the foundations of a new legality, for a new legal system is not created—we are convinced of this, gentlemen of the court—by means of manifestos, but by a real reorganization of the entire state apparatus. Because we adopted this materialist standpoint, the only correct one, we had no confidence whatever in the immanent force of the manifesto of October 17. And this we openly declared. But I do not believe that our subjective attitude as party men, as revolutionaries, determines for the court our objective attitude, as citizens of a state, to the manifesto: For the court, inasmuch as it is a court, is bound to see the manifesto as a foundation of a new legality, or else it must cease to exist. We know that in Italy there exists a bourgeois parliamentary republican party operating on the basis of the country's monarchical constitution. Socialist parties which are revolutionary by their nature legally exist and fight in all civilized countries.

The question is: does the manifesto of October 17 leave any room for us Russian republican socialists? That is the question which the court must answer. The court must say whether we social-democrats were right when we argued that the constitutional manifesto was merely a list of promises which would never be voluntarily fulfilled; whether we were right in our revolutionary criticism of those paper guarantees; whether we were right when we called upon the people to engage in open struggle for true and complete freedom. Were we right, or were we not? Let the court tell us that the manifesto of October 17 is a real legal foundation upon which we republicans could exist as persons of legality, persons who acted within the law, despite our opinions and intentions. Let the manifesto of October 17 tell us here, through the verdict of this court: "You denied my reality, but I exist for you as well as for the rest of the country."

I have already said that the Soviet of Workers' Deputies never once raised the question of a Constituent Assembly and the creation of a democratic republic at its meetings; nevertheless, as you have seen from the speeches of working-class witnesses, its attitude to those slogans was clearly defined. How could it be otherwise? After all, the Soviet did not come into being on virgin soil. It was created when the Russian proletariat had already lived through the events of January 9 (22), through Senator Shidlovsky's commission, through the whole long, too long, school of Russian absolutism. Long before the Soviet existed, the demand for a Constituent Assembly, for universal franchise, for a democratic republic, together with the eight-hour working day, had become the central slogans of the revolutionary proletariat. That is why the Soviet never had occasion to raise these issues as matters of principle: it simply included them in its resolutions, as matters which had been decided once and for all. The same, in substance, was also true of the idea of an insurrection.

What is an insurrection, gentlemen of the court? Not a palace revolution, not a military conspiracy, but an insurrection of the working masses! The president of this court addressed the following question to one of the witnesses: did he consider a political strike to be an insurrection? I forget what the witness replied, but I believe and affirm that a political strike, despite the president's doubts, is indeed, in its substance, an insurrection. That is not a paradox, although it may seem to be one from the point of view of the indictment. I repeat: my notion of an insurrection—and I shall presently demonstrate this—has nothing in common but its name with the construction which the police and the prosecution put on the term. A political strike is an insurrection, I say. For, in point of fact, what is a political general strike? It has only one thing in common with an economic strike —namely, that in both cases workers cease to work. In no other respect do the two resemble one another. An economic strike has a definite, narrow aim, that of bringing pressure to bear upon an employer by putting him, for that purpose, temporarily outside the competitive field. It interrupts work at a factory in order to achieve certain changes within the limits of that factory.

The nature of a political strike is profoundly different. It exerts no pressure on individual employers, it does not as a rule make any specific economic claims; its claims are directed, over the heads of the employers whom it hits so hard, at the state power itself. How, then, does a political strike affect the state power? It paralyzes its vital activity. A modern state, even in so backward a country as Russia, is based on a centralized economic organism turned into a single whole by the skeleton of the railways and the nervous system of the telegraph. And although the telegraph, the railway, and all the other attainments of modern technology may not serve Russian absolutism for cultural or economic ends, they are all the more essential to it for the purposes of repression. The railways and the telegraph are irreplaceable weapons for transferring troops from one end of the country to another, uniting and directing the administration's activities in suppressing sedition. What does a political strike do? It paralyzes the economic apparatus of the state, disrupts communications between separate parts of the administrative machine, isolates the government, and renders it powerless. On the other hand, it politically unites the mass of workers from the factories and plants and opposes this workers' army to the state power.

Therein, gentlemen of the court, lies the essence of an insurrection. To unite the proletarian masses within a single revolutionary protest action, to oppose them as enemies to the organized power of the state—that, gentlemen of the court, is insurrection as the Soviet understood it and as I understand it too. We saw such a revolutionary clash between two hostile sides during the October strike which broke out spontaneously, without the Soviet, which occurred before the Soviet, indeed which gave birth to the Soviet. The October strike created "anarchy," and as a result of that anarchy came the manifesto of October 17. I hope that the prosecution will not deny this, any more than do the most conservative politicians and journalists, including those of the semi-official *Novoye Vremya*. Only a few days ago *Novoye Vremya* wrote that the manifesto of October 17 was the result of governmental *panic* created by the political strike. But if this manifesto is the foundation of the whole new system in force, we must recognize, gentlemen of the court, that our present state system is based on panic, and that the panic, in turn, was based on the political strike of the proletariat. And so you see that a general strike is something more than mere cessation of work.

I have said that a political strike, as soon as it stops being a demonstration, becomes, in substance, an insurrection. It would be more accurate to say that it becomes the principal, most general method of proletariat insurrection: the principal, but not the only method. The method of the political strike has its natural limits. And this became evident as soon as the workers, following the Soviet's call, resumed work at noon on October 21 (November 3).

The manifesto of October 17 was received with a vote of no confidence; the masses feared, and with good reason, that the government would fail to introduce the promised freedoms. The proletariat saw the inevitability of a decisive struggle and instinctively turned to the Soviet as the center of their revolutionary power. On the other hand, absolutism, on recovering from its panic, began to reconstruct its half-demolished apparatus and put its regiments in order. As a result it transpired that after the October clash there were two powers: a new, popular power based on the masses—the Soviet of Workers' Deputies was such a power—and the old, official power based on the army. These two forces could not exist side by side: the strengthening of one threatened the other with extinction.

The autocracy, founded as it is on bayonets, naturally tried to bring the maximum confusion, chaos, and disintegration into the vast process, whose center was the Soviet, of unifying the popular forces. On the other hand, the Soviet, founded as it was on the confidence, the discipline, the active effort, the unanimity of the working masses, could not fail to understand the terrible threat to popular freedom, civil rights, and personal immunity embodied in the fact that the army and all material weapons of power remained in the same blood-stained hands that had wielded them up to October 17. And so a titanic struggle for influence over the army begins between these two organs of power—the second stage of the growing popular insurrection.

After the mass strike which has opposed the proletariat to the autocracy there arises a powerful movement to bring the army over to the workers' side, to fraternize with the soldiers, to win over their minds. From this movement naturally springs a revolutionary appeal to the soldiers, on whom absolutism rests. The second November strike was a powerful and splendid demonstration of solidarity between the factory and the barracks. Of course, if the army had gone over to the side of the people, there would have been no need for insurrection. But is a peaceful transition of the army into the ranks of the revolution conceivable? No, it is not. Absolutism is not going to wait with folded arms for the army, freed from every corrupting influence, to become the friend of the people. Before all is lost, absolutism will take the initiative and launch an offensive. Did the Petersburg workers realize this? Yes, they did. Did the proletariat, did the Soviet believe that open conflict between the two sides was inevitable? Yes, it did; it had no doubt of it, it knew, knew for certain, that sooner or later the fatal hour would strike.

Of course if the organization of popular forces, uninterrupted by any attacks of the armed counter-revolution, had continued to advance along the path on which it had entered under the leadership of the Soviet of Workers' Deputies, the old system would have been destroyed without the use of any force whatever. For what did we see? We saw how the workers rallied around the Soviet, how the peasants' union, embodying ever-increasing masses of the peasantry, sent its deputies to the Soviet; how the railway and postal unions united themselves with the Soviet; how the organization of the liberal professions, the Union of Unions, was drawn towards the Soviet; we saw how tolerant, how almost benevolent, was the attitude towards the Soviet even of the factory managements. It was as though the whole nation were making a heroic effort, trying to produce from its very deepest core an organ of power that might really and unchallengeably lay the foundations of a new social system pending the convening of a Constituent Assembly. If the old state power had not intervened in this organic effort, if it had not introduced real anarchy into national life, if this process of the organization of forces had been able to develop in complete freedom, the result would have been a new, reborn Russia, without the use of force and without bloodshed.

But the point is precisely that we never for a moment believed that the process of liberation would follow a smooth course. We knew too well the real nature of the old power. We social-democrats were convinced that, despite the manifesto which looked like a definitive break with the past, the old state apparatus would not withdraw of its own free will, would not hand over power to the people or surrender a single one of its principal positions; we foresaw, and openly warned the nation, that absolutism would make many more convulsive attempts to keep such power as it still possessed in its hands and even to regain what it had solemnly relinquished. That is why insurrection, armed insurrection, gentlemen of the court, was inevitable from our point of view. It was and remains a historical necessity in the process of the people's struggle against the military and police state. Throughout October and November this idea reigned at all meetings and assemblies, dominated the entire revolutionary press, filled the entire political atmosphere and, in one way or another, was crystallized in the consciousness of every member of the Soviet; and that is why, quite naturally, it formed part of the Soviet's resolutions, and why, too, there was never any need for us to discuss it.

The tense political situation we inherited from the October strike—a situation in which a revolutionary organization of the masses struggling for its existence, not founded on legality because legality did not exist, but on strength, which did exist, confronted an armed counter-revolution waiting for its moment of revenge—was, if I may put it that way, the algebraic formula of insurrection. New events merely introduced new numerical values into the formula. The idea of armed insurrection, the prosecution's superficial conclusions notwithstanding, is not only to be found in the Soviet's decision adopted on November 27, i.e., a week before our arrest, where it is expressed clearly and unequivocally: no, the idea of armed insurrection, in different forms but essentially the same, runs like a red thread from the very beginning of the Soviet's existence, through all the

Soviet's decisions—in its resolution canceling the funeral demonstration, its resolution proclaiming the end of the November strike, and in many other resolutions which spoke of armed conflict with the government, and of the final assault or the final battle as an inevitable stage in the struggle.

But what was the Soviet's own interpretation of these decisions? Did it believe that armed insurrection is an enterprise that can be prepared underground and then brought out, ready-made, into the street? Did it think that insurrection can be acted out in accordance with a preconceived plan? Did the Executive Committee elaborate a technique of street fighting?

No, of course not. And this is bound to puzzle the author of the indictment when faced with a modest few dozen revolvers which, in his eyes, are the only stage properties of an armed rising. But his view is only the view of criminal law, which knows all about conspiratorial associations but cannot understand the concept of a mass organization, which knows about assassinations and mutinies but does not and cannot know revolution.

The legal concepts on which this trial is based are decades behind the development of the revolutionary movement. The modern working-class movement in Russia has nothing whatever in common with the notion of conspiracy as interpreted by our criminal code—a notion which has not substantially changed since Speransky, who lived at the time of the Carbonari. That is why the attempt to squeeze the Soviet's activities into the narrow definition of Articles 101 and 102 is so hopeless from the point of view of legal logic.

And yet our activities *were* revolutionary. And yet we really *were* preparing for armed insurrection.

An insurrection of the masses, gentlemen of the bench, is not made: it accomplishes itself. It is the result of social relations, not the product of a plan. It cannot be created; it can be foreseen. For reasons which depended on us as little as they did on Tsardom, an open conflict became inevitable. It drew closer day by day. To prepare for it meant, for us, doing everything possible to minimize the casualties of this inevitable conflict. Did we think that for this purpose we had first of all to lay in stocks of arms, prepare a plan of military operations, assign the participants of the rising to particular places, divide the town up into sectors—in other words, do all the things which the military authorities do in anticipation of "disorders," when they divide Petersburg up into sectors, appoint colonels in charge of each sector and equip them with a certain number of machine guns and ammunition? No, that is not how we interpreted our role. To prepare for an inevitable insurrection—and, gentlemen of the court, we never *prepared an insurrection* as the prosecution thinks and says; we prepared *for* an insurrection—meant to us, first and foremost, enlightening the people, explaining to them that open conflict was inevitable, that all that had been given to them would be taken away again, that only might can defend right, that a powerful organization of the working masses was necessary, that the enemy had to be met head on, that the struggle had to be continued to the end, that there was no other way. That is what preparing for an insurrection meant to us.

Under what conditions did we think an insurrection might lead us to victory? The condition of the army's sympathy. The first requisite was to bring the army over to our side. To force the soldiers to recognize the shameful role they were playing, to persuade them to work with the people and for the people—that was the first task we set ourselves. I have already said that the November strike, a disinterested impulse of direct fraternal solidarity with the sailors under threat of the death penalty, also had tremendous political significance in that it drew the army's sympathetic attention towards the proletariat. That is where the prosecutor should have looked for preparations for armed insurrection. But, of course, a demonstration of sympathy and protest could not, by itself, settle the matter. Under what conditions, then, did we think—and do we think now—that the army can be expected to pass over to the side of revolution? What is the prerequisite for this? Machine guns and rifles? Of course, if the working masses possessed machine guns and rifles they would wield great power. Such power would even largely remove the inevitability of an insurrection. The undecided army would lay down its arms at the feet of the armed people. But the masses did not, do not, and cannot possess arms in large quantities. Does that mean that the masses are doomed to defeat? No, it does not. However important weapons are, it is not in weapons that the most essential strength lies. No, not in weapons. Not the capacity of the masses to kill, but their great readiness to die, that, gentlemen of the court, is what we believe ensures, in the last count, the success of a people's rising.

When the soldiers, sent out into the streets to repress the masses, find themselves face to face with the masses and discover that this crowd, the *people*, will not leave the streets until it has got what it wants; that it is prepared to pile corpses upon corpses; when they see and are convinced that the people have come out to fight in earnest, to the end—then the soldiers' hearts will falter, as they have always done in all revolutions, for they will be forced to doubt the stability of the order which they serve, they will be forced to believe in the triumph of the people.

It is customary to connect the idea of an insurrection with barricades. Even leaving aside the fact that barricades may loom too large in our notion of a popular rising, we should not forget that a barricade—clearly a mechanical element in the rising—plays, above all, a *moral* role. In every revolution, the significance of barricades is not at all the same as that of fortresses in a battle. A barricade is not just a physical obstacle. The barricade serves the cause of insurrection because, by creating a temporary barrier to the movement of troops, it brings them into close contact with the people. Here, at the barricades, the soldier hears—perhaps for the first time in his life—the talk of ordinary honest people, their fraternal appeals, the voice of the people's conscience; and, as a consequence of such contact between citizens and soldiers, military discipline disintegrates and disappears. This, and only this, ensures the victory of a popular rising. And this is why, in our opinion, a popular rising has been "prepared," not when the people have been armed with rifles and guns—for in that case it would never be prepared—but when it is armed with readiness to die in open street battle.

But, of course, the old besieged power, seeing the growth of this great feeling, this readiness to die for the interests of one's country, to give one's life for the happiness of future generations, seeing the masses becoming contaminated by such an enthusiasm as it could never feel or understand for itself—it could not calmly watch the moral regeneration of the people taking place before its eyes. To look on passively would have meant, for the Tsarist government, to let itself be scrapped. That much was clear. What, then, could it do? It had to fight the political self-determination of the people with its last forces, with every means at its disposal. The ignorant army, the Black Hundreds, the secret police, the corrupt press, all had to be sent into action. To set people against one another, to cover the streets in blood, to loot, rape, burn, create panic, lie, cheat and slander, that is what the old, criminal power had to do. And it did these things and is still doing them to this day. If an open conflict was inevitable, it was certainly not we but our mortal enemies who sought to bring it closer.

You have heard here many times that the workers in October and November armed themselves against the Black Hundreds. If one knew nothing of what is happening outside this court-room it would seem totally incomprehensible how, in a revolutionary country where the vast majority of the population supports the ideals of liberation, where the popular masses openly show their determination to fight to the end, how, in such a country, hundreds of thousands of workers can arm themselves to fight the Black Hundreds who represent a small and insignificant part of the population. Are they, then, so dangerous, these outcasts of society, this scum, whatever their social position? No, of course they are not. The problem would be small if it were only the pitiful gangs of the Black Hundreds that stood in the people's way. But we have heard, not only from the lawyer Bramson who appeared as a witness, but also from hundreds of workers who testified here, that the Black Hundreds are backed by a large number of government authorities, if not by all of them; that behind the gangs of thugs who have nothing to lose and who stop at nothing—neither an old man's gray hairs, nor a helpless woman, nor a child—there stand agents of the government who undoubtedly organize and arm the Black Hundreds out of the funds of the state budget.

And, finally, did we not know this before the present trial? Did we not read the papers? Did we not hear the reports of eye witnesses, did we not receive letters, did we see nothing with our own eyes? Were we not aware of Prince Urusov's shattering disclosures? But the prosecution does not believe any of it. It cannot believe it, for if it did it would have to direct its accusations against those whom today it is defending; it would have to admit that a Russian citizen who arms himself with a revolver against the police is acting in the interests of necessary self-defense. But whether the prosecution believes or not in the pogrom activities of the powers-that-be is ultimately unimportant. For this court it is sufficient that *we* believe in them, that the hundreds of thousands of workers who armed themselves at our call were convinced of them. We believed beyond any doubt that the powerful hand of the ruling clique guides the picturesque activities of the Black Hundreds. Gentlemen of the court, we can see that sinister hand even now.

The prosecution invites us to admit that the Soviet armed the workers for the struggle against the existing "form of government." If I am categorically asked whether this was so, I shall answer: Yes! Yes, I am willing to accept this accusation, but on one condition only. I do not know if the prosecution and the court will accept my condition.

Let me ask: what does the prosecution mean by "form of government"? Do we really have a form of government? For a long time past the government has not been supported by the nation but only by its military-police-Black Hundreds apparatus. What we have is not a national government but an automaton for mass murder. I can find no other name for the government machine which is tearing into parts the living body of our country. If you tell me that the pogroms, the murders, the burnings, the rapes . . . if you tell me that everything that happened in Tver, Rostov, Kursk, Siedlce . . . if you tell me that Kishinev, Odessa, Bialystok are the form of government of the Russian Empire—then I will agree with the prosecution that in October and November last we were arming ourselves, directly and immediately, against the form of government of the Russian Empire.

CHAPTER 32

<><><><><><><><><><>

There . . .

Extracts from letters

3 January 1907. We have been in the transit prison for the last two or three hours. I confess I parted from my cell in the "House of Preliminary Arrest" with nervous apprehension. I had become so used to that little ship's cabin where I had every opportunity for working! We knew that in the transit prison we were to be placed in a common cell—what can be more tiring? And after that would come the dirt, mess, and muddle of the journey into exile, which I know so well. Who knows how long it will be before we arrive at our destination? And who can tell when we shall return? Would it not have been better to stay in Cell No. 462, reading, writing, waiting? As you know, to move from one apartment to another is for me an act of moral courage. And a move from one prison to another is a hundred times worse. A new prison administration, new difficulties, new efforts to establish relations that aren't too intolerable. Ahead of us is a continually changing series of persons in authority, starting with the transit prison governor here in Petersburg and ending with the local policeman in the Siberian village that will be our place of exile. I have made this trip before and I anticipate its repetition without much relish.

We were taken here today quite suddenly, without warning. In the reception hall they made us change into prisoners' clothes. We did this with the curiosity of schoolboys. It was odd to see each other in those gray trousers, gray cloth jackets, and gray caps. However, the classic "ace of diamonds" on the back of the jacket is missing. We have been allowed to keep our own underclothes and shoes. Then, a large, excited crowd in our new get-up, we burst into our cell . . .

Despite the unfavorable rumors concerning the transit prison, the attitude of the administration seems quite decent, in certain respects actually considerate. There is reason to believe that special instructions have been issued: we are to be closely watched, but clashes are to be avoided.

The actual date of departure is still shrouded in the greatest mystery; obviously they are afraid of demonstrations and attempts to free us en route. They are afraid, and so they are taking the necessary measures; yet under the present conditions any such attempt would be senseless.

10 January. I am writing in the train. . . . Therefore please excuse the bad handwriting. It is 9:00 A.M.

We were awakened by the chief warder in the middle of the night, at half past three (most of us had only just gone to bed, so absorbed had we been in playing chess), and told that we would be leaving at 6:00 A.M. We had waited so long for this moment that the hour of departure struck us as . . . unexpected.

Afterwards everything happened as usual. We packed our belongings hurriedly and unsystematically. Then we went down to the reception hall, where the women and children joined us.

Then we were handed over to our escort, and our bags were quickly searched. A sleepy warder handed our money to an officer. Then we were placed in prison horse-carriages and taken to Nikolayevsky Station under reinforced convoy. We did not yet know where we were going. It's interesting to note that our escort was brought over specially from Moscow today: evidently they couldn't trust the Petersburg troops. The officer was very amiable throughout the proceedings, but claimed complete ignorance in response to all our questions, saying that the person in charge was a gendarmerie colonel who would issue all instructions, while he, the officer, was under orders to take us to the station and that was all. It's possible, of course, that the government is carrying caution to such a point, but on the other hand it's quite possible that this was simple diplomacy on the officer's part.

We have been traveling for about an hour and we still don't know whether the train is going to Moscow or Vologda. The soldiers don't know either—and so far as they are concerned that really is the truth.

We are traveling in a separate third-class coach, quite comfortable, with a sleeping bunk for everyone. Another coach is provided for our luggage, and the soldiers of the escort tell us that it also carries the ten gendarmes and their colonel who are accompanying us.

We have settled down and feel that we don't much care by what route we're going to travel: they'll get us there, one way or the other . . .

It appears that we are going via Vologda: one of us says he can tell by the names of the stations. That means we'll arrive at Tyumen in four days' time.

Everyone is very animated; traveling is a source of distraction and excitement after thirteen months in jail. True, the windows are barred, but directly beyond the bars is freedom, life, movement. . . . How soon shall we be traveling back along these rails? Farewell, my dear friend.

11 January. If the escorting officer is considerate and courteous, the soldiers are much more so still: nearly all of them have read reports of our trial and are extremely sympathetic towards us. An interesting detail: until the very last moment the soldiers did not know whom they were escorting and where. The precautions with which they were suddenly taken from Moscow to Petersburg made them think that they would have to deliver us to Schlisselburg for execution. In the reception hall of the transit prison I noticed that they seemed very restless and somehow unusually obliging, with a touch of guilt. It wasn't until we were in the train that I found out the reason. . . . How overjoyed they were to discover that we were "workers' deputies" condemned only to exile!

The gendarmes of the super-escort never show up in our coach. They are responsible for exterior guard duties—surrounding the coach at stations, mounting guard outside the carriage door, but most of all watching the soldiers of the escort. At least, that's what the soldiers themselves think.

Instructions to provide us with food and water for washing and drinking are sent ahead by telegraph. So far as that's concerned we are traveling in perfect comfort. It's not for nothing that the buffet manager in one of the stations we passed formed such a high opinion of us that he got the escort to ask whether we wanted thirty oysters! We had a good laugh over that, but turned down the oysters all the same.

12 January. We are leaving you further and further behind all the time.

From the first day we broke up into several "family" groups, and since the coach is crowded, each group has to live separately from the others. Only our doctor (Feit, a socialist revolutionary) doesn't belong to any group. With his sleeves rolled up, active and indefatigable, he seems to be in command of us all.

As you know, there are four children traveling with us in this coach. But their behavior is ideal, so much so that one forgets that they exist. The tenderest friendship unites them to the soldiers of the escort. The raw-boned soldiers treat them with the utmost delicacy . . .

. . . How "they" do guard us! At every station the coach is surrounded by gendarmes, and at the larger ones by policemen as well. In addition to their rifles, the gendarmes carry revolvers with which they threaten anyone who, accidentally or out of curiosity, approaches the coach. Such protection is reserved, these days, for two categories of persons: especially important "criminals" and especially well-known ministers.

Their tactics in our respect have been carefully worked out. We realized this back in the transit prison. On the one hand the most watchful vigilance, on the other hand, gentlemanly treatment within the limits of the law. This reflects Stolypin's constitutional genius. But, beyond any doubt, this cunning system will break down. The only question is, which of the two will break down first—vigilance or gentlemanly behavior?

We have arrived in Vyatka. The train is standing still. What a reception we got from the Vyatka bureaucracy! I wish you could have seen it all. Half a company of soldiers lined up on either side of the carriage, a second row of local police with rifles slung behind their backs. Officers, police inspectors, sergeants, etc. Directly by the coach, as always, the gendarmes. In short, a whole military demonstration. It seems that Prince Gorchakov, the local pompadour, has added his own special touch to the instructions from Petersburg. Some of our crowd say they're offended because there isn't any artillery. Truly it's hard to imagine anything more ridiculous or more cowardly. It's a real caricature of "strong" power. We have reason to feel proud: evidently even a "dead" Soviet still scares them.

Cowardice and stupidity—how frequently they become the obverse of vigilance and gentlemanliness! To prevent anyone knowing which way we are traveling which is anyway impossible—we are sure this is the reason, there can't be any other—we are not allowed to write letters en route. Such are the orders from the invisible colonel, based on "instructions" from Petersburg. But we started writing letters on the very first day in the hope of finding a way of posting them. And we were not mistaken. The "instructions" fail to take account of the fact that the authorities have no faithful servants, whereas we are surrounded by friends on every side.

16 January. I am writing under the following conditions: we are halted in a village twenty *versts* from Tyumen. Night. A peasant's hut. A low-ceilinged, dirty room. The entire floor, without any free space whatever, is covered with the bodies of members of the Soviet of Workers' Deputies.

No one is asleep yet, there is talk and laughter. . . . Three of us drew lots for a wide bench (something like a divan), and I won. I'm always lucky in life. We stopped in Tyumen for three days. We were met (as we are used to being, by now) by a vast number of soldiers, mounted and on foot. Those on horseback ("chasseurs") made their horses rear up to frighten away the street urchins. From the station to the prison we had to walk.

Our treatment continues to be extremely considerate, almost excessively so, but at the same time the precautionary measures are getting stricter all the time, almost to the point of superstition.

For example, we were offered by telephone a choice of goods from all the local shops, and at the same time not allowed to exercise in the prison yard. The former is an exceptional privilege, the latter a breach of the law. From Tyumen we continued in horse-drawn sleighs, the 14 of us prisoners being accompanied by 52 (fifty-two) escort soldiers, not counting their captain and a police inspector and a sergeant. This is something unheard-of. Everyone is amazed, including the soldiers, the captain, the inspector, and the sergeant. But such are the "instructions." We are now heading for Tobolsk and advancing extremely slowly. Today, for instance, we covered only twenty *versts*, arriving here at 1:00 P.M. Why not go on? Impossible.

Why not? Instructions! To avoid escapes they do not want us to travel at night, which makes a small amount of sense. But the folks in Petersburg have so little confidence in the initiative of the local authorities that they have laid down in advance the number of *versts* to be covered each day. What efficiency on the part of the Department of Police! So now we travel for three or four hours a day and halt for twenty hours. At this rate we'll reach Tobolsk (250 *versts*) in about ten days, arriving probably on January 25 or 26. How long we shall stop there and where we shall go thereafter is unknown, or rather, we aren't told.

The convoy consists of about forty sleighs. The front ones are used for carrying the luggage. Then it's us, the "deputies," in pairs. Each sleigh is drawn by one horse. Behind us is a line of sleighs carrying only soldiers. The officer and the police inspector are traveling in front of the convoy in a covered sleigh. We proceed at walking pace. For several *versts* from Tyumen we were escorted by twenty or thirty mounted "chasseurs." In short, taking account of the fact that these unheard of and never previously seen precautions are the result of orders from Petersburg, one is bound to conclude that they are determined to deliver us to the most remote place possible *at any price*. After all, this voyage with a royal escort can't simply be the result of some pen-pusher's whim. . . . This may mean that serious difficulties lie ahead . . .

Now everyone is asleep. In the kitchen next door—the door is ajar—soldiers are on guard. Sentries are walking up and down outside the windows. This night is glorious, moonlit, snowy, sky-blue. What a strange scene—these bodies scattered on the floor in deep sleep, these soldiers at the doors and windows. . . . But since I am going through all this for the second time, my impressions aren't any longer quite fresh . . . and just as Kresty prison seemed to me a replica of Odessa prison, which is built on the same model, so this voyage seems no more than a continuation, temporarily interrupted, of that first journey under escort to Irkutsk province.

In the prison at Tyumen, there were many political prisoners, especially "administrative" exiles. During exercise they collected outside our window, sang songs and even produced a red banner with the inscription "Long Live the Revolution!" The choir wasn't at all bad; obviously they've been kept together for a long time and have had plenty of opportunity for practice. . . . The scene was quite impressive and, if you like, moving in its own way. We replied with a few words of greeting through a tiny ventilation window. In the same prison, the criminal prisoners handed us a very long petition in prose and verse, begging us, "distinguished revolutionaries from Petersburg," to help them in some way. We thought we might give a little cash to the most needy ones among the politicals, some of whom lack underclothing and warm clothes, but the prison administration refused categorically. The "instructions" prohibit any contact whatsoever between the "deputies" and other politicals. Even contact through impersonal bank notes? Yes. What forethought!

We were not allowed to send telegrams from Tyumen because no one must know where we are and when. What foolishness! As if the military demonstrations all along the route didn't make it perfectly clear to every passer-by which way we're traveling!

18 January. Pokrovkoye. I am writing from our third halt. We are traveling at a rate of no more than six *versts* an hour and no more than four or five hours a day. Luckily the frost is not very severe—20, 25, or 30 degrees below zero (Réaumur). Three weeks ago the temperature went down to 52 degrees below zero. Imagine traveling with young children under such conditions!

There's another week left till Tobolsk. No newspapers, no letters, no news of any kind. We write without any certainty that our letters will arrive at their destination: we are still forbidden to post letters en route, and so we are obliged to avail ourselves of chance opportunities which are not always very reliable. But really all this is unimportant. We are all warmly dressed and we enjoy breathing the wonderful frosty air after the stinking atmosphere of solitary cells. Say what you like, the human organism wasn't intended for the conditions of solitary confinement.

Heine wrote in his Paris Letters in 1843:

In this sociable country, solitary confinement—the Pennsylvanian method—would constitute an unheard-of cruelty, and the French people are too magnanimous to agree to purchase their public safety at such a price. As a consequence I am convinced that even if the Chambers were to give their consent, the dreadful, inhuman, yes, unnatural system of solitary confinement would not be put into effect, and that the many millions spent on building the necessary premises are, God be thanked, so much money down the drain. The people will smash these castles of the new bourgeois knights with the same indignation as it once smashed the nobility's Bastille. However grim and frightening the aspect of the latter, it was a bright kiosk, a gay pavilion compared with these small, silent American caves which could only have been invented by a dull-minded pietist and approved only by a heartless shopkeeper trembling for his property.

All that is very true and very fine. But still, I prefer being in solitary.

Everything in Siberia has remained the same as it was five or six years ago, and yet everything has changed: not only Siberian soldiers (and to what an extent!) but also Siberian peasants, or "cheldony." Everybody talks politics, everybody wants to know when "this" will end. A boy sleigh-driver, about thirteen years old (he swears he's fifteen), sings at the top of his voice: *"Arise, arise you working people! Enter the struggle, starving folk!"* The soldiers, obviously well-disposed towards the singer, tease him by threatening to report him to the officer. But the lad knows very well that everyone is on his side, and that he can invite the working people to "arise" with perfect impunity . . .

Our first halt from which I wrote to you was in a wretched peasant hut. The other two have been in government buildings, no less filthy but more comfortable. There are separate premises for men and women, there are kitchens. We sleep in tiered plank-beds. Our standard of cleanliness is, of necessity, extremely relative. That, I suppose, is the most disagreeable feature of the voyage.

Peasant women and men come here, to these government transit buildings, bringing us milk, curds, suckling-pigs, griddle-cakes ("shangy") and other food. They are allowed in, which is actually against the law. The "instructions" prohibit any form of contact with the outside world. But it would be difficult for the escort to organize our food supply in any other way.

Order among us is maintained by our sovereign headman, F., whom everyone—we prisoners, the officer, the soldiers, the police, the food-selling peasant women—call simply "Doctor." He seems to have inexhaustible reserves of energy, packing, buying, cooking, feeding, teaching to sing, etc., etc. The others take turns in helping him, and all of them resemble one another in that they do practically nothing. . . . At this moment supper is being cooked, which means a lot of animation and noise. "The doctor wants a knife . . ." "The doctor needs some butter . . ." "Look, friend, would you mind taking out the slops?" . . . The doctor's voice: "Oh, you don't eat fish? I'll fry you a rissole, it's no odds to me. . . ." After supper, tea is served to the tiered beds. Our ladies are responsible for tea duties: it is so ordained by Doctor Feit.

23 January. I am writing from the last halt but one before Tobolsk. The transit house here is excellent, newly built, spacious and clean. After the filth of the other stopping-places this does good to body and soul. There are sixty more *versts* to go before Tobolsk. If you knew how, in these last days, we have been longing for a "real" prison where we shall be able at last to have a proper wash and rest! Here there is only one political exile, formerly the licensee of a liquor shop in Odessa sentenced for carrying on propaganda among soldiers. He came to bring us food and told us about living conditions in Tobolsk province. Most of the exiles are living in villages 100 to 150 *versts* from Tobolsk itself; however, there are a few exiles in Berezov district as well. Life there is incomparably harder and the poverty greater. Escapes are very frequent from everywhere. Escaped prisoners are mostly caught in Tyumen (the nearest railway station) and along the railway generally. But the proportion of those caught is small.

Yesterday we happened to read in an old Tyumen newspaper about two telegrams addressed to S. and myself at the transit prison in Tyumen and never delivered. These telegrams must have arrived just while we were there, but the prison authorities refused to accept them, again for those strange conspiratorial reasons which neither we nor they can grasp. We are being guarded very closely all along the way. The captain has quite worn out his men with excessively long hours of sentry duty, not only outside the building where we are locked up but everywhere in the village. Yet it has already become noticeable how, as we travel further north, the "regime" is gradually thawing: little by little we are being allowed to visit local shops under escort, we walk about the village in small groups, sometimes we can visit the local exiles. The soldiers help us as best they can; they feel united to us by our common opposition to the captain. The n.c.o., who represents the connecting link between the officer and the men, is in the most difficult position.

"You know, gentlemen," he once told us in front of the soldiers, "today's n.c.o. isn't what he was in the old days."

"There are some who'd like to be just what they were in the old days," a soldier riposted, "but we twist their tails for them and then they think better of it."

Everyone burst out laughing. The n.c.o. laughed too, but not very happily.

26 January. Tobolsk prison. Two halts before Tobolsk we were met by a deputy police inspector, on the one hand to ensure greater safety and, on the other, to emphasize the courtesy with which we are being treated. The guard was reinforced. We were no longer allowed out shopping. Yet the families among us were placed in covered sleighs. Vigilance and gentlemanliness! About ten *versts* from the town, two exiles came to meet us. As soon as the officer saw them he immediately "took measures": he rode past our entire convoy and ordered the soldiers to dismount (until then they had been riding in the sleighs). And that is how we proceeded for the remaining ten *versts*. The soldiers, cursing the officer for all they were worth, walked on foot on either side of the road with their rifles on their shoulders.

But here I must interrupt my description: the doctor, who has just been called to the office, tells us that we are all being sent to the village of Obdorskoye; we are to travel forty or fifty *versts* a day under military ecort. To Obdorskoye it is more than 1,200 *versts* by snow road. That means that under the best imaginable conditions, if horses are available at every changing-stage and no time is lost through illness, we shall be on the road more than a month. Once arrived, we shall receive a subsidy of 1 rouble 80 kopecks a month.

Traveling for a whole month with young children is particularly difficult just now. They say that between Berezov and Obdorsk reindeer will have to be used. This was especially alarming news for those of us who are traveling with their families. The local administration swears that the ridiculous schedule of forty *versts* a day instead of 100 has been prescribed by Petersburg, like all other details of our voyage. The wise men in their offices have thought of everything to prevent us escaping; and, to do them justice, nine out of ten measures prescribed by them are devoid of any meaning whatsoever. The wives who are following their husbands into exile voluntarily asked to be let out of prison during the three days we are stopping here in Tobolsk. The governor refused point-blank, which is not only senseless but also completely illegal. Local public opinion is a little disturbed, and a protest is being written. But what is the use of protesting when the answer is the same in every case: sorry, instructions from Petersburg.

Thus the most sinister newspaper rumors have proved justified: our place of exile is the northernmost point of the province. It is curious to note that the "equality" which found expression in the verdict has also affected the choice of the place of exile: all of us are going to the same destination.

The idea people here in Tobolsk have of Obdorsk is just as vague as yours in Petersburg. All they know is that it is a village somewhere inside the Arctic circle. The question arises: will they have to settle soldiers in Obdorsk specially to guard us? That would be only logical. And will there be any possibility at all of organizing an escape, or shall we be obliged to sit there between the North Pole and the Arctic circle waiting for the further progress of the revolution and changes in the whole political situation? There are grounds for fearing that our release will be transformed from a technical question into a political one. Very well then, we shall sit in Obdorsk and wait. And work. Just keep sending books and newspapers, newspapers and books. Who knows how events will develop in the future? Who knows how soon our calculations will prove right? Perhaps the year we shall be obliged to spend in Obdorsk will be the last revolutionary breathing-space history will ever grant us to fill the gaps in our knowledge and sharpen our weapons still more. Do you think such thoughts are too fatalistic? Dear friend, when one is traveling to Obdorsk under escort there's no harm in a little fatalism.

29 January. It's two days now since we left Tobolsk: Our escort consists of thirty soldiers under an n.c.o.'s command. We left in huge troikas on Monday morning, but after the second halt the number of horses pulling each sleigh was reduced from three to two. It was a marvelous morning, clear, bright, and frosty.

Forest all around, still and white with frost against the clear sky. A fairy-tale setting. The horses galloped at a mad pace—the usual Siberian rhythm. As we were leaving the town (the prison is in the outskirts), a crowd of local exiles, forty or fifty persons, stood awaiting us; there were many greetings, gestures, attempts to exchange a few words. . . . But we were driven away at great speed. The people here have already made up legends about us: some say that five generals and two provincial governors are being taken into exile, others that it is a count with his family, still others that we are members of the State Duma. And the woman in whose house we stopped last night asked the doctor: "Are you politicals, too?" "Yes, we're politicals." "But then you're surely the chiefs of all the politicals!"

Tonight we are staying in a large, clean room, with papered walls, American cloth on the table, a painted floor, large windows, two lamps. All this is very pleasant after those other filthy places. But we have to sleep on the floor because there are nine of us in the room. They changed our escort at Tobolsk, and the new escort turned out to be as rude and mean as the Tyumen one had been courteous and well-disposed towards us. This is due to the absence of an officer; the soldiers feel responsible for everything that may go wrong. But I must add that after only two days they have thawed considerably, and we are establishing excellent relations with most of them, which is far from being a mere detail on such a long journey.

Almost in every village since Tobolsk there have been political exiles, most of them "agrarians" (peasants exiled for rioting), soldiers, workers, and only occasionally intellectuals. Some are "administrative," a few are "settlers," i.e., exiles condemned to settle here. In two of the villages we passed, the "politicals" have organized cooperative workshops which yield a small income. Altogether we have not yet encountered really desperate poverty among the exiles. This is because life in these parts is extremely cheap; politicals pay the peasants six roubles a month for board and lodging, the minimum fixed by the local exiles' organization. For ten roubles a month you can live "quite well." The further north you go, the more expensive life becomes and the more difficult it is to find work.

We have met some comrades who used to live in Obdorsk. All of them had good things to say about the place. The village is large, with more than 1,000 inhabitants and twelve shops. The houses are built on the town model and good lodgings are easy to find. The countryside is mountainous and very beautiful, the climate very healthy. The workers among us will find jobs. It is possible to earn some money by giving lessons. Life is quite expensive, it is true, but earnings are also higher. This incomparable place has just one drawback: it is almost entirely cut off from the world. One and a half thousand *versts* from the railway, 800 *versts* to the nearest telegraph office. Mail arrives twice a week, but when the roads are bad in spring and autumn it stops coming altogether for periods of six weeks to two months. If a provisional government is formed in Petersburg today, the local policeman will still be king in Obdorsk for a long time: the fact that Obdorsk is so far from the Tobolsk highway explains its relative liveliness, for it serves as an independent center for an enormous area.

Exiles do not remain in one place for long. They wander incessantly all over the province. The regular steamships on the Ob River carry politicals free of charge. The paying passengers have to crowd into corners, while the politicals take over the whole ship. This may surprise you, dear friend, but such is the firmly established tradition. Everyone is so used to it that our peasant sleigh-drivers, hearing that we are going to Obdorsk, tell us: "Never mind, won't be for long, you'll be back again on the steamship next spring." But who knows under what conditions we of the Soviet will be placed in Obdorsk? For the time being instructions have been issued for us to be given the best sleighs and the best stopping quarters en route.

Obdorsk! A minuscule point on the globe . . . perhaps we
shall have to adapt our lives for years to Obdorsk conditions.
Even my fatalistic mood does not guarantee complete peace of
mind. I clench my teeth and yearn for electric street-lamps, the
noise of trams and the best thing in the world—the smell of fresh
newsprint.

1 February. Yurovskoye. Today was exactly the same as yesterday. We covered more than fifty *versts.* My companion in the
sleigh was a soldier who entertained me with stories of the war
in Manchuria. We are being escorted by men of the Sibirsky
regiment, which was almost completely reconstituted after the
war. This regiment suffered more losses than any other. One
part of it is stationed in Tyumen, another in Tobolsk. The
Tyumen soldiers, as I told you before, were very well disposed
towards us, those in Tobolsk are more rough; among them there
is a largish group of "conscious" Black Hundreds supporters.
The regiment is composed of Poles, Ukrainians, and Siberians.
The indigenous Siberians are the most ignorant element. But
even among them there are some splendid fellows. . . . After
only two days our new escort began softening towards us—
which is not an insignificant detail, for these warriors now rule
over our life and death.

My companion was enthusiastic over the Chinese women.
"Lovely things, they are. Their men are undersized, can't be
compared to real men, but the women are beautiful, white and
plump . . ."

"Well then," asked our sleigh-driver, an ex-soldier, "did our
fellows take up with the Chinese girls?" "No . . . not allowed
to, see. First they take the Chinese women away, then they let
the troops in. Still, some of our crowd caught a Chinese girl
in a maize field and had a go. And one of them, see, left his cap
there. So the Chinese men brought this cap along and showed it
to our officer. He lines up the whole regiment and asks: 'Whose

cap?' Nobody makes a sound, better lose your cap than get into that sort of trouble, see? In the end it all came to nothing. But the Chinese girls are lovely . . ."

We left Tobolsk in troikas, but since the second halt the sleighs have been drawn by pairs because the road is getting narrower all the time.

In the villages where we change horses there are sleighs already harnessed and waiting. The change is made outside the villages, in the middle of fields. Usually the entire population comes out to look at us. Some animated scenes take place. While the women hold the horses by their bridles, the men, under the doctor's instructions, take care of our baggage and the children run noisily and merrily around us. Yesterday some "politicals," wanting to take a photograph of us while our horses were being changed, waited for us outside the rural office building, but we were driven past at a gallop and they had no chance to do anything. Today, as we entered the village where we are now spending the night, the local "politicals" met us, carrying a red banner. There are fourteen of them, including ten or so Georgians. The soldiers became alarmed at the sight of the red banner, drew their bayonets and threatened to shoot. Finally they managed to seize the red banner and push back the "demonstrators."

In our escort there is a small group of soldiers centered around a corporal who is an Old Believer. This man is an exceptionally low and cruel brute. Nothing gives him greater pleasure than to bully a boy driver, frighten a Tatar woman or hit a horse with his rifle-butt. A brick-red face, a permanently half-opened mouth, bloodless gums, and unblinking eyes give him the appearance of an idiot. This corporal is in violent conflict with the sergeant in charge of the escort. He thinks the sergeant doesn't treat us roughly enough. When it's a question of grabbing a red flag or pushing back a political who has come a little too close to our sleighs, the corporal and his little gang are always there first. We all have to control ourselves in order to avoid sharp clashes, for in case of trouble we could hardly count on the sergeant, who is scared to death of this corporal.

2 February, evening. Demyanskoye. Despite the fact that the red banner which greeted us at Yurovskoye yesterday was seized by the troops, this morning, as we were leaving the village, there was a new one stuck on a long pole into a snowdrift. This time nobody touched it; the soldiers had only just settled into their sleighs and no one felt like getting out again. And so we paraded past it. Further on, a few hundred yards from the village, where the road dips down to the river, we saw an inscription in huge letters on the snowy slope: "Long Live the Revolution!" My driver, a fellow of eighteen or so, burst out laughing when he read the inscription. "Do you know what that means—long live the revolution?" I asked him. "No, I don't," he said after a moment's thought, "all I know is that people keep shouting these words, 'Long Live the Revolution!' " But you could tell by his face that he knew more than he was prepared to say. Altogether the local peasants, especially the young ones, are extremely well disposed towards the "politicals."

We arrived at Demyanskoye, the large village where we are stopping for the night, at 1:00 P.M. A large crowd of exiles came to meet us (there are more than sixty here). This caused great confusion among some of our escort. The corporal at once gathered his faithful around him in case of need. Luckily there was no trouble. It was obvious that they had been waiting for us here for a long time and with a good deal of nervous tension. A special commission to organize our reception had been appointed. A magnificent dinner and comfortable quarters were prepared in the local "commune." But we were not allowed to go there, and had to stop in a peasant house; the dinner was brought here. Meeting the politicals is extremely difficult; they were able to get in to see us only for a few minutes at a time, in twos and threes, carrying various parts of the dinner. Apart from that we took turns to visit the local shop, accompanied by soldiers, and on the way were able to exchange a few words with comrades who waited in the street all day long.

One of the women exiles, dressed up as a peasant woman, came to sell us milk; she played her part very well, but the owner of the house must have given her away to the soldiers and they immediately forced her to leave. The corporal was on duty at the time, worse luck. I remember how our little colony at Ust-Kut (on the Lena) used to prepare for the passage of every new lot of exiles: we used to cook *shchi*, make *pelmeni*, in short we did exactly what the people at Demyanskoye did for us today. The passage of a large batch of exiles is a tremendous event for every little colony along the route, all of whose members are impatient for news from home.

4 February, 8:00 P.M. Tsingalinsk Yurts. Our accompanying police officer, at our request, asked the Tobolsk administration whether the tempo of the journey could not be speeded up. Apparently Tobolsk asked permission from Petersburg, and as a result the police officer has received a telegram giving him freedom of action in this respect. Assuming that from now on we shall do seventy *versts* a day, the chances are that we shall arrive at Obdorsk on February 18 or 20. Of course that is only an estimate.

We are stopping in a small village called Tsingalinsk Yurts. But in reality the houses here are not yurts (nomads' tents) but peasant huts. The population consists mostly of Ostyaks, a very sharply defined Asiatic type. However, their speech and way of life are purely peasantlike; the only difference is that they drink even more than Siberian peasants. They drink every day, from early morning on, and by noon they are already drunk.

A local exile, N., a schoolteacher, has told us some curious things. It appears that the Ostyaks, hearing that unknown persons were going to pass through their village and that these persons were being received with great pomp everywhere, became very frightened, refrained from drinking and even hid away their stocks of liquor. That is why today most of them are sober. By evening, however, unless I am mistaken, our Ostyak host returned home drunk.

We have now entered fish country, and meat is difficult to get. The same teacher has organized a fishermen's team of exiles and local peasants. He has bought fishing nets, he supervises operations himself and takes the catch to Tobolsk for sale. Last summer every member of the team earned over 100 roubles. Everyone tries to adapt himself to his circumstances as best he can. . . . But N. has got a rupture as a result of his fishing initiatives.

6 February. Samarovo. We covered sixty-five *versts* yesterday and seventy-three today, and tomorrow we shall cover approximately the same distance. The agricultural region now lies behind us; the peasants here, Ostyaks as well as Russians, engage exclusively in fishing.

The extent to which Tobolsk province has been settled with "politicals" is extraordinary. There is literally not a single remote hamlet that doesn't house its exiles. The owner of the house where we stopped for the night told us that not long ago there were no exiles here at all; they began to arrive in large numbers after the manifesto of October 17. "Ever since then they've been flooding the place." Such has been the effect of the constitutional era in these parts! In many places the politicals pursue the same occupations as the indigenous population: they collect and clean cedar cones, catch fish, gather berries, hunt. The more enterprising have organized cooperative workshops, fishing gangs, shops for consumer goods. The peasants' attitude towards the exiles is extremely friendly. For example, here in Samarovo —a large trading village—the peasants have given a whole house to the politicals free of charge and gave the first to arrive a present of a calf and two sacks of flour. There is an established tradition whereby the shops sell to exiles at a cheaper price than to peasants. Some of the exiles here live in a commune in their own house, on the roof of which a red flag flies all the time. Just try raising the red flag in Paris, Berlin, or Geneva!

In passing I'd like to tell you of two or three general observations I have made concerning the condition of exile at the present time.

The fact that the social composition of the political population of prisons in Siberia is gradually becoming more democratic has been pointed out dozens, if not hundreds of times since the '90s. Workers have come to represent an increasingly high percentage of the "politicals," finally outnumbering the revolutionary intellectuals who were once accustomed to consider the Peter and Paul Fortress and Kolymsk their private and hereditary monopoly, something like an entailed estate. At the beginning of the century, I still saw members of the People's Will and People's Right parties who shrugged their shoulders in an almost offended manner when they saw chimney sweeps from Vilna or fodder merchants from Minsk arriving with the latest party of prisoners. But the exiled workman of that time was, in the majority of cases, a member of a revolutionary organization and his political and moral level was high. Almost all exiles, except possibly for workers from the Jewish Pale, had been through the sieve of the gendarmerie's interrogation, and, however coarse that sieve, it generally retained the most advanced workers. This maintained a certain level among the exiled population.

Exile in the "constitutional" period of our history bears an entirely different character. Now it is no longer a matter of organizations, but of an elemental mass movement. There are no longer gendarmerie interrogations, but wholesale street roundups. The most inconspicuous is now eligible for exile, or even for the executioner's bullet. After the suppression of a series of popular movements, a period of "guerrilla" actions began, with expropriation for revolutionary ends or simply under revolutionary pretexts, maximalists' adventures, and plain thuggeries. Whoever could not be hanged was sent by the administration to Siberia. It is easy to understand that a brawl of such colossal dimensions involved many people who had merely touched the revolution with one finger, or who were innocent onlookers, not to mention many adventurers from the underworld of our large cities. You can imagine what an effect this has had on the general level of the exiles.

There is another factor which leads in the same direction: the escapes. It is obvious what sort of people escape: the most active, most conscious ones, who know that their party and their work is waiting for them. The percentage that succeeds can be judged by the fact that out of 450 exiles in a certain part of Tobolsk province only approximately 100 are left. Only the lazy ones stay. As a result, most of the remaining exiles are a gray, politically ill-defined lot who find themselves there more or less by chance. The few active ones who, for some reason, have not managed to get away, are sometimes placed in a difficult position, since all politicals are morally bound to one another by the mutual guarantee system.

8 February. Karymkrinsk Yurts. Yesterday we did seventy-five *versts,* today ninety. We arrive at the halts tired out and go to bed early.

Tonight we are stopping in an Ostyak village, in a small, dirty hut. The soldiers of the escort, chilled to the bone, are crowding out the filthy kitchen together with some drunken Ostyaks. A lamb is bleating on the other side of the wall. . . . There is a wedding in the village—this is the season of weddings —and all the Ostyaks are drinking and, once drunk, try to get into our hut.

A little old man from Saratov, an "administrative" exile, also drunk, has been to see us. It turns out that he and another man have come here from Berezov to buy meat, which they then resell. Both are politicals.

The preparatory work which must have been done here to

ensure our transport is extraordinary. Our convoy, as I already told you, consists of twenty-two covered sleighs drawn by about fifty horses. Few villages dispose of such a number of horses and they are assembled from all over the countryside. At some stations we were given horses brought there from 100 *versts* away. Yet the coaching stages here are very short, mostly 10 or 15 *versts*. Thus an Ostyak has to drive his horse for 100 *versts* in order to transport two members of the Soviet of Workers' Deputies over a distance of 10 *versts*. Moreover, since no one knew when exactly we would arrive, some drivers had to wait a fortnight before their horses were needed. They can remember only one such case previously—when the provincial governor "himself" made a tour of these parts . . .

I have already mentioned several times how friendly the local peasants are to politicals in general and to us especially. An extraordinary thing happened to us in Belogorye, a small village in the Berezov district. A group of local peasants collectively organized a reception for us, with tea and cold food, and collected six roubles to give to us. We naturally refused the money, but accepted the invitation to tea. However, our escort protested and the party did not come off. That is to say, the sergeant agreed, but the corporal made a tremendous fuss, shouting loudly enough to be heard all over the village and threatening to denounce the sergeant. So we left again without our tea. Almost the whole village followed us; it was a proper demonstration.

9 February. Kandinskoye. We have done another 100 *versts*. Another two days and we shall reach Berezovo (on the eleventh). I got very tired today; we had nothing to eat throughout nine or ten hours of continuous travel. We are following the Ob River all the time. The right bank is hilly and wooded, the left bank low. The river is wide, the weather calm and relatively warm. Small fir trees are stuck in the snow on either side of the road to serve as beacons. Most of our drivers are Ostyaks. The sleighs are pulled by two or three horses harnessed one behind the other, since the road gets narrower the further we travel. The drivers have long rope whips on long handles. The convoy spreads over a tremendous distance. From time to time one of the drivers gives a high-pitched shout which sets the horses galloping, raising thick clouds of snow-dust. The speed takes your breath away. The sleighs almost pile up on top of one another, a horse's mouth suddenly appears from behind your shoulder and breathes into your face. Then one of the sleighs capsizes or some part of the harness breaks or comes undone. The whole convoy stops. After many hours of driving you feel as though hypnotized. The air is very still. The drivers call to one another in their guttural voices. Then the horses start up again and soon we are galloping once more. Frequent halts slow us down greatly and prevent the drivers from attaining maximum speed. We do about fifteen *versts* an hour, whereas the normal speed here is eighteen to twenty or even twenty-five *versts*.

Rapid travel in Siberia is the normal and, in a sense, necessary thing, given the enormous distances. But I've never experienced such driving as this, even on the Lena.

We arrive at a station. Beyond the village, harnessed sleighs and fresh horses are waiting; only two of our sleighs, reserved for the families with children, are "through carriages" to Berezov. We change quickly and proceed on our way. The drivers here sit in an extraordinary way. A plank is nailed across the front end of the sleigh; this place is called the "arbor," and the driver sits on top of the arbor, that is, the bare plank, his feet hanging over the side of the sleigh. When the horses are galloping and the sleigh tilts up now on one side, now on the other, the driver balances it with his body, leaning out sideways like a yachtsman and sometimes pushing off from the ground with his feet.

12 February. Berezov. The prison. Five or six days ago—I didn't write about it at the time so as not to cause you unnecessary worry—we passed through an area where there was a lot of

typhus. Now those parts are left far behind. At Tsingalinsk
Yurts, which I mentioned to you, there were typhus cases in
thirty houses out of sixty. The same in many other villages.
Many deaths. There was scarcely a driver who had not lost one
of his relations. The speeding up of our journey and the change
in the original schedule is directly connected with the typhus:
the police officer justified his telegraphic request to the authorities by the necessity to pass the danger area as quickly as possible.

During the last days we have been advancing towards the
north at a rate of 90 or 100 *versts* a day, that is to say, by almost
a whole degree. As a result, the cultural decline—if one can
speak of culture here—is especially evident. Every day we drop
a degree further into the kingdom of wildness and cold. A
climber must have a similar impression as he ascends a high
mountain, traversing one zone of altitude after another. . . .
First there were prosperous Russian peasants. Then Russified
Ostyaks who, as a result of mixed marriages, had almost lost their
Mongol look. Then we left the agricultural zone and entered the
land of Ostyak hunters and fishermen, short, shaggy-headed
creatures who speak Russian with difficulty. Horses became
more scarce and less good; horse transport does not play an
important part here, and a hunting dog is valued more highly
than a horse. The road became worse too, narrow and entirely
unsurfaced. . . . And yet the police sergeant tells us that the
"highway" Ostyaks here are models of culture compared with
those living along the tributaries of the Ob.

Their attitude towards us is vague and confused; I daresay
they imagine us to be big shots in temporary disgrace. An
Ostyak today kept asking: "Where's your general? Show me
your general . . . I wish I could see him . . . I've never seen
a general."

An Ostyak today was harnessing a broken-down nag to one
of our sleighs, and another one called out to him: "Give them a
better one than that, who do you think they are, police officers?"
But there was another, opposite case, the only one of its kind it

is true, when an Ostyak said of us: "Not very important passengers, are they?"

We arrived in Berezov last night. You will hardly expect a
description of the "town." It is like Verkholensk, Kirensk, and
a multitude of other towns with 1,000 inhabitants, a police station and a fiscal office. However, here they also show (without guarantee of authenticity) Osterman's grave and the place
where Menshikov was buried. Local wits also point out the old
lady in whose house Menshikov had his meals.

We were taken directly to the prison. The entire local garrison, some fifty men, were lined up at the entrance. It appears
that prior to our arrival the prison was washed and scrubbed for
a fortnight, all prisoners having been previously removed. In
one of the cells we found a large table with a table cloth, some
dining chairs, a card table, two candlesticks with candles and
a large hanging lamp. Such consideration is almost touching . . .

We shall rest here for a couple of days and then move on.

Move on, yes . . . but I haven't yet decided in which direction.

CHAPTER 33

❖❖❖❖❖❖❖❖❖❖❖

. . . . . and Back

During the first part of our voyage in horse-driven sleighs I looked back in dismay at every halt and saw the distance separating us from the railway line getting greater all the time. Obdorsk was not going to be the final destination for any of us, and certainly not for me. The thought of escape never left us for an instant. I had a passport and money for the return voyage skillfully hidden in the sole of my boot. But the large size of the escort and the close watch kept on us made an escape en route extremely difficult. I should say, however, that the possibility of escape existed: not for us all, but for an individual. Several by no means impractical plans were made, but we were put off by the thought of the consequences of an escape on those left behind. The soldiers of the escort, and more particularly the sergeant, were responsible for delivering us safely to our place of exile. In the previous year a sergeant from Tobolsk had been put in a punishment battalion for letting a student prisoner escape. After this the Tobolsk troops were on their guard and their treatment of exiles en route had become much less friendly. It was as though a tacit agreement had been reached between them and the prisoners: there would be no escapes en route. None of us considered this agreement to be absolutely binding. Yet it paralyzed our resolve, and one halt after another went by without anything happening. Towards the end, when we had already traveled several hundred *versts*, a certain inertia set in and I no longer looked back but forwards; I was impatient to "get there," worried about receiving books and newspapers. In short I was ready for a long stay. In Berezov this mood was immediately dispelled.

"Any chance of getting out of here?"

"In spring it's easy."

"What about now?"

"Not so easy, but it should be possible. Mind you, no one's tried it yet."

Everyone, absolutely everyone told us that to escape in the spring was simple and easy because it was physically impossible for a small number of police to control a very large number of exiles. However, controlling fifteen exiles settled in one place and enjoying special attention would not prove impossible. I would do much better to escape at once.

The first condition was to stay behind in Berezov. To continue to Obdorsk meant adding another 480 *versts* to the return voyage. I announced that I was tired and ill and would resist any attempt to force me to continue the journey at once. The police chief consulted the local doctor and decided to let me stay on in Berezov for a few days. I was put in the hospital. At this time I had no definite plans.

In the hospital I enjoyed relative freedom. The doctor advised me to walk as much as possible and I took advantage of this to size up the situation.

On the face of it the simplest way was to return by the road on which we had come, that is, the "big Tobolsk highway." But this, I decided, was too unsafe. True, along the road there were many reliable peasants who would convey me secretly from village to village. But still, the chance of unlucky encounters was too great. The entire administration either lived or traveled along the highway. Within two days, or even sooner, someone could get from Berezov to the nearest telegraph office and warn the police posts all the way to Tobolsk. I decided to reject this solution.

Another way was to travel by reindeer across the Urals and then to reach Archangel via Izhma, wait for the opening of navigation in the spring and then embark on a ship going abroad. The road to Archangel was safe, passing only through remote localities. But how safe would it be to stay in Archangel? I knew nothing of conditions there and had no way of obtaining information.

The third plan seemed to be the most attractive. This consisted of traveling by reindeer to the Ural ore mines, taking the narrow-gauge railway at Bogoslovsk mine and there changing to the Perm line. Then on to Perm, Vyatka, Vologda, Petersburg, Helsingfors . . .

It is possible to travel by reindeer to the mines straight from Berezov, along the Sosva or Vogulka rivers. Directly beyond Berezov the country is completely wild. No police for a thousand *versts*, not a single Russian village, only scattered Ostyak yurts here and there, naturally no question of any telegraph, not a horse anywhere—the road was suitable only for reindeer. All I needed was to gain a little headway, and the Berezov police would never catch me even supposing they set out in the right direction.

I was warned that the journey would be full of hardships and physical danger. In some places there was no human habitation for a hundred *versts*. The Ostyaks, sole inhabitants of the region, suffered from severe endemic diseases; syphillis was rife, typhus a common occurrence. I could expect no help from anyone. A young merchant from Berezov by name of Dobrovolsky had died that winter after two weeks of violent fever in the Ourvi yurts, which lay along the Sosva River. . . . And what if a reindeer died and could not be replaced? What if there was a snowstorm? A storm may last for several days, and anyone caught en route is doomed. And February is the month of snowstorms. Furthermore, was the road actually open at present? Few people took it, and if no one traveled along it for a few days the snow piled up and it was easy to miss one's way. Such were the warnings I received.

The danger could not be denied. Of course the Tobolsk highway offered great advantages from the point of view of physical safety and "comfort." But that was precisely why it was infinitely less safe from the point of view of getting caught. I decided to travel along the Sosva river; and I have no reason to regret my choice.

◇ ◇ ◇

It remained to find someone who would agree to drive me to the Ural mines and that was the riskiest part of the undertaking.*

"Wait a bit, I think I can help you," a young "liberal" merchant called Nikita Serapionych, with whom I was discussing my problem, told me after long reflection. "There's a Zyryan fellow living about forty *versts* from here, name of Nikifor . . . he's a real old fox, he is . . . he's got two heads instead of one, he can do it if anyone can."

"He doesn't drink, does he?" I asked prudently.

"What do you mean, doesn't drink? Of course he drinks, who doesn't, around here? Drink's been his undoing, too; he's a good hunter, used to kill a lot of sables, earn a lot of money. But never mind. If he agrees to do it, maybe he'll keep off the stuff. Let me go and see him for you. He's a real old fox, that one . . . if he can't do it, no one else can."

* The description of the escape which follows has been considerably changed and all the names used are fictitious to ensure the safety of those who helped me.

Nikita Serapionych and I worked out the details of the contract I should offer to Nikifor. I would pay for three reindeer, the best ones available, to be chosen by him. The sleigh would also be mine. If Nikifor delivered me safely to my destination, the reindeer and sleigh would become his property; and, in addition, I would pay him fifty roubles in cash.

That evening I already had the answer. Nikifor accepted the offer. He had already set out for a native tent-village, about fifty *versts* from his house, and would return at noon on the following day with three first-class reindeer. We should be able to leave the following night. By that time I would have to be equipped with good reindeer *kisy and chizhi**, a *malitsa* or a *gus*** and with provisions for ten days or so. Nikita Serapionych offered to attend to all that.

"I'm telling you," he kept assuring me, "Nikifor will get you there for sure. He can do it if anyone can."

"Yes, unless he starts drinking," I added doubtfully.

"Never worry, God grant he won't. The only thing is, he's afraid that if you take the mountain road he might miss it, it's eight years since he's been that way. You'll have to follow the river as far as Shominsk Yurts, and that's a longer way by far."

Two roads lead from Berezov to the Shominsk Yurts. The first, the "mountain road," is direct, crossing the Vogulka River in several places and passing the Vyzhnepurtym Yurts. The second road follows the Sosva River and takes you through Shaytansk and Maleyevsk Yurts and other villages. The mountain road is half the distance, but it is infrequently traveled and is liable to get completely snowed up.

Alas, we were unable to leave the following night; Nikifor had failed to turn up with the reindeer, and no one knew where he was. Nikita Serapionych was very crestfallen.

---

* *Chizhi:* reindeer-skin stockings, with fur on the inside; *kisy:* reindeer-skin boots with fur on the outside.
** A *malitsa* is a reindeer-skin overcoat worn with the fur turned inwards; in especially cold weather, a *gus* (with the fur on the outside) is worn on top.

"You didn't give him any money to buy the reindeer, by chance?" I asked.

"What do you take me for, a child? All I gave him was five roubles, and I made sure his wife saw me do it. Wait, I'll go and see him again today."

My departure was postponed by twenty-four hours at least. The police chief might insist any day on sending me to Obdorsk. A bad start!

I left on the third day, February 18.

That morning Nikita Serapionych came to see me in the hospital and, after waiting for a convenient moment when there was no one else in the room, announced resolutely:

"Tonight at 11:00 P.M. you must slip out unnoticed and come to my place. You're leaving at midnight. All my family are going to the show tonight, I'll be alone at home. You'll change and eat at my house, then I'll drive you into the forest where Nikifor will be waiting. He's decided to take the mountain road after all; he's heard that two Ostyak sleighs passed that way yesterday."

"Is this final?" I asked doubtfully.

"Yes, final and definitive."

Until evening I tramped up and down restlessly in my room. At 8:00 I went to the army barracks where the "show" was being given; I thought that this would be the best way. The assembly hall of the barracks was chock-full of people. Three large lamps hung from the ceiling, candles fixed to bayonets were lit along the walls. Three musicians were seated below the front of the stage. The front row was occupied by the administration, behind them sat the merchants and the "politicals," and simpler folk crowded the back rows—shop assistants, small tradesmen, and young people. Soldiers stood along the walls. A performance of Chekhov's *The Bear* was already in progress. The doctor's assistant, Anton Ivanovich, a tall, fat, good-natured man, played the "bear." The doctor's wife was the attractive neighbor. The doctor himself was the prompter and hissed like a goose from his little box in the center of the stage. Then the fancifully painted curtain fell and everyone clapped.

During the interval the politicals gathered into a group and exchanged the latest news. "They say the police chief is very sorry that the two families weren't allowed to stay in Berezov." "By the way, the police chief has said that no one can escape from here." "Well, he can't be completely right," someone objected, "if people arrive, that means that people can leave, too."

The three musicians fell silent and the curtain rose. The next play was *The Tragedian Despite Himself*, a drama about a husband on holiday. The hospital inspector, a former army doctor's assistant, played the part of the husband dressed in a tussore-silk jacket and a straw hat—in February by the Arctic circle! When the curtain fell once more, I complained of neuralgic pains and left.

Nikita Serapionych was waiting.

"You've just got time to have supper and change. I've told Nikifor to set out for the rendezvous when the town clock strikes midnight."

Just before midnight we went outside. After the brightly lit room the darkness seemed impenetrable, but soon I was able to make out the outlines of a sleigh with a single horse harnessed to it. I lay down on the floor of the sleigh, spreading my *gus* hastily beneath me. Nikita Serapionych covered me with a large bundle of straw and tied the whole packet with rope, as though we were carting goods for delivery. The straw was frozen and mixed with snow. My breath quickly melted the snow and wet flakes soon covered my face. My hands, too, were ice cold inside the straw; I had forgotten to pull on my gauntlet gloves, and now found it difficult to move. The town clock struck twelve. The sleigh started, we passed through the gate of the merchant's house, and the horse trotted swiftly along the street.

"At last!" I thought. "We're off!" Even my cold hands and

face gave me pleasure because they confirmed the reality of the event. We traveled at at trot for twenty minutes or so and then stopped. I heard a loud whistle, Nikita's signal. Another whistle came at once from a little distance off, followed by the sound of low voices. "Who's that talking?" I wondered in alarm. Nikita evidently shared my anxiety because he did not untie me but only muttered something under his breath.

"Who's that?" I asked quietly through the straw.

"The devil knows whom he's picked up there," Nikita replied.

"Is he drunk?"

"Well, he isn't sober."

Meanwhile a sleigh with several men in it appeared in the road.

"Never mind, don't worry, Nikita Serapionych, and tell the *character* not to worry either," I heard someone say. "This here is a friend of mine . . . and this here's my old dad . . . they'll never let on . . ."

Nikita, grumbling, untied me. Before me stood a tall muzhik wearing a *malitsa*, but hatless. He had bright red hair and a drunken but nevertheless cunning face, and looked very much like a Ukrainian. A young fellow stood silently a few yards away, and an old man teetered on his feet holding on to the sleigh, obviously very much the worse for drink.

"Never mind, sir, never mind," the red-haired fellow, whom I guessed to be Nikifor, was saying, "these are my men, I'll answer for them. Nikifor drinks, but he's got his wits about him. . . . Don't you worry. Look at these bulls here (he pointed at the reindeer), why, I could take you anywhere with these. . . . My uncle, Mikhail Yegorych, he says to me: go ahead and take the mountain road . . . two Ostyak sleighs passed that way only yesterday . . . I'd rather go by the mountain road . . . everybody knows me along the river. . . . So I invited Mikhail Yegorych to have some *pelmeni* with me . . . he's a good muzhik, he is . . ."

"Hold on a bit, Nikifor Ivanovich, pack the luggage, won't you?" Nikita Serapionych raised his voice.

Nikifor went to work, and five minutes later the new sleigh was packed and I was sitting in it.

"It's too bad, Nikifor Ivanovich," Nikita said reproachfully, "You should never have brought these other men along, didn't I tell you? Listen here," he addressed the two, "not a word out of you, eh?"

"Not a word," the young muzhik said.

The old man twirled a finger vaguely in the air. I bade a warm farewell to Nikita Serapionych.

"On your way!"

Nikifor called smartly to the reindeer and we were off.

The reindeer ran well, their tongues hanging out from the side of their mouths and their breath coming rapidly, chu-chu-chu-chu. The road was narrow, the beasts huddled together and I was amazed how they managed to run so fast without getting in each other's way.

"I'm telling you straight," Nikifor addressed me, "you won't find better reindeer than these. These are choice bulls, they are; seven hundred in a herd, and these are the best. That old man, Mikhey, he said at first: I'll never let you have those bulls, not on your life. Afterwards, when we'd cracked a bottle between us, he said, all right, take them. And when I was taking them he burst out crying. See here, he said, this leader (Nikifor pointed at the front reindeer) is priceless; if ever you get back safely, I'll buy him back for the same price. That's the sort of bulls they are! I paid good money for them, mind, but they're worth it, and that's the truth. That leader alone is worth twenty-five roubles. Only thing is, my uncle, Mikhail Osipovich, would have lent them to us for nothing at all. He told me straight, he did: you're a fool, Nikifor. That's what he said. Nikifor, he said, you're a fool, why didn't you tell me you were taking this *character*, eh?"

"What character?" I interrupted his chatter.

"Why, let's say yourself."

Later on I had many occasions to notice that the word *character* was a favorite one in my driver's vocabulary.

We had scarcely covered ten *versts* when Nikifor suddenly brought the reindeer to a halt.

"We've got to turn off here, five *versts* or so. . . . There's a tent-village where they're keeping a *gus* for me. How can I travel in just a *malitsa?* I'd freeze to death for sure. I've got a note from Nikita Serapionych about the *gus.*"

I was dumbfounded at the ridiculous idea of going out of our way to visit a tent-village ten *versts* from Berezov. From Nikifor's evasive answers I understood that he should have gone to fetch the *gus* on the previous day, but had done nothing but drink for the past forty-eight hours.

"You can do what you like," I said, "but I'm not going with you to fetch any *gus*. You should have thought of it sooner. If you feel cold, you can put my topcoat on over your *malitsa*— I'm only using it to lie on. And when we get to where we're going, I'll make you a present of the sheepskin I'm wearing, it's better than any *gus*.

"That's fine then," Nikifor agreed readily, "What do we want a *gus* for? We aren't going to freeze to death, no sir. Ho ho!" he yelled at the reindeer. "These bulls here don't need prodding, they're that good. Ho ho!"

But Nikifor's high spirits did not last long. The effects of liquor completely overcame him. He became limp, couldn't sit up straight and fell more and more deeply asleep. I woke him up several times; he shook himself, prodded the reindeer with a long pole and mumbled: "Never worry, these bulls here are first-class . . . ," then fell asleep again. The reindeer had slowed down almost to a walk and only my occasional shouts made them speed up momentarily. A couple of hours passed in this way. Then I, too, dozed off and woke up a few minutes later, realizing that the reindeer had stopped. At first it seemed to me that all was lost . . . "Nikifor!" I shouted frantically, pulling him by the shoulder. In reply he only mumbled disconnected words: "What d'you want me to do? I can't do anything . . . I want to sleep, I do . . ."

This was indeed a sorry state of affairs. We were not more than thirty or forty *versts* from Berezov, and a halt here certainly did not form part of my plans. I saw that it was no joking matter, and decided to "take measures."

"Nikifor," I screamed, pulling the hood off his drunken head and laying it bare to the frosty air, "if you don't immediately sit up straight and start driving these reindeer, I'll push you off the sleigh and go on by myself."

Nikifor woke up a little, whether because of the frost or of my words I don't know. While sleeping, he had dropped the pole he used for prodding the reindeer; now, staggering and scratching himself, he found an ax in the bottom of the sleigh, cut down a young pine tree at the side of the road and lopped off the branches. The pole was ready, and we set off once more.

I decided that Nikifor needed firm handling.

"You realize what you're doing, don't you?" I asked him as severely as I could. "Do you think this is a joke? If they catch us, you'll have nothing to laugh about."

"I understand, sir, don't think I don't," replied Nikifor, sobering up more and more. "You can be sure of that. The only trouble is, that third bull isn't up to much. The first bull's fine, the second one's fine, only the third one . . . to tell the truth, he's no damn use at all."

It was getting on for morning, and the temperature was falling noticeably. I put my *gus* on top of my sheepskin and felt perfectly comfortable. But poor Nikifor's state was becoming sorrier all the time. The heat from the alcohol was gone, the frost had crept under his *malitsa*, and the poor fellow was shivering all over.

"Why don't you put my fur coat on," I suggested.

"No, it's too late for that; I must warm myself and warm the coat first."

An hour later we saw some yurts—three or four wretched log huts—by the side of the road.

"I'll go inside for five minutes, ask about the road and warm myself a little."

Five minutes passed, then ten, fifteen, twenty. A shape wrapped in fur came near, stood awhile beside my sleigh and went away again. The moon began to rise and the forest together with those wretched huts seemed to me to take on a sinister glow.

"How will it all end?" I asked myself. "How far can I get with this drunk? At this rate they'll have no difficulty in catching us. In his drunken state, Nikifor is capable of giving everything away to the first person we meet on the road; they'll inform Berezov, and that'll be the end of me. Even if they don't catch us there and then, they'll telegraph every station along the narrow-gauge railway. Is it worth going on?" I wondered.

About half an hour had gone by. Nikifor did not appear. It was essential to find him, yet I had not even noticed which of the huts he had entered. I went up to the first hut and looked in through the window. The hearth in the corner was full of flames. On the floor stood a steaming saucepan. A group of men, with Nikifor in the center, sat on the raised plank bed; Nikifor was holding a bottle. I started drumming on the window and the adjoining wall. Nikifor appeared a minute later. He was wearing my fur coat, which emerged by two inches from underneath his malitsa.

"Get on that sleigh!" I shouted as fiercely as I could.

"Right away, right away," he replied very meekly. "Don't worry, I just had a little warm, now we'll be getting on. By nighttime we'll have gone so far, the devil himself couldn't catch us. The only trouble is, that third bull's useless, might as well not have him at all."

We drove off.

◇ ◇ ◇

It was about 5:00 A.M. The moon had risen long ago and was shining brightly, the frost had hardened, there was a smell of morning in the air. I was wearing my reindeer-fur coat on top of my sheepskin and felt warm and comfortable; Nikifor in the driver's seat seemed confident and wide awake; the reindeer ran at a spanking pace, and I dozed quietly. From time to time I woke up and saw the same unchanging picture. The area we were traversing was almost treeless marshland; a few undersized, stunted pines and birch trees punctuated the snow, the road was a narrow, almost invisible winding strip. The reindeer ran with the indefatigability and regularity of automatic machines, and their loud breathing was like the noise of a small engine. Nikifor had flung back his white hood and sat with his head bare. Tufts of white reindeer fur from the hood had stuck to his head and it looked as though it were covered with frost. "We're on our way," I thought, a wave of joy rising within me, "it may be a whole day, or even two days, before they miss me . . . we're on our way . . ." And I dozed off again.

At about 9:00 Nikifor stopped the reindeer. A *choum*, or nomad's tent, shaped like a truncated cone, made of reindeer skins, stood almost directly by the road. An Ostyak sleigh with reindeer already harnessed stood outside the tent; there was a pile of chopped logs, fresh reindeer skins hung drying on a line, a skinned reindeer head with huge antlers lay on the snow, two children wearing *malitsas* and *kisas* played with some dogs.

"What's this tent doing here?" Nikifor wondered aloud. "I didn't think we'd see any till the Vyzhnepurtym Yurts." He enquired, and was told that these were Ostyaks from Kharumpalovsk, 200 *versts* away, hunting squirrel in these parts. I gathered up our cooking utensils and provisions; we climbed into the *choum* through a small opening covered with a skin flap, and made ready to have breakfast.

"*Paisi*," Nikifor greeted our hosts.

"*Paisi, paisi, paisi!*" came the answer from all sides.

Piles of fur lay all over the floor, and human figures stirred upon them. They had been drinking here the previous night, and everyone was feeling the after-effects. A bonfire burned in the center of the tent and the smoke escaped freely through a large hole left at the top. We hung our kettle over the fire and added some logs. Nikifor was conversing freely in the Ostyak language. A woman with a baby whom she had just been nursing rose to her feet and, without concealing her bare breast, moved up to the fire. She was ugly as death. I gave her a sweet. Two other figures rose at once and moved towards us. "They want some vodka," Nikifor translated. I gave them some spirit, hellish spirit at 95 degrees. They drank, wrinkling their faces and spitting on the floor. The woman with the bare breasts also drank her share. "The old man would like some more," Nikifor explained, offering a second glass to a bald, elderly Ostyak with greasy red cheeks. Later he added: "I've hired this old man for four roubles to come with us as far as the Shominsk Yurts. He'll drive his troika ahead of us and open up the road, our reindeer will run more briskly behind his."

We drank our tea and ate our food. I gave our hosts some cigarettes as a farewell gift. Then we piled all our things into the old man's sleigh, got into ours and drove off. The sun shone high in the sky, the road now led through forest, the air was bright and cheerful. The old man drove his three white *vazhenki* (does), all of which were in calf, ahead of us. He carried a pole of immense length with a small horn knob at one end and a sharp metal point at the other; Nikifor too had taken a new pole. The *vazhenki* pulled the old man's light sleigh at great speed and our bulls kept up with them smartly.

"Why doesn't the old man cover his head?" I asked Nikifor, surprised to see the Ostyak's bald head exposed to the frosty air.

"That's the quickest way to get rid of the liquor fumes," Nikifor explained.

Half an hour later the old man stopped his *vazhenki* and came asking for more spirit.

"We'd better give him some," Nikifor decided, taking a nip

himself at the same time. "His *vazhenki* were already harnessed, didn't you see?"

"Well, and so what?"

"He was just going to Berezov for more liquor. What if he didn't keep his mouth shut? So I hired him. We'll be safer that way. He won't get to town for at least a couple of days now. I'm not afraid for myself, you understand. Why should I be? All right, so they ask me: did you drive this character? Well, how am I to know whom I'm driving? They're policemen, I'm a driver. They get their wages, I get mine. Their job is watching people, mine's driving. Am I right or not?"

"You're right!"

Today is February 19. Tomorrow is the opening of the State Duma. Amnesty! "Amnesty will be the first duty of the State Duma." Maybe . . . but it is better to wait for amnesty a few dozen degrees further west. We'll be safer that way, as Nikifor says.

◇ ◇ ◇

After passing the Vyzhnepurtym Yurts we came across a sack full of bread lying in the road. It weighed over a *poud*. Despite my protests, Nikifor insisted on putting it in our sleigh. I took advantage of his falling once more into a drunken sleep and quietly threw the sack out again; the weight could only slow down our reindeer.

On waking, Nikifor found neither the sack of bread nor the pole he had taken from the old man's tent.

These reindeer are extraordinary creatures. They seem never to get hungry or tired. They had had no food for twenty-four hours before we set out, and it will soon be another twenty-four hours that we have been traveling. Nikifor says they're "only just getting going." They run at a steady, tireless pace of about eight or ten *versts* an hour. After every ten or fifteen *versts* we stop for two or three minutes while they make water, then we drive on. This is known as a "reindeer run," and since

(441)

no one has ever counted the *versts* in this part of the world, distances are measured in terms of "runs." Five runs correspond to about sixty or seventy *versts*.

When we get to Shominsk Yurts, where we are to leave the old man and his *vazhenki*, we shall have done at least ten "runs." That's not a bad distance.

At about 9:00 P.M., as night was falling, we had our first encounter with a few sleighs coming in the opposite direction. Nikifor tried to pass them without stopping, but failed; the road is so narrow that the reindeer sink up to their bellies into the snow if you drive even slightly off it. The sleighs stopped. One of the drivers came up to us, took a close look at Nikifor and addressed him by name. "Whom are you driving? Are you going far?"

"No, not far," Nikifor replied, "He's a merchant from Obdorsk."

The meeting made him quite agitated.

"That was the devil's doing, that was. I hadn't seen that fellow for a full five years, and still he recognized me, God damn him. They're Zyryans from Lipinsk, a hundred *versts* from here, going to Berezov for goods and vodka. They'll get there by tomorrow night."

"I don't care," I said. "They can't catch us now. I only hope you won't have any trouble when you get back there."

"What trouble should there be? I'll tell them: I'm a driver, driving's my business, knowing people's names is yours. How am I to know whether a character's a merchant or a political? It isn't written on his forehead. You're a policeman, I'm a driver. Is that right?"

"That's right!"

Night fell, dark and deep. The moon rises only towards morning. The reindeer, despite the darkness, kept well on the road. We met no one more. At 1:00 we suddenly drove into a circle of bright light and stopped. A bonfire was burning brightly by the side of the road; two figures, one large, the other small, were seated beside it. Water was boiling in a pot, and an Ostyak boy was slicing chips of tea from a tea-brick and throwing them into the boiling water.

We walked into the circle of light and our sleigh was immediately lost in the surrounding darkness. I could not understand a word of the language spoken. Nikifor took a cup from the boy, put a handful of snow into it and lowered it for a moment into the boiling water; then put in another handful and lowered the cup into the water once more. It was as though he were preparing a mysterious potion at this fire lost in the depths of this dark northern wasteland. Then he drank greedily and long.

Our reindeer seem to be getting tired. Every time we stop they lie down beside one another and eat snow.

◇ ◇ ◇

At about 2:00 A.M. we reached the Shominsk Yurts. Here we decided to rest and feed our reindeer. Yurts here are not nomad dwellings but permanent log huts. But there is an immense difference between them and those in which we stopped along the Tobolsk highway. Those yurts were, in essence, peasant *izbas*, with two rooms, a Russian-type brick stove, a samovar, chairs— just a little dirtier and less prosperous than the house of any ordinary Siberian muzhik. Here there is only one "room" with a primitive hearth instead of a stove, without any furniture, a low entrance door and a slab of ice instead of a window pane. Nevertheless I felt marvelous once I had taken off my *gus*, sheepskin, and *kisy*, which an old Ostyak woman immediately hung by the hearth to dry. I had eaten nothing for almost twenty-four hours.

It was a delightful feeling to sit on the raised plank bed covered with reindeer skins, eat Nikita's cold roast veal, and wait for my tea. I drank a glass of brandy, my head reeled a little and I felt as though our voyage were already at an end. A young

Ostyak with long pigtails plaited with red cloth ribbons got off the bed and went out to feed our reindeer.

"What will he give them?"

"Moss. He'll turn them loose at a place where there's moss growing, and they'll get at it under the snow, never worry. They'll dig a hole, lie down in it and eat their fill. A reindeer doesn't want much."

"Won't they eat bread?"

"They eat nothing but moss—unless you get them used to baked bread when they're young, but that doesn't often happen."

The old woman added more logs to the fire and then woke a young Ostyak woman who, covering her face with a kerchief so that I shouldn't see her, went out to help her husband, a young fellow whom Nikifor hired for two roubles to accompany us to Ourvi. Ostyaks are a terribly lazy lot, and all their work is done by women. This is not only true of household work; many Ostyak women carry rifles and go out hunting squirrel and sable. A forestry official in Tobolsk once told me extraordinary stories about the Ostyaks' idleness and their attitude toward their wives. He had to travel around the remotest parts of Tobolsk district, the so-called "*tumany*." As guides he used to hire young Ostyaks at 3 roubles a day. And each of these young Ostyaks used to be accompanied into the "*tumany*" by his wife, or, if he was single, by his mother or sister. The woman would carry all the baggage —an ax, cooking pot, a bag with provisions. The man only carried his knife stuck into his belt. When they stopped to rest, the woman would clear a space, take the husband's belt to ease him, light a fire, and prepare tea. The man did nothing but smoke his pipe and wait.

The tea was ready, and I raised the cup greedily to my lips. But the water stank unbearably of fish. I put two spoonfuls of cranberry essence into the cup and only then was able to drink.

"Don't you mind it?" I asked Nikifor.

"No, we don't mind fish, we eat it raw, straight out of the net, while it's jumping in your hand. There's nothing tastier."

The young Ostyak woman re-entered the room, still half-covering her face, and, standing by the hearth, adjusted her clothing with divine unself-consciousness. Then her husband came in and, through Nikifor, offered to sell me fifty squirrel furs.

"I told him you were a merchant from Obdorsk, so he wants you to buy," explained Nikifor.

"Tell him I'll drop in on my way back, no point in buying now."

We drank our tea and smoked. Nikifor lay down on the raised bed to have a sleep while the reindeer were feeding. I too longed to lie down and sleep, but was afraid of sleeping through till morning; instead, I took out my exercise-book and pencil and settled by the hearth to jot down my impressions of the first twenty-four hours of the journey. How simply, how well everything was going! Too well, perhaps. . . . At 4:00 A.M. I woke up the two drivers and we left.

"I see the Ostyak men as well as their women wear pigtails with ribbons and rings; I daresay they don't plait them more than once a year?"

"Their pigtails?" Nikifor replied. "Oh no, they plait them often. When they're drunk, they always get at each other's pigtails. They'll drink and drink, then suddenly, hop! they've grabbed someone by the pigtail. The one that's weaker says, 'Let me go.' The other'll let him go. Then they'll drink together once more. They're never angry with one another, they haven't the heart for it."

After Shominsk Yurts we joined the Sosva River. The road sometimes follows the river, sometimes goes through a forest. A sharp, penetrating wind is blowing, and I am having difficulty in jotting down these notes. We are driving through open country, between a birch grove and the riverbed. The road is murderous. If I look back I can see how the wind immediately covers over with snow the tracks left by our sleigh. The third reindeer keeps stumbling off the road, sinking to its belly in the deep snow, getting back on the track by a series of desperate jumps, jostling the middle reindeer and pushing the front one off the road. When we are driving on the river ice or over frozen marshland, we have to proceed at walking pace. Worst of all, our "leader"—that self-same bull that had no equal anywhere—has gone lame. Dragging his left hind leg, he continues staunchly to run along this dreadful road, and only his lowered head and extended tongue with which he tries to lick up a little snow as he runs show what a hard time he's having.

Suddenly the road dropped down and we found ourselves between two snow walls about an *arshin* and a half in height. The reindeer huddled together and it looked as if the two outside ones were carrying the middle one on their flanks. I noticed that the leader's front leg was bloody.

"I'm something of a vet, you know," explained Nikifor. "I thought he could do with a bit of bloodletting while you were asleep."

He stopped the reindeer, took a large clasp-knife out of his belt, gripped it between his teeth and started feeling the reindeer's bad leg. "Can't make it out, can't make it out at all," he muttered, and began digging with the knife a little above the hoof. The beast lay with its legs pulled up, making not a sound while the operation proceeded. When it was over it sadly licked up the blood on the hurt leg. Patches of blood, sharply outlined against the snow, marked our stopping place. I insisted that the Ostyak's reindeer be harnessed to our sleigh while our beasts pulled his light one. The poor lame leader was tied on behind.

We have been traveling for five hours or so after leaving the Shominsk Yurts, and it is another five hours to Ourvi; only there will we be able to change our reindeer at the house of a rich reindeer breeder called Semyon Pantiuy. But will he agree to hire his beasts out for such a long journey? I discuss the matter with Nikifor. Perhaps we shall be obliged to buy two teams of three reindeer from Semyon? "Well, what of it?" says Nikifor defiantly, "so we'll buy them!" My method of traveling seems to impress him in the same way as the voyages of Phineas Fogg once impressed me. If you remember, Phineas Fogg bought elephants and steamships and, when fuel was in short supply, threw all the wooden parts of his railway train into the engine furnace. At the thought of new difficulties and expenses, Nikifor, when he is under the influence of drink, that is, nearly all the time, becomes uncontrollable. He identifies himself completely with me, winks slyly at me and says: "Ye-es, it's going to cost us a pretty penny . . . but we don't give a damn, we don't. . . . Money's no object to us. Bulls? Let'em die, we'll buy new ones. Why should I care about losing a bull? I never . . . let him run while he can, I say. Ho ho! All we care about is getting there. Am I right?"

"You're right!"

"If Nikifor doesn't get you there, no one will. My uncle Mikhail Osipovich (he's a good muzhik, that one), he says to me: 'Nikifor, you going to drive this character? Go ahead, drive him. Take six bulls from my herd if you like. Free of charge.' And Suslikov, he's a corporal in the army, he says: 'Driving him, are you? Here's five roubles for you then,' he says."

"Why did he give you five roubles?"

"For taking you away."

"Are you sure it was for that? Why should he care?"

"I swear it was for that. He loves the *brothers*, does Suslikov, he'll do anything for them. For, let's face it, whose side are you on? The community, the poor people, that's who you're for. 'Here are five roubles,' says he, 'drive him away, I give you my blessing. I'll stake my head on it,' he says."

The road enters the forest and improves immediately; the trees protect it from drifting snow. The sun is high in the sky, the forest is still, and I am so warm that I take off my *gus* and remain in just the sheepskin. The Ostyak from Shominsk keeps falling behind and we have to wait for him. Pine trees surround us on all sides. Enormously tall trunks without branches till the very top, bright yellow and straight like candles. You have the

impression of driving through an old, handsome park. The stillness is total; only very rarely a pair of white willow-ptarmigan
start up, indistinguishable from the snow, and fly off deeper into
the forest. Then the pine forest stops abruptly, the road dips
down steeply towards the river, we keel over, right ourselves,
cross the Sosva and continue over open ground. A few undersized birches protrude from the snow. We must be driving
across marshland.

"How many *versts* have we done?" I ask Nikifor.

"About 300, I daresay. Only who's to know? Whoever
measured the *versts*, hereabout? The Archangel Michael, and no
one else. . . . They say 'an old woman started measuring with
her crutch, but she soon gave up.' Never mind, sir, another three
days or so and we'll get to the ore mines, just so long as the
weather holds. Sometimes it's very bad around here. . . . Once
I got into a snowstorm near Lyapin, did no more than three
versts in three days, God protect us."

Here we are in Malye Ourvi. Three or four wretched yurts,
only one of them inhabited. Twenty years ago they were probably all full of people. The Ostyaks are dying out at a terrifying
rate. . . . Another ten *versts* or so, and we'll arrive at Bolshie
Ourvi. Will Semyon Pantiuy be there? Will he give us a change
of reindeer? Ours have become completely useless.

We're in trouble! No muzhiks are to be found at Ourvi, they
are all away in tents, two reindeer runs away; we must drive
back a few *versts* and then turn off the road. If we had stopped
at Malye Ourvi and inquired there, we should have saved ourselves several hours of travel. In a mood bordering on despair
I waited while some women tried to find us a reindeer to replace
our lame leader. As everywhere and always, the Ourvi women
were recovering from a drinking bout, and when I began un-
wrapping our provisions they asked for vodka. I converse with
them through Nikifor, who is equally fluent in Russian, Zyryan,

and two Ostyak dialects, "upper" and "lower," which are almost totally different from one another. The local Ostyaks do not know a word of Russian; however, Russian swear-words have become part and parcel of the Ostyak language, and, together with state-monopoly vodka, are the most obvious gift of Russian culture to the natives. In the midst of incomprehensible sounds, in a country where no one can even say "hello" in Russian, a familiar obscenity suddenly flashes like a meteor, pronounced perfectly clearly and without the slightest accent.

From time to time I offer my cigarettes to the Ostyaks and their women. They smoke them with respectful contempt. Their palates, annealed by the fire of almost pure spirits, are quite insensitive to my poor offerings. Even Nikifor, who has a high opinion of all the products of civilization, has confessed that he thinks my cigarettes unworthy of attention. "This horse needs stronger oats," he said in explanation of his verdict.

We are driving towards the tents. How wild this country is! Our reindeer wander among snowdrifts, stumble amid the trees of this primeval forest, and I am at a loss to guess how my driver can tell the way. He has a special sense for it, like the reindeer themselves as they negotiate their huge antlers in the most astonishing way through the thicket of pine and fir branches. The new leader they gave us at Ourvi has enormous antlers, at least five or six hand-spans long. The road, such as it is, is barred by branches at every other step and one feels sure that the antlers will get caught in them. But at the last moment the bull performs a barely noticeable movement with his head and manages to miss the branches so that not a single pine needle is disturbed. I have watched these maneuvers for a long time and they seem to me infinitely mysterious, as do all manifestations of pure instinct to our ratiocinating minds.

◇ ◇ ◇

More trouble! The old man has gone with one of his laborers to a summer camping ground where he had left some of his reindeer. He is expected back at any moment, but no one knows when exactly he will turn up. His son, a young fellow with his upper lip split in half, daren't negotiate with us in his absence. We are obliged to wait. Nikifor has put our reindeer out to graze, or rather to eat moss, and has carved his initials in the fur of their backs with his knife to make sure they don't get mixed up with the local herd. Then he mended our sleigh, which had been badly shaken up by the long drive. With a despairing heart I walked around the clearing, then entered the tent. A completely naked small boy of three or four was sitting on a young Ostyak woman's lap; his mother was dressing him. What is it like, living with children in these huts at forty or fifty degrees below zero? "At night it's not too bad," explains Nikifor, "they dig themselves into a pile of furs and go to sleep. I've wintered many a time in tents, you know. An Ostyak will strip for the night, then he'll climb in between the furs. Sleeping's all right, getting up's worse. Your breath makes your clothes stiff enough to cut with an ax. . . . Getting up's bad." The young woman wrapped the little boy in the skirt of her *malitsa* and put him to the breast. Here they breast-feed children until the age of five or six.

I boiled some water on the hearth. Before I could say anything, Nikifor had poured some tea leaves from my box on the palm of his hand (dear God, what a palm it is!) and threw them into the kettle. I didn't like to protest, and now I must drink tea that has been in contact with a hand that has seen many things, but hasn't seen any soap for a long time.

The Ostyak woman finished feeding her boy, washed him, dried him with fine wood shavings, dressed him and let him out of the tent. I was struck by the tenderness with which she handled the child. Now she is at work sewing a *malitsa* out of reindeer skins, using reindeer veins for thread. The work is not only solid but also, unquestionably, elegant. The edges of the coat are decorated all over with ornamental patterns made of pieces of white and dark reindeer fur. A strip of red cloth is woven into every seam. Every member of the family wears *pimy, malitsy, gusi* made by the women of the house. What an appalling amount of labor goes into all this!

The eldest son has been lying sick in the corner of the tent for over two years. He gets medicines where he can, takes them in vast quantities and spends the winters here, in the tent with its pierced roof. The sick man has an unusually intelligent face; disease has carved lines into it which resemble traces of thought. I recall that it was here, among the Ourvi Ostyaks, that Dobrovolsky, the young merchant from Berezov who had come to buy furs, died a month ago. Before he died he tossed in fever, without any help, for many days . . .

Old Pantiuy for whom we are waiting owns about 500 reindeer. He is known throughout the countryside for his wealth. A reindeer here is everything—food, clothing, transport. A few years ago the price of a reindeer was six to eight roubles, now it is ten to fifteen. Nikifor explains this by the incessant epidemics which kill off hundreds of beasts.

◇ ◇ ◇

The light is going fast. It is obvious to me that no one is going to catch any reindeer for us before nightfall, but I am reluctant to abandon the last hope and I wait for the old man more impatiently, perhaps, than anyone has ever waited for him in his long life. It was already quite dark when he arrived at last with his hired men. He entered the tent unhurriedly, greeted us, and sat down by the hearth. His face, intelligent and commanding, struck me greatly. Obviously the five hundred reindeer he owns make him feel a king from head to foot.

"Talk to him, won't you?" I nudged Nikifor. "What's the use of wasting time!"

"It's too soon, they've got to have supper first."

The laborer, a tall, wide-shouldered muzhik, came in, greeted us in a nasal voice, changed his wet foot-cloths in a corner and moved up to the fire. What a dreadful face! The nose has completely vanished, the upper lip is raised high, the mouth is always half-open, baring a set of white, powerful teeth. I turned away, terrified, from this unfortunate.

"Perhaps the time has come to offer them some spirits?" I asked Nikifor, whose authority in these matters I have come to respect.

"Couldn't be a better time for it," he agreed.

I took out the bottle. The daughter-in-law, who had begun covering her face since the old man's return, lit a piece of tree bark at the fire and, using it as a torch, found a metal drinking bowl in a trunk. Nikifor wiped the drinking bowl with the hem of his shirt and filled it to the brim. The first portion was offered to the old man. Nikifor explained to him that this was 95 degree spirit; the old man nodded gravely and emptied the large bowl in one gulp; not a muscle quivered in his face. Then the younger son, the one with the split lip, had a bowlful; he forced himself to drink, wrinkled his poor face, and then took a long time spitting into the fire. Then the laborer drank, and his head began rocking uncontrollably from side to side. Then the bowl was offered to the sick man; he failed to drain it and returned the bowl. Nikifor threw the remainder into the fire to show the quality of the product: the alcohol burned with a bright flame.

"*Taak*," * the old man said calmly.

"*Taak*," confirmed his son, expelling a long jet of spittle from his mouth.

"*Saka taak*," ** added the laborer.

Then Nikifor had a drink and also found that it was too strong. The spirit was diluted with tea. Nikifor stuck his finger in the neck of the bottle and shook it. Everyone had another drink. Then they diluted it once more and had one more drink. At last Nikifor began to explain our business.

"*Saka khosa*," said the old man.

"*Khosa, saka khosa*," the others chimed in.

* Strong.
** Very strong.

"What are they saying?" I asked impatiently.

"They say it's very far. . . . He wants thirty roubles to the ore mines."

"How much does he want to go as far as Nyaksimvol?"

Nikifor muttered something, obviously displeased (I was not to know the reason until later), but translated my question to the old man and replied: "Thirteen roubles to Nyaksimvol, thirty to the ore mines."

"Well, when will he round up the reindeer for us?"

"As soon as it's dawn."

"Why not now?"

Nikifor, with an ironical look, translated my question. Everyone laughed and shook their heads negatively. I understood that a night halt could not be avoided and went out into the fresh air. It was still and warm. I walked in the clearing for half an hour and then lay down to sleep in our sleigh.

Wearing my sheepskin and *gus* I lay as if in an animal's lair made of fur. A circular segment of sky above the tent was lit up with the light of the dying fire.

Total stillness everywhere. The stars hung high and clear in the sky. The trees stood motionless. The smell of reindeer furs moistened by my breath was a little suffocating, but the warmth was pleasant, the stillness of the night had a hypnotizing effect and I fell asleep with the firm resolve to arouse the muzhiks at the crack of dawn and to leave as soon as possible. So much time lost! A disaster!

I woke up with a start several times, but it was still dark. Soon after 4:00, when the sky was just beginning to brighten, I went inside the tent, groped my way through to Nikifor and shook him awake. He aroused all the others. It is evident that forest life during the icy winters has left its mark on these people: after waking they coughed, hacked, and spat on the floor for so long that I was unable to go on watching the scene and got out into the fresh air. At the entrance to the tent a boy of about ten was pouring water from his mouth onto his dirty hands and then spreading it over his dirty face; having completed this operation, he dried himself meticulously with a handful of wood shavings.

Soon thereafter the laborer without a nose and the son with a split lip went off on skis, accompanied by dogs, to round up the reindeer. A good half hour passed before the first group of animals approached the tent.

"That's all right then," said Nikifor, "the whole herd'll be here in a moment."

But this was not the case. Two hours went by before a sufficient number of reindeer had collected in the clearing. They walked quietly around the outside of the tent, dug the snow with their muzzles, gathered into groups, and lay down. The sun had already risen above the forest and shone over the snow-covered clearing. The silhouettes of the reindeer, large and small, dark and white, with antlers and without, stood out sharply against the snow—a fantastic sight that seemed unreal and that I will never forget. The reindeer are controlled by dogs. These small, shaggy creatures hurl themselves at groups of fifty reindeer or more as soon as they wander away from the tent—and the huge beasts, panic-stricken, return at once.

But even this could not drive away thoughts of the time lost. This day, the opening day of the State Duma, was proving an unlucky day for me. I waited with feverish impatience for the roundup to be completed. It was already past 9:00, but the herd was not yet all there. We had lost twenty-four hours; obviously we could not leave before 11:00 or midday, and then there was the return journey to Ourvi, twenty to thirty *versts* on an almost non-existent road. If things went badly, they might catch up with me before night. If the police had missed me the day after I had left and had got one of Nikifor's innumerable drinking companions to disclose what route we had taken, a search party might have set out on the night of the nineteenth. We had traveled no more than 300 *versts*. This distance could be covered in twenty-four to thirty-six hours. In other words, we had just given the enemy sufficient time to catch us. The present delay might prove fatal.

I began nagging Nikifor. Hadn't I told him the night before that we should go out and look for the old man instead of waiting for him? We should have paid out a few more roubles rather than waste all night. If only I could speak Ostyak myself, I'd have fixed it all . . . but that was what Nikifor was supposed to do, that was his job . . . etc., etc.

Nikifor looked past me with a sulky face.

"What's one to do with them when they don't want to start before morning? And their reindeer, too, are spoiled and overfed, no hope of rounding them up in the middle of the night. But never fear," he added suddenly, turning his gaze upon me, "we'll get there!"

"Are you sure?"

"We'll get there!"

I too became suddenly convinced that all would be well, that we would *get there*. The more so as the whole clearing was now filled with reindeer and the two Ostyaks on skis appeared between the trees.

⬦ ⬦ ⬦

"Watch, they're going to pull in the reindeer now," said Nikifor.

I saw each of the Ostyaks take up a lasso. The old man slowly arranged the loop over his left arm. Then all three of them talked together in loud voices, apparently working out a plan and choosing the first victim. Nikifor, too, was let into the plot. His job was to set a particular group of reindeer galloping down the wide space between the old man and his son. The laborer stood a little further along. The frightened beasts rushed in a solid mass, a stream of heads and antlers. The men seemed to be watching out for a pinpoint in the stream. Now! The old man threw his lasso and shook his head in disappointment. Now! The young Ostyak missed too. But the noseless man, standing on open ground in the midst of the stream of reindeer, looked so confident, so elementally powerful, that, as I watched the movements of his hand, I felt sure he would succeed. The reindeer all shied back from the rope, but a large, white bull, after making two or three leaps, stopped and began to twist and turn on the spot: the loop had caught him around the neck and antlers.

Nikifor explained to me that the animal which had been caught was the most cunning of the reindeer, who caused constant trouble by leading the whole herd away when it was most wanted. Now the white rebel would be tied up and things would go more smoothly. The Ostyaks picked up their lassos again, looping them around the left arm, and exchanged loud remarks, working out a new plan of action. I, too, was seized by the disinterested passion of the hunt. Nikifor told me that they were now going to catch that big *vazhenka* over there, with the short horns, and I joined the military operations. We began driving a group of reindeer in the direction where the three men stood waiting with their lassos. But the *vazhenka* seemed to know what was awaiting her. She darted off to one side and would have disappeared in the forest if the dogs had not taken up the pursuit. An encircling movement had to be executed. This time the noseless man was again the one who succeeded in choosing the right moment and throwing the loop over the *vazhenka*'s neck.

"This one's barren, she's never had a calf," explained Nikifor; "that's why she's specially good for work."

The hunt was exciting, although long drawn-out. After the *vazhenka* a huge reindeer with the look of a real bull was caught by two lassos at once. Then there was a lull because the group of reindeer that was wanted escaped into the forest. The laborer and the younger son went off once more on their skis, and we had to wait for half an hour or so. Towards the end things went better, and, with concerted effort, we managed to catch thirteen reindeer—seven for Nikifor and me, six for our hosts. At last, at about 11:00, in four sleighs drawn by three reindeer each, we set off in the direction of Ourvi. The Ostyak laborer will accompany us as far as the ore mines. A seventh, spare reindeer is tied on behind his sleigh.

◇ ◇ ◇

The lame bull, left behind at Ourvi while we went to the tent village, never recovered. He lay limply on the snow and let himself be caught without a lasso. Nikifor let his blood once more, but to no better purpose than before. The Ostyaks said he must have dislocated a leg. Nikifor stood over him for a while, not knowing what to do, and then sold him for eight roubles to one of the locals for meat. The man dragged the poor brute away on a rope. Such was the melancholy end of the bull "which had no equal anywhere in the world." Curiously, Nikifor sold the animal without asking my consent; yet our agreement had been that the reindeer would become his property only after he had safely delivered me to my destination. I was very reluctant to let the knacker take away an animal that had served me so well, but I hadn't the courage to protest. Having completed his business transaction, Nikifor turned to me, put the money in his purse, and said: "That's twelve roubles' pure loss." What a funny fellow he is! He has forgotten that it was I who paid for the reindeer, and that he had assured me that they would transport us the whole way. Yet here am I, obliged to hire new ones after only 300 *versts*.

Today the weather is so warm that a slight thaw has set in. The snow has softened, and the reindeer's hooves set wet lumps of it flying in all directions. This makes it harder for the deer to run. Our "leader" is a bull with only one horn and of rather mediocre appearance. The barren *vazhenka*, working hard, is on the right. Between them is a fat, not very large young bull who has never been in harness before. Escorted on right and left, he is performing his duties conscientiously. The Ostyak is in front, driving a sleigh loaded with my luggage. On top of his *malitsa* he is wearing a bright-red smock, which makes an absurd, and yet central, patch of color against the background of white snow, gray forest, gray reindeer, and gray sky.

The road is so difficult that the traces on the front sleigh have already broken twice: the skids freeze to the road at every halt and it is difficult to set the sleighs in motion. After only two "runs" the reindeer are already noticeably tired.

"Shall we be stopping at Nildinsk Yurts for a drink of tea?" Nikifor asked. "The next yurts are a long way off."

I could see that both drivers wanted tea, but I was anxious to lose no more time after the twenty-four hours lost at Ourvi, I said we would not stop.

"You're the boss," said Nikifor, and gave an angry prod to the barren *vazhenka*.

◇　◇　◇

We traveled in silence for another forty *versts* or so. When Nikifor is sober, he is surly and taciturn. The weather turned colder, the road froze and hardened. At Sangi-tur-paul we decided to stop. The yurt here is marvelous, with benches and a table covered with American cloth. At supper Nikifor translated for me part of the noseless man's conversation with the women who served us, and I learned a number of interesting things. About three months ago this Ostyak's wife had hanged herself. And what had she used? A bit of frayed old hempen rope, which she had tied to the end of a branch. The man had been away in the forest hunting for squirrel together with the other Ostyaks. The rural policeman, another Ostyak, had come to find him saying his wife was very sick (the thought flashed through my mind: so they, too, don't tell you straight away). The Ostyak had said: "What's her mother there for? Let her make a fire in the hearth, that's why we keep her with us." But the policeman had insisted that he should come. The husband had arrived at the tent, but the wife was already "a goner." "That's the second wife he's lost," Nikifor concluded.

"Don't tell me the other one killed herself too!"

"No, that one died a natural death, from a sickness."

It transpired that the two pretty children whom, to my great horror, our Ostyak had kissed good-bye on the mouth when leaving Ourvi, were his children by his first wife. He had lived with the second one for about two years.

"Maybe they forced her to marry him? You only have to look at him," I said.

Nikifor made inquiries.

"No, he says she came to him of her own free will. Later he paid her old folk thirty roubles and then they all lived together. No one knows why she hanged herself."

"I don't suppose it often happens that way, does it?"

"You mean, Ostyaks not dying a natural death? Why, they're always doing it. Last summer, near my home, an Ostyak shot himself with a rifle."

"What, deliberately?"

"No, by accident. And another time, a police clerk in our district town shot himself. You'll never guess where—on top of the police tower! Climbed up to the very top and said, take that, you sons of bitches—and then he shot himself."

"An Ostyak, was he?"

"No, a Russian character, Nikita Mitrofanovich Molodtsovatov."

When we left the Sangi-tur-paul night had already fallen. It had stopped thawing long before, but the weather continued very warm. The road was excellent, soft yet dry—a good working road, Nikifor said. The reindeer trod the ground noiselessly and seemed to be pulling without any effort. In the end the third one had to be unharnessed and tied on behind; when reindeer haven't enough work to do, they tend to swerve from side to side and may end by smashing up a sleigh. The sleigh skidded along smoothly and noiselessly, like a boat on the glassy surface of a pond. In the gathering darkness the forest looked even more gigantic than before. I could not see the road and hardly felt the motion of my sleigh. It was as though the trees were under a spell and came running towards us, bushes slipped away, old tree stumps covered with snow flew past—everything seemed filled with mystery. The only sound was the fast, regular chu-chu-chu-chu of the reindeers' breathing. Thousands of long-forgotten sounds filled my head in the midst of the silence. Suddenly I heard a sharp whistle in the depth of the dark forest. It seemed mysterious and infinitely remote. Yet it was only our Ostyak signaling to his reindeer. Then silence once more, more whistling far away, more trees rushing noiselessly out of darkness into darkness.

In my somnolent state an anxious thought occurs to me. The Ostyaks must figure that I am a rich merchant. We are in the depths of the forest, the night is dark, not a man nor a dog anywhere for fifty *versts* round. What is to stop them . . . ? Luckily I have a revolver. But it is locked in my suitcase, which in turn is roped to the Ostyak's sleigh—the same noseless Ostyak who, at this particular moment, seems to me strangely suspicious. I decide that at the next halt I must take out the revolver and keep it next to myself.

This driver of ours in his red mantle is an extraordinary creature. The lack of a nose does not seem to have affected his sense of smell in the least; it is as though he could scent the road. He knows every tree, every bush, and is as much at home in the forest as he was in his master's tent. Now he shouts something to Nikifor. It appears that there should be some moss under the snow just here; we can stop and feed our reindeer. We stop and unharness. It is 3:00 A.M.

Nikifor says that Zyryan reindeer, unlike these Ostyak ones, are cunning and he would never let them loose at a halt but would feed them tied up. Letting a reindeer loose isn't any trouble, he says, but what if you can't catch him again when you want him? However, the Ostyak has a different opinion and is willing to release his beasts on parole. I am impressed by his noble-mindedness, but nevertheless gaze at the animals' muzzles with some anxiety. What if they are more attracted by the moss that grows around the Ourvi tent-village? That would be regrettable indeed. However, before allowing the reindeer to depart on the basis of a gentleman's agreement, my two drivers cut down two tall pines and cut them into seven lengths of about an *arshin* and a half. These logs, supposed to act as a restraining influence, are hung around the necks of each reindeer. Let us hope that they will not prove too light . . .

After releasing the reindeer Nikifor cut some firewood, trod down a circular patch of snow and dug a hollow in which he laid a fire, placing a pile of fir branches around the fire for us to sit on. Two cooking pots were hung over the fire on two green branches stuck in the snow, and we filled them with handfuls of snow. I daresay this tea-drinking party around a bonfire in February would have seemed a good deal less attractive if there had been a frost of forty or fifty degrees below zero. But we were exceptionally lucky, and the weather was warm and still.

I was afraid of oversleeping and so decided not to lie down, but sat on by the fire for two hours or so, feeding it and noting down my traveling impressions in its flickering light.

At first dawn I woke the drivers. They caught the reindeer without any difficulty. While they were being harnessed it became fully light and everything around us took on a perfectly prosaic aspect. The pines became smaller, the birches stood still. The Ostyak looked sleepy and last night's suspicions vanished like smoke. At the same time I remembered that there were only two cartridges in the ancient revolver I had acquired before leaving, and that the person who had sold it to me had urged me not to use it, saying that "there might be an accident." So it remained inside the suitcase.

We drove on through thick forest—pines, firs, birches, powerful larches, cedars and, by the river, willow. The road is good. The reindeer are running well but without friskiness. The Ostyak on the front sleigh has hung his head low and is singing a melancholy song consisting of only four notes. Perhaps he is remembering the frayed old hempen rope that his second wife used to hang herself with.

Forest, nothing but forest . . . monotonously uniform over a vast area, yet infinitely diverse in its internal combinations. Here, a pine has rotted and its upper part has fallen right across the road, forming a kind of arch. It is enormous, and snow covers it like a shroud which hangs down over our heads. And here, it seems, there must have been a forest fire last autumn. Dry, straight trunks without bark or leaves stand like telegraph poles planted in the ground without rhyme or reason, or like bare ship's masts in a frozen harbor. The area of the fire covers several *versts*. Then we travel through nothing but fir, branchy, dark and dense. The old giant trees jostle one another, their tops meet and stop the sunlight getting in. The branches are covered with a web of green thread, like a coarse spider's web. Men and reindeer seem smaller amid these centenarian firs. Then, suddenly, the trees became much smaller, as though hundreds of young firs had run out on a snowy plain and formed rows at a regular distance from one another. At a turn of the road we almost collided with a small sleigh pulled by three dogs and driven by a little Ostyak girl. A boy of about five walked at the side. The children were very pretty; I have noticed that Ostyak children are often good-looking. But why, then, are the adults so repulsively ugly?

Forest, forest. . . . Here again there has been a forest fire, though not so recently; young shoots are growing among the burned trunks. "How do these fires start?" I ask. "By people lighting bonfires?" "Never," says Nikifor, "in summer there's not a soul comes here, all the traveling's done by river. No, the fires are caused by a cloud: a cloud comes over and sets the forest alight. Or else one tree rubs against another in the wind until they strike sparks; in summer the trees are dry. Put out the fires? Who's there to do it? The wind starts a fire, the wind puts it out. The resin and bark burn away, the needles burn away, the trunk stays up. In a couple of years' time the roots will be dry and then the trunk will fall too."

There are many trunks here which are ready to fall. Some are held up only by the thin branches of the adjacent tree. This one here has nearly fallen across the road but something, heaven knows what, is keeping its top up, three *arshins* or so above the ground; we have to duck to avoid cracking our heads. Now again, for the space of several minutes, there is a zone of mighty firs, then suddenly we are in a cutting that leads down to the river.

"Such cuttings are handy for catching duck in the spring-time. In spring they fly downwards, you know. Before sunset you have to stretch a net right across the cutting, between the trees right to the very top. A large net, like a fighting net, see? Then you lie down under a tree. The duck come flying into the cutting and when it gets dark, they can't see the net, so they get caught in it. You just pull a string, the net'll fall down and cover them right up. You can bag fifty duck at once, that way. All you have to do is keep snapping them."

"How, snapping them?"

"You've got to kill'em before they've a chance of flying away, haven't you? So you get your teeth around their necks, and snap! that's the quickest way, blood pouring down your lips and all. Of course you can smash their heads with a stick, too, but snapping'em is safer."

At the beginning all reindeer, like all Ostyaks, seemed to me identical with one another. But I soon found out that each of our seven deer has a physiognomy of its own, and I have learned to distinguish between them. Sometimes I feel waves of tenderness for these wonderful animals which have already brought me five hundred *versts* nearer to the railway line.

Our alcohol supplies have given out. Nikifor is sober and glum. The Ostyak keeps singing his song about the hempen rope. There are moments when I find it unspeakably hard to realize that it is I, I, not anyone else, lost here amid this immeasurable wasteland. Two sleighs, seven reindeer and two men, all making this journey because of me. Two men, adults, fathers of families, have left their homes and are suffering all the hardships of the road because I—a third person, a total stranger to them both— require it.

Such relations exist everywhere, all over the world. But I doubt whether anywhere else but here, in the primeval taiga, where they are exposed in all their crassness, one's imagination could be so vividly struck by them.

After the night bivouac we passed the Saradeisk and Menk-i-paul yurts, stopping only at Khanglaz, further along the road. Here the people are, if anything, still more savage than in the other places we have seen. Everything is a novelty to them. My eating utensils, my scissors, my stockings, the blanket I keep in my sleigh, all evoke admiration and astonishment. Everyone makes approving noises whenever I produce anything new. At one point I spread out a map of Tobolsk province and read out the names of all the adjacent yurts and rivers. All listened with gaping mouths and when I had finished declared in unison that everything I had said was exactly right. Having run out of small change, I gave every man and woman three cigarettes and a sweet as thanks for their hospitality. Everyone was highly satis-fied. An old Ostyak woman, less repulsive-looking than the rest and very lively, literally fell in love with me, or rather with my belongings. You could see from her smile that her feeling was one of purely disinterested admiration of these phenomena from another world. She helped me wrap my legs in the blanket, we shook each other affectionately by the hand and each said a few agreeable words in their own language.

"Well, is the Duma going to meet soon?" Nikifor unexpectedly asked me.

"It met the day before yesterday."

"I wonder what it'll do. . . . I hope it makes *them* see reason. *They've* got us down properly, they have. Take flour—it used to be a rouble fifty, now, an Ostyak tells me, it's gone up to one eighty. How do you expect us to live at such prices? Especially we Zyryans. They've got it in for us. You fetch a cartload of straw and you have to pay. You put up a pile of firewood, you have to pay. The Russians and the Ostyaks both say the land is theirs, see. The Duma ought to do something about that. Our police sergeant isn't a bad character at all, but the inspector is a different proposition altogether."

"The Duma won't have much to say. They'll dissolve it, you'll see."

"That's true, they'll dissolve it," Nikifor agreed, adding a few strong words whose energy Stolypin might have envied.

We arrived at the Nyaksimvoli yurts at night. Here it was possible to change reindeer, and I decided to do this despite Nikifor's objections. He kept insisting that we should continue with the Ourvi reindeer, using the most absurd arguments and interfering with my negotiations. I was surprised at his behavior until I understood that he was thinking of the return journey: if we kept the Ourvi reindeer he could go back to where he had left his own beasts without incurring further expense. But I refused to give in, and we hired fresh beasts for eighteen roubles as far as Nikito-Ivdelskoye, a large gold-mining village by the Ural mountains. That is the last point on the reindeer road; beyond it we still had to travel a hundred and fifty or so *versts* in horse-driven sleighs till we got to the railway line. The distance from Nyaksimvoli to Ivdelskoye is about 250 *versts*—twenty-four hours of fast travel.

Here we had a repetition of the same business as at Ourvi: the reindeer could not be rounded up at night and we had to wait till morning.

We stopped in a poor Zyryan house. Our host was once a merchant's clerk, but quarreled with his employer and is now without work. He surprised me at once by his literary, not at all peasantlike, speech. We got into conversation. He spoke with perfect understanding about the possibilities of the Duma being dissolved, the government's chances of obtaining a new loan, etc. Among other things he asked me whether all Herzen's works had been published yet. And yet this educated person is a complete barbarian. He wouldn't move a finger to help his wife, who keeps the entire family. She bakes bread for the Ostyaks, two ovenfuls a day. She fetches wood and water; in addition, she takes care of the children. The night we spent in her house she never went to bed at all. A small lamp burned behind the partition, and we could hear sounds of her hard at work, kneading and shaping bread dough. In the morning she was still on her feet; she boiled the samovar, dressed the children, and handed her just-awakened husband his reindeer-skin boots, which she had dried overnight.

"Why doesn't your man help you?" I asked her when we happened to remain alone.

"There isn't any real work for him to do, you see. There's no fishing here, and he's not used to hunting. The land hereabouts isn't plowed, last year was the first time anyone tried doing it. So what's he to do? Our men don't work in the house, never. They're lazy, you see, scarcely any better than the Ostyaks. That's why Russian girls will never marry a Zyryan, what's the point of putting your head in a noose, they say. Only we Zyryan women will do it. It's a matter of what you're used to."

"And do Zyryan girls marry Russians?"

"Oh yes, lots. Russian muzhiks like marrying our girls because no one's a better worker than a Zyryan woman. But never the other way around. I don't think there's ever been a case of a Russian girl marrying a Zyryan."

"You were saying someone in this village tried plowing the land last year. What came of it?"

"It was very good, really. One man sowed a *poud* and a half of rye, and collected a crop of thirty *pouds*. Another sowed a *poud* and collected twenty. About forty *versts* from here, that was."

Nyaksimvoli is the first place along the road where I have heard of any attempts at agriculture.

⬦ ⬦ ⬦

We didn't leave until the afternoon; the new driver, like all drivers in general, promised to bring his reindeer "at the crack of dawn" but in fact did not turn up till midday. He is not traveling himself but has sent a young lad along with us.

The sunshine was dazzling; I could hardly open my eyes, and even through closed lids the snow and the sun shone like molten metal. At the same time a steady, cold wind prevented the snow from thawing. It wasn't until we entered the forest that I could rest my eyes a little. The forest is the same as before, and there is the same large number of animal tracks, which Nikifor has taught me to distinguish. A hare's silly loops that he weaves without any rhyme or reason. Hares are particularly plentiful because nobody hunts them. Here a whole circle of ground has been trampled by hares' paws, with tracks radiating out in all directions. You might think the hares had held a night meeting and, surprised by a police patrol, had scattered in panic. Partridges, too, are plentiful, the tracks of their pointed feet clearly visible in the snow. A fox's track forms a cautious, regular line, as though drawn with a ruler, thirty paces to the side of the road. The scarcely noticeable tracks of forest mice are everywhere. In many places the tracks of ermine, like tightly stretched pieces of string with knots tied at regular intervals along them. Here the road is pitted with a series of large holes, made by a heavy-footed elk.

At night we stopped once more, set loose our reindeer, made a bonfire and drank tea, and again in the morning I waited for the reindeer's return in a feverishly impatient state. Before going for them, Nikifor warned me that the piece of wood had come untied from the neck of one of them.

"Does that mean he's gone?"

"No, the bull's here all night," said Nikifor and immediately proceeded to curse the reindeer's owner for giving us neither lassos nor lengths of ordinary rope for emergencies en route. I gathered that things were not going too well.

The first to be caught was the bull. To try and win the animal's confidence, Nikifor simulated the rattling noise reindeer make in their throats. The reindeer came quite close, several times, but as soon as Nikifor made any movement, it darted back into the forest. This scene was repeated two or three times. Finally Nikifor tied loops into a piece of rope he had found in the bottom of the sleigh, spread it on the ground, and covered it over with snow. Then he started making rattling and bubbling noises once more to ingratiate himself with the bull. When the animal warily approached, Nikifor suddenly tugged at the rope and the piece of wood hanging from the bull's neck got caught in one of the loops. The captured bull was pulled into the forest to act as a decoy for the other reindeer. A good hour passed after this, and the forest grew fully light. From time to time I heard human voices in the distance, then silence fell again. What would they do about the reindeer that had shaken off its piece of wood, I wondered? I had heard that it sometimes took three days to catch an escaped reindeer.

No, they were coming.

First they had caught all the reindeer except the "free" one, which roamed close by and refused to be tempted into coming nearer. Then suddenly it joined the reindeer which had already been caught, and started eating snow together with them. Nikifor crept close and grabbed the "free" animal by the leg. It pulled away, fell over and knocked Nikifor over in the process; but, in the end, the man won.

◇ ◇ ◇

At about 10:00 A.M. we arrived at Sou-vada. Three yurts here were boarded up, only one was inhabited. An enormous carcass of a she-elk lay on a pile of wood, another, of a wild reindeer, lay on the ground a little further along. Lumps of blue meat were to be seen on the smoke-blackened roof, among them two dead elk calves taken from the mother elk's belly. All the inhabitants of the yurt were drunk and asleep. No one returned our greeting. The house was quite large but incredibly dirty, without any furniture. A cracked piece of ice propped up with sticks served as a window-pane. On the walls were the Twelve Apostles, portraits of various monarchs and a colored advertisement from a rubber factory.

Nikifor made a fire in the hearth. Then an Ostyak woman, swaying and stumbling, rose to her feet. Three children, one of them a babe in arms, slept beside her. During the last few days the family had hunted with great success: besides the she-elk, they had killed seven wild reindeer; six carcasses were still in the forest.

"Why are there so many empty yurts hereabouts?" I asked Nikifor after we had set off once more.

"For many reasons. An Ostyak won't live in a house where there's been a death. He'll either sell it or board it up or transfer it to another bit of ground. Same thing, if a woman that's unclean enters a house then that's the end of it, the house's got to go. Their women live separately during those times, you see, in huts made of branches. Another thing, the Ostyaks are dying out pretty fast. That's why their yurts stand empty."

"Listen, Nikifor Ivanovich, don't tell people any more that I'm a merchant. As soon as we reach the ore mines, say that I'm an engineer from the Göte expedition. Have you heard about it, yourself?"

(469)

"No, I haven't."

"Well, there's a plan to build a railway from Obdorsk to the Arctic Ocean; they want to be able to export Siberian goods abroad without going through Central Russia first, you see. So remember to say that this was the business I went to Obdorsk on."

The day was ending. It was less than fifty *versts* to Ivdel. We came to the Vogul settlement of Oika-paul. I asked Nikifor to go into one of the houses to reconnoiter. He returned ten minutes later. The house, he said, was full of people, all drunk. The local Voguls had been having a party with some Ostyak carters taking goods to Nyaksimvoli. I refused to enter the house for fear that Nikifor would get drunk at this final stage of our journey. "I shan't drink," he assured me, "I'll just buy a bottle for the road."

A tall muzhik came up to our sleigh and started questioning Nikifor in Ostyak. I could not follow their conversation until both began cursing one another in the purest Russian. The man was not quite sober. Nikifor too was no longer quite himself after the few minutes he had spent indoors. I joined in the conversation. "What does he want?" I asked Nikifor, taking his interlocutor for an Ostyak. But the man replied in Russian. He had only put the usual questions to Nikifor—whom was he driving and where —and Nikifor had told him to go to hell, which had been the cause for the further exchange of views.

"Are you an Ostyak or a Russian, then?" I asked in my turn.

"Why, a Russian, sure enough. Shiropanov, my name is, from Nyaksimvoli. And you, you wouldn't be from Göte's crowd, by chance?"

I was astounded.

"Yes, I am. But how do you know about it?"

"They wrote to me from Tobolsk asking me to join; that was when they were going out to prospect for the first time. There was an Englishman with them at the time, can't remember the name . . . Charles Williamovich."

"Putman?" I prompted at random.

"No, that's something else, wasn't there something about Putman's wife? No, this one's name was Cruse, I just remembered."

"And now what are you doing?"

"I'm a clerk at the Shulgins' in Nyaksimvoli; it's their goods we're carting. Trouble is, I haven't been well the last three days, pains all over my body."

I offered him some medicines, and was obliged to enter the house.

◇ ◇ ◇

The fire in the hearth was dying; no one bothered to revive it, and the room was almost completely dark. It was full of people, sitting on the plank beds and on the floor; some were standing. As always, the women half-covered their faces with their kerchiefs on seeing a stranger. I lit a candle and gave Shiropanov some sodium salicylate, whereupon I was immediately surrounded by drunk and half-drunk Ostyaks and Voguls, all complaining of various diseases. Shiropanov acted as interpreter, and I treated everyone impartially with quinine and sodium salicylate.

"Is it true you live where the Tsar lives?" a little old desiccated Vogul asked me.

"Yes, in Petersburg," I replied.

"I've been there too, at the exhibition. I've seen everybody, the Tsar, the Chief of Police, the Grand Duke, everybody."

"Oh, did you go in a deputation, in Vogul national dress?"

"Yes, yes," everybody began to nod affirmatively.

"I was younger then, and stronger. Now I'm an old man, always sick."

I gave him some medicine, too. The Ostyaks were very pleased with me, shook my hand, invited me for the tenth time to drink some vodka and were very much upset by my refusal. Nikifor sat by the hearth downing one cup after another of tea and vodka alternately. I gave him several meaningful looks, but he kept his eyes glued to the cup and pretended not to see me.

There was nothing for it but to wait while Nikifor finished his "tea."

"We've taken three days to cover the forty-five *versts* from Ivdel, the Ostyaks have been drinking the whole time. At Ivdel we stopped at Mitry Mitrich Lyalin's, a very good man, that. He's brought some new books back from a trip to the ore mines —the People's Calendar, and some recent newspapers. The calendar tells you what everybody's salary is, some get 200 thousand, you know, some 150. What do they get all that money for, I ask you? I don't hold with any of that, I've never seen you before, sir, but I'm telling you straight: I don't like any of that, I don't care for it. They say the Duma met on the twentieth: I'll bet this one is as bad as the last, or worse. Well, let's see what those socialists can do. There'll be about fifty socialists in the Duma, plus a hundred and fifty Narodniks, plus a hundred Kadets or so . . . hardly any Blacks at all."

"Would you mind if I asked what party you sympathize with?"

"Me? I'm a social democrat by conviction . . . because the social-democratic party puts everything on a scientific basis."

I felt like rubbing my eyes. The depths of the taiga, a dirty native hut, a crowd of drunken Voguls, and here was some petty merchant's clerk telling me that he was a believer in social democracy because of its "scientific basis!" I must admit I felt a sudden upsurge of party pride.

"It's a pity you've buried yourself in these dark and drunken parts," I said to him with genuine regret.

"What is there to be done? I used to work in Barnaul, then I got sacked. I'm a family man, I hadn't any choice but to come here. And, you know, when in Rome, do as the Romans do—or, as we say more aptly, live among wolves, howl like a wolf. I turned down the offer to go north with Göt's expedition, and now I'm sorry. If I should be needed again, drop me a line."

I felt embarrassed, and wanted to tell him that I was no

engineer and not a member of any expedition, but an escaped "socialist" . . . but I thought it over and abstained.

The time had come to get back into our sleighs. The Voguls crowded around us in the courtyard, holding up the lighted candle which I had given as a parting present. The air was so still that the candle did not go out. We said good-bye over and over again; a young Ostyak even tried to kiss my hand. Shiropanov packed a wild reindeer's skin in my sleigh as a present. He absolutely refused to accept payment, and in the end I gave him a bottle of rum I had been carrying with me "in case." At last we set off.

◇ ◇ ◇

Nikifor had regained his loquacity. For the hundred and first time he told me how he had been sitting at his brother's house, how Nikita Serapionovich had come in—"a sly muzhik, that one!"—and how he, Nikifor, had at first refused, and Suslikov, the corporal, had given him five roubles and told him to accept, and his uncle Mikhail Yegorych—"a good muzhik, that"—had said, "You fool, why didn't you say straight away that you are going to drive that character." As soon as he had finished, Nikifor would start all over again: "Now I'll tell you the whole story just how it was. There was I sitting at my brother Panteley Ivanovich's house, not drunk, mind, but having had a few, certainly. . . . Well then, Nikita Serapionovich comes in and says to me . . ."

"Look here, now Nikifor Ivanovich, we'll soon be getting there. I want to thank you, and tell you that I'll never forget what you did for me. If only it were possible, I'd print it in the newspapers: 'I want to express my sincere gratitude to Nikifor Ivanovich Khrenov, without whose help my escape could not have taken place.' "

"Well, why don't you print it?"

"What about the police?"

(473)

"That's true, I'd forgotten them. But it would be nice, and no mistake. I was in the paper once before, you know."

"How was that?"

"That's how it was. There was a merchant from Obdorsk, and, well, he pinched his sister's money, and I, to tell the truth, helped him a bit. Well, not exactly helped, but sort of backed him up. If the money's in your hand, I said, that means God's on your side. Is that right?"

"Well . . . not quite."

"Never mind, then. Anyway I backed him up, sort of. Nobody knew about it, just the one character, Pyotr Petrovich Vakhlakov, a really sly one. And so he goes and prints all about it in the newspaper: 'A thief, the merchant Adrianov, stole the money, and another thief, Nikifor Khrenov, helped to cover the deed up.' All printed black on white, and every word of it the truth!"

"You ought to have sued him for slander," I said. "There was a minister once, by the name of Gurko, can't remember if he stole something or only helped someone else to steal something, anyway, when he was found out he sued for slander. You should have done the same."

"I did think of it! But I couldn't do it, because, you see, this Vakhlakov, he's my best friend. He didn't do it to hurt, just for a joke, see? He's a clever muzhik, a jack-of-all-trades. Not a man but a regular price-list."

◇ ◇ ◇

At about 4:00 A.M. we arrived at Ivdel and stopped at the house of Dmitry Dmitrievich Lyalin, whom Shiropanov had recommended to me as a "Narodnik." He proved to be a most amiable and warm-hearted person, and I am happy to have this opportunity of expressing my most sincere thanks to him.

"Our life here is a quiet one," he told me over the samovar. "Even the revolution barely touched us. Of course we're interested in the events, we read the newspapers, we sympathize with the progressive movement, our representatives to the Duma are left-wingers, but I couldn't say the revolution has properly stirred us up here. At the ore mines, yes, there were some strikes and demonstrations, but nothing here, we lead a quiet life, we don't even have any police, just the one officer to look after the mines. The telegraph doesn't start till the Bogoslovsky mine, a hundred and fifty *versts* from here, and the railway line starts there too. Exiles? Yes, there are a few—three from Liflandia, a schoolmaster, a circus artist. All of them are working on the dredger, no one's particularly badly off here. They lead a quiet life like the rest of us. We prospect for gold, in the evenings we drop in at each other's houses. From here you can continue to Rudniki without any fear, no one'll stop you: you can take the postal coach, or hire your own if you like; I'll find you a driver."

When I said good-bye to Nikifor he could hardly stand up.

"Take care, Nikifor Ivanovich," I said—"make sure the drink doesn't get you into trouble on the way back."

"Never worry . . . if the belly's safe, the backbone's sound," he retorted.

❖   ❖   ❖

The "heroic" phase of my story, the journey by reindeer over seven or eight hundred *versts* of taiga and tundra, comes to an end here. Even at its most hazardous moments, my escape turned out to be much easier and more prosaic—because of good luck —than it appeared to me in the planning stage, or to other people if one may judge by certain newspaper reports. The rest of the voyage in no way resembled an escape. My traveling companion for a large part of the way to Rudniki was an excise official on a tour of government liquor shops in the area.

At Rudniki I went to see a number of people to inquire whether it was safe to take the railway. The local conspirators did their best to frighten me with tales of local spying activities and advised me, after waiting at Rudniki for a week, to travel to Solikamsk, where everything would, they assured me, be much easier. I did not follow their advice, and have no reason to regret it. On the night of February 25 I took the narrow-gauge railway from Rudniki without the least trouble and after twenty-four hours' slow travel changed, at Kushva station, into a train on the Perm railway. Then I continued via Perm, Vyatka, and Vologda and arrived in Petersburg on the evening of March 2. Thus, after twelve days of travel, I was driving in a cab down Nevsky Prospect. That is not long at all; the journey to Berezov had taken a month.

While I was traveling on the narrow-gauge Ural railway, I was not yet safely out of danger; on a local branch every "foreigner" is noticed at once and, had the appropriate instructions been received by telegraph from Tobolsk, I might well have been arrested at any station. But when I had changed and was traveling in a comfortable carriage of the Perm railway I knew that I had won. The train passed the same stations at which we had been met, so recently, by so many gendarmes, police and troops. But now I was going in the opposite direction, and my feelings, too, were entirely different. At first the spacious, almost empty carriage seemed close and stuffy to me. I went and stood on the open connecting platform between two coaches; it was dark, a strong wind was blowing, and a loud cry burst spontaneously from my breast—a cry of happiness and freedom!

Meanwhile the train of the Perm-Kotlass railway was carrying me forward, forward, always forward.

Index

(477)

Index

(479)